# THE MONMOUTH REBELS
## 1685

# THE MONMOUTH REBELS
## 1685

Compiled by
W. MACDONALD WIGFIELD, M.A.

ALAN SUTTON

This volume, also published as volume 79 of the Somerset Record Society, has been prepared for publication by the Honorary General Editor of the Somerset Record Society, Dr R.W. Dunning, who has also compiled the index. The information from the Barbados records has been provided by Mr Ronnie Hughes.

Alan Sutton Publishing Limited
30 Brunswick Road
Gloucester GL1 1JJ

First published 1985

*British Library Cataloguing in Publication Data*

Wigfield, W.M.
  The Monmouth rebels.—(Somerset record
  series; v. 79)
  1.  Monmouth's rebellion, 1685  2.  Soldiers,
  England—History—17th century
  I.  Title    II.  Series
  942.06'7    DA448.9

ISBN 0-86299-234-6

.

Printed in Great Britain

# CONTENTS

# INTRODUCTION

The popular uprising in the West Country known as the Monmouth Rebellion must be one of the best documented of all similar events in English history. Between 11 June 1685, when the Duke of Monmouth landed at Lyme in Dorset with a party of just over eighty men, and the defeat of his army at Sedgemoor, in the heart of Somerset, on 6 July, a significant proportion of the population of West Dorset, East Devon and Somerset rose up in arms against the government of James II. Exactly how many took part will never be known: estimates of those who fought for Monmouth at Sedgemoor by those present vary between 3,200 and 7,000,[1] and by that time, it must be assumed, some men who had joined the rebel army had already gone home. There were others in the countryside who were sympathetic to the rebel cause; claims of 10,000 Clubmen waiting near Axbridge and of 500 horsemen in Wiltshire[2] proved in the event rather empty, but in the months which followed the rebel defeat, men from Wiltshire to Devon found themselves in trouble on minor charges of uttering treasonable words. Such support for the cause throughout the West was both the reason why the government reacted with such savagery against those rebels caught and convicted for taking up arms, and why also so many men were reported to be 'at large' or 'not taken', having disappeared into a countryside prepared to shelter them.

The 'roll call' of rebels published in this volume comprises almost 4,000 names. It has been compiled largely from a number of lists (see below) made either in preparation for or during the Assizes conducted in the West Country in September and October 1685, or from the records of other courts held in various towns and villages during the summer of that year. Some few prisoners were sent up to London for interrogation and were subsequently returned to stand trial at one of the four Assize towns where most rebels were tried: Dorchester, Exeter, Taunton and Wells. To give each rebel-suspect trial with at least two witnesses against him would have been difficult and time-consuming. Those responsible for planning the trials, therefore, agreed to try to get the rebels to plead guilty, thereby obviating the need to procure witnesses. There are at least three accounts of this exercise and John Whiting, a Quaker prisoner at Ilchester, recorded in his autobiography on 3 September 1685[3]

> I cannot forbear to mention what I observed passed at Ivelchester while I was a prisoner in the ward . . . There came David Trimm of Wells and took account of the prisoners (which perhaps was his place as county-clerk to do), with the causes of their commitment; but not only so, but wheedled them to confess how far they were concerned; pretending, if they would confess,

they would do them all the kindness they could at the assizes; so drew out of them all they could, under hopes of favour, and then went in and writ down their examinations; which I was eye-witness of . . . The like they did at the common gaol . . . It was such a piece of treachery to betray them out of their lives . . . Some were terrified into confessing in hopes of pardon, and then hanged, whom otherwise they could have had little against.

The Autumn Assizes on the Western Circuit were conducted by the country's most brutal judge, Lord Chief Justice George, Baron Jeffreys of Wem, together with four other senior judges. Jeffreys seems to have conducted proceedings as if the other judges were not needed. After Salisbury, he made at each Assize an address in which he stressed the king's eagerness to pardon rebels provided that they pleaded guilty. To make the point as clearly as possible he arranged at Dorchester first to try a batch of 30 rebels who were determined to plead not guilty. Of these 29 were found guilty on Saturday 5 September and were sentenced to be hanged; 13 died at Dorchester two days later.

Public hangings and the subsequent gruesome business of burning entrails, quartering the corpses, boiling them in salt and dipping them in pitch for long-term exhibition were proceedings designed to strike awe into the West Country. The sheriff's instructions to the mayor of Bath to prepare for executions in the city,[4] printed Broadsheets listing names and places of execution,[5] and the accounts of costs of placing severed limbs in various parts of the twin boroughs of Weymouth and Melcombe Regis[6] are examples of the ways in which the government deliberately set out to ensure submission.

An alternative to hanging was transportation. It had become known in London by the beginning of August that some rebels would be shipped for service in the colonies, and courtiers with business interests in the West Indies began to make bids for them. The Secretary of State wrote to Jeffreys early in September outlining his instructions: 200 were to be given to Sir Philip Howard, Governor of Jamaica, 200 to Sir Richard White, 100 each to Sir William Booth, a Barbados merchant, to Sir James Kendall, later Governor of Barbados, to Sir Jerome Nipho, the queen's Italian Secretary, to Sir William Stapleton, Governor of the Leeward Islands, and to Sir Christopher Musgrave. These grantees, and later the queen herself and William Bridgeman, were to be responsible for taking the prisoners from custody within ten days to 'some of his Majesties southern plantations, viz. Jamaica, Barbados, or any of the Leeward Islands in America',[7] and to keep them there for ten years.

Each prisoner was worth between £10 and £15, and Jeffreys argued that the arrangement, allowing re-sale in the islands, would put money in the pockets of the merchants, men who had in no way to bear the costs incurred by the rebellion. His protest was ignored, but great care was taken to record each detail of the transactions, thus providing the remarkable information on many of the rebels. The purchasers were obliged to certify the number of prisoners handed over, and a total of 890 is recorded. Each was then required to send an invoice of shipment, giving names and destinations. Not all of these invoices have survived, but a total of at least 612 prisoners sailed either from Weymouth or Bristol in eight ships, one, the *John*, a converted frigate, another the inappropriately-named *Happy Return*. The governor of each of the colonies was warned to expect the new arrivals, was required to see that the island assemblies passed a law to ensure their ten-year servitude, and was asked to notify the arrival and disposal of the prisoners in each colony. Lieutenant-Governor Stede of Barbados recorded the safe disposal of 304 out of 329 men who left Weymouth.

Prisoners on the islands were to become indentured servants for ten years, and the Barbados assembly was the first to pass laws which imposed heavy fines and imprisonment on any purchaser who freed them. Any prisoner caught escaping was to be branded a Fugitive-Traitor, wearing the letters F.T. on his forehead.

The change of government at home in 1689 forced a revision of policy towards the prisoners. Early in January 1690 the laws concerning them were disallowed, and in February free pardons were issued. But Governor Kendall of Barbados wrote in June expressing the reluctance of the planters – he himself among them – who had invested money in these men on the understanding that they would serve for ten years and had taught them the skill of boiler, distiller and refiner on their estates. Kendall, who had originally been assigned 100 men, assigned 10 to his manager John Burston. He and his estate were thus financially involved.[8]

In the event the Barbados prisoners were theoretically freed in January 1691, but since they were not to receive the usual cash reward at the end of servitude, how could they return home? Half the Jamaican prisoners had already been released by this time and the rest entered voluntary service. How many settled permanently there and on the other islands can perhaps now be discovered as the names of those transported are found in the records of Barbados and the other islands. Already searches in Barbados have uncovered some settlers (*see* Enoch Gold) who within a generation were well established in the West Indies, and there are families, such as the Austins, who claim by probabilities rather than by precise proofs, that their ancestors were brought to the island as rebels.

The causes and course of Monmouth's Rebellion have been exhaustively studied. This list will provide material not only to establish a better analysis[9] of the economic background of many of the rebels, but also will allow a more comprehensive study of, for instance, the significance of Nonconformity in the West Country scene. The question of motive will always be the hardest to answer. The handsome face of the Duke of Monmouth is unlikely, the fear of unemployment in the cloth trade not demonstrated. But the last letters of eight of the rebels and 'dying speeches' of a dozen more are surely some indication of personal opinions. Those dozen speeches were printed within half a dozen years of the executions while some salient points could still be remembered. John Spragg of Colyton was quoted as saying that he 'believed that no Christian ought to resist a lawful power; but this case being between popery and protestantism altered the matter; and the latter being in danger, he believed it was lawful for him to do what he did'. The fear that the protestant religion might be subverted might well have been the prime cause of the rebellion, and was closely linked with the hope of freedom of worship for protestant nonconformists. That, Monmouth promised as he landed at Lyme. That, so John Whiting, Quaker in Ilchester gaol but related to several rebels and sharer of his quarters with many more, was indeed a factor: 'Had liberty of conscience been granted sooner', he wrote, 'there might have been no rebellion in the west'. It is an opinion which needs to be tested afresh; tested, for instance, in the light of men and women of Lyme who were fined in May and June 1685 for non-attendance at church. Among them were nine men who so very soon afterwards were to join Monmouth's cause.[10]

### The Records

There are at least eight incomplete lists of the Westcountrymen who served in Monmouth's army. After Sedgemoor the constables of the hundreds were required to submit lists of the men of the villages in their jurisdictions who were 'absent from their homes during the rebellion of James Scott late Duke of Monmouth'. This Presentment of the Rebels, known as The Monmouth Roll, lists 2,611 men, with their villages of origin and sometimes their occupations. The Gaol Delivery Book gives the names of 1,573 who were brought from several prisons to be tried at the Assizes at Dorchester, Exeter, Taunton and Wells. The Report of Lord Chief Justice Jeffreys to King James gives the sentences he imposed, and his warrant to the High Sheriff of Somerset details the places where those not already hanged were to be executed. Ship lists show whither convicted rebels were to be transported and, in some cases, to whom they were sold. Among the Treasury Books is a list of rebels' lands declared forfeit to the Crown and for sale. The last major list is of 135 men and 43 women excepted from the General Pardon issued on 10 March 1686. The women included the Maids of Taunton who had made banners for Monmouth; among the men were some rebels who had not been caught, and some Whigs who were suspected of conspiring against the king. There are also shorter lists from Quarter Sessions records and a few rolls of courts leet of individual manors, notably Taunton Deane and North Curry, which give several names not among the records of the Assizes.

To have printed these documents in full would have entailed countless repetitions and would then have given the reader the severe and lengthy task of searching through each list with the likelihood, in the common event of several men with the same name, of creating utter confusion. It has been thought wiser to print the names alphabetically, with information culled from each of the lists and identified where possible. The standard entry runs: surname; forename; age; occupation; parish or village; constables' presentment; assize at which tried; sentence; place of execution or ship of transportation, destination and purchaser.

For many rebels all the information to survive is the village of origin and the constable's presentment. The lack of further facts implies *either* that the rebel was killed and buried at Sedgemoor *or*, more probably, that he managed to stay concealed until the General Pardon was proclaimed. It is impossible to compile a list of those killed at Sedgemoor. A few are mentioned in the constables' presentments, a few more in the court leet presentments. A few more may be deduced from the list of forfeited lands whose owners were not presented for trial. Another batch may be named by comparing a list of those who came from Holland with Monmouth with the list of those excepted from the General Pardon. King James had declared there would be no pardon for those who invaded the kingdom with Monmouth; so, if any known 'invader' was not excepted from the General Pardon, there is a clear presumption that he did not survive the battle. Nathaniel Wade, whose narrative[11] is the best contemporary account of the rebellion, made a list of those officers whom Monmouth commissioned on board ship. Wade 'remembered' those the king could not arrest: a few killed at Sedgemoor; a few like Colonel Holmes already tried and hanged; a few like Colonel Venner and Major Manley already safe abroad. When Wade, badly wounded, was brought to Windsor Castle, his life depended on a disclosure of information. Allowed to send out his washing, Wade smuggled out a letter begging for the names of men known to have been killed. The names reached him tucked in the pleats of his 'good holland shirt', and when submitted to the king, who came in person to see him, provoked the comment 'Your friends, Mr Wade, seem to be among the dead'.

Monmouth's steward, William Williams, was captured after the battle and was brought to the Gatehouse in Westminster for examination. He had none of Wade's inhibitions, and ten days after the battle he gave the names of 20 who had come with the duke.[12] A third list, of 34 names, mostly officers, was found in the pocket of 'Young Hewling' when he was captured by Captain Richardson.[13]

In most of the entries the village and presentment come from the Presentment of the Rebels (or The Monmouth Roll). The ship list of 67 rebels sentenced at Taunton, given to the Queen, and transported to Barbados, gives their ages and occupations. In a few other instances the age has been calculated from an entry in a parish register. The ship list of 90 rebels, 67 from Somerset and 23 from Devon, tried at Taunton, given to Sir William Booth and transported to Barbados, gives their villages. The schedule of lands forfeit and for sale names the villages where the rebels had lived or held land.

The Gaol Delivery Book shows the assize at which the rebels were presented for 'levying warr against the King'. The Taunton men and a very small minority of others were accused of 'aydeing and assisting the rebells against the King'. At Dorchester the first 30 presented were marked *Po. se, cul.* and the next 4 *Po. se, non cul.*, contractions for *Ponit se, (non) culpabilis* – he places himself (on the evidence) (not) guilty. The selection of prisoners and rapid sentence were designed to frighten the rest of the accused into pleading guilty, in hope of the king's mercy. In the Dorchester list, after this first group, there follow 276 names (except one marked *pardonatus*) with the word *cogn.* for *cognovit*, he pleaded guilty. Those sentenced to death at Dorchester and Exeter are marked *Tr. et ss.* for *Trahetur et suspendatur*, let him be drawn and hanged.

At Taunton on Friday, September 18 the first four presented, 'for levying warr' and one for 'aydeing and assisting', pleaded not guilty and were sentenced to death. The clerk marked their names *Tr. etc.* and with a huge star, which has been interpreted as 'for execution'. Three of them were hanged on Monday, September 21. The other had the additional mark *Reprd. per Judic.*, Reprieved by the Judge. The rest of the accused, all marked *cogn.*, were sentenced to death, but Jeffreys did not specify until he had reached Wells which were to be hanged and which transported. Possibly he consulted the king before he confirmed the death penalty for 145, of whom one was subsequently reprieved. From Wells Jeffreys sent his warrant to Edward Hobbes, sheriff of Somerset:[14]

Whereas the severall (persons) in the schedules herewith annexed at the Sessions of Oyer and Terminer and (General Gaol) Delivery holden for this country were (convicted of) high treason and have received judgment of death to be drawne, hanged and quartered.

These are to will and require you immediately on sight hereof to putt the same judgment in Execution in the severall places in the said schedules annexed. And for yor soe doing This shall be yor sufficient Warrant. Given under my hand and seale the six and twentyeth day of September Ao 1 Jacob 2di Regis 1685.

Lett the Sheriff of the County of Somersett dispose of the heads and quarters . . . in the severall places where they are to be executed or in the neighbouring parishes . . . The sheriffe is to begin at Taunton this day and to-morrow at Wellington . . .

As the Lord Chief Justice had left Taunton before he made his decision, the clerk of the court could not add the stars to the names, and their absence has made some historians suggest that only three rebels had been hanged at Taunton.

Among Jeffreys' lists[15] for each Assize are five shorter lists of considerable interest. First is a list of 'Prisoners who had Certificates allowed pursuant to his Majesties gratious Proclamacion': 27 men at Dorchester, 20 at Taunton, and six at Wells. Two letters from the Earl of Sunderland, the Secretary of State, to the Earl of Feversham, commander-in-chief, concern the issue of the proclamation:

Windsor, June 24. The King having thought fit to have a proclamation prepared promising pardon to such of the rebels as lay down their arms, I send you several of the said proclamations, which his Majesty leaves to you to publish *when* and *where* as you shall find best for his service. I send you also a form of the certificate to be given to such rebels as shall lay hold of the benefit of the said proclamation.

Windsor, July 2 . . . and if you think it may be of any service to his Majesty to give poor people who have been deluded more time to come in, he (the king) leaves it to you to prolong the term limited, and what you shall promise, he wil make good.

The proclamation has not been found, but one certificate survives:

William White of this place [Lyme Regis], latterly in the camp of James Scott, late Duke of Monmouth, hath laid down his arms and is returned to his obedience, and craves the liberty of his Majesties most gracious pardon.[16]

Next in Jeffreys' report come 28 names from Dorset, 'Prisoners humbly proposed for his Majesties Gracious pardon'. There was only one so proposed at Exeter, 22 at Taunton, and 26 at Wells. The current price for a pardon was £60, and several local lawyers were described as pardonmongers, some of them exacting £250 or even £400 from terrified relatives for captured rebels. One of the most notorious of these lawyers was Andrew Loder of Dorchester, 'whom', wrote Lord Ailesbury, 'I knew well to be a very rascal'.[17]

'Prisoners remayning in Custody till further Order' (six at Dorchester) and 'Prisoners continued in Gaole not indicted' come next (nine at Dorchester) of whom the first was subsequently hanged at Taunton. At Exeter there were four 'Prisoners convicted remayning in Custody' of whom two were reprieved and two transported. At Taunton 22 were so listed, of whom 25 were later transported, one was marked 'runn away' and one was proposed for pardon. At Wells ten were listed 'till further order', of whom one was hanged and six transported. It is possible that they remained in custody to see whether their relatives would pay for a pardon. Seven more remained in custody 'for want of evidence', whereas at Dorchester 14 or 15 prisoners were 'discharged for want of evidence'. Another Wells list of 14 men were 'Witnesses for the King left in Custody'.

Fifteen men at Taunton and five at Wells were described as 'Prisoners in Gaole omitted in the Warrant for Execution, altho designed to be executed'. This was neither through carelessness nor through incompetence. One of the Taunton group, John Pacey, managed to escape from prison one morning and of his own free will returned in the evening, having then more trouble to get in than he had to get out. He had made good use of his hours of freedom, and had made it worthwhile for someone to omit his name from the warrant for execution.[18] He was granted a pardon under the Privy Seal in December. Ten of the Taunton 15 were subsequently transported with a late batch from Wells; and one of the five at Wells was transported to fill a gap in another list, in place of a man reprieved.

Two other lengthy lists complete the Assize Rolls. At the end of the Exeter papers is one headed 'The Names of the severall persons who are indicted of High Treason and are at large'. There are 343 names, all from Devon, all described as yeomen, and all in the same order as in the Presentment of the Rebels. Therein lies a mistake, for the copying clerk failed to notice the village name Musbury, and included the first 14 Musbury men as if they came from Axminster. Moreover, there was little or no attempt at collation; ten of those reported at large had already been, or were shortly to be, hanged. At least five others were in prison rather than at large and four others had been killed in action.

There were too many rebels to be tried at Wells so, having dealt with 556 prisoners there, Jeffreys contented himself with binding over the remaining 140 'each for the other for theire appearance at the next Assizes and for the(ir) good behaviour in C$^l$ [£100] each'. If their names appear in the 1686 lists they are marked as 'pardoned by the proclamation of our

Lord the King' or 'pardoned and dismissed'.

Quarter Sessions[19] were held at Bridgwater eight days after the battle at Sedgemoor and were concerned mainly with presentments 'for takeing up Armes against the King, as wee are very credibly informed by our neighbors, and are yet absent'. The adjourned sessions were held at Bruton on August 4th. As the named rebels had not by then returned, the constables would hardly have known who was alive and who dead. The constables were required to submit a presentment of those absent from home during the rebellion. Some of those presented at Quarter Sessions were not on the list prepared for the Assizes, and this omission suggests that those presented at the Quarter Sessions a week after the battle and not presented at the Assizes two months later were found to have been killed at Sedgemoor. Some of the names presented at the Court Leet at North Curry on October 27th were annotated: fled, wounded, mort, killed at Norton or transported.

[1] W. MacDonald Wigfield, *The Monmouth Rebellion* (1980), 63.

[2] Ibid. 51–2, 58–9.

[3] J. Whiting, *Persecution Exposed* (1st end. 1715), 322.

[4] J. Collinson, *History and Antiquities of Somerset* (1791), I, xlvii.

[5] *Somerset & Dorset Notes and Queries*, viii, 224–9.

[6] J. Hutchins, *History and Antiquities of Dorset*, ii, 448.

[7] Abbot Emerson Smith, *Colonists in Bondage: White Servitude and Convict Labor in America* (1947), 188–95.

[8] For details of Kendall's interest I am indebted to Mr Ronnie Hughes of Barbados.

[9] Peter Earle, *Monmouth's Rebels* (1977), was the first seriously to attempt an analysis of the social and economic background of the rebels. For a simplified study of the present list see Robert Dunning, *The Monmouth Rebellion* (1984), 61–4.

[10] Dorset Record Office, Lyme Regis Misdemeanour Book (B.7 A 3/1), pp. 7–8.

[11] Printed in Wigfield, *The Monmouth Rebellion*, 149–71.

[12] British Library, Lansdowne MS 1152A.

[13] Historical MSS. Commission, Stopford-Sackville MSS. I (1904), 23.

[14] British Library, Additional MSS. 34516: printed in *The Bloody Assize*, ed. J.G. Muddiman (1929), 226–31.

[15] Ibid. Additional MSS. 90337: printed in Muddiman, 195–225.

[16] Dorset Record Office, Photo 182.

[17] *Memoirs of Thomas, Earl of Ailesbury* (Roxburgh Club 1895), I, 122.

[18] *Newsletter*.

[19] Somerset Record Office, Q/SR, 162–3.

# APPENDIX I: THE GENERAL PARDON

The General Pardon was issued on 10 March 1685/6. The text of the Proclamation has been taken from a copy in the British Library (Proclamations, 2 James II, shelfmark 816. m. 3 (10)), the list of exceptions from G. Roberts, *Life of the Duke of Monmouth* (1844), ii. 258–60. These exceptions include the names of known rebels, some not tried, others not captured; the Maids of Taunton whose ransoms had not then been negotiated; and some Whigs whom the government was unwilling to release. A second 'Gracious and General Pardon' was issued on 2 October 1688, from which were excepted all those transported for treason, all fugitives not returning, seven named surviving rebels, and ten prominent Whigs.

A Proclamation of the King's Majesties most Gracious and General Pardon.

JACOBUS REX Whereas soon after our coronation We had given Order for preparing of a Bill, containing Our most gracious, general, and Free Pardon to Our Loving subjects, with intention to have passed the same into an Act in the first session of our Parliament, but were unhappily prevented therein, by the late most Unnatural Rebellion, which since it hath pleased Almighty God by his Blessing upon Our Arms, to suppress, We have thought fit to renew Our Princely Intentions of Grace and Mercy to Our Subjects, especially considering the steadfast Loyalty of the far greater number of Our Subjects, who continued firm in their Obedience to Us notwithstanding that Rebellion; and being perswaded that many of those who joyned themselves in that Rebellion being poor Labourers and Handicraftsmen, were drawn and seduced thereinto by the subtile and crafty Insinuations of some Ill-disposed Persons of greater Note and Quality than themselves, and not from their own Evil Rancour of mind, and Traiterous Aversion to Us or our Government, whose Condition We in Our Princely Clemency commiserating; And to the end their fears and dispair of Our Mercy, may not betray them to evil and lewd courses of Life, but that they may with safety return to their Obedience to Us, and to their former Habitations, Labours, and Imployments. And that the minds of other Our Subjects may be quieted; and that all Fears and Jealousies which may concern their security for any matter since Our Reign, or in the Reign of Our late Dearly beloved Brother, be removed and wholly taken away, as much as in Us lies, We of Our especial Grace and Tenderness to Our People, do hereby Publish and Declare this Our most Royal and Gracious Pardon; and We do hereby for Us, Our Heirs and Successors Pardon, Acquit, Release and Discharge all and every Our subjects (except Bodies Politick and Incorporate, and such other Persons who shall be herein or hereby excepted) of this Our Realm of England, Dominion of Wales, and the Town of Berwick upon Tweed, their Heirs, Executors and Administrators, them and every of them against Us, Our Heirs and Successors, of, and from all manner of Treasons, Felonies, Misprisions of Treason or Felony, Treasonable or Seditious Words or Libels, Seditious and unlawful Meetings and Conventicles, all Offences Whereby any Person may be Charged with the Penalty and Danger of Praemunire; all Riots, Routs, Offences, Contempts, Trespasses, and Misdemeanours, and all Judgements and Convictions for not coming to church, and of and from the Forfeitures and Penalties for the same, or any of them heretofore had, committed or done, except as herein or hereby after is excepted. And Our Will and Pleasure is, That neither Our Said Subjects, nor any of them, nor the Heirs, Executors or Administrators of any of them, be, or shall be sued, vexed or disquieted in their Bodies, Goods or Chattels, Lands or Tenements, for any manner etc. etc.

Excepted: Treasons overseas; Counterfeiting seal or money; Murders and Poysonings; Piracies; Highway robbery and Burglaries; Rape etc. Perjury etc. Taking War-stores; Frauds re revenue; Transportees for Treason.

Except also all and every person and Persons who in a Traiterous and Hostile manner Invaded this Our Realm with James Scott late Duke of Monmouth, and all and every other person or persons who in the time of the late Rebellion under the said late Duke of Monmouth were officers or had the name or Repute of being Officers in his Army. Except also all Fugitives and persons fled from our Justice of into parts beyond the Seas or out of this Our Realm who shall not return and render themselves to Our Chief Justice or some Justice of the Peace before the 29th day of September next ensuing.

And also excepted out of this Our Pardon the Persons hereafter particularly mentioned viz

| | |
|---|---|
| George Speke, of White Lackington, Esq. | John Parsons,    ditto |
| Mary Speke, his wife | Thomas Cram, Warminster |
| John Speke, their son | Thomas Place, Edington |
| Samuel Townsend, Ilminster | Robert Gee, Martock |
| Reginald Tucker, Long Sutton | Hugh Chamberlain |
| James Hurd, Langport | William Savage, Taunton |
| George Pavior,  ditto | Richard Slape,  ditto |
| Gabriel Sprat, Ash Priors | John Palmer, Bridgwater |
| George Cary, Glastonbury | John Webber,  ditto |
| John Lewis, Babcary | Henry Herring, Taunton |
| Thomas Lewis,  ditto | Thomas Hurd, Langport |

Christopher Cooke, Wilton, clothier
Amos Blinham, Galhampton
Mrs. Musgrave, Schoolmistress
    Sarah Wye
    Elizabeth Wye
    Catherine Bovet
    Scading
    Mary Blake
    Elizabeth Knash
    Mary Bird
    Mary Mead
    Susan Peck
    Elizabeth Barns
    Mary Burridge
    Hannah Burridge
    Grace Herring
    Anne Herring
    Mary Waters
    Sarah Waters
    Elizabeth Germain
    Grace Germain
    Hannah Whetham
    Esther Whetham
    Susan Tyler
    Mary Goodwyn
Mrs. Sarah Longham
    Margery Sympson
    Sarah Reynolds
    Mary Hucklebridge
    Margaret Hucklebridge
    Mary Baker
    Mary Tanner
    Anne Tanner
    Elizabeth Gammon
    Sarah Stacy
    Hannah Stacy
    Elizabeth Dyke
    Elizabeth Baker
    Mary Smith
    Mary Page
    Elizabeth March
    Hannah Grove
    Elizabeth Bigswood, Taunton

John Tucker, Shepton Mallet
John Bennet, Alisbeere, gent.
John Greenaway, Crewkerne
Thomas Skinner, Dawlish, Esq.
John alias Rob Moor, Haychurch
William Way, Coomb St. Nicholas
Robert Hucker, Taunton
Robert Penny, Shepton Mallet
Thomas Hooper
Edward Keetch
William Parbury
William Green
William Husey
William Strode, of Street, Esq.
Mary Bath, Wrington

George Legg, ditto
Edward Rogers, Banwell
John Rogers, ditto
Ralph Green
William Jobbins
William Manning
William Whinnell
John Baker, Banwell
John Worms, Warminster
John Worms, ditto
William Pardoe
Nicholas Smith
John Edwards
John Collier
Henry Coles, Bridgwater
Richard Bluecock, Stokegursey
Henry Ireton
John Cragg, alias Smith
Mrs Mary Jennings
James Hooper
John Bennet
Joseph Gatch
William Thompson, London
Humphrey Aldwin, ditto
Thomas Love, alias Alexander, ditto
Richard Tucker, Bishop's Hull
William Crab, Ashill, Gent.
Francis Gough, ditto
Francis Vaughan, Criston, Esq.
Lawrence French, Chard
Edward Matthews, Lincoln's Inn, Esq.
Hugh Cross, sen., Bishop's Hull
Samuel Bernardiston
Benedick Hack, Culliton
Henry Quick, Upottery
John Comb, Luppit
Henry Gatchil
Nich. Hore
George Pippen, Dulverton, Gent.
Abraham Cairie, Taunton.
John Huish, ditto
Peter Terry, ditto
Richard Raw, ditto
Maurice Frith, Wincanton, Gent.
William Tiggens, Ford
John Kerridge, Lyme Regis, mariner
Robert Parsons
Samuel Venner
Andrew Fletcher
John Fowke
Robert Bruce
Anthony Bruce
James Fox
Joseph Gaylard
William Oliver
John Woolters
Nathaniel Hook, clerk
Richard Lucas, Dalverton
John Bettiscomb, near Lyme Regis

George Stucky, White Lackington
Thomas Saxon
John Jesse
George Nipe, Cheddar
Joseph Francklyn, Worle, clerk
Joseph Dore, late mayor of Lymington
James Carrier, Ilminster
Nicholas Covert, Chichester, Gent.
John Tripp, Shipham
Joseph Hearse, Badgeworth
Francis Creswick, Fanham, Esq.
Francis Fudge, Wedmore
Colonel John Rumsey
Joshua Lock, jun.
Stephen Lobb, clerk
William Gaunt
Ralph Alexander
Bartholomew Vermeuyden
Major John Manley
Izaack Manley, his son

Walter Thimbleton
Aaron Smith, London, Gent.
Sir William Waller
Slingby Bethel, Esq.
Francis Charlton, Esq.
Richard Goodenough
Nathaniel Wade
John Tellier
Richard Edghill
Samuel Story
John Jones
John Vincent
George Bowyer
John Dutton, Colt.
Charles Earl of Macclesfield
John Trenchard Esq,
John Wildman, Esq,
Titus Oates, clerk
Robert Ferguson, clerk

Provided always, That this our General Pardon shall not extend to any person that were in actual Arms against Us in the late Rebellion in the West, who being now within this Realm shall not within 3 Months after the Publication hereof, lay hold of this Our Pardon, and Testifie the same by their peaceable returning to their former Habitations, Labours and Imployments.

Given at Our Court at Windsor the 10th day of March 1685 In the 2nd Year of Our Reign.

GOD SAVE THE KING.

# APPENDIX II: THE PURCHASERS OF THE MONMOUTH REBELS IN BARBADOS

Adamson, Richard
Alchorne, John
Allamby, William
Allen, Major Abel
Austin, Thomas

Baron, William
Battyn, Doctor
Bawden, John
Beal, Rebecca
Beresford, Thomas
Bird, Benjamin
Bishop, Robert
Bond, Francis
Browne, John
Burke, Thomas
Burston, John
Bushell, Major George

Chace, John
Chapman, Mattheww
Chater, Barnabas
Cheesman, Richard
Chester, William
Child, Michael
Colleton, Colonel Thomas

Denner, John
Duesbury, Daniel
Dvorax, Stephen

Estwicke, Thomas

Farmer, Colonel John
Fenton, Agnes
Forstall, Richard
Foster, Elizabeth
Foster, Hester

Fousher, Philip
Frere, Captain Tobias
Fretwell, Ralph
Flewilling, Peter

Gallop, Ann
Gibbs, Captain John
Gibbs, Nicholas
Gibbs, Stephen
Gibbs, Thomas
Goldingham, John
Gray, John
Gray, Matthew

Haggatt, Othniell
Hallett; Colonel John
Hannay, George
Harper, George
Harrison, Captain Robert
Harwood, Richard
Haviland, Captain Matthew
Hayse, Thomas
Haywood, John
Henley, Edward
Hethersell, John
Holeman, Thomas
Holder, John
Holder, William
How, John
Hurlstone, Edward

Jackman, John
Johnson, Archibald
Johnson, Major John
Jones, Joseph
Jourdan, Edward

Kelly, Robert

Kershall, Captain William
King, Captain John

Lane, Ralph
Lewgar, William
Lillington, Major George
Linton, Thomas
Lintott, Richard

Marchant, Silas
Marchant, William
Marshall, Captain William
Maynard, Nicholas
Middleton, Benjamin
Morris, Captain Thomas

Palmer, Anthony
Parnell, Captain John
Parsons, Daniel
Pearce, Thomas
Prideaux, Nicholas
Prothero, Thomas

Quintyne, Henry

Sadler, Thomas
Salter, Major Richard
Sampson, Colonel John
Scott, Richard

Scott, Captain Walter
Shahany, John
Slograve, William
Smart, John
Smart, Samuel
Springham, Doctor John
Stewart, Captain John
Stoaks, Captain
Summers, John
Sutton, Captain John

Terwight, Captain George
Thomas, Charles
Thorpe, James
Titcombe, Colonel Samuel

Vinter, Lieutenant Colonel Richard

Walford, Muse
Walters, Ann
Walters, Richard
Warner, Samuel
Waterman, Colonel John
Weaver, William
Williams, Christopher
Williams, Hugh
Williams, Colonel Richard

Young, Francis

# ABBREVIATIONS

ACWA
: Axminster Churchwardens' Accounts, printed in G.P.R. Pulman, *The Book of the Axe* (reprinted 1969), 648.

Albemarle's List
: List of officers notified by the Duke of Albemarle: British Library, Harleian MS 7006.

Axe
: Narrative of the Revd. Thomas Axe: British Library, Harleian MS 6485

BA
: *The Bloody Assize*, ed. J.G. Muddiman (1929)

BJo
: Barbados, records of St. John's parish.

BMi
: Barbados, records of St. Michael's parish.

Br
: Broadsheet entitled 'A List of the Names of the Rebels that were executed' (1696).

CL
: Somerset Record Office, Presentments at Courts Leet of the Manor of Taunton Deane (DD/SP 18/61) and North Curry (DD/CC 113586).

CM
: J. Coad, *Memorandum of the Wonderful Providences of God* . . . (1849).

CP
: Constables' Presentments of 2,611 names intended for the Assizes at Dorchester, Exeter and Taunton (also called the Monmouth Roll): British Library, Additional MS 30077.

CSPC
: *Calendar of State Papers, Colonial* (H.M.S.O.), xi (1681–5); xii (1685–8); xiii (1689–92).

CSPD
: *Calendar of State Papers, Domestic* (H.M.S.O.) C2 (Charles II); J2 (James II); W & M (William and Mary).

Dep
: Depositions in the case Gardner v. Loder (printed in *Somerset and Dorset Notes and Queries* ix, 59–61) and the defence of Joseph Holmes, *penes* Mr J. Stevens Cox, Guernsey.

DLD
: List compiled for the Deputy Lieutenant of Devon of men in prison in Wiltshire, Somerset, Dorset and Devon: Churchill College, Cambridge, Erle MS 4/2 (photocopy in SRO T/PH/wig).

DNB
: *Dictionary of National Biography*

Dummer
: Edward Dummer's Journal, Pepysian Library, Magdalene College, Cambridge; copy in British Library, Additional MS 31956. Printed in J. Davis, *The History of the Second Queen's Regiment* (1895), 45–50.

Ecc.
: *Ecclesiastica, The Book of Remembrance of the Independent Congregations of Axminster and Chard* (1874); see also

|  | *Somerset Archaeology and Natural History*, 119, 51–5. |
|---|---|
| GD | Gaol Delivery Book for the Western Circuit, 1685: Public Record Office Asz 1/23/3. Printed, not entirely accurately, in F.A. Underwick, *Sidelights on the Stuarts* (2nd edn. 1891); Gaol Delivery Book for the Western Circuit, 1686: Public Record Office. |
| GJP | Grand Jury Presentments. |
| GP | General Pardon: printed Appendix I, p. xv–xviii. |
| H | 'A Paper found in young Hewling's poukett by Capt. Richardson': Historical Manuscripts Commission, *Stopford-Sackville MSS*. I (1904), 23. |
| Hist. MSS. Comm. | Historical Manuscripts Commission. |
| JB/JD | John Burd's letter to John Dunton, printed in *Bloody Assize*, ed. Muddiman, 131–6. |
| JR | Jeffreys' Report to King James: British Library, Additional MS 90337; copy in Harleian MS 4689. Printed in *Bloody Assize*, ed. Muddiman, 195–225. |
| JR2 | Jeffreys' later Report to King James: British Library, Additional MS 31957. Printed in *Calendar of Treasury Books*, VIII (H.M.S.O.), 414–25. |
| JW | Jeffreys' Warrant to the Sheriff of Somerset: British Library, Additional MS 34516. Printed in T. Salmon, *A Collection of Proceedings and Trials against State Prisoners* (1741) and *Bloody Assize*, ed. Muddiman, 226–31. |
| L | Interrogation of rebels: British Library, Lansdowne MS 1152A. |
| Lo | Richard Locke, *The Western Rebellion* (1782, reprinted 1927). |
| LRCB | Lyme Regis Court Book: Dorset Record Office B.7 D.1/3a. |
| LRMB | Lyme Regis Misdemeanour Book: Dorset Record Office B.7 A 3/1. |
| NL | Newsletter |
| Oldmixon | J. Oldmixon, *The History of England during the Reigns of the Royal House of Stuart* (1730). |
| OR | *Original Records of Early Nonconformity*, ed. G. Lyon Turner (1911–14). |
| P | Presumption. |
| Pa | Account of the Revd. Andrew Paschall, rector of Chedzoy. A contemporary copy of the longer version is in British Library, Harleian MS 4162; another, both from a common original, is in Lambeth Palace Library. The shorter version, from a manuscript discovered at Hoare's Bank, London, is printed in *Somerset and Dorset Notes and Queries*, xxviii, 15–21. |
| PE | Peter Earle, *Monmouth's Rebels* (1977). |
| PR | Parish Register. |

| | |
|---|---|
| PRO | Public Record Office. |
| Pulman, *Book of the Axe* | G.P.R. Pulman, *The Book of the Axe* (reprinted 1969). |
| PW | *A Relation of the Great Sufferings and Strange Adventures of Henry Pitman, Chyrurgion to the late Duke of Monmouth* (1689), reprinted in *Stuart Tracts*, ed. C. Firth. The *Relation* includes a letter from John Whicker. |
| QS | Quarter Sessions. |
| QSR | Quarter Sessions Rolls or Indictments. |
| SL | Sailing and Shipping lists: Public Record Office, Colonial Office (CO) 1/57, 58, 66. Partly printed in *The Original Lists of Persons of Quality, Emigrants, Religious Exiles, Political Rebels . . . who went from Great Britain to the American Plantations, 1600–1700*, ed. J.C. Hotten (Reprinted 1974). |
| SRO | Somerset Record Office. |
| T | Tradition. |
| TB | *Calendar of Treasury Books* (H.M.S.O.) Volume VIII, pp. 2002–6, is a schedule of people whose lands were forfeit and in some cases were for sale. |
| W | The Narrative of Nathaniel Wade: British Library, Harleian MS 6845. Printed in W.M. Wigfield, *The Monmouth Rebellion* (1980), 150–71. |
| WB | Joseph Winter's bill for the treatment of rebel prisoners: SRO DD/PH (Phelips MSS) 212/40. |
| Whiting | John Whiting, *Persecution Exposed* (1715). |

# ROLLCALL OF THE REBELS
## 1685

# ROLLCALL OF THE REBELS 1685

AARON, probably a negro servant, 'Mr. Palmer's man,' of Bishop's Hull, absent, (CP), not taken (CL).

ABBOTT, Edward, tried at Wells, transported thence for Bridgeman (JR) on Oct. 31 by White on the *Constant Richard* to Jamaica (SL).

ABBOTT, Michael, cordwainer (TB), of Honiton, 'a rebel' (CP), imprisoned in the Devon workhouse (DLD) tried at Dorchester, hanged (JR) at Sherborne, Sept. 15 (NL); land forfeit and for sale (TB).

ABBOTT, Robert, junior, of Somerton, 'in the late rebellion and not come home' (CP).

ABBOTT, William, of Honiton, 'rebel, not taken' (CP).

ABRAHAMS, Isaac, yeoman (JR), of Colyton, absent (CP), presented at Exeter, at large (JR). Father of John (PR).

ABRAHAMS, John, aged 14 (PR), of Colyton, absent (CP); presented at Exeter, at large (JR). Survived; returned to Colyton and married c. 1695; son baptised 1696 (PR).

ACASTLE (Attcastle), Robert, of Kingston St Mary, wanting from his home (CL); 'absent' (CP); tried at Wells, remaining in custody (JR), but transported by T. Heywood on the *Constant Richard* to Jamaica (SL).

ADAMS, Abraham, of Leigh on Mendip, 'supposed in Monmouth's army' (CP).

ADAMS, Edward, tried at Dorchester, transported for Booth (JR) on Sept. 25 from Weymouth to Barbados on the *Happy Return*; sold to James Thorpe (SL).

ADAMS, George, tried at Wells, hanged (JR) at Pensford (JW).

ADAMS, Jacob, of Leigh on Mendip, 'supposed in Monmouth's army' (CP), tried at Wells, transported for Stapleton (JR) on Oct. 20 on the *Indeavour* from Bristol to Nevis or St Kitts (SL).

ADAMS, John, yeoman, of Lopen (TB), tried at Dorchester, transported for Booth, (JR) Sept. 25 from Weymouth to Barbados on the *Happy Return*; sold to James Thorpe (SL); land forfeit and for sale (TB).

ADAMS, John, worsted comber, of Taunton St James, 'assisting' (CP), Blue Regt. (P), tried at Taunton, transported for the Queen (JR) Dec. 9 on the *Jamaica Merchant* to Barbados; sold to Richard Forstall, Mar. 12. (SL).

ADAMS, Nicholas, tried at Taunton, hanged (JR) at Crewkerne (JW).

ADAMS, Richard, tried at Wells, remaining in custody, 'humbly proposed for his Majesties most gracious pardon' (JR).

ADAMS, Robert, of Creech St Michael, 'absent and not taken' (CP).

ADAMS, Samuel, of Taunton St James, 'aiding' (CP), Blue Regt. (P); tried at Taunton, remaining in gaol (JR).

ADAMS, Thomas, weaver, of Taunton St Mary, 'aiding'(CP), Blue Regt. (P); tried at Taunton, transported for Musgrave (JR) on the *Jamaica Merchant* from Weymouth to Barbados, there by March 12 (SL).

ADDER, John, weaver, of Taunton St Mary, 'aiding' (CP), Blue Regt. (P).

ADLAM, Benjamin, captain, of the Wilts. Horse (W); mortally wounded at Sedgemoor, hanged outside Westonzoyland church (T).

ADLAM, Timothy, yeoman, of West Woodlands, 'in the rebellion and at large' (CP).

ADWELL, Will, of Bishop's Hull, 'absent and not taken' (CL).

AIRE, Edward, of Croscombe, 'in Scott's army and not taken' (CP).

ALDERSEY, Hugh, probably of Gloucestershire, at Sedgemoor, escaped to Lothersdale, Yorkshire, married and settled there (T).

ALDRIDGE, Ralph, of Westbury, 'in the rebellion' (GJP, Wilts. QSR).

ALEXANDER *see* Love.

ALFORD, Benjamin, carpenter, of Taunton St James, 'aiding' (CP), Blue Regt. (P).

ALLFORD, Richard, of Othery, absent (CP).

ALLAMBRIDGE, John, tried at Dorchester, transported for Booth (JR) on the *Happy Return* from Weymouth, Sept. 25, to Barbados; sold to Col. Richard Williams (SL).

ALLEN, George, tried at Wells, transported for Howard (JR) on *Port Royal Merchant* Oct. 25, to Jamaica (SL).

ALLEN, Henry, of Shepton Mallet, 'in prison for rebellion' (CP); perhaps died there (P).

ALLEN, John, tried at Dorchester, transported for Booth (JR) on the *Happy Return* from Weymouth, Sept. 25, to Barbados; sold to Capt. John Parnell (SL).

ALLEN, Richard, of Creech St Michael, 'in the rebellion and taken' (CP), tried at Taunton, transported for Booth (JR) from Taunton Bridewell via Bristol, Oct. 24, on the *John* to Barbados; sold to Capt. W. Scott (SL).

ALLEN, Richard, tried at Dorchester, transported for Booth (JR) on the *Happy Return* from Weymouth, Sept. 25, to Barbados; sold to William Lewgar, Esq. (SL).

ALLEN, Robert, tried at Taunton, hanged (JR) at Somerton (JW).

ALLEN, Thomas,⎫ both tried at Dorchester and transported for Booth
ALLEN, Thomas,⎭ (JR), on the *Happy Return* from Weymouth Sept. 25, to Barbados and sold, one to Richard Lintott, the other to Col. Richard Williams, Dec. 1685.

ALLER, John, of Crewkerne, 'rebel in Monmouth's army and not taken' (CP). Perhaps John Allen.

ALSOP, Benjamin, late of London, 'engaged in the late rebellion'; pardon May 31, 1687 (CSPD J2, II, 1833).

ALSTON, John, tried at Dorchester, transported for Booth (JR) on the *Happy Return* from Weymouth, Sept. 25, to Barbados; sold to Col.

John Hallett. Named on the 1689 Petition for return (CSPD, W&M, I, 43).

ALSTON, William, tried at Dorchester, hanged (JR) at Sherborne, Sept. 15. (NL).

ALTROGE, Christopher, 'committed to the County Gaol, confessing that he landed at Lime with the Rebells as servant to one Capt. Bruce and that he rune away from Bridgwater on Munday last' (Wilts. QSR July 14, 1685).

AMEREY, John, yeoman, of Somerset: pardon, May 5, 1686 (CSPD J2, II, 513).

AMEREY, Simon, worsted comber, of Taunton St Mary, 'aiding' (CP), Blue Regt. (P).

ANDERSEY, Thomas, of Othery, absent, taken, (CP); tried at Wells, to be transported for Howard (JR) recommended for pardon; reprieved and Roger Drower transported instead in *Port Royal Merchant* to Jamaica (JR in TB).

ANDREWS (Androse), Ames, of Bishop's Hull, 'absent, not taken' (CL).

ANDREWS, Henry, junior, of Creech St Michael, 'absent and not taken' (CP).

ANDREWS, James, of Bishop's Hull, 'absent, not taken' (CL).

ANDREWS, John, senior, of Frome, clothworker, 'in the rebellion and at large' (CP), presented at Wells and bound over (JR).

ANDREWS, John, junior, aged 27, woolcomber (SL), tried at Taunton, transported for the Queen (JR) from Taunton on the *Jamaica Merchant* Dec. 9 to Barbados March 12; sold to Richard Forstall (SL).

ANDREWS, Jeremiah, yeoman, of Frome, 'in the rebellion and at large' (CP).

ANDREWS, John, of Thornfalcon, 'taking up arms against the king' (CL).

ANDREWS, Joseph, of Lovington, 'absent and not returned' (CP).

ANDREWS, Philip, of Shaftesbury, 'for being in the rebellious army of James Duke of Monmoth as it is reported' (CP); tried at Dorchester; certificate (of laying down his arms) allowed (JR).

ANDREWS, Robert, of Wellington, 'absent' (CP).

ANDREWS, Samuel, comber, of Taunton St Mary, 'aiding' (CP), Blue Regt. (P).

ANDRIDGE, William, tried at Exeter 'for assisting Roger Bryant to make his escape'; pleaded guilty; fined and whipped (GD, JR).

ANNESLEY (Angeley, Ansley) Abraham, an Independent, Captain of Foot (dying speech); taken to Newgate, London, July 16 (CSPD J2, I, 1249); tried at Taunton and hanged there (JR, JW) Sept. 30 (Lo); last letter and dying speech in BA.

APLYN, William, of Durston (CL), of North Petherton (CP) 'in the rebellion and in prison' (CP); tried at Wells, remaining in custody (JR); transported by Heywood in the *Constant Richard* to Jamaica (SL).

APPLEDORE *see* Jennings.

APPLIN, John, of Glastonbury, 'from home in the time of rebellion' (CP).

APREPOLLING, William, of Durston, 'having taken up armes against his present Majesty' (CL).

ARCHETT, *see* Orchard.

ARNOLD, Francis, thatcher, of Taunton St James, 'aiding' (CP), Blue Regt. (P).

ARNOLD, John, of Nether Compton, 'absent, suspected' (CP), tried at Wells, transported thence Oct. 31, for Bridgeman (JR) by White on the *Constant Richard* to Jamaica (SL).

ARNOLD, William, labourer, of Glastonbury; land forfeit and for sale (TB). Presumably killed at Sedgemoor (P).

ASCOUGH, ASCUE *see* Askew

ASH, William, weaver, of Taunton St Mary, 'aiding' (CP), Blue Regt. (P); recently married (PR).

ASHE, Richard, tried at Taunton, hanged (JR) at Castle Cary (JW).

ASHFORD, Ambrose, yeoman, of Musbury, 'in the late rebellion, in prison' (CP) at Ilchester (DLD), tried at Dorchester, transported for Booth (CP) on the *Happy Return* from Weymouth Sept. 25 to Barbados; sold to Capt. Walter Scott (SL).

ASHFORD, Thomas, carpenter, of Staplegrove (CL), of Taunton St James, 'aiding' (CP); Blue Regt. (P); presented at Wells and bound over (JR).

ASHFORD, William, junior, carpenter, of Staplegrove (CL), of Taunton St James, 'aiding' (CP); Blue Regt. (P); tried at Wells, recommended for the king's pardon (JR).

ASHLEY, Hugh, tried at Taunton, hanged (JR) at Stogursey (JW).

ASHLEY, John, worsted comber, of Taunton St Mary, 'aiding' (CP), Blue Regt. (P).

ASHPOOLE, Ellis, pardoned 'for all treasons,' April 17, 1687 (CSPD J2, II, 417).

ASHTON, Samuel, presented at Wells, 30 March, 1686, as 'convicted at the last sessions'. No other note [of 8 so presented, 4 were rebels.]

ASHWOOD, John, student, son of nonconformist minister of Axminster, marched as far as Norton St Philip, returning thence was taken (Ecc.), tried at Wells, to be hanged (JR) at Shepton Mallet (JW). Reprieved and pardoned (JR2); became Congregational minister at Exeter.

ASKEW (Ascue), Josias, of Long Acre, London (L), Ensign, commanded Rear Guard at Bridport (W); after Sedgemoor taken to the Gatehouse, Westminster, July 16 (CSPD J2, I, 1250) and interrogated (L); tried at Dorchester and hanged (JR) at Lyme, Sept. 12 (NL). Last letter to his mother, signed J. Askew, printed in BA.

ASSELFORD, Henry, of Beaminster, 'absent in the time of the rebellion' (CP).

ATKINS, Jeremiah, husbandman, of Taunton (TB), Blue Regt. (P); in the Bridewell at Taunton (SL); tried there, transported for Booth

(JR) from Bristol, Oct. 24 on the *John* to Barbados; sold to John Browne (SL). Land forfeit and for sale (TB). Atkins escaped from Barbados with Dr Pitman, but was captured by Spanish pirates and died of malaria on the deck of their ship (PW).

ATKINS, John, of Chardland, 'absent, believed in the rebellion' (CP).

ATKINS, John, of Knowle St Giles, 'in the rebellion and not come in'. (CP).

ATKINS, John, sergemaker, of Taunton St Mary, 'aiding' (CP); Blue Regt. (P). Escaped to Holland; in scheme to manufacture English cloth there; pardon, June 2, 1686: 'if he return within 2 months with his goods and effects' (CSPD J2, II, 626).

ATKINS, Joseph, worsted comber (DLD) of Chard, 'absent, believed in the rebellion' (CP); in the High Gaol, Devon (DLD).

ATKINS, Philip, glazier, of Taunton St Mary, 'aiding' (CP), Blue Regt. (P).

ATTCASTLE, *see* Acastle.

ATTWOOD, John, shoemaker, of Rode, 'in the rebellion' (CP); tried at Wells, transported for Howard (JR) Oct. 25 in the *Port Royal Merchant* to Jamaica (SL).

ATTWOOD, Richard, weaver, of West Woodlands, 'in prison for the late rebellion' (CP), tried at Wells, transported for Stapleton (JR), Oct. 20, in the *Indeavour* from Bristol to Nevis or St Kitts (SL).

AUDLER, Christine, 'in the late rebellion, confessed,' in Newgate, London, July 16; taken to the Earl of Middleton, July 17 (CSPD J2, I, 1249, 1252).

AULER the younger, 'was very busy entering all the arms at Amsterdam' (L, interrogation of Kidd). [Did he come with Monmouth?]

AUSTIN, Thomas, aged 27, mercer (SL), tried at Taunton, transported for the Queen (JR) on Dec. 9 on the *Jamaica Merchant* to Barbados, Mar. 12 sold to Charles Thomas and Thomas Sadler (SL). He was to have escaped with Dr Pitman but stayed (PW). ? married 1694; Austin family in island from 1720s onwards (Barbados records).

AVANT, Francis, of Wootton Fitzpaine, 'suspected of being in the rebellion' (CP).

AVOAKE, John, tried at Taunton (JR), transported from Bridgwater for Booth (SL).

AXE, Andrew, yeoman, of Stoke under Ham, 'absent' (CP).

AYLER, Edward, of Donyatt, 'out in the rebellion' (CP).

AYMES, James, tried at Wells (JR), transported for Howard in the *Port Royal Merchant* on Oct. 25 to Jamaica (SL).

BABB, Edward, of Trull, 'absent' (CP), Blue Regt. (P). Pardon 31 May 1687 (CSPD J2, II, 1833).

BABB, Robert, of Barrington, 'in the rebellion and not come in' (CP).

BABBINGTON, Ensign Babbington of the Red Regt. came from Holland with Monmouth (W) and was probably killed at Sedgemoor (P).

BABINGTON, Randall, was tried at Taunton, and to be transported for the Queen (JR). He was not on the *Jamaica Merchant*, but was on the list (Oct. 12) to be transported by John Rose of London (SL).

BABINGTON, Randolph, probably the same man, claimed to have been tried at Taunton by Jeffreys and sentenced to transportation to Barbados for Booth. He paid £28 to Sir John Knight of Bristol to travel as a free passenger, paying £4 to Capt. Stoakes of the *John* and £2 'for better usage'. After 9 or 10 days' freedom in Barbados he was arrested and examined by the Lieut. Governor, Edwin Stede. He claimed to be a warehouseman from Cripplegate, who was in the West collecting a debt when Monmouth arrived. A spectator only, he was arrested on suspicion and tried, pleading guilty as the others did. Stede reported on Jan. 8 1686 that the list of the second shipload, on the *John*, was not in accordance with the warrant of the Lord Chief Justice. Stede kept Babington in custody. (CSPC, xii, 561). If the Ensign was also the London warehouseman and not killed at Sedgemoor, he was a skilful liar. Buried 1686 St Michael's, Barbados (BMi).

BACALAR, Richard, sent to prison by Axminster churchwardens, but not brought to trial (Pulman, *Book of the Axe*).

BACHER *see* Butcher.

BADCOCK, John, of Bampton, 'supposed to be a rebel' (CP).

BADCOCK, William, tailor, of Lyme Regis, 'absent and supposed' (CP).

BADD (Badoe, Baddy), George, tried at Taunton, hanged (JR) at Keynsham (JW).

BADGE, Richard, tried at Wells and bound over (JR).

BADSETTY, Joseph, of Bishop's Hull, 'absent, not taken' (CL).

BAGG, Edward, of South Petherton, 'in the rebellion and not come in' (CP).

BAGG, George, of Wootton Fitzpaine, 'suspected to be in the rebellion' (CP).

*And see* Bragg.

BAGG, Richard, of Thurloxton, 'in the rebellion and in prison' (CP). Perhaps he died there (P).

BAGG, Robert, of Taunton St James, 'aiding' (CP). Blue Regt. (P).

BAGLEY, Thomas, tried at Taunton, 'remaining in gaol' (JR); transported Oct. 9 by Thomas Heywood, gent. to Jamaica (SL).

BAGWELL, Amos, aged 31 (PR), yeoman, of Colyton, 'absent' (CP); presented at Exeter, but at large (JR).

BAGWELL, Francis, sergeweaver, of Colyton, wounded at Sedgemoor, imprisoned at Wells (DLD); tried there and transported for Stapleton (JR), in the *Indeavour* from Bristol Oct. 20 to Nevis or St Kitts (SL).

BAGWELL, John, yeoman, of Colyton, 'absent' (CP); cordwainer, in Bridgwater prison (DLD), tried at Dorchester, transported for Musgrave (JR) on the *Jamaica Merchant* from Weymouth to Jamaica, there 12 March 1686. Named on the 1689 petition for return (CSPD, W&M, I, 43).

BAGWELL, Peter, yeoman, of Colyton, 'absent' (CP), in Bridgwater prison (DLD), tried at Dorchester, transported for Nipho (JR) from Dorchester gaol on the *Betty* to Barbados; sold to Nicholas Maynard (SL); escaped with Dr Pitman and returned to England (PW). Probably aged 33; died 1693 (PR).

BAGWELL, Walter, yeoman, of Colyton, 'absent' (CP); presented at Exeter but at large (JR). Aged 42; married 1684; a son christened in 1688; died Jan. 1695/6 (PR).

BAGWELL, William, aged 20 (PR), yeoman, of Colyton, 'absent' (CP); presented at Exeter but at large (JR).

BAILES *see* Beales.

BAILEY, Samuel, of Beaminster, 'wanting from home' (CP).

BAKEHOUSE, George, of Shepton Mallet, 'in prison for rebellion' (CP). Perhaps he died there (PR).

BAKER, Bartholomew, yeoman, of Axmouth, 'reported to be in arms' (CP); presented at Exeter but at large (JR).

BAKER, Caleb, fuller, of Taunton St Mary, 'aiding' (CP); Blue Regt. (P).

BAKER, Charles, tried at Wells, transported for Stapleton (JR), on the *Indeavour* from Bristol Oct. 20, to Nevis or St Kitts (SL).

BAKER, Edward, presented at Wells and bound over (JR).

BAKER, George, carpenter, of Lyme Regis, 'absent and supposed' (CP).

BAKER, George, of Westonzoyland, 'absent.'

BAKER, Jacob, presented at Dorchester, certificate allowed (JR).

BAKER, James, of Milverton, 'absenting himself' (CP), tried at Taunton, transported for Booth (JR) from Exeter via Bristol, Oct. 24, on the *John* to Barbados; sold to Capt. Stoaks (SL).

BAKER, James, tried at Wells, to be transported for Howard (JR); 'humbly proposed for pardon'; John Rossiter transported instead (JR2).

BAKER, John, of Banwell, excepted from GP.

BAKER, John, senior, of Buckland St Mary, 'out in the rebellion and not taken' (CP), tried at Taunton and transported thence for the Queen (JR) on the *Jamaica Merchant* Dec. 9 to Barbados March 12; a sergeworker aged 35, sold to Major George Bushell (SL).

BAKER alias Barrett, John of Dowlishwake, 'in the rebellion and not come in' (CP).

BAKER alias Wood, John, of Honiton, 'a rebel' (CP), worsted comber, imprisoned in the High Gaol, Devon (DLD), tried at Wells, transported for Howard (JR) Oct. 25 to Jamaica (SL). Named in petition for return (CSPD, W&M, I, 43).

BAKER, John, yeoman, of Musbury, 'in the rebellion' (CP); (wrongly 'of Axminster' in JR); presented at Exeter but at large (JR). Pardoned at the Exeter Assize, March 1686 (GD).

BAKER (Barker), John, of Shaftesbury 'in the rebellious army' (CP), tried at Dorchester, transported for Nipho (JR) from Dorchester gaol on the *Betty* to Barbados; sold to Ralph Lane (SL).

BAKER, John, of Wellington, 'in prison for rebellion' (CP), tried at Taunton, transported for the Queen (JR) from Taunton on the

*Jamaica Merchant*, Dec. 9, to Barbados March 12; a mason, aged 27, sold to Col. Thomas Colleton (SL).

BAKER, Marke, carpenter, of Sheldon, wounded at Sedgemoor, imprisoned at Wells (DLD) and perhaps died there. (P).

BAKER, Roger, of South Petherton, 'in the rebellion and not come in' (CP). Presented at Wells and bound over (JR).

BAKER, Thomas, yeoman, of Kingsbury Episcopi, 'absent and believed' (CP). Pardoned, May 12, 1686 (CSPD, J2, II, 530).

BAKER, Walter, of Ruishton, 'absent' (CP), 'absent' (CL) Oct. 27.

BAKER, Walter, senior, of Westonzoyland, 'absent' (CP).

BAKER, Walter, junior, of Westonzoyland, 'absent' (CP). [*See below*]. [One Walter Baker was tried at Wells and hanged at Bath, Nov. 18 (JR, JW).]

BAKER, William, of Sheldon, worsted comber, imprisoned in Taunton (DLD); tried at Taunton, 'remaining in gaol' (JR); transported from Wells, Oct. 31, by White on the *Constant Richard* to Jamaica (SL).

BAKER, William, of Stowell, 'out in the rebellion and at large' (CP), 'absent' (CL). *And see* Long.

BALCH, Thomas of Staple Fitzpaine, 'out in the rebellion' (CP).

BALE, John, pardoned at Dorchester Assizes, March 1686 (GD).

BALL, James, of Norton Fitzwarren, 'absent' (CP).

BALL, William, of Norton Fitzwarren, 'absent' (CP).

BALLER, Francis, of Pitminster, 'absent, supposed' (CP).

BALLY *see* Bayly.

BALSON, John, of Sherborne, 'taken at Lyme Regis and sent to Dorchester gaol', July 14 (LRMB).

BALSTER, Isaac, prisoner, charged for 'running from his Colours' in the Lord Fitzharding's troop of Horse, committed July 17th (Som. QSR, adjourned from Bridgwater, July 14 to Bruton, August 4, 1685).

BALSTER *see* Bollster.

BALSTON, John, weaver, of East Woodlands, 'in the rebellion and at large' (CP).

BALSTON, John, ostler, of Lyme Regis, 'absent and supposed' (CP). [One John Balston was presented at Wells and bound over (JR)].

BANBURY, Thomas, tried at Taunton, transported for the Queen (JR). [Not on the *Jamaica Merchant* but on John Rose's list, Oct. 12 (SL).]

BANFIELD (Bampfeild), Thomas, junior, of Bradford on Tone, 'absent' (CP).

BANTON, Hugh, tried at Wells, transported for Howard (JR) Oct. 25, on the *Port Royal Merchant* to Jamaica (SL).

BARBER, Edward, yeoman, of Colyton, 'absent' (CP); presented at Exeter but at large (JR); escaped from Exeter Workhouse (*London Gazette*). He returned to Colyton and his child was baptized there in 1688, although Edward had died in January 1687/8 (PR).

BARD *see* Bond.

BARGE, Bartholomew, tried at Dorchester, 'remaining in custody' (JR); pardoned at Dorchester Assize, March 1686 (GD).

BARGE (Burge), Robert, husbandman, of Broomfield, 'in the rebellion and taken', (CL); tried at Taunton, transported for Musgrave (JR) from Weymouth on the *Jamaica Merchant* to Barbados, reached by March 12 (SL).

BARKER *see* Baker.

BARNARD, Richard, of Huish Episcopi, 'absent and believed' (CP).

BARNARD, Samuel, of Puriton, 'actively a soldier in the Duke of Monmouth's army' (CL).

BARNARD, Thomas, tried at Taunton, hanged (JR) at Ilminster (JW).

BARNARD, William, yeoman, of Colyton, 'absent' (CP), presented at Exeter but at large (JR).

BARNARD, William, of Huish Episcopi, 'absent and believed' (CP), tried at Taunton, transported for Booth (JR) from Taunton Bridewell via Bristol, Oct. 24, on the *John* to Barbados; sold to Col. John Sampson (SL).

BARNARDISTON, Samuel, from Holland with Monmouth (H), 'Reformade' [ex officer re enlisted]. Excepted from the GP.

BARNARDISTON 'young', from Holland with the Duke (H); not excepted from the GP, and therefore presumably killed at Sedgemoor (P).

BARNES, Ralph, of Chardland, 'absent and believed' (CP).

BARNES, Robert, of Symondsbury, 'suspected' (CP).

BARNETT, William, of Long Sutton, 'in the rebellion and not come home' (CP).

BARR *see* Bond.

BARRELL, Robert, of Wedmore, 'absent and in the late rebellion' (CP).

BARRETT, Giles, of Chard, 'in the late rebellion' (CP).

BARRETT, John, of Chard, 'in the late rebellion' (CP).

BARRETT, John, junior, of Ilminster, 'in the late rebellion' (CP).

BARRETT, Osmond, soapboiler (DLD), husbandman of Colyton, absent (CP), imprisoned at Exeter (DLD), presented there but at large (JR), tried at Taunton and hanged (JR) at Ilchester (JW). Land forfeit and for sale (TB).

BARROW *see* Burrough.

BARTLETT, Francis, mason, of Taunton St Mary, 'aiding' (CP), tried at Taunton, to be hanged (JR) at Minehead (JW) where 3 of 6 so sentenced were hanged (NL).

BARTLETT, James, of Bruton, 'in James Scott's army and not yet taken' (CP).

BARTLETT, John, junior, of North Curry (CL), of Stoke St Gregory (CP), 'in arms, aiding and assisting James Scott in the time of the rebellion' (CP).

BARTLETT, John, of Pitminster (SL), tried at Taunton, transported for Booth (JR) from Taunton Bridewell via Bristol, Oct. 24, on the *John* to Barbados; sold to Capt. W. Scott (SL).

BARTLETT, John, of Stratton, South Petherton, 'in the rebellion and not come in' (CP); tried at Wells; transported for Stapleton (JR), Oct. 20, from Bristol in the *Indeavour* to Nevis or St Kitts (SL).

BARTLETT, John, of Abbott's Wootton, 'suspected' (CP); pardoned at
Exeter Assizes, 1686 (GD).

BARTLETT, Josiah, yeoman, of Axmouth, 'reported to be in arms in the
late rebellion' (CP); presented at Exeter but at large (JR). LRMB
says husbandman, 'compelled by William Cox, his master, to drive
his plough [cart] to Lyme and Bridgwater, and was at Norton St
Philip fight, and continued with his plough until they were taken by
the King's party; he laid hidden; to Dorchester gaol, Jan. 5;
pardoned at Dorchester Assizes, 1686 (GD).

BARTLETT, Nicholas, presented at Dorchester, certificate allowed
(JR).

BARTLETT, Thomas, of Pitminster, 'absent' (CP); tried at Taunton,
'humbly proposed for his Majesty's gracious pardon'. 'Remaining
in gaol' deleted (JR).

BARTLETT, William, of Corfe, 'absent' (CP).

BARTON, Richard, of Wilton, 'absent' (CP); hanged in Taunton by Col.
Kirke on July 9 (P), buried on July 10 by the Vicar of St James's
(PR).

BARTRAM, Peter, joiner, of Cullompton, in the High Gaol, Devon
(DLD).

BASELEY (Basleigh) John, tried at Taunton, to be hanged (JR) at
Dulverton (JW), where 2 of the 3 so sentenced were hanged on Dec.
8 (NL).

BASELEY, Richard, of Stockland, 'suspected' (CP).

BASLEIGH, Robert, yeoman, of Colyton, 'absent' (CP), presented at
Exeter but at large (JR), pardon granted May 12, 1686 (CSPD J2, II,
530).

BASSETT *see* Bovet.

BATES, John, yeoman, of Axminster, 'supposed', (CP), presented at
Exeter but at large; tried at Taunton, to be hanged, but omitted
from the warrant (JR); 'humbly proposed for pardon' (JR2) but
transported, Oct. 9, on the *Constant Richard* to Jamaica (SL).

BATT, Robert, tried at Wells, transported for Nipho (JR); on Penne's list
for the *Rebecca* (SL).

BATT, Stephen, of South Petherton, 'in the rebellion and not come in'
(CP).

BATTEN, Robert, of Chard, 'absent and believed' (CP).

BATTINS, James, yeoman, of Colyton, 'absent' (CP), presented at
Exeter but at large (JR).

BATTISCOMBE, Christopher, gentleman, lawyer, of Symondsbury and
London, on the fringe of the Rye House Plot; came from Holland
with Monmouth (W). Captain in the Red Regiment (W); taken after
Sedgemoor and sent from Exeter to Newgate, London, July 16,
(CSPD J2, I, 1236), interrogated Aug. 23, gave nothing away (L);
tried at Dorchester (JR), hanged at Lyme Regis, Sept. 12 (NL).
Short dying speech (BA); land forfeit and for sale (TB).

BAUNTON, Alexander, of Chard, 'absent and believed' (CP).

BAUNTON, Gamaliel, of Chardland, 'absent and believed' (CP).

BAYLY, William, of Milverton, 'absenting himself' (CP); tried at Taunton, transported for Musgrave (JR) on the *Jamaica Merchant* from Weymouth to Barbados, there March 12 1686 (SL).

BAYNHAM, Jacob, of Kingston St Mary, 'absent' (CP); of Nailsbourne, 'by report in the late rebellion' (CL).

BEACH, Zachary, of Combe St Nicholas, 'absent and believed' (CP).

BEADON, Richard, presented at Wells, recommended for the king's pardon (JR).

BEALE, Robert, tried at Wells, transported for Howard (JR), Oct. 25 to Jamaica (SL).

BEARD, Richard, of Ottery St Mary, 'in the late rebellion as supposed' (CP).

BEARD, Roger, of Crewkerne, 'rebel in Monmouth's army' (CP).

BEASELEY, Henry, blacksmith, of Shute (DLD), presented at Dorchester, 'humbly proposed for his Majesty's gracious pardon' (JR).

BEATES, John, sergeweaver, of Axminster (DLD); examined by JPs at Lyme, gave 17 names; sent to Dorchester gaol (LRMB).

BEATON, Edward, of Nether Compton, 'absconding and suspected' (CP).

BEATON, Nathaniel, tried at Wells, transported for Nipho (JR). On Penne's list for the *Rebecca*, Oct. 21 (SL).

BEATON, Robert, tried at Wells, transported for Howard (JR), Oct. 25 on the *Port Royal Merchant* to Jamaica.

BEAUMONT, John senior, of Lyme Regis, tried at Dorchester, hanged (JR) at Bridport (JW) on Sept. 12 (NL).

BEAUMONT, John junior, tried at Dorchester, 'humbly proposed for pardon' (JR).

BEAUMONT, Robert, tried at Wells, hanged (JR) at Frome (JW).

BEAVIS, Francis, weaver, of Taunton St Mary, 'aiding' (CP); of Extraportam (CL); Blue Regt. (P).

BEAVIS, Francis [another], weaver, of Taunton St Mary, 'aiding' (CP); Blue Regt. (P).

BEAVIS, John, of Sidbury, 'joined in the rebellion' (CP).

BEAVIS, John, of Abbott's Wootton, 'suspected' (CP); tried at Dorchester, hanged (JR) at Weymouth or Melcombe Regis (JW) on Sept. 15 (NL).

BEAVIS, Nathan, of North Curry, 'absent' (CP), 'in arms' (CL).

BEAVIS, Preston, of Chardland, 'absent and believed' (CP); tried at Wells, hanged (JR) at Pensford (JW).

BEAVIS, Stephen, seaman, of Lyme Regis, 'absent and supposed' (CP).

BEAVIS, Thomas, of Combe St Nicholas, 'absent and believed' (CP).

BEAWAY, William, yeoman, of Axminster, presented at Exeter, but at large (CP).

BEDFORD, Joseph, junior, cardmaker, of Frome, 'for a ryott and amongst the Clubmen' (CP).

BEDLER, Henry, presented at Wells and bound over (JR).

BEDLOW, Samuel, presented and pardoned at Dorchester Assizes, 1686 (GD).

BEEDLE, Henry, of Tiverton, 'with the late Duke of Monmouth' (CP).

BEERE, John, taken to prison (Pulman, *Book of the Axe*); presented and pardoned at Exeter Assizes, 1686 (GD).

BELLAMY, Edward, aged 27, carpenter (SL), tried at Taunton, transported for the Queen (JR) from Taunton to Barbados on the *Jamaica Merchant*, arriving March 12, 1686; sold to John Hethersell, Esq. (SL).

BELLAMY, Joseph (or Joshua), tried at Taunton, to be hanged (JR) at Bridgwater (JW) but reprieved (JR) 'under the gallows' (Lo).

BELLAMY, Simon, of Thurloxton, 'absconded' (CP).

BELLET, Matthew, presented and pardoned by proclamation at Wells, 1686 (GD).

BELLEW, John, presented and pardoned by proclamation at Dorchester, 1686 (GD).

BELLIS, Thomas, of Chard, 'absent and believed' (CP).

BELLRINGER, John, of Taunton St Mary, 'aiding' (CP); Blue Regt. (P).

BEMAN, Robert, weaver, of Rode, 'thought to be in the rebellion' (CP).

BENCHFIELD, Stephen, presented at Wells, 'recommended for pardon' (JR).

BENDICK, Simon, of Combe St Nicholas, 'absent and believed' (CP).

BENGFIELD, Thomas, of Bruton, 'in James Scott's army and not yet taken' (CP).

BENJAMIN, late servant to Mr Robert Bobbett of Creech St Michael, 'took up arms against his Majesty' (CL).

BENNETT, Charles, junior, of Wellington, 'in prison for rebellion' (CP); tried at Taunton, to be transported for the Queen (JR); on John Rose's receipt, Oct. 12 (SL).

BENNETT, Henry, of Winsham, 'absent and believed' (CP).

BENNETT, John, gentleman, of Aylesbeare, exceppted from the General Pardon, but pardon 'renewed', Oct. 31, 1686 (CSPD, J2, II, 1041).

BENNETT, John [another], excepted from GP. [Possibly the J.B. of Street and Leigh *below*.]

BENNETT, John senior at Lyme Regis, a pauper, 'absent and supposed' (CP). Locke says tried at Dorchester; Jeffreys: 'I will ease the parish of the burden'; hanged Locke did not know where (LO). [Possibly confused with John Beamont senior.]

BENNETT, John junior, of Lyme Regis, 'absent and supposed' (CP). He offered to die in his father's place (LO).

BENNETT, John, of Street and Leigh tithing, Winsham, 'in the rebellion and not come in' (CP).

BENNETT, John senior, comber, of Taunton St Mary, 'aiding' (CP); Blue Regt. (P). A John Bennett was tried at Taunton, transported for the Queen (JR); on John Rose's receipt, Oct. 12 (SL).

BENNETT, John junior, comber, of Taunton St Mary, 'aiding' (CP); Blue Regt. (P).

BENNETT, John, weaver, of Wellington, 'in prison for rebellion' (CP); tried at Wells, transported for Howard (JR) Oct. 12 for Jamaica, but escaped between Wells and Sherborne (SL).

BENNETT, John, of West Buckland, 'at large' (CP).

BENNETT, John, carpenter, of Wellington, 'absent' (CP).

BENNETT, Joseph, of Bishop's Hull, 'absent' (CP); 'dead' (CL).

BENNETT, Richard, of Curry Rivel, 'out in the rebellion and not taken' (CP).

BENNETT, Simon, presented and pardoned at Exeter Assizes, 1686 (GD).

BENNETT, Thomas, tried at Dorchester, transported for Booth (JR), from Weymouth, Sept. 25, on the *Happy Return* to Barbados; sold to John Hethersell (SL). Buried 1690 St Johns, Barbados (BJo).

BENNETT, Thomas, of Salisbury, pardon for all treasons, Oct. 3, 1686 (CSPD, J2, II, 1041).

BENNETT, William, of Chardland, 'absent and believed' (CP), presented at Dorchester and discharged for want of evidence (JR).

BENNETT, William, mercer, of Crewkerne, tried at Dorchester, to be transported for Booth (JR) but reprieved (JR2). Land forfeit and for sale. Mumford to keep pardon money (TB).

BENNETT, William, of North Petherton, 'in the rebellion and in prison' (CP); 'humbly proposed for pardon' (JR2). Land forfeit but not for sale (TB).

BENNETT, William, of Taunton St Mary, 'aiding' (CP); Blue Regt. (P).

BENNETT, William, of Winsham, 'absent and believed' (CP).

BEREMAN, John, of Whitelackington, 'out in the rebellion' (CP).

BERRY, John, of Bampton, 'supposed to be a rebel' (CP).

BERRY, Joseph, yeoman, of Upottery, 'absent' (CP); presented at Exeter but at large (JR).

BERRY, Thomas, tried at Dorchester, 'humbly proposed for pardon' (JR).

BESSOM, Blose, of Milverton, 'absenting himself' (CP).

BESSON, James, hanged at Taunton by Col. Kirke (P) July 9; buried by the vicar of St James's, July 12 (PR).

BEST, James, tried at Wells; transported for Howard (JR) Oct. 25 on the *Port Royal Merchant* to Jamaica (SL).

BEST, Robert, of Lopen, 'in the rebellion and not come in' (CP); tried at Wells; transported for Howard (JR) Oct. 25 on the *Port Royal Merchant* to Jamaica (SL).

BEST, Thomas, tried at Dorchester; transported for Booth (JR) on the *Happy Return* from Weymouth Sept. 25 to Barbados; sold to John Burston (SL).

BEST, William, tried at Wells; transported for Howard (JR) Oct. 25 to Jamaica (SL).

BETTISCOMB, John, near Lyme Regis, excepted from the GP.

BEVIS *see* Beavis.

BICKHAM, Richard, of Wellington, 'in prison for rebellion' (CP); tried at Taunton; transported for Booth (JR) from Taunton Bridewell via

Bristol, Oct. 24, on the *John* to Barbados; sold to Capt. W. Scott (SL).

BICKLEY (Beckley), James, tried at Wells; transported for Stapleton in the *Indeavour* from Bristol, Oct. 20, to Nevis or St Kitts (SL).

BIDDLE, William, of Stoke St Gregory, 'in arms, aiding and assisting James Scott' (CP); of Curry Load, 'a tenant, fled' (CL).

BIDGOOD, Humphrey, 'proposed for pardon' at Devon Assizes, 1685 (JR2).

BIDGOOD, Thomas, of Frome Selwood; land forfeit and for sale (TB). Probably killed at Sedgemoor (P).

BIGG, James, junior, of Wellow, 'in the late rebellion and not returned' (CP).

BIGGOTT (Bigwood), Thomas, senior, of East Woodlands, 'in the rebellion, in prison' (CP); tried at Wells; transported for Stapleton (JR) Oct. 20, to Nevis or St Kitts (SL). Of Frome Selwood, land forfeit and for sale (TB). *See* Brigwood.

BIGGOTT, Thomas, junior, weaver, of East Woodlands, 'in the rebellion and at large' (CP).

BIGGS, William, tried at Wells; transported for Nipho (JR) on the *Betty* Sept. 26 to Barbados; sold to Richard Walters (SL).

BILLDIN, Thomas, of Staple Fitzpaine, 'out in the rebellion' (CP).

BILLEN, Andrew, of Clapton, 'rebel and not taken' (CP); tried at Dorchester and 'proposed for pardon' (JR).

BILLEN, John, of Clapton, 'rebel and not taken' (CP).

BILLEN, Daniel, of Bridport, 'in the Rebellion as we are informed' (CP).

BILLING, William, presented at Dorchester; no note of sentence (JR), perhaps he died in gaol before sentence.

BRIMSTONE, Abraham, yeoman, of Axminster, 'supposed' (C); presented at Exeter but at large (JR).

BINDON, Josias, of Alstone, Huntspill, 'being in arms in the late Rebellion' (CP).

BINGHAM, Samuel, of Lyme Regis, baker, 'absent and supposed' (CP).

BIRD, Bernard, yeoman, of Luppitt, 'supposed' (CP); presented at Exeter but at large (JR).

BIRD, John, yeoman, of Musbury, 'in the rebellion' (CP); presented at Exeter but at large (JR). Wrongly said to be of Axminster (JR).

BIRD, John, yeoman, of Luppitt, 'out in the rebellion' (CP); presented at Exeter but at large (JR).

BIRD, John, mercer, of Taunton St Mary, 'aiding' (CP); Blue Regt. (P); tried at Wells; sentenced to be hanged, but omitted from the warrant (JR); 'remaining in gaol, recommended for pardon' (JR2). The pardon-money to be kept by Richard Cridland; land forfeit but not for sale; granted to the lawyer-agents, Brent, Loder and Clarke (TB).

BIRD, Nathaniel, yeoman, of Luppitt, 'absent' (CP); presented at Exeter but at large (JR).

BIRD, Peter, tried at Exeter, transported for Nipho (JR) from Exeter gaol in the *Betty* towards Barbados, but died at sea, Jan. 1 1685/6. (SL).

BIRD, Thomas, carrier, of Taunton St Mary, aiding (CP); Blue Regt. (P). *And see* Burd.

BIRDLE, John, of Charmouth, suspected (CP).

BISHOP, Edward, presented and bound over at Wells (JR).

BISHOP, Henry, of Over Compton, 'absconding and suspected' (CP).

BISHOP, Humphrey, husbandman, of Langport, 'absent' (CP).

BISHOP, John, of Corscombe, 'suspected' (CP) tried at Wells (JR); see below.

BISHOP, John, tailor, of Minehead, 'in the late rebellion' (CP); 'for bearing arms against his Majesty' (CL); tried at Wells (JR). One of these two was recommended for pardon; the other was transported for Bridgeman (JR) from Wells to Jamaica on the *Constant Richard* (SL).

BISHOP, Thomas, apothecary, of Bridport, 'in the rebellion as informed' (CP); presented at Wells; 'remaining in custody for want of evidence' (JR); pardoned July 4, 1686 (CSPD, J2, II, 768). A Quaker.

BISHOP, Thomas, yeoman, of Upottery, 'absent' (CP); presented at Exeter but at large (JR).

BISHOP, William, of Churchstanton, 'absconding, suspected' (CP).

BISHOP, William, of Wellington, 'absent' (CP).

BISSE, George, of Martock, 'aiding' (GD). He wanted to plead not guilty, but was persuaded to plead guilty (Dep.); tried at Wells for aiding and assisting (GD); remaining in custody (JR); later: reprieved and 'humbly proposed for pardon' (JR2); pardon at Wells, March 30 1686 (GD). Loder charged £400 for this pardon (Dep.) and secured the keeping of the money by royal grant. Some of Bisse's land was confiscated and granted to Loder and his partners (TB). Bisse had been licensed as a General Teacher [Nonconformist Preacher] in 1672 (OR). Brass tablet to his memory in Martock church.

BISSE, John, of Wellington, 'in prison for rebellion' (CP); tried at Taunton; remaining in gaol (JR) transported from Wells by Sir Richard White to Jamaica in the *Constant Richard* (SL).

BISSE *see* Thomas.

BISSELL *see* Bushell.

BLACKALTER, Richard, pardoned at Exeter Assizes, March 1686 (GD).

BLACKLEY, John, presented at Wells and bound over (JR).

BLACKMORE, Richard, weaver, of Taunton St Mary, 'aiding' (CP); Blue Regt. (P).

BLACKMORE, Samuel, tried at Wells; transported for Stapleton (JR) in the *Indeavour* from Bristol on Oct. 20 to Nevis or St Kitts (SL).

BLACKMORE, Thomas, tried at Taunton; hanged at Cothelstone (JR, JW).

BLACKMORE, William, senior, yeoman, of Colyton, 'absent' (CP); presented at Exeter but at large (JR).

BLACKMORE, William, junior, yeoman, of Colyton, 'absent' (CP); imprisoned in the workhouse at Exeter but escaped (*London*

*Gazette*); presented at Exeter but at large (JR). Returned to Colyton; his child baptized there in summer of 1688 (PR).

BLAKE, Ensign in the Green Regt.; came with Monmouth (W); Lieutenant, killed at Norton St Philip (W).

BLAKE, William, merchant, of Taunton St Mary, 'aiding' (CP); Blue Regt. (P).

BLANCHFLOWER, George, weaver, of Taunton St Mary, 'aiding' (CP), Blue Regt. (P); presented at Wells; recommended for pardon (JR).

BLATCHFORD, Alexander, of Whitelackington, 'out in the rebellion' (CP).

BLATCHFORD, George, yeoman, of Axminster, 'supposed' (CP); presented at Exeter but at large (JR).

BLATCHFORD, William, yeoman, of Axminster, 'supposed' (CP); presented at Exeter but at large (JR).

BLEW, Walter, of Thurloxton, 'in the rebellion and in prison' (CP); tried at Taunton; transported for Musgrave (JR) on the *Jamaica Merchant* from Weymouth to Barbados, there by March 12 (SL).

BLINMAN, Ames, of Galmington, excepted from the GP, but pardoned on Oct. 2, 1686 (CSPD, J2, II, 1035).

BLUECOCK, Richard, of Stogursey, excepted from the GP.

BLUNT, William, of North Curry, 'absent' (CP); of Wrantage, 'in arms' (CL).

BOAD, Thomas, Monmouth's groom, pardoned; 'now the Duke of Somerset's groom' (CSPD, J2, I, 862).

BOARD, Robert, carrier, of Lyme Regis, 'absent and supposed' (CP).

BOCHER see Butcher.

BODLEY, Christopher, of Langford Budville, 'absenting himself' (CP).

BODY, Henry, seaman, of Lyme Regis, 'absent and supposed' (CP); tried at Wells; hanged at Bath (JR, JW) on Nov. 18; a married man; dying speech in BA.

BODY, Thomas, of Glastonbury, 'from home' (CP); tried at Wells; to be hanged, but omitted from the warrant (JR). Transported (JR2).

BOILES, Edward, of Bath Forum, 'in Monmouth's army and not yet taken' (CP).

BOLE see Boole.

BOLLETT see Bovett.

BOLLSTER, Edward, weaver, of Stoke Trister, 'at large or killed' (CP).

BOLLSTER, Israel, weaver, of Stoke Trister, 'at large or killed' (CP); tried at Wells; transported for Howard (JR), Oct. 25 to Jamaica (SL).

BOLLSTER, James, weaver, of Stoke Trister, 'at large or killed' (CP).

BOLTING, John, of Yarley, Wookey, 'supposed' (CP).

BOND, Abraham, of Chardland, 'absent and believed' (CP); tried at Wells; hanged there (JR, JW).

BOND, George, 'millard', of Taunton St James, 'aiding' (CP); Blue Regt. (P).

BOND (Barr), John, of Axminster, 'supposed' (CP); yeoman, of Shute, in Bridgwater prison (DLD); presented, as Barr, at Exeter but at large (JR).

BOND, John, of Chard, 'absent and believed' (CP).

BOND, John, aged 26, son of Thomas senior (below) (PR); 'in the rebellion' (CP).

BOND, Josiah, of Northcote, Honiton, 'a rebel' (CP).

BOND, Nathaniel, of Bridport, 'in the rebellion' (CP).

BOND, Philip, aged 20, son of Thomas senior (below) (PR); of Taunton St Mary, 'aiding' (CP); Blue Regt. (P).

BOND, Robert, of Chard, 'absent and believed' (CP).

BOND, Robert, of Thurloxton, 'absconded' (CP).

BOND, Samuel, aged 20, sergeweaver (SL); of Sandford, Crediton; imprisoned at Taunton (DLD) and tried there; transported for the Queen (JR) from Taunton to Barbados on the *Jamaica Merchant*, Dec. 9; sold to Daniel Parsons.

BOND, Thomas senior, aged 50+ (PR), woolcomber, of Taunton St Mary, 'aiding' (CP); Blue Regt. (P).

BOND, Thomas, junior, aged 28 (PR), woolcomber, of Taunton St Mary, 'aiding' (CP); Blue Regt. (P). Son of Thomas senior (PR).

BOND, Thomas, of Ottery St Mary, 'in the rebellion as supposed' (CP).

BOND, Thomas, yeoman, of Upottery, 'absent' (CP); presented at Exeter but at large (JR).

BOND, William, of Glastonbury, 'from home at the time of rebellion' (CP).

BOOBY, Charles, of Pitminster, 'absent' (CP).

BOOLE (Bole), Richard, yeoman, of Ditcheat, 'in prison, being in arms in Scott's army' (CP); tried at Wells; hanged at Bruton (JR, JW). Land forfeit and for sale (TB).

BOONE, Robert, weaver, of Taunton St Mary, 'aiding' (CP); Blue Regt. (P).

BOONE, Samuel, tried at Taunton; transported for Booth (JR) from Taunton Bridewell, via Bristol, Oct. 24, to Barbados on the *John*: sold to John Browne (SL).

BORGES, John, hanged at Taunton by Col. Kirke (P); buried, July 9, by the Vicar of St James's (PR).

BORMAN, Amos, of Pitminster, 'absent' (CP).

BOROUGHS *see* Burrow.

BOULSTONE, Robert, presented at Dorchester, discharged for want of evidence (JR).

BOULTER, John, of Queen Charlton, 'absent and not returned' (CP).

BOUND, Joseph, of Glastonbury, 'from home' (CP).

BOVETT, Clement, yeoman, of Yarcombe, 'wanting; slain in the service' (CP). Presented at Exeter as at large (JR).

BOVETT, Edmund, Honiton area of Devon, tried at Exeter; to be transported for Nipho (JR); 'wounded, remaining in Exeter gaol'; sailed in the *Betty* Oct. 21, to Barbados; sold to Richard Walters (SL). Named on the 1689 petition for return (CSPD, W&M, I, 43).

BOVETT, John, senior, 'excise', of Taunton St Mary, 'aiding' (CP); Blue Regt. (P). [*See below.*]

BOVETT, John, junior, combmaker, of Taunton St Mary, 'aiding'; (CP); Blue Regt. (P). [One of these two was tried at Dorchester and transported for Nipho from Dorchester gaol on the *Betty* to Barbados and sold to Charles Thomas and Co. The other was pardoned on May 31 1687 (CSPD, J2, II, 1833)].

BOVETT, Philip, of Wellington, a Lieutenant in 1659; Captain in Albemarle's list; tried at Taunton; hanged at Wellington (JR, JW) on Oct. 1 (NL).

BOVETT, Richard, combmaker, of Taunton St Mary, 'aiding' (CP); Blue Regt (P).

BOVETT (Buffett), Richard, of Bishop's Hull, 'absent' (CP); tried at Taunton; hanged at Cothelstone (JR, JW). Colonel of the Blue (Taunton) Regt. (W). He was Colonel of Somerset Militia during the Protectorate, and sequestrator of Lord Stawell's estate at Cothelstone. [His name was misspelt Buffett (letter in *Calendar of Committee for Compounding*, i, p. 754). Buffett was misread as Bassett].

BOVETT (Bollett), Thomas, yeoman, of Axminster, 'supposed' (CP).

BOVETT, Thomas, yeoman, of Membury, 'wanting from his habitation' (CP). [One of these two was tried at Dorchester and transported for Booth (JR) on the *Happy Return* from Weymouth on Sept. 25 to Barbados, and sold to Philip Fousher (SL). He was named on the 1689 petition for return. (CSPD W&M, I, 43)]. [Both of the above were presented at Exeter and reported at large.]

BOVETT, William, of Stockland, 'suspected' (CP).

BOWDEN, George, of Bishop's Hull, 'absent' (CP), 'not taken' (CL).

BOWDEN, Richard, tried at Taunton, hanged at Keynsham (JR, JW).

BOWDEN, Thomas, of Bampton, 'supposed' (CP); tried at Wells; hanged at Wincanton (JR, JW).

BOWDITCH (Bowdage, Bowdidge), Alexander, mariner, of Lyme Regis, 'absent and supposed' (CP).

BOWDITCH (Bowdage, Bowdidge) Daniel, yeoman, of Thorncombe, 'wanting from his habitation'; (CP); presented at Exeter but at large (JR).

BOWDITCH (Bowdidge), Edward, of Wootton Fitzpaine, 'suspected' (CP).

BOWDITCH (Bowdidge), John, tailor, of Lyme Regis, 'absent and supposed' (CP); member of Lyme Corporation (LRCB).

BOWDITCH (Bowdage), John senior, yeoman, of Membury, 'wanting' (CP); presented at Exeter but at large (JR).

BOWDITCH (Bowdage), John junior, yeoman, of Membury, 'wanting' (CP); presented at Exeter but at large (JR).

BOWDITCH (Bowdage), John, yeoman, of Thorncombe, 'wanting' (CP); presented at Exeter but at large (JR).

BOWDITCH (Bowdidge), John, of Wootton Fitzpaine, 'suspected' (CP). [One of these Johns was presented at Dorchester and had his certificate (of laying down his arms) allowed (JR)].

BOWDITCH, Joseph, presented at Dorchester; 'proposed for pardon' (JR).

BOWDITCH (Bowdidge), Matthew, yeoman, of Wootton Fitzpaine, 'suspected' (CP); 'entered Monmouth's camp at Taunton, June 18, and went with the carriages'; apprehended Dec. 26; in Dorchester gaol, Jan. 5 (LRMB); presented and pardoned at Dorchester, March 1686 (GD).

BOWDITCH, Michael, of Oathill, Wayford, 'rebel and not taken' (CP).

BOWDITCH (Bowdidge), Nathaniel, yeoman, of Axmouth, 'reported in arms' (CP); presented at Exeter but at large (JR).

BOWDITCH (Bowdidge), William, of Wootton Fitzpaine, 'suspected' (CP).

BOWELL, William, of Thornfalcon, 'taking up arms against the King' (CL).

BOWNE, William, hanged at Taunton by Col. Kirke on July 9 (P); buried July 10 by the Vicar of St James's (PR).

BOWRING, John, presented at Wells and bound over (JR).

BOWRING, William, of Wellington, 'absent' (CP).

BOWYER, George, excepted from the GP; but pardoned August 2 (CSPD, J2, I, 862).

BOYCE, David, of Combwich, 'taking up arms against his Majesty' (CL); tried at Wells; hanged at Wrington (JR, JW).

BOYTE, Andrew, of Wellington, 'in prison for rebellion' (CP); tried at Taunton; transported for Musgrave (JR) on the *Jamaica Merchant* from Weymouth to Barbados; there by March 12 (SL).

BRADDICK, John, yeoman, of Luppitt, 'out in the rebellion' (CP); presented at Exeter but at large (JR).

BRADDON, Nicholas, no record of trial but named on the 1689 petition for return from exile (CSPD, W&M, I, 43).

BRADLEY, George, yeoman, of Luppitt, 'out in the rebellion' (CP); presented at Exeter but at large (JR).

BRADLEY, James, yeoman, of Luppitt, 'out in the rebellion' (CP); presented at Exeter but at large (JR).

BRAGG, Caleb, yeoman, of Axminster, 'supposed' (CP); presented at Exeter but at large (JR); 'taken to prison' (Pulman, *Book of the Axe*); presented and pardoned at Exeter Assize, March 1686 (GD).

BRAGG, Elias, of North Curry, 'absent' (CP).

BRAGG, John, carpenter (DLD), of Thorncombe (SL); imprisoned in the High Gaol, Devon (DLD); tried at Taunton; transported for Booth (JR) from Exeter via Bristol, Oct. 24, on the *John* to Barbados, sold to Henry Quintyne Esq. (SL).

BRAGG, Matthew, attorney, of Thorncombe and Dorchester, presented at Dorchester for 'levying war against the king,' pleaded not guilty, found guilty Sept. 5; hanged at Dorchester Sept. 7 (GD, JR). Land not for sale (TB). Bragg was not in Monmouth's army, but was conscripted to guide a party to the house of the Roman Catholic priest (BA).

BRAGG, Matthew junior, of Thorncombe, 'wanting' (CP); apparently not presented at the Assizes.

BRAGG, William, presented at Wells and bound over (JR).

BRAINE, Henry junior, yeoman, of Yarcombe, 'wanting' (CP); presented at Exeter but at large (JR).

BRAINE (Brayne) Hugh, of Stratton, South Petherton, 'in the rebellion and not come in' (CP).

BRAINE (Brane), John, of Chard, 'thought to be in the late Rebellion' (CP).

BRAINE, William of Kingsbury Episcopi, 'absent and believed' (CP).

Van BRAKELL, Cornelius Abraham, commanded Monmouth's ship, 'levying war against his Majesty and invading the kingdom'; taken to the Marshalsea Prison, June 21, 1686; pardoned (CSPD, J2, II, 792).

BRAMBLE, Giles, tried at Wells; hanged at Shepton Mallet (JR, JW).

BRAMBLE, James, tried at Wells; transported for Bridgeman (JR) by White Oct. 31 on the *Constant Richard* to Jamaica (SL).

BRAMBLE, John, tried at Wells; transported for Bridgeman (JR) by White Oct. 31 on the *Constant Richard* to Jamaica (SL).

BRAND, Mr, from London, Captain of Horse, killed at Keynsham (W).

BRANSCOMBE, Osmund, husbandman, of Taunton St Mary, 'aiding' (CP); Blue Regt. (P).

BRASSEY, William, at Wells, witness for the king; left in custody (JR).

BRAY, Christopher, presented at Wells as 'a prisoner, for the King's pardon' (JR).

BRAY, John, of Kittisford, 'absconding' (CP).

BRAY, John, of North Petherton, 'absconded' (CP).

BRAY, John, of Batcombe; tried at Taunton; transported for Booth (JR) from the Bridewell at Taunton (SL). He was one of eleven on Booth's receipt but not on the ship-list of the *John* nor on the sales list. His wife came from North Curry and returned there, but was chivvied back to Batcombe, and thence to North Curry (Som. QS minutes).

BRAY, Thomas, yeoman, of North Petherton, land forfeit and for sale (TB). Probably killed at Sedgemoor (P).

BRAY, Thomas, sergemaker, of Taunton St Mary, 'aiding' (CP); Blue Regt. (P); tried at Taunton; transported for Musgrave (JR) on the *Jamaica Merchant* from Weymouth to Jamaica; died at sea. Pardon authorised March 26 and April 14, 1686 (CSPD, J2, II, 357).

BREFFETT (Brisset), John, tried at Taunton; to be transported for Booth (JR); from Taunton Bridewell. On Booth's receipt, but not on the *John* list or sale-list (SL).

BRESTER, Peter, of Stoford, 'in the late rebellion' (CP).

BREWER, John, glazier, of Axminster, in the High Gaol, Devon (DLD); presented at Exeter for 'wilfully suffering George Legg to escape'; pleaded and found not guilty (GD), but presented at Wells and bound over to appear at next Assize (JR); freed by GP, from which George Legg was excepted.

BREWER, Peter, of Chard, 'absent and believed' (CP), presented at Wells, and bound over (JR).

BREWER (Brener), Thomas, fuller, of Lyme Regis, 'absent and supposed' (CP).

BREWER, William, of Chard, 'absent and believed' (CP).

BRIANT (Bryant), Bernard, clothworker, of Thorncombe, imprisoned in Wilts (DLD); tried at Dorchester; transported for Booth (JR) on the *Happy Return* from Weymouth, Sept. 25, to Barbados; sold to John Burston (SL). Buried 1687 St John's, Barbados (BJo).

BRIANT, Gerrard, husbandman, of Taunton St Mary, 'aiding' (CP); Blue Regt. (P); tried at Wells; hanged at Bath (JR, JW) Nov. 18 (NL).

BRIANT, Hugh, worsted comber, of Taunton St Mary, 'aiding' (CP); Blue Regt. (P).

BRIANT (Bryant), Israel, yeoman, of Glastonbury, (TB), tried at Wells; hanged at Glastonbury (JR, JW); land forfeit and for sale (TB); a Quaker.

BRIANT (Bryant), Richard, weaver, of East Woodlands, 'in the rebellion and at large' (CP).

BRIANT (Bryant), Roger, alias Hooper, pipemaker, of Lyme Regis, 'absent, supposed' (CP); tried at Dorchester; transported for Nipho (JR) from Dorchester Gaol on the *Betty* to Barbados; sold to Thomas Linton (SL).

BRIANT (Bryant), Roger. At Exeter Assizes, William Andridge pleaded guilty to 'assisting Roger Bryant to make his escape', and was fined and whipped (JR). [Were there two Roger Bryants? or was Roger recaptured in time for Dorchester Assize?].

BRIANT (Bryant), William, of Durston, 'in arms against his Majesty' (CL).

BRIANT, William junior, of Minehead, 'in arms in the rebellion of James Scott' (CP).

BRICE, John, presented at Wells for 'aydeing and assisting the rebels against the King' (GD); transported for Nipho (JR) Dec. 8 on the *Jamaica Merchant* to Barbados; sold to Francis Bond (SL).

BRIDDELL, Thomas, of Winsham, 'absent and believed' (CP).

BRIDLE, John, tried at Dorchester; transported for Booth (JR) on the *Happy Return* from Weymouth, Sept. 25, to Barbados; sold to John Burston (SL).

BRIDGOOD, Humphrey, mercer, of Tiverton; imprisoned in the High Gaol, Devon (DLD).

BRIGHT, John, of Kingsbury Episcopi, 'absent and believed' (CP), tried at Wells; transported for Stapleton (JR) on the *Indeavour* from Bristol Oct. 20, to Nevis or St Kitts (SL).

BRIGWOOD (Bridwood), Thomas, tried at Wells; transported for Stapleton (JR) in the *Indeavour* from Bristol Oct. 20, to Nevis or St Kitts (SL). *See* Biggott.

BRINSDON (Brunsdon), William, yeoman, of Membury, 'wanting from his habitation' (CP); presented at Exeter but at large (JR).

BRINSCOMBE, Lieut. in the Red Regt; commanded flank guard at Bridport (W); probably killed at Sedgemoor or hanged there when captured (P). [Was he the Lieutenant given as Perniscombe in Albemarle's list?]

BRISTOWE, Christopher, carpenter, of Taunton St James, 'aiding' (CP); Blue Regt. (P).

BROADBEARE, John, of Taunton St Mary, 'aiding' (CP); Blue Regt. (P).

BROADBEARE, Robert, tried at Taunton; transported for Musgrave (JR) on the *Jamaica Merchant* from Weymouth to Barbados; there by March 12, 1686 (SL).

BROADBEARE, Thomas senior, of Leigh tithing, Pitminster, 'absent' (CL).

BROADBEARE, Thomas junior, his son, of Pitminster, 'absent' (CP).

BROADBEARE, William, of North Curry, 'out in the late rebellion and in prison' (CP); tried at Wells and transported thence for Bridgeman (JR) by White on the *Constant Richard*, Oct. 31, to Jamaica (SL).

BROADRIDGE, Thomas, presented, pardoned and dismissed at Exeter, March 1686 (GD).

BROCAS, Samuel, cutler, of Taunton St Mary, 'aiding' (CP); Blue Regt. (P).

BROCK, James, of West Monkton, 'out in the rebellion and at large' (CP).

BROCK, John, of Langford Budville, 'absenting' (CP); presented at Wells; 'recommended for pardon' (JR).

BROCK, Thomas junior, of West Monkton, 'out in the rebellion and at large' (CP); tried at Taunton; transported for Booth (JR) from Taunton Bridewell via Bristol, Oct. 24, on the *John* to Barbados; sold to Col. John Hallett (SL).

BROCK, William, of Langford Budville, 'absenting' (CP).

BROOKE *see* Furze.

BROOKE, Robert, tried at Taunton; transported for Musgrave (JR) on the *Jamaica Merchant* from Weymouth to Barbados; there by Mar. 12 (SL).

BROOKE, Simon, fuller, of Taunton St Mary, 'aiding' (CP); Blue Regt. (P).

BROOKE, Thomas, of Crediton, 'absent' (CP).

BROOKE, William, of Barrington, 'in the rebellion and not come in' (CP).

BROOME, John junior, yeoman, of Dulverton, 'being in the late rebellion' (CP).

BROOME, John, of Luppitt, 'out in the rebellion' (CP).

BROOME, John, of Horton near Ilminster with estate of £18 per annum, husbandman; tried at Wells; to be hanged (JR) at Glastonbury (JW) but died before execution. His widow petition to have the estate (CSPD, J2, II, 1417, Feb. 4, 1687).

BROOME, Thomas, brother of John, 'in the rebellion but hid till the General Pardon', and then occupied his late brother's farm; husbandman (CSPD, J2, II, 1417).

BROUGHTON, Charles, tried at Dorchester; transported for Nipho (JR) from Dorchester gaol, Sept. 26, on the *Betty* to Barbados; sold to Daniel Deusbury (SL).

BROUGHTON, James, tried at Wells; transported for Stapleton (JR) on the *Indeavour* from Bristol on Oct. 20, to Nevis or St Kitts (SL).

BROUGHTON, Thomas, tried at Exeter JR; hanged at Axminster Sept 14 (NL).

BROWNE, Bernard, mason and alehouse keeper, of Lyme Regis, 'absent and supposed' (CP); seen with a musket on his shoulder and heard to say 'the Duke is come, blessed be God'; joined the Duke at Lyme; survived (LRMB).

BROWNE, Frank, presented at Dorchester in March 1686, pardoned by the King's Proclamation (GD).

BROWNE, James junior, yeoman, of Axminster, 'supposed' (CP); presented at Exeter but at large (JR).

BROWNE, James, of Taunton St Mary, 'aiding' (CP); Blue Regt. (P).

BROWNE, alias Baller, John, of Croscombe, 'in Scott's army and in prison' (CP).

BROWNE, John, yeoman, of Luppitt, 'out in the rebellion' (CP); presented at Exeter but at large (JR).

BROWNE, John, worsted comber, of Taunton St Mary, 'aiding' (CP); Blue Regt. (P).

BROWNE, John, of Wilton, 'absent' (CP). [Of the above four Johns one was presented at Taunton and had his certificate (of laying down his arms) allowed (JR). Another was tried at Dorchester and transported for Booth (JR) on the *Happy Return* from Weymouth, Sept. 25, to Barbados; and sold to Benjamin Bird (SL). The other two were tried at Wells and transported for Stapleton (JR) in the *Indeavour* from Bristol on Oct. 20 to Nevis or St Kitts (SL)].

BROWNE, Jonas, plowman [carter], tried at Taunton; transported thence for the Queen (JR) on Dec. 9 on the *Jamaica Merchant* to Barbados and sold on March 12 to Major George Lillington (SL).

BROWNE, Philip, presented at Wells and bound over (JR).

BROWNE, Richard, yeoman, of Musbury, 'in the rebellion' (CP); presented at exeter but at large (JR). [Wrongly of Axminster in BL Add. MS 90337].

BROWNE, Thomas, of Chardstock, 'suspected guilty' (CP).

BROWNE, Thomas, of Norton sub Hamdon, 'in the late rebellion and not taken' (CP). [One of these two was tried at Wells and transported for Stapleton (JR) in the *Indeavour* from Bristol on Oct. 20 to Nevis or St Kitts (SL). The other was presented at Wells and bound over (JR).]

BROWNE, William, yeoman, of Axmouth, 'reported in arms' (CP); tried at Dorchester; transported for Booth (JR) on the *Happy Return* from Weymouth, Sept. 25, to Barbados; sold to Col. John Hallett. Named in the 1689 petition for return (CSPD, W&M, I, 43).

BROWNE, William, husbandman, of Axmouth, presented at Exeter but at large (JR). At Lyme on Feb. 6 George Stokes swore that 'William Browne joined Monmouth at Lyme and served in arms under his command.' Browne was sent to Dorchester gaol, Feb. 8 (LRMB).

BROWNE, William, carpenter, of Knowle in Somerset, land forfeit and for sale (TB). Probably killed at Sedgemoor (P).

BROWNING, Jasper, of Glastonbury, 'from home in time of rebellion' (CP).

BROWNSEY, William, of Honiton, 'a rebel' (CP).

BROXWELL, Thomas, woodman, of Frome, 'for a riot and amongst the Clubmen' (CP).

BRUCE, Anthony, excepted from the GP.

BRUCE *see* Brice.

BRUCE, Robert, of Fife, Scotland, came from Holland with Monmouth, after 14 years in the Brandenburg army; a Captain in the Blue Regt.; confined in the Gatehouse at Westminster; interrogated July 16 (L); sent to Scotland to give evidence against Fletcher of Saltoun (CSPD, J2, I, 1512). Excepted from the GP.

BRUFORD, John, of Pitminster, 'for taking up arms against his Majesty' (CL).

BRUNSDON, William, yeoman, of Membury, presented at Exeter but at large (JR).

BRYANT *see* Briant.

BRYER, John, aged 25, mason (SL); tried at Taunton; transported for the Queen (JR) from Taunton to Barbados on the *Jamaica Merchant*; sold on March 12 to Francis Bond, Esq. (SL).

BUCKLER, Henry, of Wellow, 'in the late rebellion and not returned' (CP); presented at Wells and bound over (JR).

BUCKLER, William, presented at Wells, certificates allowed (JR).

BUCKNOLL (Buckerell), Thomas, yeoman, of Membury, 'wanting from his habitation' (CP); presented at Exeter but at large; presented at Wells and bound over (JR).

BUCKNOLL, William, of Honiton, 'a rebel' (CP).

BUCKRELL, Humphrey, of Barrington, 'in the rebellion and not come in' (CP).

BUDD, Richard, mason, of Dunster, 'in arms in the rebellion of James Scott' (CP).

BUDGE, John, of Chardstock, 'suspected guilty' (CP); tried at Taunton; transported for Booth (JR) from Bridgwàter prison via Bristol, Oct. 24, to Barbados on the *John*; sold to John Burston (SL).

BUFFETT *see* Bovet.

BUFFETT, Thomas, of Charmouth, 'suspected' (CP).

BUGLER, Thomas, of Beaminster, 'wanting from home' (CP).

BUGLER, Thomas, of Pitminster, 'absent' (CP).

BUGLER, Thomas, of Trull, 'absent' (CP); tried at Taunton; transported for the Queen (JR) on the *Jamaica Merchant* to Barbados; sold to Col. Thomas Colleton (SL).

BUGLER, William, of Beaminster, 'wanting from his home' (CP).

BUGLER, William, of Crewkerne, 'rebel and not taken' (CP).

BULL, John, husbandman, of Axminster, 'supposed' (CP); 'scriber' imprisoned in Wiltshire (DLD); tried at Dorchester (JR); hanged at Bridport on Sept. 12 (NL). Presented at Exeter and misreported at large (JR). Land forfeit and for sale (TB).

BULL, Joseph, of Thurloxton, 'absconded' (CP).

BULL, Richard, of Trull, 'absent' (CP).

BULL, Robert, aged 19, yeoman, of Axminster, 'supposed' (CP); in prison in Wilts. (DLD); tried at Dorchester (JR); hanged at Bridport on Sept. 12 (NL). At Exeter misreported at large (JR).

BULL, Thomas, of Honiton, 'a rebel' (CP).

BULL, Thomas, of Martock, 'absent' (CP).

BULL, William, tried at Taunton; transported for Musgrave (JR) on the *Jamaica Merchant* from Weymouth to Barbados, there March 12 (SL).

BULLMAN, James, yeoman, 'late of Chard', land forfeit and for sale (TB). Presumably killed at Sedgemoor (P).

BURBRIDGE, Osmund, presented at Taunton; certificate allowed (JR).

BURCH, Edward, of Ottery St Mary, 'in the late rebellion as supposed' (CP).

BURCH, Walter junior, of Ottery St Mary, 'in the late rebellion as supposed' (CP).

BURD, John, of Beckington, taken after Sedgemoor but escaped, recaptured, imprisoned at Bath (JB/JD); tried at Wells; to be hanged, but omitted from the warrant (JR); reprieved but had to pay for his pardon (JB/JD).

BURFORD *see* Durden.

BURFORD, Edmund, of Buckland St Mary (TB), tried at Taunton; hanged at Ilchester (JR, JW); land forfeit and for sale (TB). [Edward in GD].

BURFORD, John, son of William, of Bradford on Tone, 'absent' (CP).

BURGE *see* Barge.

BURGE, William, of Marnhull, 'absent' (CP).

BURGEN, John senior, worsted comber, of Taunton St Mary, 'aiding' (CP); Blue Regt. (P); tried at Taunton; hanged at Ilminster (JR, JW).

BURGES, John, of Taunton (SL); Blue Regt. (P); tried at Taunton; transported for Booth (JR) from Taunton Bridewell via Bristol, Oct. 24, to Barbados on the *John*; sold to Ann Gallop (SL).

BURGES, Peter, fuller, of Taunton St Mary, 'aiding' (CP); Blue Regt. (P).

BURGES, Thomas senior, of Taunton St Mary, 'aiding' (CP); Blue Regt. (P).

BURGES, Thomas, worsted comber, of Taunton St Mary, 'aiding' (CP); Blue Regt. (P).

BURGIS, Thomas, of West Pennard, 'from home in time of the rebellion' (CP).

BURIMAN, Charles, of Pitminster, 'absent' (CP).

BURNARD *see* Barnard.

BURNEHAM, John senior, of Pitminster, 'absent' (CP).

BURNEHAM, John, of Pitminster, 'absent' (CP).

BURNELL, Roger, tried at Taunton; hanged at Crewkerne (JR, JW).

BURNESTER, Edward, of Isle Abbots, 'out in the rebellion and not taken' (CP).

BURNETT, John, tailor, of Taunton St Mary, 'aiding' (CP); Blue Regt. (P).

BURRIDGE (Burrage), Charles, aged 27, comber, of Taunton (SL); tried at Taunton; transported thence for the Queen (JR) to Barbados on the *Jamaica Merchant*, Dec. 9 to March 12; sold to Edward Hurlstone (SL).

BURRIDGE (Burrage), Daniel, of Crewkerne, 'charged to be in rebellion with the late Duke of Monmouth'; William Moore, deputy tithingman of Trowbridge, 'did suffer D.B. to escape out of his custody' (Wilts. QSR).

BURRIDGE, George, of Chardland, 'absent and believed' (CP).

BURRIDGE, James, of Milverton, 'absenting himself' (CP).

BURRIDGE (Burrage), John, of Donyatt, 'out in the rebellion' (CP).

BURRIDGE, John, tried at Dorchester (JR); hanged at Weymouth or Melcombe Regis on Sept. 15 (NL).

BURRIDGE, John, presented at Dorchester, certificate allowed (JR).

BURRIDGE (Burrage), Richard, of Chard, 'absent and believed' (CP); presented at Dorchester, certificate allowed (JR).

BURRIDGE, Robert, tried at Dorchester; transported for Booth (JR) on the *Happy Return* from Weymouth on Sept. 25 to Barbados; sold to Major John Johnson (SL).

BURRIDGE, Robert, tried at Wells; transported for Howard (JR) on Oct. 25 to Jamaica (SL).

BURRIDGE, Thomas, tried at Dorchester; transported for Booth (JR) on the *Happy Return* from Weymouth on Sept. 25 to Barbados; sold to John Hethersell, Esq. (SL).

BURRIDGE (Burrage), William, cutler, of Chard, 'absent and believed' (CP).

BURROUGH (Barrow), Ezekiel, yeoman, of Luppitt, 'out in the rebellion' (CP); presented at Exeter but at large (JR).

BURROUGH (Burrow), Christopher, of Wellington, 'absent' (CP).

BURROUGH (Burroughs), George, comber; of Taunton; pardon dated June 2, 1686, 'if he returns from abroad with his goods and effects within two months' (CSPD, J2, II, 626), which implies that he got to Holland and joined the attempt to manufacture English cloth in Friesland.

BURROUGH (Burrow), John, yeoman, of Wick, Luppitt, 'out in the rebellion' (CP); presented at Exeter but at large (JR).

BURROUGH, John, of Wootton Fitzpaine, 'suspected' (CP).

BURROUGH (Burrowe), Joseph, of Charmouth, 'suspected' (CP).

BURROUGH (Burrow), Thomas, of Ilminster, 'believed to be in the late rebellion' (CP).

BURROUGH (Burroughs), William, of Corfe, 'absent' (CP); tried at Taunton; transported for Booth (JR) from Taunton Bridewell via Bristol, Oct. 24, to Barbados on the *John*; sold to John Burston (SL).

BURSTON, John, of Milverton, 'absenting himself' (CP).

BURT, Edward, presented and pardoned at Exeter, March 1686 (GD).

BURT, William, presented at Dorchester; discharged for want of evidence (JR).

BURTEN, John, of Bridport, 'in the rebellion' (CP).

BURTON, James, of London, came from Holland with Monmouth; Lieutenant in Capt. Jones's troop of Horse; escaped to London, arrested on August 2; in Newgate; interrogated Sept. 24 and Oct. 2, gave away several names (L); turned King's Evidence against two who had sheltered him: Elizabeth Gaunt, who was burnt at the stake, and John Fernley, who was hanged. Warrant to Keeper of Newgate to set Burton at liberty under the GP, March 18 (CSPD, J2, II, 292).

BURY, John, of Crewkerne, 'rebel and not taken' (CP).

BUSH, James, of Bath Forum, 'in Monmouth's army and not taken' (CP).

BUSH, William, tried at Wells; transported for Stapleton (JR) in the *Indeavour* from Bristol Oct. 20, to Nevis or St Kitts (SL).

BUSHELLS, John, weaver, of Whitford (TB); imprisoned at Taunton (DLD); probably died in prison (P); land forfeit and for sale (TB).

BUSSELL, Francis, of Wedmore, 'absent and in the late rebellion' (CP).

BUSSELL, John, of Northcote, Honiton, 'a rebel' (CP); tried at Taunton; hanged at Crewkerne (JR, JW).

BUSSON, John, of Milverton, tried at Taunton; transported for Booth (JR) from Taunton Bridewell via Bristol, Oct. 24, to Barbados on the *John*; sold to Othniell Haggat (SL).

BUTCHER, Benjamin, of Hinton St George, 'rebel and not taken' (CP).

BUTCHER, George, tried at Wells, transported thence for Bridgeman (JR) by White to Jamaica on the *Constant Richard* (SL).

BUTCHER, James, of Crewkerne, 'in prison for being in arms with the Duke', was offered a pardon if he would swear against Edmund Prideaux. He refused (*Commons' Journal* x, 113–6).

BUTCHER, John senior, of Lyme Regis, 'absent and supposed' (CP); presented at Dorchester; certificate allowed (JR).

BUTCHER, John junior, of Lyme Regis, mariner, 'absent and supposed' (CP); presented at Dorchester; certificate allowed (JR).

BUTCHER, John junior, of Clapton, 'taken at Lyme Regis and sent to Dorchester gaol', July 14 (LRMB); reprieved (JR2).

BUTCHER, John, yeoman, of Colyton, presented at Exeter but at large (JR); tried at Wells; to be transported for Howard (JR) Oct. 25 but escaped between Wells and Sherborne (SL); presented at Dorchester and pardoned, March 1686 (GD).

BUTCHER, John, of Hinton St George, 'rebel and not taken' (CP); tried at Wells; hanged at Axbridge (JR, JW).

BUTCHER, Joseph, presented at Dorchester, March 1686, and pardoned by proclamation (GD).

BUTCHER, Richard, yeoman, of Musbury, 'in the rebellion' (CP); presented at Exeter but at large (JR). Wrongly 'of Axminster' in BL Add. MS. 90337.

BUTCHER, Roger, of Pitminster, 'absent' (CP).

BUTFIELD, John, tried at Taunton; transported for Musgrave (JR) on the *Jamaica Merchant* from Weymouth to Jamaica; there by 12 Mar. (SL).

BUTLER, Richard, 'taken at Hindon upon suspicion that he was going to join with the late Duke of Monmouth and other traitors (Wilts. QSR).

BUTSON, Robert, presented at Dorchester: not guilty (GD).

BUTTER, Bartholomew, aged 58 (PR), yeoman, of Colyton, 'absent' (CP); presented at Exeter but at large (JR); returned to Colyton and died, Jan. 1687 (PR).

BUTTER, Daniel, presented at Dorchester; certificate allowed (JR).

BUTTER, John, of Kingsbury Episcopi, 'absent and believed' (CP).

BUTTER, John, yeoman, of Colyton, 'absent' (CP); presented at Exeter but at large (JR).

BUTTLEY, Edward, carpenter, of Taunton St Mary, 'aiding' (CP); Blue Regt. (P).

BUTTLEY, Thomas, worsted comber, of Taunton St Mary, 'aiding' (CP); Blue Regt. (P).

BUXTON, Edward, of Wedmore, 'absent and in the late rebellion' (CP).

BUYSE, Anton, 'the Brandenburger', Captain, came with Monmouth from Holland, to command the Artillery (L); left Sedgemoor with Monmouth (Oliver, in Oldmixon); captured in Hampshire, taken to the Tower (CSPD, J2, I, 1212); thence by ship to Scotland (ibid. 1512) to give evidence against Fletcher of Saltoun. Pardoned (P).

BYNUM, Jacob, of Kingston St Mary, 'wanting from home' (CL).

CABLE, Benjamin, tried at Wells; transported for Stapleton (JR) on the *Indeavour* from Bristol Oct. 20, to Nevis or St Kitts (SL).

CALLAWAY, Edward, of Ilminster, 'in the late rebellion' (CP).

CALLAWAY, Robert, of Ilminster, 'in the late rebellion' (CP).

CALLAWAY, William, of Ilminster, 'in the late Rebellion' (CP).

CALWAY, Thomas, presented at Dorchester, certificate allowed (JR).

CAMBDEN (Combden), William, clothier, of Netherbury (TB); tried at Dorchester; transported for Musgrave (JR) on the *Jamaica Merchant* from Weymouth to Barbados or Jamaica (SL). Land forfeit and for sale (TB).

CAMBRIDGE, Philip, of Gloucestershire, tried at Wells; to be hanged at Redcliffe Hill, Bristol, on Oct. 9 (JR, JW) where 3 of 6 so sentenced were hanged; 2 died of smallpox (NL).

CAME, Francis, of Huntspill, 'active soldier in Monmouth's army' (Som. QSR); tried at Taunton; transported for Booth (JR) from Bridgwater prison via Bristol, Oct. 24, on the *John* bound for Barbados; died at sea (SL).

CAMM, John, weaver, of Taunton St Mary, 'aiding' (CP); Blue Regt. (P).

CAMP, Joshua, of West Chinnock, 'in the late rebellion' (CP).

CAMRE, William, presented at Wells, pardoned by proclamation (JR2).

CANDY, Christopher, tried at Wells, to be transported for Howard (JR) on Oct. 25 but escaped between Wells and Sherborne (SL).

CANNADAY, William, presented at Wells and bound over (JR).

CANTLEBURY, John, of Beaminster, 'wanting from his home' (CP).

CANTLEBURY, John, of Sampford Peverell, tried at Taunton; transported for Booth (JR) from Bridgwater prison via Bristol, Oct. 24, on the *John* to Barbados; sold to John and William Holder (SL).

CAPP *see* Clapp.

CAPRON, Christopher, of Gittisham, 'went to Monmouth and is yet in rebellion' (CP).

CARD, John, of Staplegrove, 'for taking up arms against the king and is yet absent' (Som. QSR).

CARDEN, Thomas, tried at Wells; transported for Howard (JR) Oct. 25 to Jamaica (SL).

CARDY, Abraham, brewer, of Taunton St Mary, 'aiding' (CP); Blue Regt. (P). Excepted from GP.

CAREW alias Hillard, Francis, of Glastonbury, 'from home at the time of rebellion' (CP).

CARNELL, John, junior, of Bampton, 'supposed to be a rebel' (CP).

CARNER, Alexander, of Ilminster, 'in the late rebellion' (CP).

CARNER, Edward, of Ilminster, 'in the late rebellion' (CP).

CARPENTER, Thomas, presented at Wells and bound over (JR).

CARRIER (Carner, Corner), James, blacksmith, of Ilminster; 'in the late rebellion' (CP); Ferguson's letter about Monmouth's impending arrival was directed to him (B.L. Harl. 6845, f. 284) and he went to Forde Abbey for weapons (Dep.); excepted from GP, but pardoned 31 May, 1687 (CSPD, J2, II, 1833).

CARROW, George, of Bridgwater (SL), tried at Taunton; transported for Booth (JR) from Bridgwater prison via Bristol, Oct. 24, to Barbados on the *John*; sold to Capt. W. Scott (SL).

CARSWELL, Roger, of Wellington, 'in prison for rebellion' (CP); presented at Taunton, 'remaining in gaol till further order'; transported from Wells by White (JR) Oct. 31 on the *Constant Richard* to Jamaica (SL).

CARSWELL, Robert, of Kingston St Mary, 'for taking up arms against the king and yet absent' (Som. QSR).

CARTABROOKE *see* Eastabrooke.

CARTER, Alexander, scrivener, of Beckington, 'in the rebellion, out of Beckington, at large' (CP).

CARTER, Frank, in Ilchester gaol, tried at Wells; transported for Howard (JR), Oct. 25, to Jamaica (SL).

CARTER, James, mason, of Ottery St Mary, in the High Gaol, Devon (DLD); presented at Dorchester, discharged for want of evidence (JR).

CARTER, John, of Coxley, 'supposed' (CP); tried at Wells; hanged at Bath (JR, JW).

CARTER, Robert, husbandman, of Broadway in Somerset; land forfeit and for sale (TB). Presumably killed at Sedgemoor (P).

CARTER, Robert, of Stockland, 'suspected' (CP); tried at Wells; transported thence for Bridgeman (JR) by White on the *Constant Richard*, Oct. 31, to Jamaica (SL).

CARTER, Thomas, of Sidmouth, 'went to Monmouth' (CP).

CARTER, William, of Chard; land forfeit and for sale (TB). Presumably killed at Sedgemoor (P).

CARTER, William, of Wedmore, 'absent' (CP).

CARVER, Daniel, of Chilton Polden, 'out in the rebellion and at large' (CP).

CARVER, John, of Chilton Polden, 'out in the rebellion and at large' (CP).

CARY, Daniel, weaver, late of London, pardoned July 18, 1686, and Sept. 16 (CSPD, J2, II, 822, 988). [*See below.*]

CARY, George, senior, of Glastonbury, 'from home in the time of rebellion' (CP). Excepted from the GP. [*See below.*]

CARY, Captain of Horse, missed Sedgemoor by being sent with Captain Hewling to Minehead to fetch some guns (W). [Captain Cary might have been either of the above, or a third Cary.]

CASE, Matthew, weaver, of East Woodlands, 'in the rebellion and in prison' (CP). Land forfeited and for sale (TB). Not presented at Assizes so presumably died in prison (P).

CASE, William, weaver, of Taunton St Mary, 'aiding' (CP). Blue Regt. (P).

CASLIN (Castland), Jeffery, of Chard, 'absent and believed' (CP); presented at Wells and bound over (JR).

CASS, William, of Somerton, 'being in the late rebellion and not come home' (CP).

CASSELL, Richard, of Glastonbury, 'from home in time of the rebellion' (CP).

CASWELL (Casewell), John, tried at Wells; hanged at Norton St Philip (JR, JW).

CASWELL, Lawrence, tried at Wells; transported for Nipho (JR) on the *Betty* to Barbados; sold to Capt. John Gibbs (SL).

CASWELL, Robert, of Nailsbourne, Kingston St Mary, 'absent and by report in the late rebellion' (CL).

CASWELL, Roger, presented at Taunton, 'remaining in gaol till further order'; transported from Wells by White (JR) Oct. 31, on the *Constant Richard* to Jamaica (SL).

CHADWICK (Chaddock), Tom, from London, a gentleman private in the Life Guards, Captain, first in the Green Regt., then in the Horse, accidently killed at Norton St Philip (W).

CHAFER, Samuel, sergeweaver, of Cullompton, in the High Gaol, Devon (DLD).

CHAFFY, Benjamin, of South Petherton, 'in the rebellion and not come in' (CP).

CHAMBERLAIN, Hugh, 'Reformade', came from Holland with Monmouth (HL), landed with Dare at Chideock; excepted from the GP, but pardoned for all treasons, June 10, 1686 (CSPD, J2, II, 652).

CHAMBERLAIN, 'young', his son, came from Holland; probably killed at Sedgemoor (P).

CHAMBERLAINE, John, aged 20, shoemaker, of Haytors Castle, East Budleigh, 'joined in the rebellion' (CP); of Broad Clyst, imprisoned in Devon workhouse (DLD); tried at Taunton, transported thence for the Queen (JR) on Oct. 12 to Barbados on the *Jamaica Merchant*; sold on Mar. 12 to William Baron (SL). Buried 1687 St Michael's, Barbados (BMi).

CHAMBERS, Henry, aged 25, woolcomber (SL), of Wellington, 'in prison for rebellion' (CP); tried at Taunton; transported for the Queen (JR) Oct. 12 to Barbados on the *Jamaica Merchant*; sold on Mar. 12 to Major Richard Salter (SL).

CHAMBERS, John, of West Buckland, 'absent' (CP). [His wife, Elizabeth, was buried on 12 Sept. 1686 (PR).]

CHAMBERS, Ralph, of Chardland, 'absent and believed'(CP).

CHAMP, Richard, yeoman, of Axminster, 'supposed' (CP); presented at Exeter but at large (JR).

CHAMPION, Edward, of West Pennard, 'from home in time of the rebellion' (CP).

CHANCEY, Icabod, of Bristol, pardon for all treasons, Mar. 22, 1686 (CSPD, J2, II, 308, 354).

CHANNELL, Humphrey, weaver, of Taunton St James, 'aiding' (CP); Blue Regt. (P).

CHANNING, John, of Chard, 'absent and believed' (CP).

CHANNING, Matthias, presented at Wells and bound over (JR).

CHANNING, Robert, of Chard, 'absent and believed' (CP).

CHANNING, Roger, tried at Wells; to be transported for Howard (JR) Oct. 25; escaped between Wells and Sherborne (SL).

CHANNING, Thomas junior, of Chard, 'absent and believed' (CP); tried at Wells; to be transported for Howard (JR) Oct. 25; escaped between Wells and Sherborne (SL).

CHANNING, William, presented at Wells and bound over (JR).

CHANNON, Caleb, of Churchstanton, 'for flying from his Colours' (CP).

CHANNON, John, weaver, of Ottery St Mary, 'in the late rebellion as supposed' (CP).

CHAPLE, John, of Thurloxton, 'in the rebellion and in prison' (CP); tried at Taunton; 'designed for execution but omitted from the warrant' (JR); transported from Taunton by Thomas Heywood, Nov. 12, on the *Constant Richard* to Jamaica (SL).

CHAPPELL, John, of Petherton (SL), tried at Taunton; transported for Booth (JR) from Taunton Bridewell via Bristol, Oct. 24, on the *John* to Barbados; sold to William Allamby (SL).

CHAPPLE, Charles, tried at Taunton; hanged at Keynsham (JR, JW).

CHAPPLE, James, of Oathill, Wayford, 'rebel and not taken' (CP).

CHAPLIN (Chaplaine), Richard, of Ditcheat, 'in prison; being in Scott's army' (CP); tried at Wells; transported for Stapleton (JR) on the *Indeavour* from Bristol, Oct. 20, to Nevis or St Kitts (SL).

CHAPMAN, John, of Chard, 'absent and believed' (CP).

CHAPMAN, Joseph, of Chardland, 'absent and believed' (CP).

CHAPMAN, Thomas, of Chardstock, 'suspected guilty' (CP); presented at Exeter, March 1686, and pardoned (GD).

CHAPMAN, Thomas, cardmaker, of Frome, 'for a riot and amongst the Clubmen' (CP).

CHAPMAN, William, of Chard, 'in the late rebellion' (CP).

CHARE, Samuel, fuller, of Taunton St Mary, 'aiding' (CP); Blue Regt. (P).

CHARELL, John, of Wedmore, 'absent and in the late rebellion' (CP).

CHARLTON, Francis, Esq., excepted from the GP, 1686 and 1688; estate of £250 per annum forfeited (TB).

CHARNOCK, Robert, pardoned May 25, 1686 (CSPD, J2, II, 597).

CHEDZOY, Edward, of Stoke St Gregory, 'in the rebellion and in prison' (CP); tried at Wells; transported thence for Bridgeman (JR) by White on the *Constant Richard* to Jamaica (SL).

CHEDZOY, Robert junior, of Stoke St Gregory, 'in the rebellion and in prison' (CP). Not presented at Assize, so perhaps died in prison (P).

CHEDZOY, Robert, worsted comber, of Taunton St James, 'aiding' (CP); Blue Regt. (P).

CHEEKE, Jonas, of Thornfalcon (CL), of North Curry, 'absent' (CP).

CHEEKE, Philip, aged 16, plowman [carter] (SL); of Thornfalcon (CL), of North Curry, 'out in the rebellion and in prison' (CP); tried at Taunton and transported thence for the Queen (JR) on the *Jamaica Merchant*, Dec. 9, to Barbados; sold on Mar. 12 to Edward Hurlston (SL).

CHEEK alias Chick, William, tried at Wells; hanged at Pensford (JR, JW).

CHICK, John, of Ilminster, 'in the late rebellion' (CP).

CHICK, Stephen junior, of Ilminster, 'in the late rebellion' (CP).

CHIBBETT alias Kidnor, Thomas, of Minehead, 'in the late rebellion' (CP).

CHILCOTT, John, of Tiverton (SL); tried at Taunton; transported for Booth (JR) from Bridgwater prison via Bristol, Oct. 24, on the *John* to Barbados; sold to Ann Gallop (SL).

CHILLCOTT, William, of Ruishton, 'absent' (CP); tried at Wells; transported thence for Bridgeman (JR) by White, Oct. 31, on the *Constant Richard* to Jamaica (SL).

CHIN, Thomas junior, of Othery, 'taken' (CP); tried at Wells; transported for Nipho (JR) from Ilchester gaol, Oct. 21, on the *Rebecca* to Barbados (SL). Reprieve granted, probably too late (JR2).

CHIN, William, tried at Wells; transported for Howard (JR) Oct. 25 in the *Port Royal Merchant* to Jamaica (SL).

CHINN, Richard, of Wells, husbandman, 'supposed' (CP); tried at Wells; hanged at Shepton Mallet (JR, JW); land forfeit and for sale (TB).

CHINN, Simon, tried at Wells; transported for Howard (JR), Oct. 25 on the *Port Royal Merchant* to Jamaica (SL).

CHRISTOPHER, Thomas, porter, of Taunton St Mary, 'aiding' (CP); Blue Regt (P).

CHUBB, Richard, of Crewkerne, 'rebel and not taken' (CP).

CHUBB, Thomas junior, of Martock, 'absent' (CP).

CHURCHILL, William, of Somerton, 'in the late rebellion and not come home' (CP).

CHURCHHOUSE, Thomas, of Tiverton, tried at Wells; transported thence for Stapleton (JR) on the *Indeavour* from Bristol to Nevis or St Kitts (SL).

CLAPP, Edward, yeoman, of Sidbury, 'joined in the rebellion' (CP); in the High Gaol, Devon (DLD).

CLAPP, John, aged 51, mercer, of Colyton, 'absent' (CP); a married man with ten children (PR); 'seen in Monmouth's camp' by John Baites (LRMB); presented (as yeoman) at Exeter but at large (JR); came home from Sedgemoor and hid in the roof when the house was searched (T). In May 1689 he and four friends organised a petition for the return of men from Colyton and Honiton who had been transported (CSPD, W&M, I, 43).

CLAPP, Thomas, comber, of Sidmouth, 'went to Monmouth' (CP); imprisoned in Wilts. (DLD); tried at Dorchester (JR); hanged at Bridport on Sept. 12 (NL). Land forfeit and for sale (TB).

CLAPP, William, of Sidmouth, 'went to Monmouth' (CP).

CLARE, Daniel, soapboiler, of Lyme Regis, 'absent and supposed' (CP).

CLARKE, Abraham, clothier, of Axminster, 'supposed' (CP); presented as a yeoman at Exeter but at large (JR); 'seen in Monmouth's camp' by John Baites (LRMB).

CLARKE, Adam, carrier, of Honiton, 'a rebel' (CP); in the High Gaol, Devon (DLD); presented at Dorchester, certificate allowed (JR).

CLARKE, Benjamin, on the Gaol Delivery list for Wells; no sentence recorded.

CLARKE, George, of Barrington, 'in the rebellion and not come in' (CP).

CLARKE, George, of Northcote, Honiton, 'a rebel' (CP).

CLARKE, James, of Honiton, 'a rebel' (CP).

CLARKE, James, of Northcote, Honiton, 'a rebel' (CP).

CLARKE, John senior, yeoman, of Axmouth, 'reported' (CP); presented at Exeter but at large (JR).

CLARKE, John junior, yeoman, of Axmouth, 'reported' (CP); wounded at Sedgemoor, imprisoned and tried at Wells (DLD); transported for Stapleton (JR) Oct. 20 on the *Indeavour* from Bristol to Nevis or St Kitts (SL). He had been presented at Exeter and reported at large (JR).

CLARKE, John, of Chard, 'absent and believed' (CP).

CLARKE, John, brazier, of Taunton St Mary, 'aiding' (CP); Blue Regt. (P).

CLARKE, John, of Wellington, 'in prison for rebellion' (CP);? died (P).

CLARKE, Richard, of Ilminster, 'in the late rebellion' (CP).

CLARKE, Robert, yeoman, of Axminster, 'supposed' (CP); presented at Exeter but at large (JR); transported [*See below*]

CLARKE, Robert, bonelace maker (DLD) of Honiton, 'a rebel' (CP); imprisoned in the Devon workhouse (DLD); transported. [*See below*]

CLARKE, Robert, transported. [*See below*]

CLARKE, Robert, transported. [*See below*] All 4 Robert Clarkes were transported. One was tried at Dorchester, transported for Nipho

(JR) to Barbados on the *Betty*, and sold to Peter Frewilling (SL). Another was tried at Taunton and remained in gaol (JR) but was transported by White from Wells on the *Constant Richard* to Jamaica (SL). The other two were tried at Wells and transported (JR), one for Stapleton on the *Indeavour* from Bristol on Oct. 20 to Nevis or St Kitts; the other for Howard on Oct. 25 to Jamaica (SL).

CLARKE, Samuel, tried at Wells; transported for Stapleton (JR) on the *Indeavour* from Bristol Oct. 20, to Nevis or St Kitts (SL).

CLARKE, Thomas senior, woolcomber, of Thornfalcon, 'in the rebellion and in prison' (CP) at Bridgwater; 'for taking away the parish's arms of North Curry' (Som. QSR); tried at Taunton; remaining in gaol (JR); transported, Nov. 12, by White on the *Constant Richard* to Jamaica (SL). Land forfeit and for sale (TB).

CLARKE, Thomas junior, of Thornfalcon, 'absent' (CP); 'in arms' (Som. QSR).

CLARKE, Tristram senior, yeoman, of Honiton, 'a rebel' (CP); imprisoned in Bath (DLD); tried at Wells; to be hanged on Redcliffe Hill, Bristol (JR, JW), where 3 of 6 so condemned were hanged (NL). Land forfeit and for sale (TB).

CLARKE, William, of Taunton St James, 'aiding' (CP); Blue Regt. (P).

CLARKE, William, tailor, of Lyme Regis, 'absent and supposed' (CP); taken at Lyme Regis and sent to Dorchester gaol, July 14 (LRMB); tried at Dorchester and transported (JR). [*See below*].

CLARKE, William, of Wareham, 'absent' (CP); tried at Dorchester and transported (JR). [*See below*]. One William Clarke was given to Booth (JR) and shipped on the *Happy Return*, Sept. 25, from Weymouth to Barbados; sold to Capt. William Marshall (SL). The other was given to Nipho (JR) and sailed on the *Betty* to Barbados; sold to Ralph Lane (SL). One William Clarke was named on the 1689 petition for the return of transported rebels (CSPD, W&M, I, 43).

CLASSEY, John, tried at Wells; transported for Stapleton (JR) on the *Indeavour* from Bristol on Oct. 20 to Nevis or St Kitts (SL).

CLATWORTHY, Hugh, of Wellington, 'in prison for rebellion' (CP). Not named in Assize Rolls of 1685, but presented at Wells in March 1686 as convicted at last session (GD); presumably pardoned by proclamation (P).

CLATWORTHY, Marmaduke, worsted comber, of Taunton St Mary, 'aiding' (CP); Blue Regt. (P).

CLATWORTHY, Nicholas, presented at Dorchester; discharged for want of evidence (JR).

CLATWORTHY, Reginald, edgetool maker, of Honiton, imprisoned in Wilts. (DLD); presented at Dorchester and proposed for pardon (JR).

CLATWORTHY, Robert, shoemaker, of Taunton St Mary, 'aiding' (CP); Blue Regt. (P).

CLATWORTHY, Thomas, of Wellington, 'in prison for rebellion' (CP); tried at Wells; hanged at Bath (JR, JW) on Nov. 18 (NL).

CLATWORTHY, William, tried at Wells; transported for Howard (JR). Oct. 25, to Jamaica (SL).

CLAY, John, wire drawer, of West Woodlands, 'in the rebellion and in prison' (CP); not presented at Assize.

CLEEVES, Joseph, pointmaker, of Lyme Regis, 'absent and supposed' (CP).

CLEGG, John, presented at Exeter, March 1686, pardoned and dismissed (GD).

CLEGG, John [another], presented at Exeter, March 1686, pardoned and dismissed (GD).

CLEGG, William, aged 46, weaver, of Colyton, 'absent' (CP); tried at Exeter; hanged at Colyton (JR) in Oct. (NL). Land forfeit and for sale (TB).

CLEGG, (Cligg), William, yeoman, presented at Exeter, but at large (JR).

CLEMENT, George, of Wilton, 'absent' (CP).

CLEMENT, William, tried at Wells; hanged at Frome (JR, JW).

CLEWES, George senior, yeoman, of Axminster, 'supposed' (CP); presented at Exeter but at large (JR).

CLIFT, James, aged 20, weaver (SL); of Westbury, 'in the rebellion' (Wilts. QSR); tried at Taunton; transported thence for the Queen (JR); shipped Dec. 9 on the *Jamaica Merchant* to Barbados; sold there March 12 to Major Abel Allen (SL).

CLODE, Edward, of Chardstock, 'suspected guilty' (CP).

CLODE, John, yeoman, of Upottery, 'absent' (CP); presented at Exeter but at large; tried at Taunton; transported for Booth (JR) from Exeter, via Bristol, Oct. 24, to Barbados on the *John*; sold to John Burston (SL). Named on the 1689 petition for return(CSPD, W&M, I, 43).

CLODE, Robert, yeoman,, of Upottery, 'absent' (CP); presented at Exeter but at large (JR); presented at Exeter, March 1686, pardoned and dismissed (GD).

CLOGG, Thomas, tailor, of Taunton St Mary, 'aiding' (CP); Blue Regt. (P).

CLOTHIER, Michael, of West Pennard, 'from home in time of the rebellion' (CP).

CLOUD, John, worsted comber, of Taunton St Mary, 'aiding' (CP); Blue Regt (P).

CLOUD, Ralph junior, of Beaminster, 'wanting from home' (CP).

COAD, Thomas or John, carpenter, of Stoford; called up in militia; joined Monmouth at Axminster, Red Regt.; 'came to push of pike' at Keynsham; wounded in lung and hand at Norton St Philip; surrendered to Col. Sir Edward Phelips; imprisoned at Ilchester; treated by Dr Winter (CM); tried at Wells; to be hanged at Wells (JR, JW) but marched with transportees to Weymouth; thence to Jamaica; sold to Col. Bach; lay preacher on Sundays; freed in 1690 and paid his fare home (CM). Land forfeit and for sale (TB). His Memorandum was published, as by John Coad, in 1849. In all other contemporary records he is Thomas Coad.

COADE, George, yeoman, of Axmouth, 'reported' (CP); presented at Exeter but at large (JR).

COCKE *see* Cooke.

COCKRAM, James, aged 21, comber (SL); of Tiverton, 'with the late Duke of Monmouth' (CP); tried at Taunton; transported thence for the Queen (JR) on the *Jamaica Merchant*, Dec. 9, to Barbados; sold on March 12 to Nicholas Gibbs (SL).

COCKRAM, John, aged 18, comber (SL); of Tiverton, 'with the late Duke of Monmouth' (CP); tried at Taunton; transported thence for the Queen (JR) on the *Jamaica Merchant*, Dec. 9, to Barbados; sold on March 12 to George Hannay, Esq. (SL). Buried 1687 St John's, Barbados (BJo).

COCKRAM, Richard, soaper, of Taunton St Mary, 'aiding' (CP); Blue Regt. (P).

CODNER, Jeremiah, weaver, of Taunton St Mary, 'aiding' (CP); Blue Regt. (P).

COFFIN, William, white baker, of Dunster, 'in arms in the rebellion of James Scott' (CP).

COGAN, Richard, of Coaxdon Hall, Axminster; returned from Sedgemoor; was concealed at the Green Dragon, Axminster, by Elizabeth Gray, whom he subsequently married (T).

COGGAN, Barnard, of Street and Leigh tithing, Winsham, 'in the rebellion and not come in' (CP).

COLBORNE, John, of Wellington, 'in prison for rebellion' (CP); tried at Taunton; 'proposed for pardon' (JR); land forfeit and for sale (TB). Transported for Stapleton on the *Indeavour* from Bristol Oct. 20 for St Kitts or Nevis (SL).

COLBORNE, Roger, of Milverton, a captain, 'absenting' (CP).

COLBORNE, William, of Wellington, 'in prison for rebellion' (CP); tried at Taunton; proposed for pardon (JR); land forfeit and for sale (TB).

COLE, Daniel, of Wellington, 'absent' (CP).

COLE, David, presented at Wells and bound over (JR).

COLE, Edward, haberdasher, of Taunton St Mary, 'aiding' (CP); Blue Regt. (P).

COLE, Henry, excepted from the GP.

COLE, James, presented at Wells and bound over (JR).

COLE, John, presented at Wells and bound over (JR); in 1686 presented at Exeter, pardoned and dismissed (GD).

COLE, Roger, tried at Wells; transported for Howard (JR) on Oct. 25 to Jamaica (SL).

COLE (Coles), William, weaver, of Taunton St Mary, 'aiding' (CP); tried at Wells; transported for Stapleton (JR) on the *Indeavour* from Bristol on Oct. 20 to Nevis or St Kitts (SL).

COLE, William, presented at Wells and bound over (JR).

COLEBART, Robert, seaman, of Lyme Regis, 'absent and supposed' (CP).

COLEMAN, Edward, prisoner in the County Gaol 'upon suspicion of High Treason' (Wilts. QSR).

COLEMAN, James, yeoman, of Luppitt, 'out in the rebellion' (CP); presented at Exeter but at large (JR).

COLEMAN, John, of Axmouth, 'reported in arms' (CP). [*See below.*]

COLEMAN, John, of Milverton, 'absenting' (CP). [*See below.*]

COLEMAN, John junior, of Stoke St Mary, 'absent and in the late rebellion' (CL). [*See below.*]

COLEMAN, John, of Ruishton, 'absent' (CP). [*See below*] One of these 4 was tried at Wells; transported for Stapleton (JR) on the *Indeavour* from Bristol on Oct. 20 to Nevis or St Kitts (SL).

COLEMAN, Joseph, yeoman, of Axmouth, 'reported in arms' (CP); presented at Exeter but at large (JR).

COLEMAN, Richard, of Bishop's Hull, 'absent' (CP); 'not taken' (CL).

COLEMAN, Thomas, of West Hatch, 'out in the late rebellion' (CL).

COLEMAN, William, of Bridgwater, yeoman, pardon March 22, 1686 (CSPD, J2, II, 309).

COLLENDER, Ferdinand, of Chard, 'absent and believed' (CP).

COLLENS *see* Collins

COLLICK, John, worsted comber, of Taunton St Mary, 'aiding' (CP); Blue Regt (P).

COLLIER, Henry, blacksmith, of Lyme Regis, 'absent and supposed' (CP); of Uplyme, 'being in the late rebellion' (LRMB).

COLLIER, John, excepted from the GP.

COLLIER, Robert, of Chardstock, 'suspected guilty' (CP).

COLLIER, William, tried at Wells; transported thence for Bridgeman (JR); by White, Oct. 31, on the *Constant Richard* to Jamaica (SL).

COLLIER, William, presented at Exeter, March 1686, pardoned and dismissed (GD).
*And see* Collyer.

COLLINS, Emanuel, of Stockland, 'suspected' (CP); tried at Dorchester; transported for Booth (JR) on the *Happy Return* from Weymouth Sept. 25 to Barbados; sold to Richard Lintott (SL).

COLLINS, Henry, of Chard, 'absent and believed' (CP); tried at Wells; transported for Stapleton (JR) in the *Indeavour* from Bristol Oct. 20, to Nevis or St Kitts (SL).

COLLINS, John, of Chard, 'absent and believed' (CP); tried at Wells; transported for Nipho (JR) on the *Betty*, Sept. 26, to Barbados; sold to Capt. John Sutton. Pardon granted May 31, 1687, when several other transportees were pardoned but not released (CSPD, J2, II, 1833).

COLLINS, John, of Ditcheat, 'in arms in Scott's army and not taken' (CP). [*See below.*]

COLLINS, John, of Stockland, 'suspected' (CP). [*See below.*]

COLLINS, John, yeoman, of Upottery, 'absent' (CP); presented at Exeter but at large (JR). [*See below.*] One of these 3 was tried at Wells and transported for Stapleton (JR) on the *Indeavour* from Bristol Oct. 20, to Nevis or St Kitts (SL).

COLLINS, Nicholas senior, of Chardland, 'absent and believed' (CP); tried at Taunton; hanged at Ilminster (JR, JW).

COLLINS, Nicholas junior, aged 20, weaver (SL) of Chardland, 'absent and believed' (CP); tried at Taunton; transported for the Queen (JR) from Taunton, Dec. 9, to Barbados on the *Jamaica Merchant*; sold on March 12 to Col. Thomas Colleton (SL).

COLLINS, Philip, of Chardland, 'absent and believed' (CP).

COLLINS, Philip, of Yeovil, 'absent and not returned' (CP).

COLLINS, (perhaps Philip) of Tiverton, 'with the late Duke of Monmouth' (CP).

COLLINS, Samuel, tried at Taunton; transported for the Queen (JR). He is on John Rose's receipt, Oct. 12, but not on any of the ship lists so far discovered.

COLLINS, Thomas, goldsmith, of Taunton St Mary, 'aiding' (CP); Blue Regt. (P); tried at Wells; hanged at Bath (JR, JW) on Nov. 18 (NL).

COLLINS, William, of Walton, 'absent' (CP).

COLLINS, William, of Uplyme, weaver, with Monmouth at Axminster and Taunton; said he left the rebel army at Taunton to see his sick grandfather; hid with John Wyatt, 'taken' Feb. 4; sent to Dorchester gaol Feb. 8 (LRMB); presented at Dorchester in March, pardoned by proclamation (GD).

COLLINS, William, clothworker, of Frome, 'for a riot and amongst the Clubmen' (CP).

COLLWAY, John, clothier, of Lyme Regis, 'absent and supposed' (CP).

COLLYER, George, feltmaker, of Uplyme, imprisoned in Wilts. (DLD); tried at Dorchester (JR); hanged at Bridport on Sept. 12 (NL). *And see* Collier.

COMBDEN (Cumden), William, clothier of Netherbury (PR); tried at Dorchester; to be transported for Musgrave (JR) from Weymouth on the *Jamaica Merchant* to Barbados (SL) but died in Dorchester gaol; buried at All Saints', Feb. 16 (PR).

COMBE, COME *see* Coombe.

COMMER (Cumer), John, presented at Wells; 'recommended for pardon' (JR) but transported, Nov. 25, from Weymouth on the *Betty* to Barbados (SL).

CONDICK, George junior, of Bridgwater, tried at Taunton; hanged at Somerton (JR, JW).

CONNETT, James, of Gittisham, 'went to Monmouth and yet in rebellion' (CP).

CONNETT (Conant), John, of Gittisham, 'trained soldier, went to Monmouth and yet in rebellion' (CP); tried at Dorchester; transported for Nipho (JR) on the *Betty* to Barbados; sold to William Marchant (SL). Named in the 1689 petition for return (CSPD, W&M, I, 43).

CONNETT, Matthew, of Gittisham, 'went to Monmouth and yet in rebellion' (CP).

CONNETT, Richard, of Gittisham, 'trained soldier, went to Monmouth and yet in rebellion' (CP).

CONNETT, Thomas, presented at Exeter for 'aiding and assisting James Scott', convicted, 'remaining in custody' (JR); 'proposed for pardon' (JR2), land forfeit but not for sale; granted to Brent, Loder and Clarke. Pardon money to be kept by its recipient (TB).

CONNORY, Brian, 'engaged in the late rebellion'; pardon granted May 31, 1687 (CSPD, J2, II, 1833).

COODRIS, Walter, in Newgate July 16, 1685, 'in the late rebellion, confessed' (CSPD, J2, I, 1249).

COOKE, Christopher, clothier, of Wilton and aulnager at Taunton; to him Ferguson addressed the letter alerting Taunton. It was intercepted (Axe) and therefore Cooke was excepted from the GP. He took no part in the rebellion, 'having withdrawn himself'; but got away to Holland and took a leading part in establishing the manufacture of English cloth there. His pardon, dated May 5, 1686, specifies 'if he return from the parts beyond the seas with his goods and effects within 2 calendar months after the date thereof, or else have no benefit thereby' (CSPD, J2, II, 306, 512).

COOKE, Henry, of Mells, 'supposed' (CP); tried at Wells; to be transported for Howard (JR) Oct. 25, but escaped between Wells and Sherborne (SL).

COOKE, John, of Chard, 'absent and believed' (CP); tried at Wells; transported for Nipho (JR) on the *Betty* to Barbados; sold to Thomas Pearce (SL); escaped with Henry Pitman and reached England in 1688 (PW).

COOKE, John, of Wookey, 'supposed' (CP); tried at Wells; transported for Nipho (JR) from Ilchester gaol on the *Rebecca* to Barbados (SL).

COOKE, Jonathan, tailor, of Wincanton, 'absent, so informed' (CP).

COOKE, Joshua, of Colyton, 'supposed' (CP).

COOKE, Matthew, aged 21, carter [plowman] (SL), tried at Taunton; transported thence for the Queen (JR) on the *Jamaica Merchant*, Dec. 9, to Barbados; sold there March 12 to Col. Thomas Colleton (SL). Buried 1702 St John's, Barbados (BJo).

COOKE, Robert, yeoman, of Colyton, presented at Exeter but at large; tried at Wells; hanged at Norton St Philip (JR, JW).

COOKE, Stephen, clothier, of Wilton, 'actually a rebel in arms' (Wilts. QSR); in Newgate July 16 'in the late rebellion confessed' (CSPD, J2, I, 1249); tried at Dorchester; 'proposed for pardon' (JR); land forfeit and for sale (TB).

COOKE, Thomas, clothier, of Kilmington (TB), imprisoned in Wilts. (DLD); tried at Dorchester (JR); hanged at Bridport on Sept. 12 (NL); land forfeit and for sale (TB).

COOKENEY (Cookney), John senior, tailor, of Lyme Regis, 'absent and supposed' (CP).

COOKENEY (Cookney), John, junior, tailor, of Lyme Regis, 'absent and supposed' (CP).

COOKENEY, Nicholas, husbandman, of Lyme Regis, 'absent and supposed' (CP).

COOKENEY, Robert, carpenter, of Lyme Regis, 'absent and supposed' (CP).

COOKENEY (Cookney), Thomas, of Sidmouth, 'went to Monmouth' (CP); of Plymtree, woolcomber, imprisoned at Taunton (DLD); presented at Dorchester; and proposed for pardon (JR).

COOKESLEY, William, of Chardland, 'absent and believed' (CP).

COOKESLEY (Cooksley) John, husbandman, of Taunton St James, 'aiding' (CP); Blue Regt. (P).

COOLING, Edward, of North Barrow, 'rebel, in custody' (Som. QSR).

COOLING, Henry junior, of North Barrow, 'absent and not returned' (CP).

COOMBE, Hugh, yeoman, of Upottery, 'absent' (CP), presented at Exeter but at large (JR).

COOMBE, James, of Pitminster, 'a rebel' (CL); tried at Taunton; transported for Musgrave (JR) on the *Jamaica Merchant* from Weymouth to Jamaica, there March 12 (SL).

COOMBE, John, yeoman, of Luppitt, 'supposed' (CP); presented at Exeter but at large (JR); excepted from the GP.

COOMBE, John, of Huntspill, 'active soldier in the Duke of Monmouth's army' (Som. QSR), tried at Wells. [*See below.*]

COOMBE, John (another) tried at Wells. [*See below.*] One of these Johns was hanged at Shepton Mallet (JR, JW); the other was transported for Stapleton (JR) on the *Indeavour* from Bristol Oct. 20, to Nevis or St Kitts (SL).

COOMBE, Richard, comber, of Taunton St Mary, 'aiding' (CP); Blue Regt. (P).

COOMBE, Robert, tried at Taunton; hanged at Wiveliscombe (JR, JW).

COOMBE, William, of Broadwindsor, 'out in the horrid rebellion' (CP); tried at Taunton; transported for Booth (JR) from Exeter via Bristol, Oct. 24, on the *John* to Barbados; sold to John Burston (SL).

COOMBE, William, presented at Wells and bound over (JR). Perhaps a Congregationalist of Axminster, or possibly a Quaker of Stoke St Gregory.

COOPER, Christopher, pipemaker (DLD), of Honiton, 'a rebel' (CP), imprisoned in Devon workhouse (DLD); tried at Exeter; transported for Nipho (JR) from Exeter gaol on the *Betty* to Barbados; sold to Charles Thomas & Co. (SL). Buried 1686 St Michael's, Barbados (BMi).

COOPER, John, gentleman, of Beckington, 'in the rebellion, out of Beckington and at large' (CP).

COOPER, Joseph, tried at Taunton, pleaded not guilty; sentenced to be hanged, but omitted from the warrant (JR); transported, Nov. 12, by T. Heywood on the *Constant Richard* to Jamaica (SL).

COOPER, William, joiner, of Bridgwater (TB), tried at Taunton, pleaded not guilty; hanged at Taunton (JR, JW) on Sept. 21 (NL); land forfeit and for sale (TB).

COOPER, William, of Croscombe, 'in Scott's army and not taken' (CP).

COPP, Peter, of Crewkerne, 'rebel and not taken' (CP).

CORDILION, Peter, of Ilchester, 'in the late rebellion' (CP); tried at Wells; transported for Nipho (JR) on the *Betty* to Barbados; sold to John Jackman (SL).

CORNELIUS, Joseph, of Ilminster, 'in the late rebellion' (CP).

CORNELIUS, Richard, presented at Taunton; certificate allowed (JR).

CORNELIUS, Richard, presented at Wells and bound over (JR).

CORNELIUS, Roger, tried at Wells; hanged at Pensford (JR, JW).

CORNELIUS, Thomas, tried at Dorchester; transported for Booth (JR) from Weymouth, Sept. 25, on the *Happy Return* to Barbados; sold to Col. John Farmer (SL).

CORNER, *see* Carrier.

CORNISH, James, of Thornfalcon, 'absent' (CP); 'taking up arms against the king, and taking away arms from Mrs. Courte of Lillesdon in the parish of North Curry' (Som. QSR).

CORNISH, Nicholas, cordwinder, of Taunton St Mary, 'aiding' (CP); Blue Regt (P).

CORNISH, Philip, yeoman, of Taunton St Mary, 'aiding' (CP); Blue Regt. (P).

CORNISH, Philip, yeoman, of Kingston, pardoned March 22 (CSPD, J2, II, 310).

CORNISH, Philip, of East Street, Taunton St Mary, 'aiding' (CP), Blue Regt. (P).

CORNISH, Philip, of Stoke St Mary, 'in the late rebellion' (CL).

CORNISH, Thomas, tried at Taunton; 'remaining in gaol' (JR); transported by Heywood, Nov. 12, on the *Constant Richard* to Jamaica (SL).

CORNAWELL, John, of Creech St Michael, 'absent and not taken' (CP).

COSSENS, Samuel, presented at Dorchester; certificate allowed (JR).

COSSINS, *see* Ellis.

COTTERELL, Emanuel, breaker, of Cullompton, in the High Gaol, Devon (DLD).

COTTERELL, John, presented at Wells, 'recommended for pardon' (JR).

COUNSELL, Edward, husbandman, of Chapel Allerton (TB, SL), tried at Taunton; transported for Booth (JR) from Bridgwater prison via Bristol, Oct. 24, on the *John* bound for Barbados; died at sea (SL). Land forfeit and for sale (TB).

COUNSELL, John, of Wedmore, 'absent and in the late rebellion' (CP).

COURSE (Cowes), Joseph, tried at Wells; transported for Stapleton (JR) in the *Indeavour* from Bristol Oct. 20, to Nevis or St Kitts (SL).

COURT, James, weaver, of Taunton St James, 'aiding' (CP); Blue Regt. (P).

COURT, Robert, yeoman, of Frome, 'in the rebellion and in prison' (CP); tried at Wells; transported for Stapleton (JR) on the *Indeavour* from Bristol Oct. 20, to Nevis or St Kitts (SL).

COURT, William, presented at Taunton, 'proposed for pardon' (JR).

COVERT, Nicholas, gentleman, of Chichester, excepted from the GP.

COWARD, John, of Wanstrow, 'in the rebellious army of Monmouth' (CP).

COWARD, Robert, of Rode, tried at Taunton; transported for Booth (JR) from Bridgwater prison via Bristol, Oct. 24, on the *John* to Barbados; sold to Ann Gallop (SL).

COWES, *see* Course.

COX, James, yeoman, of Axmouth, 'reported' (CP); presented at Exeter, proposed for pardon; misreported 'at large' (JR).

COX, John, yeoman, of Axmouth, 'reported' (CP); presented at Exeter but at large (JR).

COX, John, yeoman, of Combpyne, 'with Monmouth' (CP); presented at Exeter but at large (JR).

COX, John senior, fuller, of Taunton St Mary, 'aiding' (CP), Blue Regt. (P).

COX, John junior, worsted comber, of Taunton St Mary, 'aiding' (CP); Blue Regt. (P).

COX, John, of West Hatch, 'absent' (CP); transported (CL); tried at Wells; transported for Stapleton (JR) on the *Indeavour* from Bristol Oct. 20 to Nevis or St Kitts (SL).

COX, Lancelot, of Beaminster, 'wanting from his home' (CP); presented at Wells and bound over (JR).

COX, Philip, husbandman or yeoman, of Colyton, 'absent' (CP); tried at Dorchester; transported for Nipho (JR) on the *Betty* bound for Barbados; died at sea Dec. 19 (SL). Also presented at Exeter and misreported 'at large' (JR). Land, estate worth £30 p.a., forfeit and for sale. Widow and daughter, reduced to begging, petitioned for the estate, which was granted to them (TB).

COX, Richard, yeoman, of Musbury, 'in the rebellion' (CP); 'went with his plough [cart]' (DLD); wounded, his hand broken, at Norton St Philip; captured and put in Ilchester gaol, where Dr Winter set the bones (WB); presented at Dorchester, 'remaining in gaol' (JR). Also presented at Exeter and misreported 'at large' (JR).

COX, Robert, of Wedmore, 'absent and in the late rebellion' (CP).

COX, Robert, yeoman, of Axmouth, 'reported' (CP); presented at Exeter but at large (JR).

COX, Samuel, tried at Wells; hanged at Ilchester (JR, JW).

COX, Thomas, of Chetnole, 'supposed' (CP).

COX, Thomas, yeoman, of Colyton, 'absent' (CP); presented at Exeter but at large (JR). Petitioned unsuccessfully for his brother Philip's estate (TB).

COX, Thomas, yeoman, of Musbury, 'in the rebellion, at large' (CP); presented at Exeter but at large (JR). Mistakenly said to be of Axminster in BL. Add. MS. 90337).

COX, Thomas, worsted comber, of Taunton St Mary, 'aiding' (CP); Blue Regt. (P).

COX, William senior, husbandman, of Musbury, 'in the rebellion' (CP); went with his plough [cart], imprisoned at Ilchester (DLD); tried at Dorchester (JR); hanged at Wareham on Sept. 22 (NL). Land, estate of £32 p.a., forfeit and for sale (TB). Mistakenly presented at Exeter and reported at large (JR).

COX, William, junior, yeoman, of Musbury, 'in the rebellion' (CP); went with his plough [cart], imprisoned at Ilchester (DLD); presented at Dorchester, remaining in custody (JR). Mistakenly presented at Exeter and reported at large (JR).

COX, William senior, sergemaker, of Taunton St Mary, 'aiding' (CP); Blue Regt. (P). Escaped to Holland and helped to manufacture English cloth there. Pardon dated June 2, 1686 'if he return with his goods and effects within 2 calendar months' (CSPD, J2, II, 625).

COX, William junior, sergemaker, of Taunton St Mary, 'aiding' (CP); Blue Regt. (P). Pardon dated May 12, 1686 (CSPD, J2, II, 531).

COZENS, William, tried at Dorchester; transported for Booth (JR) on the *Happy Return* from Weymouth, Sept. 25, to Barbados; sold to Ralph Fretwell (SL).

COZENS, William, presented at Wells and bound over (JR).

CRABB, William, gentleman, of Ashill, 'out in the rebellion' (CP); excepted from the GP.

CRABB, ——, of Northcote, Honiton 'a rebel' (CP).

CRAGG alias Smith, Robert, messenger between William Disney and Major Wildman in London and Monmouth in Holland (W). Warrant for his arrest, July 13 (CSPD, J2, I, 1218). Prisoner in Newgate, May 3 1686 (CSPD, J2, II).

CRAGG, alias Smith, John, his son Ensign in the Red Regt. (W); in Newgate, July 16; ordered to Dorchester (CSPD, J2, I, 1249) and presented there (GD); no note of sentence, but excepted from the GP. Did he escape from custody?

CRAISE (Cruse), William, tried at Wells; hanged at Shepton Mallet (JR, JW).

CRANDON, William, of Burstock, 'suspected' (CP).

CRANE, Giles, of Street, 'absent' (CP); tried at Taunton; transported for Musgrave (JR) from Weymouth on the *Jamaica Merchant* to Jamaica; there by March 12 (SL).

CRANE, John, of Street, 'absent' (CP); tried at Taunton; transported for the Queen (JR) from Taunton, Oct. 12. On John Rose's list (SL).

CRANE, William, of Street, 'absent' (CP).

CRAY, Richard, presented at Wells, 'remaining in custody' for want of evidence (JR).

CRAYDON, Edward, presented at Wells and bound over (JR).

CREED, George, of Bishop's Hull, 'absent' (CP); 'not taken' (CL).

CREED, Laurence, baker, of Wincanton, 'absent, and, as informed, in Scott's army' (CP).

CREW (Crow), Benjamin, husbandman, constable of Combpyne, 'in Dorchester gaol for being with Monmouth' (CP, DLD); tried at Dorchester; transported for Booth (JR) on the *Happy Return* from Weymouth, Sept. 25, to Barbados; sold to Col. John Hallett (SL). Land forfeit and for sale (TB). Also presented at Exeter and misreported at large (JR).

CREW, Thomas, of Thurloxton, 'in the rebellion and in prison' (CP); presented at Taunton and proposed for pardon (JR).

CRITCHELL, Hugh, presented at Dorchester; discharged for want of evidence (JR).

CROCKER, John, of Bishop's Hull, 'absent' (CP); presented at Wells; recommended for pardon (JR). Dead (CL Sept. 24).

CROCKER, Thomas, of Milverton, 'absenting' (CP).
*And see* Crooker

CROFT, Matthew, aged 19, weaver (SL), of Thorncombe, 'wanting from his habitation' (CP); tried at Taunton; transported thence for the Queen (JR) on the *Jamaica Merchant*, Dec. 9, to Barbados; sold on March 12 to Capt. Thomas Morris (SL).

CROFT, William, of Curry Rivel, 'out in the rebellion and not taken' (CP); tried at Taunton; transported for Musgrave (JR) on the *Jamaica Merchant* from Weymouth to Barbados, there by March 12 (SL).

CROOKE, William, carrier, of Taunton St Mary, 'aiding' (CP); Blue Regt. (P).

CROOKER, Andrew, of Bishop's Hull, 'absent, not taken' (CL).
*And see* Crocker

CROOTE, John junior, of Honiton, 'a rebel' (CP).

CROSS, Christopher, mason, of Taunton St James, 'aiding' (CP); Blue Regt. (P).

CROSS, Hugh senior, sergemaker, of Bishop's Hull, excepted from the GP; got away to Holland and helped to manufacture English cloth. Pardon dated June 2, 1686 'if he return from abroad with his goods and effects within two months' (CSPD, J2, II, 627); pardon of all treasons, dated August 21 (CSPD, J2, II, 916). He declared that he had taken no part in the rebellion (PE).

CROSS, James, 'a boy in Bridgwater prison' (DLD).

CROSS, John, of Trull, 'absent' (CP); 'a rebel' (CL).

CROSS, John, of Wellington, aged 18, plowman [carter] (SL), 'in prison for rebellion' (CP); tried at Taunton; transported thence for the Queen (JR) on the *Jamaica Merchant* Dec. 9 to Barbados; sold there on March 12 to Francis Bond, Esq. (SL).

CROSS, Jonas, of Colyton, tried at Taunton; transported for Booth (JR) from Exeter prison via Bristol, Oct. 24, on the *John* bound for Barbados; died at sea (SL).

CROSS, Matthew, tried at Taunton; hanged at Ilchester (JR, JW).

CROSS, Nicholas, shoemaker, of Taunton St Mary, 'aiding' (CP); Blue Regt. (P).

CROSS, Robert, yeoman, of Axminster, 'supposed' (CP); 'seen in Monmouth's camp by John Baites' (LRMB); presented at Exeter but at large (JR).

CROSS, Simon, of Wellington, 'in prison for rebellion' (CP); tried at Taunton; hanged at Chard (JR, JW).

CROSS, Thomas, of Wootton Fitzpaine, 'supposed' (CP); tried at Taunton; transported for Musgrave (JR) on the *Jamaica Merchant* from Weymouth to Jamaica; died at sea (SL).

CROSS, William, tried at Taunton; transported thence for the Queen

(JR); Dec. 9 on the *Jamaica Merchant* to Barbados; sold there on March 12 to Francis Bond, Esq. (SL).

CROSS, William senior, of West Horrington, 'supposed' (CP).

CROSS, William junior, of West Horrington, 'supposed' (CP).

CROSSEMAN, John, of Stoke St Gregory, 'absenting' (CP).

CROW, *see* Crew.

CROWDER, John, tried at Wells; transported for Howard (JR), Oct. 25 to Jamaica (SL).

CRUISE, Edward, husbandman, of North Bradley (TB); tried at Wells; hanged at Norton St Philip (JR, JW). Land forfeit and for sale (TB).

CUFF, John, innkeeper, of Ashill, 'out in the rebellion' (CP). A Quaker who attended Quarterly Meeting regularly from 1672 till 1683. He received relief in 1684, and again in 1697, when his house was burnt down (Som. Record Soc. 75, pp. 96–7, 149, 164, 248.)

CULVERWELL, John, tried at Taunton; transported for the Queen (JR); on John Rose's list, Oct. 12 (SL).

CULVERWELL, Richard, of Durleigh, 'in the rebellion and taken' (CP); tried at Taunton; hanged at Nether Stowey (JR, JW).

CUMDEN, *see* Combden.

CUMER, *see* Commer.

CUMINS (Cumming), Nicholas, weaver, of Cullompton, imprisoned in Wilts. (DLD), tried at Wells; transported thence for Stapleton (JR) Sept. 26; put on board *Indeavour* of Bristol Oct. 20 for Nevis or St Kitts (SL).

CURRIER, *see* Scurrier.

CURRY, Robert, of North Curry, 'absent' (CP); 'a tenant and holds a cottage, fled, not yet apprehended' (CL).

CURTIS, Thomas, tried at Taunton; transported for Musgrave (JR) on the *Jamaica Merchant* from Weymouth to Barbados; there March 12 (SL).

CUTLER, Thomas, tried at Taunton; transported for Musgrave (JR) on the *Jamaica Merchant* from Weymouth to Barbados; there by March 12 (SL).

CUTTLER, John, tailor, of Wincanton, 'absent, in Scott's army, as informed' (CP).

DABIN, William, of Glastonbury, 'from home at the time of the rebellion' (CP).

DABINETT, John, of Chardstock, 'suspected guilty' (CP).

DAGG, Francis, of Westbury, 'in the rebellion as we are informed' (Wilts. QSR).

DALBY (Dolly), Jacques, from Holland with Monmouth, Lieut. in the Red Regt. (W). Pardon July 18, 1686 (CSPD, J2, II, 822).

DALE, Robert, presented at Dorchester, 'proposed for pardon' (JR).

DALLAMAN, William, of Hardington, 'in the late rebellion' (CP).

DALLEY, John, of Chard, 'in the late rebellion' (CP).

DALLY, Henry, of Beaminster, 'absent at the time of the rebellion' (CP).

DAMMER, Richard, of Lyme Regis, taken at Lyme and sent to Dorchester gaol 14 July (LRMB); presented at Dorchester; certificate allowed (JR). Member of Lyme Corporation (LRCB).

DANIEL, Ambrose, yeoman, of Colyton, 'absent' (CP); presented at Exeter but at large (JR).

DANIEL, George, collier, of Beckington, 'in the rebellion, out of Beckington; at large' (CP).

DANIEL, James, of Beaminster, attorney, nonconformist; joined Monmouth at Lyme, present at Sedgemoor; returned home, where he hid, and then to a barn at Knowle. He died in 1711 aged 100 and was buried (like his descendants) on the site of the barn (Pulman, *Book of the Axe*, 117–18).

DANIEL, Richard, of Colyton, 'supposed' (CP); tailor, of Beer, imprisoned in the High Gaol, Devon (DLD); tried at Dorchester; transported for Nipho (JR) on the *Betty* from Weymouth, Nov. 25, to Barbados; sold to Charles Thomas & Co. (SL).

DANIEL, Thomas, clothworker, of Frome, 'for a riot and among the Clubmen' (CP).

DANIEL, Thomas, of Wilton, 'absent' (CP); tried at Wells; transported for Stapleton (JR) on the *Indeavour* from Bristol Oct. 20, to Nevis or St Kitts (SL).

DARBY, Philip, of Sidmouth, 'went to Monmouth' (CP).

DARE, George, yeoman, of Membury, 'absent' (CP); presented at Exeter but at large (JR); at Exeter March 1686 presented, pardoned and dismissed (GD).

DARE, Gideon, husbandman, of Luppitt, 'in prison, supposed' (CP); in the High Gaol, Devon (DLD); presented at Exeter but 'at large'; tried at Taunton; to be hanged but omitted from the warrant (JR); transported by Heywood, Nov. 12, on the *Constant Richard* to Jamaica (SL). Land forfeit and for sale (TB). Named on the 1689 petition for return (CSPD, W&M, I, 43). Returned with Coad 1690 (CM).

DARE, John, aged 23 (PR), yeoman, of Colyton, presented at Exeter but at large (JR).

DARE, John, of Crewkerne, 'rebel in Monmouth's army and not taken' (CP).

DARE, Samuel, tried at Taunton; 'to be hanged but omitted from the warrant' (JR); sick of the smallpox; transported by Heywood, Nov. 12, on the *Constant Richard* to Jamaica (SL).

DARE, Thomas, goldsmith, of Taunton, in prison in Taunton in 1680 for seditious words; escaped to Holland; one of the chief Whig plotters there; appointed Paymaster by Monmouth; came with him and landed at Chideock; brought 40 horses to Lyme; shot there by Fletcher on June 13 (W).

DARE, Thomas, son of Thomas Dare also of Taunton and Holland; Ensign in the Red Regt. (W). Witness for the king, left in custody at Wells (JR).

DARE, William, of Stockland, 'suspected' (CP).

DARSON, Joseph, of Trull, 'absent' (CP).

DAUPHIN, Robert, tucker, of Taunton St Mary, 'aiding' (CP); Blue Regt. (P).
*And see* Dolphin.

DAVEY, Edward, weaver, of Taunton St James, 'aiding' (CP); Blue Regt. (P).

DAVEY, John, presented at Dorchester, not indicted but continued in gaol (JR); presented, pardoned and dismissed at Exeter, March 1686 (GD).

DAVEY, Richard, yeoman, of Stockland, 'suspected' (CP); presented at Exeter but at large (JR).

DAVEY, William, of Stockland, 'suspected' (CP).

DAVIDGE, Nicholas, cordwiner, of Wincanton, in Ilchester prison (CP); presented at Wells; transported for Howard (JR) Oct. 25, to Jamaica (SL).

DAVIS, Isaiah, woolcomber, of Bampton, imprisoned at Bridgwater (DLD); tried at Taunton; hanged at Bridgwater (JR, JW).

DAVISON, Jeremiah, glazier, of Frome, 'for a riot and among the Clubmen' (CP).

DAVISON, Samuel, miller, of Sutton, Somerset (TB); presented at Wells; remaining in custody (JR); transported (JR2); land forfeit and for sale (TB).

DAVISON, William, tried at Taunton and hanged there (JR, JW) on Sept. 30 (NL).

DAVY, Bartholomew, of Milverton, 'absenting' (CP); tried at Taunton; transported for Musgrave (JR) on the *Jamaica Merchant* from Weymouth to Barbados; there by March 12 (SL).

DAVY, Godfrey, of Oathill, Wayford, 'rebel and not taken' (CP).

DAVY, Jacob, yeoman, of Sampford Courtney, in the High Gaol, Devon (DLD).

DAVY, Miles junior, of Colyton, 'supposed' (CP). Survived and returned for he had daughters christened in 1694 and 1696 (PR).

DAVY, Richard, yeoman, of Axminster, 'supposed' (CP); presented at Exeter but at large (JR).

DAVY, William, yeoman, of Upottery, 'absent' (CP); in Bridgwater prison (DLD); presented at Exeter, but at large; tried at Taunton; hanged at Chard (JR, JW).

DAVYS, Elisha, tried at Taunton; transported for Musgrave (JR); on the *Jamaica Merchant* from Weymouth to Barbados; there by March 12 (SL).

DAVYS, Humphrey, yeoman, of Frome, 'in the rebellion and in prison' (CP); tried at Wells; transported for Howard (JR) in the *Port Royal Merchant* Oct. 25 to Jamaica (SL).

DAVYS, Thomas, of Croscombe, 'in Scott's army and not taken' (CP); tried at Taunton; hanged at South Petherton (JR, JW).

DAVYS, Thomas, presented at Wells and bound over (JR).

DAVYS, William, of Bridport, 'in the rebellion, as informed' (CP); presented at Dorchester, 'continuing in gaol, not indicted' (JR).

DAWBNEY, James, presented and pardoned by proclamation at Dorchester, March 1686 (GD).

DAWE, John, of Chardland, 'absent and believed' (CP).

DAWE, Robert, of Chardland, 'absent and believed' (CP).

DAWE, Robert, of Wellington, 'absent' (CP); tried at Wells; 'remaining in custody' (JR); transported by Heywood on the *Constant Richard* to Jamaica (SL).

DAWE, William, of Taunton (SL), Blue Regt. (P); tried at Taunton; transported for Booth (JR) from the Bridewell, Taunton, via Bristol, Oct. 24, to Barbados on the *John*; sold to Anthony Palmer (SL). Buried 1709 St Michael's, Barbados (BMi); son Pitman Dawe (B).

DAY, Edward, presented at Wells, 'recommended for pardon' (JR).

DEANE, Abraham, of Chard, 'absent and believed' (CP).

DEANE, Francis, of Chardland, 'absent and believed' (CP); presented at Taunton, certificate allowed (JR).

DEANE, John, of Chardland, 'absent and believed' (CP).

DEANE, John, of Thornfalcon, 'in arms against the king' (Som. QSR).

DEANE, Robert, of Chardland, 'absent and believed' (CP).

DEARING, John, woolbreaker, of Lyme Regis, 'absent and supposed' (CP).

DEBNAM, Thomas, clothworker, of Frome, 'in the rebellion and in prison' (CP); tried at Taunton; transported for Musgrave (JR) on the *Jamaica Merchant* from Weymouth to Jamaica; there by March 12 (SL).

DEEME, John, of Axmouth, yeoman, 'reported' (CP); presented at Exeter but at large (JR).

DEEME, John senior, yeoman, of Luppitt, 'out in the rebellion' (CP); presented at Exeter but at large (JR).

DEEME, John junior, yeoman, of Luppitt, 'out in the rebellion' (CP); presented at Exeter but at large (JR).

DEFOE *see* Foe.

DELL, Samuel, goldsmith, of Taunton St Mary, 'aiding' (CP); Blue Regt. (P). Pardon May 12, 1686 (CSPD, J2, II, 530).

DEMSTER, Roger, of Donyatt, 'out in the rebellion' (CP).

DENHAM, Hugh, of Combe St Nicholas, 'absent and believed' (CP).

DENHAM, John, of Combe St Nicholas, 'absent and believed' (CP); presented at Wells [*See below*].

DENHAM, John, (another) presented at Wells. [*See below*.] Of these two John Denhams, one had his certificate allowed (JR). The other was transported for Nipho (JR) Sept. 26 on the *Rebecca* to Barbados. Reprieve granted. Was it too late? (JR2).

DENHAM, Richard, tried at Wells; transported for Stapleton (JR), on the *Indeavour* from Bristol Oct. 20, to Nevis or St Kitts (SL).

DENHAM, Samuel, tried at Wells; transported for Howard (JR), Oct. 25, to Jamaica (SL).

DENNICK, Nathan, of Norton sub Hamdon, 'in the late rebellion' (CP).

DENNICK, Timothy, of Norton sub Hamdon, 'in the late rebellion, not taken' (CP).

DENNING, John, of Beaminster, 'wanting from his home' (CP); presented at Wells; transported for Stapleton (JR) on the *Indeavour* from Bristol Oct. 20, to Nevis or St Kitts (SL).

DENNING, Nathaniel, of Stockland, 'suspected' (CP); tried at Wells; transported for Howard (JR) Oct. 25, to Jamaica (SL).

DENNING, Philip, of Beaminster, 'wanting from his home' (CP).

DENNING, Richard, yeoman, of Axminster, 'supposed' (CP); presented at Exeter but at large (JR).

*And see* Dining; Dunning.

DENNIS, Samuel, of Coleford, 'absenting' (CP).

DENNIS, Thomas, of Bridgwater (SL), tried at Taunton; transported for Booth (JR) from Bridgwater prison via Bristol, Oct. 24, on the *John* to Barbados; sold to Capt. W. Scott (SL).

DEON, Lawrence, of West Buckland, 'absent' (CP).

DERNCOMBE *see* Verncombe.

DEVERICKS (Devereux) Barnaby, tried at Taunton; hanged at Yeovil (JR, JW).

DEW, James, tried at Wells; transported for Stapleton (JR) on the *Indeavour* from Bristol Oct. 20, to Nevis or St Kitts (SL).

DEW, William, tried at Wells; transported for Stapleton (JR) on the *Indeavour* from Bristol Oct. 20, to Nevis or St Kitts (SL).

DEWDNEY, Samuel, of Taunton, woolcomber; served under Capt. Matthews; present at Norton St Philip but did not fight and 'often endeavoured to make his escape from the Army but could not for the watches'. Appeared at Exeter City Sessions 21 Aug. 1685 (Exeter City Sessions Bk.).

DIAMOND, Jasper, tried at Dorchester; transported for Booth (JR) on the *Happy Return* from Weymouth, Sept. 25, to Barbados; sold to Richard Harwood, Esq. (SL).

DICK, John, of Ashill, 'out in the rebellion' (CP).

DICKER, George, tailor, of Taunton St Mary, 'aiding' (CP); Blue Regt. (P).

DIER *see* Dyer.

DILLANY (Dilling), William, sergeweaver, of Honiton, imprisoned in the High Gaol, Devon (DLD); tried at Dorchester (JR); hanged at Poole Sept. 21 (NL).

DINHAM, Oziah, weaver, of Dunster, 'in arms' (CP).

DINHAM, Thomas, of Taunton St James, 'aiding' (CP); Blue Regt. (P).

DINNETT *see* Dunnett.

DINNING, Elias, of Taunton St Mary, 'aiding' (CP); Blue Regt. (P).

DINNING, Philip, of Wellington, 'absent' (CP).

DINNING, William, of Taunton St James, 'aiding' (CP); Blue Regt. (P).

*And see* Denning, Dunning.

DITTEE, Henry, of Axminster, 'supposed' (CP).

DOBB, Henry, of Donyatt, 'out in the rebellion' (CP).

DODD, William, of East Brent, 'absent' (CP).

DODDS, John, badly wounded at Norton St Philip, taken to Ilchester gaol, treated there by Dr Winter (WB); tried at Wells; transported for Nipho (JR) on the *Betty* from Weymouth, Nov. 25, to Barbados; sold to John Smart (SL).

DODRIDGE, *see* Spiller.

DOELING, John, presented at Wells and bound over (JR).

DOLBEARE, Samuel, pipemaker, of Honiton, in Bridgwater prison (DLD); tried at Dorchester; transported for Nipho (JR) on the *Betty* from Weymouth, Nov. 25, to Barbados; sold to William Marchant (SL).

DOLBEARE, Thomas, shoemaker, of Honiton, land forfeit and for sale (TB), which suggests that he was killed at Sedgemoor (P).

DOLEMAN, Robert, husbandman, of Langport, 'absent' (CP); tried at Wells and hanged there (JR, JW).

DOLEMAN, Thomas, tried at Wells; transported thence for Bridgeman (JR) by White on the *Constant Richard* to Jamaica (SL).

DOLLING (Doling, Polling), Silvanus, yeoman, of Thorncombe, presented at Exeter but at large (JR); 'wanting from this habitation' (CP).

DOLLING, Thomas, tried at Dorchester; transported for Nipho (JR) on the *Betty* from Weymouth, Nov. 25, to Barbados; sold to William Chester, Esq. (SL).

DOLLY *see* Dalby.

DOLPHIN, Thomas, fuller, of Taunton St James, 'aiding' (CP); Blue Regt. (P). *And see* Dauphin.

DOMAN, John, tobacco cutter, of Taunton St Mary, 'aiding' (CP); Blue Regt. (P).

DOMETT *see* Donnett.

DOMMER (Dommett) Richard, fuller, of Lyme Regis, 'absent and supposed' (CP); taken at Lyme Regis and sent to Dorchester gaol, July 14 (LRMB).

DONN, Henry, of Beaminster, 'wanting from his home' (CP).

DONNETT (Domett), James, yeoman, of Upottery, 'absent' (CP); presented at Exeter but at large; tried at Taunton; hanged at Chard (JR, JW).

DONNETT, Samuel, yeoman, of Upottery, 'absent' (CP); presented at Exeter but at large (JR).

DORCHESTER, John senior, tried at Wells; hanged at Shepton Mallet (JR, JW).

DORCHESTER, John junior, tried at Wells; recommended for pardon' (JR); Reprieved (JR2).

DORE, Thomas, Mayor of Lymington, 1683–4 and 1684–5; said to be hovering about the New Forest with about 80 horse and foot in support of Monmouth (CSPD, J2, I, 958). Dore, late Mayor of Lymington, was excepted from the GP; and pardon for Dore, late of Lymington, of all treasons, etc. was granted on August 2, 1686 (CSPD, J2, II, 864, 1936).

DOUCH, William, of Halstock, 'for flying from his colours' (CP).

DOWELL, John, weaver, of East Woodlands, 'in the rebellion and at large' (CP).

DOWER *see* Drower.

DOWNE, Hugh, presented for high treason at Exeter in March 1686; pardoned and dismissed (GD).

DOWNE, John, of Croscombe, 'in Scott's army and not taken' (CP).

DOWNE, John, of Bridport, 'in the rebellion, as informed' (CP); tried at Dorchester; transported for Booth (JR) on the *Happy Return* from Weymouth, Sept. 25, to Barbados; sold to Stephen Devorax (SL).

DOWNE, Joseph, of Sherborne, 'absconding and suspected' (CP).

DOWNE, Roger, presented at Dorchester, March 1686; pardoned by the king's proclamation (GD).

DOYER, *see* Dyer.

DRACOTT, Henry, of London, 'concerned in the rebellion in the West'; petition for pardon, June 1 (CSPD, J2, II, 617). Report: not excepted in GP, July 10. Pardon approved, August 2 (CSPD, J2, II, 862).

DRAKE, Ambrose, of Donyatt, 'out in the rebellion' (CP).

DRAKE, Andrew, joiner, of Lyme Regis, 'absent and supposed' (CP).

DRAKE, Daniel, of Buckland St Mary, 'out in the rebellion and not taken' (CP).

DRAKE, George, of Buckland St Mary, 'out in the rebellion and not taken' (CP).

DRAKE, Henry, of Buckland St Mary, 'out in the rebellion and not taken' (CP).

DRAKE, Richard, tried at Taunton; transported for Musgrave (JR) on the *Jamaica Merchant* from Weymouth to Barbados, there by March 12 (SL).

DRAKE, Robert, of Buckland St Mary, 'out in the rebellion and not taken' (CP).

DRAKE, Samuel, of Pitminster, 'absent' (CP).

DRAYTON (Dranton), Peter junior, of Leigh tithing, Pitminster, 'absent' (CL); tried at Wells; transported for Stapleton (JR) on the *Indeavour* from Bristol to Nevis or St Kitts (SL).

DREDGE, John, twister, of Frome, 'for a riot and among the Clubmen' (CP).

DREDGE, John, of Marston Bigot, 'in the rebellion and not taken' (CP).

DREW, Jonathan, tried at Wells; transported for Howard (JR) to Jamaica (SL).

DREW, William, of Goathurst (CP); of Bridgwater (SL); 'in the rebellion and taken' (CP); tried at Taunton; transported for Booth (JR) from Bridgwater via Bristol, Oct. 24, on the *John* to Barbados; sold to John Burston (SL).

DREWER, George, of Seavington St Mary, 'in the rebellion and not come in' (CP).

DREWER, Joseph, of Seavington St Michael, 'in the rebellion and not come in' (CP).

DROVER, Isaac, yeoman, of Colyton, 'absent' (CP); presented at Exeter but at large (JR). Returned; buried at Colyton in 1712 (PR).

DROVER, Zachary, aged 21, son of Isaac (PR), joiner (TB), 'absent' (CP); after Sedgemoor hid under the wheel of the water-mill (T);

taken and imprisoned at Ilchester (DLD); presented at Dorchester and 'proposed for pardon' (JR). Land forfeit and for sale (TB). Also presented at Exeter and misreported at large (JR). Returned. A son buried at Colyton in 1704 (PR).

DROWER (Dower), Robert, yeoman, of Axminster, 'supposed' (CP); tried at Exeter pleaded not guilty, convicted, 'remaining in custody'; was to be hanged on Sept. 14 but reprieved (JR). Two of Howard's rebels being reprieved, 'he is to have out of Exeter gaol Robert Drower and Elias Holmes' (SL). Locke records him as transported. The Exeter list misrecords him as at large (JR). To Jamaica (SL).

DRYER, John, of Glastonbury, 'from home at the time of rebellion' (CP). [*See below.*]

DRYER, John, of Taunton St Mary, 'aiding' (CP); Blue Regt. (P). [*See below.*] One John Dryer was tried at Taunton and hanged there (JR, JW) Sept. 30 (NL).

DRYER, Toby, tried at Taunton; transported for Musgrave (JR) on the *Jamaica Merchant* from Weymouth to Barbados; there by March 12. (SL).

DUCE, John, of Colyton, 'absent' (CP).

DUDDERIDGE, John, of Chard, 'in the late rebellion' (CP).

DUDLEY, Edward, of Aller, 'in the late rebellion and not come home' (CP).

DUNCARTON, George, of Pilton, 'in arms in Scott's army and not taken' (CP).

DUNKIN, Timothy, in Exeter gaol, tried at Exeter, to be hanged, but reprieved (JR).

DUNN, Robert, of Chard, 'in the late rebellion' (CP); presented at Taunton, certificate allowed (JR).

DUNN, Samuel, of Seavington St Mary, in the rebellion and not come in (CP).

DUNNE, Amos, of Hinton St George, 'rebel and not taken' (CP).

DUNNE, John senior, of Hinton St George, 'rebel and not taken' (CP).

DUNNE, John junior, of Hinton St George, 'rebel and not taken' (CP).

DUNNETT, John, shoemaker, of Axminster, wounded at Sedgemoor, imprisoned at Wells (DLD); tried there; transported thence for Bridgeman (JR) by White on the *Constant Richard* to Jamaica, Oct. 31 (SL).

DUNNING, Francis, tried at Wells; transported for Stapleton (JR) on the *Indeavour* from Bristol Oct. 20, to Nevis or St Kitts (SL).

DUNNING, Robert, narrow weaver, of Beckington, 'in the rebellion, out of Beckington, at large' (CP).

*And see* Denning; Dinning.

DUNSCARTON, Edward, of Shepton Mallet, 'rebel, not taken' (CP).

DUNSTAR, John, of Wilton, 'absent' (CP).

DUNSTER, Henry, of Donyatt, 'out in the rebellion' (CP).

DURDANT, John, of Merriott, 'rebel and not taken' (CP).

DURDEN (Burden), Peter, tried at Wells; transported for Howard (JR) on the *Port Royal Merchant* to Jamaica (SL).

DURNHAM, Thomas, of Crewkerne, 'rebel and not taken' (CP).

DURSTON, Thomas, yeoman, of Axbridge, tried at Wells; hanged there (JR, JW). Land forfeit and for sale (TB).

DURSTON, William, tried at Wells and hanged there (JR, JW).

DUSTON, Joseph, of North Trendle, Trull, 'rebel' (CL).

DUTCH, John, yeoman, of Frome, 'in the rebellion and in prison' (CP); presented at Taunton and 'proposed for pardon' (JR).

DUTTON, John, excepted from the GP, his name followed by the word Colt (GP).

DWELLY, Samuel, presented at Wells and bound over (JR).

DYER (Dier, Doyer), Bartholomew, of Taunton St Mary, 'aiding' (CP); Blue Regt. (P).

DYER (Dyker), George, weaver, of Taunton St James, 'aiding' (CP); Blue Regt. (P). Pardon, March 26, 1686 (CSPD, J2, II, 351). (He was married in 1680, PR).

DYER, Isaac, aged 25, comber (SL); tried at Taunton; transported for the Queen (JR) from Taunton to Barbados on the *Jamaica Merchant*, Dec. 9 to March 12; sold to Daniel Parsons (SL).

DYER, James, of Hillfarrance, 'absent' (CP).

DYER, John junior, of Staplegrove, 'absent' (CP).

DYER, Richard, weaver, of Cullompton, imprisoned in Wilts. (DLD); tried at Wells; transported for Stapleton (JR) in the *Indeavour* from Bristol to Nevis or St Kitts (SL).

DYER, Robert, yeoman, of Colyton, imprisoned in the High Gaol, Devon (DLD); presented at Taunton and proposed for pardon (JR).

DYER, Robert, of North Curry, 'absent' (CP); of Wrantage, 'in arms'; a sergeant (Som. QSR).

DYER, Simon, tried at Wells, transported for Stapleton (JR) in the *Indeavour* from Bristol, Oct. 20, to Nevis or St Kitts (SL).

DYER, Thomas, of Bishop's Hull, 'absent, not taken' (CL).

DYER, Thomas, of Stoke St Mary, 'absent' (CP).

DYER, William, of Hillfarrance, 'absent' (CP).

DYER, William, of Taunton St James, 'aiding' (CP); Blue Regt. (P).

DYKE, James, of Dowlishwake, 'in the rebellion and not come in' (CP).

DYKE, John or Jonathan, of Dowlishwake, 'in the rebellion and not come in' (CP).

DYKE, Richard, tried at Wells; transported for Nipho (JR) on the Rebecca (SL).

DYMICK, Caleb, yeoman, of Stoke under Ham, 'absent' (CP).

DYMOCK, William, presented at Wells and bound over (JR).

DYMOND, John, of Martock, 'absent' (CP).

EADES, William, presented at Wells, 'remaining in custody for want of evidence' (JR).

EAMES, Maurice, of Ilminster, 'in the late rebellion' (CP).

EARLE, Robert, aged 24, plowman [carter] (SL), of Stoke St Mary, 'absent' (CP); tried at Taunton; transported thence for the Queen

(JR) on the *Jamaica Merchant* Dec. 9, to Barbados; sold on March 12 to Capt. John Sutton (SL).

EASON *see* Easton.

EASTABROOKE (Cartabrooke, Easterbrook), Henry, sergeworker, of Kenton, imprisoned in the High Gaol, Devon (DLD); tried at Taunton; hanged at Chard (JR, JW).

EASTABROOKE, Richard, of Taunton St Mary, 'aiding' (CP); Blue Regt. (P).

EASTMOUNT, John, tried at Dorchester; transported for Nipho (JR) on the *Betty* from Weymouth, Nov. 25, to Barbados; sold to Thomas Gibbs (SL).

EASTON, Christopher, of Chard, 'engaged in the late rebellion'; pardon May 31, 1687 (CSPD, J2, II, 1833).

EASTON, John, of Chard, 'absent and believed' (CP).

EASTON, Richard, tried at Wells; transported for Stapleton (JR) in the *Indeavour* from Bristol Oct. 20, to Nevis or St Kitts (SL).

EASTON, Robert, of Taunton (SL), tried at Taunton; transported for Booth (JR) from Taunton Bridewell via Bristol, Oct. 24, on the *John* to Barbados; sold to Capt. W. Scott (SL).

EASTWOOD, John, of West Chinnock, 'in the late rebellion' (CP).

EBDEN, George, of Sidmouth, woolcomber, 'went to Monmouth' (CP); in Bridgwater prison (DLD); tried at Dorchester; transported for Nipho (JR) from Dorchester gaol, Oct. 21, on the *Rebecca* to Barbados (SL).

EDGAR, Richard, of Mosterton [SL adds Devon]; tried at Taunton; transported for Booth (JR) from Taunton Bridewell via Bristol, Oct. 24, on the *John* to Barbados; sold to John and William Holder (SL).

EDGHILL, Richard, victualler, of Beckington, 'in the late rebellion, out of Beckington, at large' (CP). [*See below.*]

EDGHILL, Richard, tailor, of Rode, 'in the rebellion' (CP). [*See below.*] One Richard Edghill was presented at Taunton and remained in gaol (JR). He, or possibly a third Richard Edghill, was excepted from the GP. The other Richard Edghill was tried at Wells and transported for Stapleton (JR) on the *Indeavour* from Bristol on Oct. 20 to Nevis or St Kitts (SL).

EDMONDS, Henry, of South Petherton, 'in the rebellion and not come in' (CP).

EDMONDS, Humphrey, tried at Wells; hanged at Pensford (JR, JW).

EDMONDS, James, tried at Taunton, remaining in gaol (JR); transported from Wells by White, Nov. 12, on the *Constant Richard* to Jamaica (SL).

EDMONDS, John junior, of South Petherton, 'in the rebellion and not come in (CP).

EDMONDS, Jonathan, of South Petherton, 'in the rebellion and not come in' (CP).

EDMONDS, Robert, of Chardland, 'absent and believed' (CP).

EDNEY, Henry, tried at Taunton; hanged at Porlock (JR, JW) in December (NL).

EDWARDS, David, of East Brent, 'absent' (CP).

EDWARDS, John, comber, of Axminster, 'supposed' (CP); imprisoned in Wilts. (DLD); tried at Dorchester; transported for Booth (JR) on the *Happy Return* from Weymouth, Sept. 25, to Barbados; sold to Capt. Matthew Haviland (SL). Land forfeit and for sale (TB). Named on the 1689 petition for return (CSPD, W&M, I, 43). Also presented at Exeter and misreported at large (JR).

EDWARDS, John, yeoman, of Dipford, Trull, 'rebel prisoner', tried at Taunton; transported for Booth (JR) from Taunton Bridewell to York, Virginia, in the *Exchange* of Topsham (CSPC, xii. 442; SL). Land forfeit and for sale (TB). He died in Maryland. His pardon was approved May 31, 1687 (CSPD, J2, II, 1833). His widow, Sarah, (with 6 children) petitioned the lord of the manor of Taunton Deane, the Bishop of Winchester, for permission to succeed to her husband's lands on payment of the fine. Granted, 19 April, 1692 (SRO, DD/SP H/62).

EDWARDS, John junior, of Bishop's Hull, 'absent' (CP); 'not taken' (CL). [*See below.*]

EDWARDS, John senior, of Wilton, 'absent' (CP) of Galmington (CL). [*See below.*]

EDWARDS, John junior, of Wilton, 'absent' (CP). [*See below.*] One John Edwards was excepted from the GP. He or another was pardoned on Oct. 2, 1686 (CSPD, J2, II, 1035).

EDWARDS, Stephen, of Lyme Regis, carrier, 'absent and supposed' (CP).

EDWARDS, William, of Winsham, 'absent and believed' (CP); tried at Taunton; transported for Musgrave (JR) from Weymouth on the *Jamaica Merchant* to Jamaica; there by March 12 (SL).

EGLIN, Thomas, tried at Wells; transported thence for Bridgeman (JR) by White on the *Constant Richard* to Jamaica (SL).

ELLBY, Robert, of Crewkerne, 'rebel and not taken' (CP).

ELLERY, Thomas, of Nether Compton, 'absconding and suspected' (CP).

ELLET, Robert, of Holford, 'absent' (CL).

ELLFORD, James, tried at Wells; transported for Howard (JR), Oct. 25 in the *Port Royal Merchant* to Jamaica (SL).

ELLFORD (Elford), James, tried at Wells; transported for Stapleton (JR) in the *Indeavour* from Bristol Oct. 20, to Nevis or St Kitts (SL).

ELLIOTT, Cornelius, tried at Wells; transported for Stapleton (JR) in the *Indeavour* from Bristol Oct. 20, to Nevis or St Kitts (SL).

ELLIOTT, Edward junior, blacksmith, of Beckington, 'in the rebellion, out of Beckington, at large' (CP).

ELLIOTT, Ezekiel, husbandman, of Cannington, 'absent and believed aiding the rebels' (CP).

ELLIOTT, Matthew, tailor, of Sidmouth, 'went to Monmouth' (CP); imprisoned in Dorset (DLD); tried at Dorchester; transported for Musgrave (JR) from Weymouth on the *Jamaica Merchant* to Jamaica (SL).

ELLIOTT, Robert, of Ruishton, 'absent' (CP).

ELLIOTT, Tristram, tried at Dorchester (JR); hanged at Weymouth or Melcombe Regis on Sept. 15 (NL).

ELLIS, alias Cossins, Andrew, of Thorncombe, 'wanting from his habitation' (CP); tried at Dorchester (JR); hanged at Poole, Sept. 21 (NL).

ELLIS, Cornelius, of Berkley and Standerwick, 'in the rebellion and in prison'. Not presented at Assize, so perhaps he died in prison.

ELLIS, Thomas, yeoman, of Willand, imprisoned in Wilts. (DLD); presented at Wells and bound over (JR).

ELLORY, Robert, weaver, of Taunton St James, 'aiding' (CP); Blue Regt. (P).

ELLWORTHY, Samuel, worsted comber, of Cullompton, imprisoned in Ilchester (DLD); tried at Wells; transported for Howard (JR) to Jamaica (SL).

ELLSTONE see Hoope.

ENGLAND, Allen, tried at Dorchester; transported for Nipho (JR) on the *Betty* from Weymouth, Nov. 25, to Barbados; sold to Col. John Waterman. (SL).

ENGLAND, John, of Chard, 'absent and believed' (CP). [*See below.*]

ENGLAND, John, of Chardland, 'absent and believed' (CP). [*See below.*]

ENGLAND, John, of Taunton St Mary, 'aiding' (CP); Blue Regt. (P). [*See below.*] One John England was tried at Taunton; transported for the Queen (JR); received by John Rose, Oct. 12 (SL).

ENGLAND, Jonathan, tried at Taunton; hanged there (JR, JW), Sept. 30 (NL).

ENGLAND, Philip, tried at Wells; transported for Stapleton (JR) in the *Indeavour* from Bristol Oct. 20, to Nevis or St Kitts (SL).

ENGLAND, Robert, joiner, of Taunton St Mary, 'aiding' (CP); Blue Regt. (P).

ENGLAND, Robert, of Trull, 'absent' (CP).

ENGLAND, Samuel, of Chardland, 'absent and believed' (CP).

ENGLAND, Thomas, of Bridport, 'in the rebellion as we are informed' (CP); tried at Dorchester; transported for Musgrave (JR) from Weymouth on the *Jamaica Merchant* to Barbados; there by March 12 (SL).

ENGLAND, Thomas, of South Petherton, 'in the rebellion and not come in' (CP); tried at Taunton; to be hanged (JR) but no place specified, which suggests he died in prison (P).

ENGLAND, William senior, barber, of Taunton St Mary, 'aiding' (CP); Blue Regt. (P). [*See below.*]

ENGLAND, William junior, comber, of Taunton St Mary, 'aiding' (CP); Blue Regt. (P). [*See below.*] One William England was tried at Wells; transported for Stapleton (JR) in the *Indeavour* from Bristol Oct. 20, to Nevis or St Kitts (SL).

ENTICOTT, James, yeoman, of Axminster, 'supposed' (CP); presented at Exeter, but at large (JR).

ERBURY, William, cardmaker, of Frome, 'for a riot and among the Clubmen' (CP).

ERVIN, John, tried at Wells; transported for Stapleton (JR) in the *Indeavour* from Bristol Oct. 20, to Nevis or St Kitts (SL).

EVAN, Griffen, of Knowle St Giles, 'in the rebellion and not come in' (CP).

EVANS, Edward, yeoman, of Luppitt, 'absent' (CP), presented at Exeter but at large (CP).

EVANS, John, scrivener, of Beckington, 'in the rebellion, out of Beckington, at large' (CP).

EVANS, John, yeoman, of Wilton (TB), tried at Taunton; hanged at Keynsham (JR, JW). Land forfeit and for sale (TB).

EVANS, Richard, Doctor in Physic, of Cotleigh (TB); tried at Wells; to be hanged at Redcliffe Hill, Bristol (JR, JW) but escaped from the cloisters at Wells; recaptured in Devon in Jan. 1686 'a dangerous rebel engaged in the late rebellion' (Devon QS Book) and hanged in Somerset (NL). A Nonconformist minister. Land forfeit and for sale (TB). Bounty paid for his arrest to a sergeant in Lord Cornbury's Regt. (Devon QS Book).

EVANS *see* Jones

EVANS, William, of Berkley and Standerwick, 'in the rebellion and not taken' (CP).

EVERARD, Arthur, tried at Wells; transported for Howard (JR), Oct. 25 in the *Port Royal Merchant* to Jamaica (SL).

EVERARD, William senior, comber, of Taunton St James, 'aiding' (CP); Blue Regt. (P).

EVERARD, William junior, comber, of Taunton St James, 'aiding' (CP); Blue Regt. (P).

EVERDALL, John, of Walton, 'absent' (CP).

EVERY, George, of Leigh, Pitminster, 'absent' (CP); presented at Court Leet of Taunton Deane, Sept. 24, as 'out, and wanting from his home' (CL).

EVERY, James, cheesemonger, of Honiton, 'a rebel' (CP); imprisoned in the High Gaol, Devon (DLD); tried at Taunton; hanged at Crewkerne (JR, JW); land forfeit and for sale (TB).

EVERY, Richard, of Ashill, 'out in the rebellion' (CP).

EVERY, Simeon, of Leigh, Pitminster, 'wanting from his home' (CL).

EVES, Edward, tried at Taunton; transported for Musgrave (JR) on the *Jamaica Merchant* from Weymouth to Jamaica; there by March 12 (SL).

EWIN, Robert, pardon dated May 25, 1686 (CSPD, J2, II, 597).

EXON, Bernard, of Creech St Michael, 'absent and not taken' (CP).

EYRES, Matthew, weaver, of East Woodlands, 'in the rebellion and at large' (CP); 'took up arms against his majesty' (Som. QSR).

EYRES, William, tried at Wells; transported for Howard (JR) Oct. 25; escaped between Wells and Sherborne (SL).

FACEY, Bartholomew, of Durleigh, 'absent and not taken' (CP).

FACEY, John, yeoman, of Colyton, imprisoned in the High Gaol, Devon (DLD); tried at Dorchester; transported for Nipho (JR) on the

*Betty* from Weymouth, Nov. 25, to Barbados; sold to Michael Child (SL).

FALLSTON, Thomas, weaver, of Frome, 'in the rebellion and at large' (CP).

FANAM, William, of Long Sutton, 'in the rebellion and not come home' (CP).

FANE, Joseph, of Taunton St Mary, 'aiding' (CP); Blue Regt. (P).

FARILS, George, of Milverton, 'absenting' (CP).

FARMER, Isaac, of Kittisford, 'absenting' (CP).

FARMER, John, of Taunton (SL); tried at Taunton; transported for Booth (JR) from Taunton Bridewell via Bristol, Oct. 24, on the *John* to Barbados; sold to Capt. W. Scott (SL).

FARMER, Joseph, yeoman, of Luppitt, presented at Exeter but at large (JR).

FARMER, Joseph, of Taunton St Mary, 'aiding' (CP); Blue Regt. (P).

FARMER, Samuel, tried at Wells; transported for Stapleton (JR), in the *Indeavour* from Bristol Oct. 20, to Nevis or St Kitts (SL).

FARMER, William, of Milverton, 'absenting'; a sergeant (CP) presented at Taunton and 'proposed for pardon' (JR).

FARNDIN, George, pardon dated May 25, 1686 (CSPD, J2, II, 597).

FARR, Thomas, presented at Wells and bound over (JR).

FARRANT, George junior, yeoman, of Colyton, 'absent' (CP); presented at Exeter but at large (JR); presented at Exeter, March 1686, pardoned and dissmissed (GD). A married man whose son was christened in 1672. George was buried in March 1699/1700 (PR).

FARTHING, John, of Staplegrove, 'taking up arms against the king, and yet absent' (Som. QSR).

FARTHING, William, of Kingston St Mary, 'wanting; we do allow of his certificate' (CL).

FATHERS, John, from Ilchester gaol to be tried at Wells; transported for Howard (JR), Oct. 25, to Jamaica (SL).

FAULKNER, John, of Taunton St Mary, 'aiding' (CP); Blue Regt. (P).

FAWNE (Foane), John, of Corscombe, tried at Dorchester, pleaded not guilty, Sept. 5 (JR); hanged at Dorchester, Sept. 7 (NL).

FAWNE, Robert, of Corscombe, 'suspected' (CP); tried at Taunton; hanged at Ilminster (JR, JW).

FAWNE, Robert, of Powerstock, 'absent' (CP); tried at Dorchester; transported for Nipho (JR) on the *Betty* from Weymouth, Nov. 25, to Barbados; sold to Ralph Lane (SL).

FAWNE, William, chandler, of Powerstock, 'absent' (CP).

FEADE, William, tried at Dorchester; to be transported for Booth (JR). One of 10 of Booth's 100 not shipped on the *Happy Return*.

FEARE, John, of Glastonbury, 'from home at the time of rebellion' (CP).

FEARE, Nicholas, of Wedmore, 'absent, in the late rebellion' (CP).

FEARE, William, of Glastonbury, 'from home' (CP); tried at Wells; transported for Stapleton (JR) in the *Indeavour* from Bristol Oct. 20, to Nevis or St Kitts (SL).

FEDDELL, John, husbandman, of Langport, 'absent' (CP).

FERGUSON, Robert, Presbyterian minister, came from Holland with Monmouth; chaplain to the army; at Sedgemoor; escaped with Wade to N. Devon; excepted from the GP of 1686 and 1688. Returned with William of Orange. Wrote a not entirely trustworthy account of the rebellion for Eachard's *History*.

FERRER, Joseph, of Luppitt, 'absent' (CP).

FERRIS, Thomas, of Milverton, 'absenting' (CP); tried at Wells; transported for Stapleton (JR) in the *Indeavour* from Bristol Oct. 20, to Nevis or St Kitts (SL).

FIDOE, Walter, presented at Wells and bound over (JR).

FIELD, James senior, blacksmith, of Long Sutton, 'in the rebellion and not come home' (CP); tried at Wells; hanged at Bruton (JR, JW). Land forfeit and for sale (TB).

FIELD, James junior, blacksmith, of Long Sutton, 'in the rebellion and not come home' (CP); tried at Wells; to be transported for Howard (JR), Oct. 25, but escaped between Wells and Sherborne (SL).

FIELD, John, tried at Wells; to be transported for Howard (JR), Oct. 25, but escaped between Wells and Sherborne (SL).

FINEERE (Finnier), Richard, of Leigh on Mendip, 'absent' (CP); tried at Wells; hanged at Pensford (JR, JW).

FINNIMORE, John, tailor, of Tiverton, imprisoned in the High Gaol, Devon (DLD); tried at Taunton; transported for Musgrove (JR) from Weymouth on the *Jamaica Merchant* to Jamaica; there, March 12 (SL).

FIRTH, *see* Frith

FISHER, Charles, of Wedmore, 'absent' (CP).

FISHER, John, tried at Dorchester; transported for Booth (JR) on the *Happy Return* from Weymouth, Sept. 25, to Barbados; sold to Col. Richard Williams (SL).

FISHER, Robert, presented at Wells, certificate allowed (JR).

FLEMING, Ensign, on Albemarle's list of rebel 'commission officers'.

FLEMING, Thomas, 'of Taunton St Mary, aiding' (CP); Blue Regt. (P).

FLETCHER, Andrew, of Saltoun, landowner, came with Monmouth; Lt Col. of Horse; shot Thomas Dare at Lyme; dismissed; went to Spain and Hungary; excepted from GP of 1686 and 1688 *in absentia* in Scotland and sentenced to death. Attainder reversed by Scots Parliament. Fletcher sat in the Scots Parliament, and opposed the Act of Union in 1707 (*Dictionary of National Biography*).

FLIGHE, Joseph, of Broad Street, London, Cornet of Horse (L).

FLITTCHETT, Thomas, of Crewkerne, 'rebel and not taken' (CP).

FLOWER, William, saddler, of Taunton St Mary, 'aiding' (CP); Blue Regt. (P).

FLOYD, Thomas, tucker, of Taunton St Mary, 'aiding' (CP); Blue Regt. (P).

FOANE *see* Fawne

FOE, Daniel, of Stoke Newington, rode from London, 'engaged in the late rebellion'. 'I who followed the Duke of Monmouth in arms' (Defoe). Pardon 31 May 1687 (CSPD, J2, II, 1833).

FOLLETT, George, of Charmouth, 'suspected' (CP).

FOLLETT, John, worsted comber, of Taunton St Mary, 'aiding' (CP); Blue Regt. (P); tried at Exeter; transported for Nipho (JR) from Exeter gaol on the *Betty* from Weymouth, Nov. 25, to Barbados; sold to Capt. Robert Harrison (SL). Mariner, will 1703/4 (Barbados records).

FOLLETT, Nathaniel, fuller, of Taunton St Mary, 'aiding' (CP); Blue Regt. (P).

FOLLETT, Richard, presented, pardoned and dismissed at Exeter, 1686 (GD).

FOOT, John, of Nether Compton, 'absent, suspected' (CP); tried at Wells; transported for Nipho (JR) on the *Betty* from Weymouth, Nov. 25, to Barbados; sold to Capt. John Gibbs (SL).

FORD, Arthur, of Bishop's Hull, 'absent' (CP); 'in prison' (CL); tried at Wells; transported for Stapleton (JR) in the *Indeavour* from Bristol Oct. 20, to Nevis or St Kitts (SL).

FORD, Benjamin, of Taunton St James, 'aiding' (CP); Blue Regt. (P).

FORD, Edward, of Shepton Mallet, 'in prison for rebellion' (CP); tried at Wells; transported for Stapleton (JR) in the *Indeavour* from Bristol Oct. 20, to Nevis or St Kitts (SL).

FORD, Edward junior, of Milverton, 'absenting' (CP).

FORD, Henry, tried at Dorchester, pleaded not guilty on Sept. 5; hanged there on Sept. 7 (JR & NL).

FORD, John, yeoman, of Axmouth, 'reported in arms' (CP); presented at Exeter but at large (JR).

FORD, John senior, weaver, of Taunton St James, 'aiding' (CP); Blue Regt. (P).

FORD, John junior, weaver, of Taunton St James, 'aiding' (CP); Blue Regt. (P).

FORD, Joseph, of Taunton St James, 'aiding', (CP); Blue Regt, (P).

FORD, Joseph, shoemaker, of Lyme Regis, 'absent, supposed' (CP).

FORD *see* Goad.

FORD, Samuel, of Taunton St James, 'aiding' (CP); Blue Regt. (P).

FORD, Thomas, of Stockland, 'suspected' (CP); presented at Wells (1685) and pardoned by proclamation (GD).

FORNECOMBE *see* Verncombe

FORSEY, Thomas, yeoman, of Thorncombe, 'wanting from his habitation' (CP); tried at Dorchester; transported for Nipho (JR) on the *Betty* from Weymouth, Nov. 25, to Barbados; sold to Lt. Col. Richard Vinter (SL). Also presented at Exeter and misreported at large (JR).

FORSTER, Thomas, presented at Wells and bound over (JR).

FORT, Edward or Edmund, of Chard, 'absent and believed' (CP); tried at Taunton; hanged at Chard (JR, JW).

FORT, George, yeoman, of Axminster, 'supposed' (CP); a clothier, 'seen in Monmouth's camp' by John Bailes (LRMB); presented at Exeter but at large (JR).

FORT, James, of South Petherton, 'in the rebellion and not come in' (CP).

FORT, Thomas, of Chardland, 'absent and believed' (CP). [*See below.*]

FORT, Thomas, of Combe St Nicholas, 'absent and believed' (CP). [*See below.*]

FORT, Thomas, of Ilminster, 'in the late rebellion' (CP). [*See below.*] One Thomas Fort or Forte was tried at Dorchester and sentenced to death on Sept. 10 (JR); hanged at Weymouth or Melcombe Regis, Sept. 15 (NL).

FORWARD, Nicholas, of Ottery St Mary, woolcomber; White Regt., fought at Norton St Philip and Sedgemoor; in Exeter prison after City sessions 25 July (Exeter City Sessions Bk.); presented at Wells and bound over (JR).

FOSTER, John, tried at Wells; transported for Stapleton (JR) to Nevis or St Kitts (SL).

FOULER, William, of Dulverton, 'for harbouring rebels' (CP).

FOULKES, John, Colonel, commanding the White Regiment, came from Holland, where he had been an officer in one of the English regiments in the service of William of Orange; cashiered at the request of King James. He escaped abroad after Sedgemoor; was excepted from the GP. He returned to command a battalion in William III's army and served in the Battle of the Boyne.

FOWERACRES, James, of Northcote, Honiton, 'a rebel' (CP).

FOWERACRES, John, cordwainer, of Honiton, imprisoned in Devon Workhouse (DLD); tried at Exeter on Sept. 14; pleaded not guilty; hanged the same day at Exeter (GD, JR, NL).

FOWERACRES, Richard, tried at Wells; transported for Stapleton (JR) in the *Indeavour* from Bristol Oct. 20, to Nevis or St Kitts (SL).

FOWLER, Henry, yeoman, of Combpyne, 'with Monmouth in the late rebellion' (CP); presented at Exeter but at large (JR).

FOWLER, James, blacksmith, of Honiton, imprisoned in the Devon workhouse (DLD); of Northcote, Honiton, 'a rebel' (CP); tried at Dorchester; transported for Booth (JR) on the *Happy Return* from Weymouth, Sept. 25, to Barbados; sold to Col. John Farmer (SL). Named on the 1689 petition for return (CSPD, W&M, I, 43).

FOWLER, John senior, of Williton, 'a copyholder of this [Williton Hadley] manor, who is convicted of high treason, for which his copyhold estate is forfeited unto the lord of this manor' (SRO DD/L); tried at Taunton; transported for Musgrave (JR) on the *Jamaica Merchant* from Weymouth to Jamaica; there by March 12 (SL).

FOWLER, John junior, sergeman, of Taunton St James, 'aiding' (CP); Blue Regt. (P); tried at Taunton; transported for Musgrave (JR) on the *Jamaica Merchant* from Weymouth towards Jamaica; died at sea (SL). Land forfeit and for sale (TB).

FOWLER, John, seaman, of Lyme Regis, 'absent and supposed' (CP); tried at Wells; transported for Stapleton in the *Indeavour* from Bristol Oct. 20, to Nevis or St Kitts. (SL).

FOWLER, William, yeoman, of Axminster, 'supposed' (CP); presented at Exeter but at large (JR).

FOX, James, a Lieut. in the Dutch Service, came from Holland with Monmouth; Major and Second in Command, Yellow Regt.; wounded at Keynsham (W); excepted from the GP. He served in William III's army under Col. Foulkes (CSPD, W&M, I, 370).

FOX, Robert, of Taunton St Mary, 'aiding' (CP); Blue Regt. (P).

FOXWELL, Francis, of Honiton, 'a rebel' (CP); a bodicemaker, imprisoned at Taunton (DLD); tried there; hanged at Yeovil (JR, JW).

FOXWELL, John, presented, pardoned and dismissed at Exeter, March 1686 (GD).

FOXWELL, William, of Ilminster, 'in the late rebellion' (CP).

FOYLE, Ralph, of Allston Moris [Huntspill], 'in arms in the late rebellion' (CP).

FRANCIS, Robert, tried at Wells; hanged at Bridgwater (JR, JW).

FRANCKLEN, Joseph, of Martock, 'absent' (CP).

FRANCKLIN, Nicholas, of West Monkton, 'out in the rebellion and at large' (CP); a Nicholas Franking buried at Norton St Philip 13 July 1685 (PR).

FRANCKLIN, Thomas, husbandman, of Luppitt, 'supposed; in prison' (CP) in Wilts. (DLD); tried at Dorchester; transported for Nipho (JR) on the *Betty* from Weymouth, Nov. 25, to Barbados; sold to Thomas Pearce (SL). Also presented at Exeter and misreported at large (JR). Land forfeit and for sale (TB). Named on the 1689 petition for return (CSPD, W&M, I, 43).

FRANCKLYN, James, and Francis Greenfield, 'upon suspicion that they came into England with the late Duke of Monmouth, and that one of them was a commission officer in his army' (Wilts. QSR).

FRANCKLYN, Joseph, clerk, of Worle, excepted from the GP.

FREAR *see* Quinton

FREKE, Peter, of Chardland, 'absent and believed' (CP).

FRENCH, Daniel, of Colyton, 'supposed' (CP).

FRENCH, George senior, worsted comber, of Taunton St Mary, 'aiding' (CP); Blue Regt. (P).

FRENCH, George junior, worsted comber, of Taunton St Mary, 'aiding' (CP); Blue Regt. (P).

FRENCH, George, of Trull, 'absent' (CP).

FRENCH, John, aged 34 (PR), of Colyton, 'supposed' (CP).

FRENCH, Joshua, of Chard, 'absent and believed' (CP); tried at Wells; hanged at Wrington (JR, JW).

FRENCH, Laurence, of Chard Town, 'absent and believed'; excepted from the GP, but pardoned Nov. 4, 1686 (CSPD, J2, II, 1114).

FRENCH, Maurice, of Merriott, 'rebel in Monmouth's army and not taken' (CP).

FRENCH, Richard, yeoman, of Musbury, 'in the rebellion' (CP); presented at Exeter but at large (JR). [Wrongly, of Axminster in BL. Add. MS. 90337; rightly, of Musbury in BL. Add. MS. 30077.]

FRENCH, Roger, aged 36 (PR), of Colyton, 'supposed' (CP); imprisoned at Ilchester (DLD); tried at Dorchester; transported for Booth (JR) on the *Happy Return* from Weymouth, Sept. 25, to Barbados. Omitted from sale (SL). A Roger French was buried at Colyton in 1698 (PR).

FRENCH, Roger, yeoman, of Seaton, 'a prisoner', died in Dorchester Gaol; buried at All Saints, Dorchester, Jan. 8 (DLD & PR).

FRENCH, William, of Musbury, 'in the rebellion' (CP); presented at Exeter but at large (JR). [Wrongly, of Axminster in BL. Add. MS. 90337; rightly, of Musbury in BL. Add. MS. 30077.]

FRESTON, Walter, tried at Wells; transported for Stapleton (JR) in the *Indeavour* from Bristol Oct. 20, to Nevis or St Kitts (SL).

FRICKER, John, tried at Taunton; hanged there, Sept. 30 (JR, JW & NL).

FRITH, Maurice, gentleman, of Wincanton, 'in arms in the rebellion; returned from Norton fight' (CP); excepted from GP.

FROST, Abraham, of Ilminster, 'in the late rebellion' (CP).

FROSTON, William, weaver, of Rode, 'in the late rebellion' (CP).

FRY, John, of Chard, 'absent and believed' (CP).

FRY, John, of Croscombe, 'in Scott's army and not taken' (CP).

FRY, John, mason, of Orchardleigh, 'in the rebellion and not taken' (CP).

FRY, John, of Burland tithing, Staplegrove, 'absent' (CP); 'in arms against the king' (Som. QSR); 'under condemnation' (SRO, DD/SP).

FRY, Robert, of West Buckland, 'absent' (CP).

FRY, Thomas, of Bishop's Hull, 'absent' (CP), 'not taken' (CL).

FRY, Thomas, of Croscombe, 'in Scott's army and not taken' (CP).

FRY, William, of Donyatt, 'out in the rebellion' (CP).

FRY, William, of Taunton St Mary, 'aiding' (CP); Blue Regt. (P).

FRY, William, of Wayford, 'rebel in Monmouth's army and not taken' (CP).

FRYER, Isaac, of Frome, 'in the rebellion and in prison' (CP). Not presented at Assize; did he die in prison?

FUDGE, Francis, of Wedmore, excepted from GP.

FUDGE, Richard, of Bampton, 'supposed to be a rebel' (CP).

FUELL, William, of Bishop's Hull, 'absent' (CP).

FULFORD, Robert, presented at Taunton for 'levying war against the king'; pleaded guilty, but was 'humbly proposed to his Majesty for his gracious pardon' (GD & JR).

FURBER (Turber), John, tried at Taunton; transported for Musgrave (JR) on the *Jamaica Merchant* from Weymouth to Jamaica; there by March 12 (SL).

FURNIVAL, Randall, alias John Sexton, at Wells Assize, a witness for the king, left in custody (JR).

FURZE, Joseph, of North Curry, 'wanting' and in the late Duke of Monmouth's service; dead' (CL).

FURZE (or Vosse alias Brooke), Morris, of Milverton, 'absenting' (CP); tried at Taunton; transported for Booth (JR) from Taunton Bridewell via Bristol, Oct. 24, on the *John* to Barbados; sold to Dr Battyn (SL).

FURZE, Thomas junior, of Stoke St Gregory, 'in arms, aiding and assisting James Scott in the time of the rebellion' (CP); of Thornfalcon, a sergeant (Som. QSR).

FURZE, William, of Stoke St Gregory, 'absenting' (CP), and 'in the late Duke of Monmouth's service' (CL).

FUSSELL *see* Russell.

FYLDY, Edmund, yeoman, of Membury, presented at Exeter but at large (JR).

GAITCH, Benjamin, yeoman, of Axmouth, 'reported to be in arms in the late rebellion' (CP); presented at Exeter but at large (JR).

GAITCH, Joseph, mariner, of Lyme Regis, 'absent and supposed' (CP); a captain (L); excepted from GP; member of Lyme Corporation (LRCB).

GAITCH, Joseph, yeoman, of Axmouth, 'reported' (CP); tried at Dorchester; transported for Nipho (JR) on the *Betty* from Weymouth, Nov. 25, to Barbados; sold to Capt. Robert Harrison (SL). Also presented at Exeter and misreported at large (JR).

GALE, Edward, of Taunton St Mary, 'aiding' (CP); Blue Regt. (P).

GALE, James, weaver, of Taunton St Mary, 'aiding' (CP); Blue Regt. (P); tried at Taunton; hanged at Porlock in December (JR, JW & NL).

GALE, John, of Corscombe, 'supposed' (CP); tried at Taunton; transported for Booth (JR) from Taunton Bridewell via Bristol Oct. 24, on the *John* to Barbados; sold to John Burston (SL).

GALE, Joseph, bodicemaker, of Bridport, 'in the rebellion' (CP); tried at Wells; transported for Stapleton (JR) in the *Indeavour* from Bristol Oct. 20, to Nevis or St Kitts (SL). Land forfeit and for sale (TB).

GALE, Thomas, of Wilton, 'absent' (CP).

GALHAMPTON, Thomas, of Westonzoyland, 'absent and taken' (CP); tried at Taunton; transported for Booth (JR) from Bridgwater prison via Bristol, Oct. 24, on the *John* towards Barbados; died at sea (SL).

GALLER, William, of Martock, 'absent' (CP).

GALLER, William junior, of Martock, 'absent' (CP).
   *And see* Gawler.

GALLOP *see* Gollopp.

GAMAGE, Stephen, tried at Dorchester; transported for Booth (JR) on the *Happy Return* from Weymouth, Sept. 25, to Barbados; sold to Richard Lintott (SL).

GAMAGE, Thomas senior, worsted comber, of Taunton St Mary, 'aiding' (CP); Blue Regt. (P); tried at Dorchester; 'humbly proposed for pardon' (JR).

GAMAGE, Thomas junior, worsted comber, of Taunton St Mary, 'aiding' (CP); Blue Regt. (P); tried at Taunton; transported for Booth (JR) from Exeter via Bristol, Oct. 24, on the *John* to Barbados; sold to Ann Gallop (SL).

GAME, John, tried at Dorchester on Sept. 5, pleaded not guilty; hanged at Dorchester on Sept. 7 (JR & NL).

GAME, Robert, of Ilchester, 'in the late rebellion' (CP); presented at Wells and bound over (JR).

GAMLING (Gamlyn), Francis, tried at Wells; transported for Stapleton (JR) in the *Indeavour* from Bristol Oct. 20, to Nevis or St Kitts (SL).

GAMLING, Thomas, tried at Wells; transported for Stapleton (JR) in the *Indeavour* from Bristol Oct. 20, to Nevis or St Kitts (SL).

GAMLING *see* Lease.

GAPE, Walter, clothier, of Axmouth, land forfeit and for sale (TB). This suggests that he was killed at Sedgemoor (P).

GARD, William, of High Ham, 'absent' (CP).

GARDINER, David, shoemaker, of Lyme Regis, 'absent and supposed' (CP); presented at Dorchester, certificate allowed (JR).

GARDINER, Draper, of Haselbury Plucknett, 'in the late rebellion' (CP).

GARDINER, Francis senior, husbandman, of Broomfield, 'absent and not taken' (CP).

GARDINER, Francis junior, of Broomfield, 'in the rebellion and taken' (CP); tried at Taunton, 'remaining in gaol till further order' (JR); transported from Wells by White, Nov. 12, on the *Constant Richard* to Jamaica (SL).

GARDINER, John, husbandman, of Broomfield, son of Francis, 'absent' (CP); 'took up arms against his Majesty' (Som. QSR); tried at Taunton; transported for Musgrave (JR) from Weymouth to Barbados (SL).

GARDINER, John, of Martock, 'absent' (CP); son of a Nonconformist minister (ejected from Staplegrove); a captain, 'very active in the rebellion'; hidden for seven months in the house of Dorothy Jeanes in Martock, where George Bishop brought him provisions daily. His mother paid Loder £300 for a pardon (which cost Loder £60). Gardiner was called, appeared and was discharged by the Proclamation of the General Pardon at Wells in March 1686. The pardon Loder obtained was dated May 22. After the Revolution Gardiner brought an action against Loder for restitution (Dep.) After ministering to a Nonconformist congregation at Barrington for some time after 1689 (PR), he applied to Bishop Kidder for ordination in 1692. Kidder speaks highly of him in his autobiography (Somerset Record Soc. xxxvii, 184).

GARDINER, John, of Milborne Port, yeoman, 'in the rebellion and at large' (CP).

GARDINER, John, of Pilsdon, 'supposed' (CP); tried at Dorchester; transported for Musgrave (JR) from Weymouth on the *Jamaica Merchant* to Jamaica; there by March 12 (SL).

GARDINER, Nicholas, of Wootton Fitzpaine, 'supposed' (CP).

GARDINER, Robert, of Wilton, 'absent' (CP).

GARLAND, Edward, labourer, of West Woodlands, 'in the rebellion and at large' (CP).

GARNISH, Samuel, tried at Taunton; to be hanged at Castle Cary (JR, JW) but reprieved (JR2).

GARNLEY, John, of West Dowlish, 'in the rebellion and at large' (CP).

GARNLEY, Sydeock, of Knowle St Giles, 'in the rebellion and not come in' (CP).

GARNSEY, Edward, of Croscombe, 'in Scott's army and not taken' (CP).

GARRETT, Richard, mason, of Frome, 'for a riot and amongst the Clubmen' (CP).

GARRIDGE, Thomas, 'actually a rebel in arms against his Majesty'; Henry Shrapnill was committed for entertaining him (Wilts. QSR).

GARROWN, Garrett, in Newgate, July 16, 'in the late rebellion, confessed'; taken to the Earl of Middleton, July 17 (CSPD, J2, I, 1249, 1252).

GATCHELL, William, yeoman, of Angersleigh, tried at Taunton on Sept. 18 'for aiding and assisting the rebells with provisions'; pleaded not guilty; hanged at Taunton on Sept. 21 (GD, JR, NL). Land forfeit and for sale (TB).

GATCHIEL, Henry, excepted from GP.

GATES, John, yeoman, of Uplyme, imprisoned in Wilts; dead (DLD);

GATTLEY, William, of Stoke St Gregory, 'absenting' (CP); of Thornfalcon, 'took up arms against the king' (Som. QSR).

GAUNT, William, of Wapping, 'engaged in the late rebellion'; excepted from GP, but pardoned on May 31 (CSPD, J2, II, 1833).

GAWLER, Samuel, of South Petherton, 'in the rebellion and not come in' (CP).

GAWLER, William, presented at Wells; certificate allowed (JR).
*And see* Galler.

GAY, Isaac, weaver, of East Woodlands, 'in the rebellion and at large' (CP).

GAY, John, weaver, of East Woodlands, 'in the rebellion and at large' (CP); presented, pardoned and dismissed at Exeter in March 1686 (GD).

GAY, John, of Monkton Wyld, 'suspected' (CP); tried at Dorchester; transported for Booth (JR) on the *Happy Return* from Weymouth, Sept. 25, to Barbados; sold to Col. John Hallett (SL). Named on the 1689 petition for return (CSPD, W&M, I, 43).

GAY, Robert, presented for high treason, pardoned and dismissed at Exeter, March 1686 (GD).

GAYLAND, Joseph, late of Exeter 'engaged in the late rebellion', excepted from GP, but pardoned May 31, 1687 (CSPD, J2, II, 1833).

GEE, John, of Martock, 'absent' (CP).

GEE, Robert, of Martock, 'absent' (CP); excepted from GP.

GEER, Christopher, of Southarp, South Petherton, 'in the rebellion and not come in' (CP).

GENT, Christopher, of Curload, 'wanting and in the late Duke of Monmouth's service'; killed at Norton St Philip (CL).

GEORGE, Richard, yeoman, of West Woodlands, 'in the rebellion and not taken' (CP).

GEORGE, William, husbandman, of West Woodlands, 'in the rebellion and at large' (CP).

GERARD, John, of Beaminster, 'wanting from his home' (CP).

GIBBONS, Henry, fuller, of Taunton St Mary, 'aiding' (CP); Blue Regt. (P); tried at Taunton; transported for Booth (JR) from Taunton

Bridewell via Bristol, Oct. 24, on the *John* to Barbados; sold to Dr John Springham (SL). Buried 1687 (BMi).

GIBBONS, James junior, wiredrawer, of Frome, 'for a riot and among the Clubmen' (CP).

GIBBS, Christopher, tinman, of Taunton St Mary, 'aiding' (CP); Blue Regt. (P).

GIBBS, John, aged 19, plowman [carter], (SL), tried at Taunton; transported thence for the Queen (JR) Oct. 12 on the *Jamaica Merchant*, Dec. 9 to Barbados; sold to Michael Child (SL).

GIBBS, John, tried at Taunton; transported for Musgrave (JR) on the *Jamaica Merchant* from Weymouth to Barbados; there by March 12 (SL).

GIBBS, Philip, of Glastonbury, 'from home at the time of rebellion' (CP).

GIBBS, Richard, presented at Wells and bound over (JR).

GIBBS, Robert, weaver, of Taunton St Mary, 'aiding' (CP); Blue Regt. (P).

GIBBS *see* Giles.

GIFFARD, John, of Lillesdon, North Curry, 'absent' (Som. QSR).

GIFFORD, John, of Kingsbury Episcopi, 'absent and believed' (CP). [*See below.*]

GIFFORD, Simon, of West Buckland, 'absent' (CP). [*See below.*] One of these two may have been the Gifford who, escaping from Sedgemoor, hid in a hollow tree and was found by an old woman gathering sticks, who fed him with eggs till he could move on. A traditional story, which links the fugitive with Bishop's Hull.

GILBERT, Edward, weaver, of Wincanton, 'in arms in the rebellion'; in the Bridewell at Shepton (CP); 'a Munmouth Rebell in custody (Som. QSR); tried at Wells; transported for Howard (JR), Oct. 25, to Jamaica (SL).

GILBERT, William, of Stogursey, glover, 'absent and believed' (CP).

GILES, Richard senior, of Wellington, 'in prison for rebellion' (CP). Not presented at Assize; did he die in prison?

GILES, Richard junior, of Wellington, 'absent' (CP).

GILES, Richard, cloth drawer, of Beckington, 'in the rebellion; out of Beckington; and at large' (CP).

GILES (Gibbs), William, yeoman, of Axminster, 'supposed' (CP); tried at Dorchester; transported for Nipho (JR) on the *Betty* from Weymouth, Nov. 25, to Barbados; sold to Michael Child (SL). Also presented at Exeter and misreported at large (JR).

GILHAM, John junior, tried at Wells; hanged at Shepton Mallet (JR, JW).

GILHAM, Josiah, tried at Wells; transported thence for Bridgeman (JR) by White on the *Constant Richard* to Jamaica (SL).

GILL, Hugh, tried at Taunton; transported for Musgrave (JR) on the *Jamaica Merchant* from Weymouth to Jamaica; there by March 12 (SL).

GILL, John senior, weaver, of Taunton St James, 'aiding' (CP); Blue Regt. (P). [*See below.*]

GILL, John junior, of Taunton St James, 'aiding' (CP); Blue Regt. (P).

GILL, John senior, of Wellington, 'in prison for rebellion' (CP); tried at Wells; hanged at Axbridge (JR, JW).

GILL, John junior, of Wellington, 'in prison for rebellion' (CP); tried at Wells; transported for Nipho (JR) on the *Betty* from Weymouth, Nov. 25, to Barbados; sold to Rebecca Beal (SL).

GILL, John, yeoman, of Somerset, pardoned May 12 (CSPD, J2, II, 530). This might be one of the John Gills of Taunton.

GILL, Nicholas, of Creech St Michael, 'in the rebellion and taken' (CP) to Ilchester gaol; tried at Wells; transported for Howard (JR), Oct. 25, to Jamaica (SL).

GILL, Richard, of Chard, 'absent and believed' (CP); presented at Taunton; certificate allowed (JR).

GILL, Robert, of Taunton St James, 'aiding' (CP); Blue Regt. (P).

GILL, William, of Milverton, 'absenting' (CP).

GILL, William, of Pitminster, 'absent' (CP); of South Trendle, 'a rebel' (CL).

GILLARD, Christopher, of North Curry, 'absent' (CP).

GILLARD, Edmund, chirurgeon, came with Monmouth from Holland (L); tried at Taunton; hanged at Yeovil (JR, JW).

GILLARD (Hillard), George, yeoman, of Pitminster, 'absent' (CP); of South Trendle 'a rebel' (CL); tried at Taunton; hanged at Stogumber (JR, JW). Land forfeit and for sale (TB).

GILLARD, Humphrey, weaver, of Taunton St Mary, 'aiding' (CP); Blue Regt. (P); tried at Taunton, 'remaining in gaol till further order' (JR); transported from Wells Oct. 31, by White on the *Constant Richard*, Nov. 12 to Jamaica (SL).

GILLETT, Henry, of Lopen, 'in the rebellion and not come in' (CP).

GILLETT, Nicholas, of Chardstock, 'suspected guilty' (CP).

GILLETT, Samuel, weaver, of Taunton St Mary, 'aiding' (CP); Blue Regt. (P).

GILLETT, William, of Crewkerne, 'rebel in Monmouth's army and not taken' (CP); tried at Taunton; hanged at Somerton (JR, JW).

GILLING, John, husbandman, of Chilton Polden, tried at Taunton, 'remaining in gaol till further order' (JR). Land forfeit and for sale (TB). Did he buy his release with his land?

GILLING, Thomas, presented at Wells and bound over (JR).

GITTON, John, 'millard', of Minehead, 'in the late rebellion' (CP).

GLANVILLE, David, weaver, of Taunton St Mary, Extraportam tithing, 'aiding', (CP & CL); Blue Regt. (P).

GLANVILLE, James, tried at Taunton; transported for Musgrave (JR) on the *Jamaica Merchant* from Weymouth to Barbados; there by Mar. 12 (SL).

GLANVILLE, John, of Taunton Extraportam tithing, 'absent' (CL).

GLASSE, John, mercer, of Dunster, 'in arms in the rebellion of James Scott' (CP).

GLISSON, John, weaver, of Wincanton, 'absent; informed in Scott's army' (CP).

GLISSON, Samuel, of Yeovil, a Baptist, 'absent and not returned' (CP); to Newgate, London, July 16 (CSPD, J2, I, 1249); tried at Dorchester; hanged at Sherborne, Sept. 16 (JR & NL). His wife was a sister of Sarah Hurd, John Whiting's fiancée.

GLOVER, John, presented at Dorchester and 'proposed for pardon' (JR).

GLOVER, John, alias Tucker, woolcomber, of Tiverton, imprisoned in Devon Workhouse (DLD); tried at Taunton; to be hanged at Redcliffe Hill, Bristol, but died before execution (JR, JW & NL).

GOAD alias Ford, Richard, presented and pardoned at Dorchester in March, 1686 (GD).

GODDARD, Martin, 'engaged in the late rebellion', pardon May 31, 1687 (CSPD, J2, II, 1833)

GODDEN, Edward, of Kingsbury Episcopi, 'absent and believed' (CP).

GODDEN, John, of South Petherton, 'in the rebellion and not come in' (CP).

GODFREY alias Newman, Richard, farm labourer, of Chedzoy, the guide to Sedgemoor (Pa); presented at Exeter, March 1686, pardoned and dismissed (GD).

GODFREY, Thomas, blacksmith, of Lyme Regis, 'absent and supposed' (CP).

GODFREY, Thomas, of Westonzoyland, 'absent' (CP).

GODFREY, William, husbandman, of Chilton Polden (TB); a captain, captured in the moors by Lieut. Withers (CSPD, J2, I, 1466); tried at Taunton; hanged at Chard (JR, JW). Land forfeit and for sale (TB).

GODFREY, William, of Stoke St Gregory, 'absenting' (CP).

GODINS, Francis, of Pawlett, 'being in the rebellion' (Som. QSR).

GODSALL, John, aged 27, butcher, (SL); tried at Taunton; transported for the Queen (JR) from Taunton, Dec. 9, on the *Jamaica Merchant* to Barbados, Mar. 12, sold to Muse Walford (SL). Buried 1686 (BMi).

GODWIN, Edward, wiredrawer, of West Woodlands, 'in prison for the late rebellion' (CP). Not presented at Assize; did he die in prison?

GOFFE (Gough), Nehemiah, tried at Wells; transported for Stapleton (JR), in the *Indeavour* from Bristol Oct. 20, to Nevis or St Kitts (SL).

GOFFE, Roger, of Stockland, 'suspected' (CP).
*And see* Gough,

GOLD (Gould), Enoch, aged 15, weaver (SL), of Wilton, 'absent' (CP); tried at Taunton; transported thence for the Queen (JR), Dec. 9, on the *Jamaica Merchant* to Barbados; sold on Mar. 12 to Major Abel Allen (SL). Married 1696 in St James's, Barbados; will 1720. Merchant of Bridgetown; friend of Richard King (Barbados Records).

GOLD, John, of Cheddon, 'absent' (CP).

GOLD, John, fuller, of Taunton St Mary, 'aiding' (CP); Blue Regt. (P). [*See below.*]

GOLD, John, 'concerned in the rebellion in the West' (TB); Blue Regt. (P). One of these Johns was tried at Wells and transported for Nipho (JR) from Ilchester gaol on the *Rebecca* to Barbados (SL). 'He being convicted and outlawed', Henry Hodson petitioned for the grant of

John Gold's estate (TB viii, 919). Another John 'prayed to have the benefit of his Majesty's pardon', June 1 1686; was reported 'Not excepted from the General Pardon' on July 10; pardon authorised, Aug. 2, and granted Oct. 2 (CSPD, J2, II, 617, 791, 862, 1035, 1291).

GOLD, Robert, yeoman, of Axminster, 'supposed' (CP); presented at Exeter but at large (JR).

GOLD, Thomas, aged 35, tailor (SL), tried at Taunton; transported thence for the Queen (JR), Dec. 9, on the *Jamaica Merchant* to Barbados; sold on March 12 to Archibald Johnson (SL).

GOLD, William, of Puriton, 'active soldier in the Duke of Monmouth's army' (Som. QSR); tried at Taunton; to be transported for the Queen (JR). On the receipt of John Rose, merchant, of London. Gold broke out of prison; involved in a riot at Huntspill on 29 June 1688 (Som. QSR).

GOLDSWORTHY (Golsery), Richard, weaver, of Taunton St Mary, 'aiding' (CP); of Extraportam tithing, 'absent' (CL); Blue Regt. (P).

GOLLOPP, James, of Pilsdon, 'suspected' (CP).

GOLLOPP, Robert, innholder, of Taunton St Mary, 'aiding' (CP); Blue Regt. (P).

GOODEN, Abraham, of Chardland, 'absent and believed' (CP); tried at Wells; transported for Nipho (JR) on the *Betty* from Weymouth, Nov. 25, to Barbados; sold to Richard Scott (SL).

GOODENOUGH, Hugh, tried at Wells; hanged at Ilchester (JR, JW).

GOODENOUGH, Francis, formerly Under Sheriff of London; came from Holland with Monmouth; Captain in the White Regt.; commanded a company in the skirmish at Bridport (W). Killed at Sedgemoor (P).

GOODENOUGH, Richard, formerly Under Sheriff of London, came with Monmouth from Holland; Captain in the Red Regt.; Paymaster after Dare's death; left Sedgemoor with Wade (W); captured in Devon by Capt. Prideaux's troop (L); sent to London; imprisoned in Newgate; interrogated and gave some names (L); excepted from GP; King's Evidence against Alderman Cornish and Lord Delamere; sent to Elizabeth Castle, Jersey, 'for life', but released on May 30, 1687; went to Ireland; pardon, Oct. 3 (CSPD, J2, II, 792, 1731, 1827).

GOODERIDGE, Laurence, of North Curry, 'absent' (CP).

GOODFELLOW, Richard, of Merriott, 'rebel in Monmouth's army and not taken' (CP).

GOODGROOME, Peter, tried at Wells; transported for Stapleton (JR) in the *Indeavour* from Bristol Oct. 20, to Nevis or St Kitts (SL).

GOODING, Isaac, of Taunton St James, 'aiding' (CP); Blue Regt. (P).

GOODING, Robert, of Stoford, 'in the late rebellion' (CP).

GOODING, Thomas, presented at Taunton for levying war against the King; pleaded guilty but was 'humbly proposed to his Majesty for his gracious pardon' (GD & JR). Mistress Gooding was excepted from GP as one of the Maids of Taunton.

GOODLAND, John, of Westonzoyland, 'absent' (CP).

GOODLAND, William, tried at Taunton; transported for Musgrave (JR), on the *Jamaica Merchant* from Weymouth to Jamaica; there by Mar. 12 (SL).

GOODLANE, John, of Donyatt, 'out in the rebellion' (CP).

GOODLANE, Thomas, of Ilminster, 'in the late rebellion' (CP).

GOODMAN, Edward, tried at Wells; transported for Stapleton (JR) in the *Indeavour* from Bristol Oct. 20, to Nevis or St Kitts (SL).

GOODMAN, Matthew, tried at Wells; transported thence for Bridgeman (JR) Oct. 31 by White, on the *Constant Richard* to Jamaica (SL).

GOODSON, Thomas, tried at Wells; transported for Howard (JR), Oct. 25 on the *Port Royal Merchant* to Jamaica (SL).

GOOTE *see* Gough

GORETT, John senior, of Wellington, 'absent' (CP).

GORETT, John junior, of Wellington, 'absent' (CP).

GOSLING, John, tried at Exeter, sentenced to be hanged but reprieved (JR).

GOTRELL, John, hanged for treason by Kirke in Taunton; buried at St James's on July 9 (PR).

GOTTERELL, George, of Hillfarrance, 'absent' (CP).

GOUGE, Stephen, of Chard, 'in the late rebellion' (CP).

GOUGH (Goote), Francis, of Ashill, 'out in the rebellion' (CP); excepted from GP.

GOUGH, John, of Hinton St George, 'rebel in Monmouth's army and not taken' (CP).

GOUGH, Seth, presented at Dorchester; certificate allowed (JR). *And see* Goffe.

GOULD *see* Gold.

GOYCE, Thomas, of Westbury, 'in the rebellion', presented at Warminster, July 14 (Wilts. QSR).

GRABHAM, Richard, of Woolavington, 'out in the rebellion and at large' (CP).

GRACE (Grise), John, mason, of Colyford (DLD), imprisoned and tried at Taunton; transported for Musgrave (JR) on the *Jamaica Merchant* from Weymouth to Barbados; there by March 12 (SL).

GRANGE, Henry, presented at Wells, 'proposed for pardon' (JR).

GRANGE, John, yeoman, of Axminster, 'supposed' (CP); presented at Exeter but at large (JR); presented again in March and pardoned (GD).

GRANGE, Thomas, of Curry Rivel, 'out in the rebellion and not taken' (CP).

GRANGE, William, of Isle Abbots, 'out in the rebellion and not taken' (CP).

GRAUNT, Richard, of Taunton St Mary, 'aiding' (CP); Blue Regt. (P).

GRAVENER, Thomas, of Woolminstone, 'rebel in Monmouth's army and not taken' (CP).

GRAVES, John senior, of Chardland, 'absent and believed' (CP).

GRAVES, John junior, clothworker, of Chard, tried at Wells; hanged at Shepton Mallet (JR, JW); land forfeit and for sale (TB).

GRAY, Benjamin, of Bridport, 'in the rebellion, as informed' (CP); tried at Dorchester, Sept. 5; pleaded not guilty; hanged at Dorchester, Sept. 7 (JR, GD, NL).

GRAY, Christopher, tried at Wells; transported for Howard (JR) Oct. 25 on the *Port Royal Merchant* to Jamaica (SL).

GRAY, George, tried at Taunton, transported for Booth (JR) from Taunton Bridewell (on Booth's receipt).

GRAY, John, yeoman, of Ruishton, presented at Taunton and proposed for pardon (JR). Land forfeit but not for sale as it was granted to Brent, Loder and Clarke (TB). Gray was pardoned, July 4, 1686 (CSPD, J2, II, 768). Pardon money to be kept by Giles Clerk (TB).

GRAY, Roger, presented at Wells and bound over (JR).

GREEDY, Robert junior, of West Buckland, 'absent' (CP).

GREEN, Ralph, excepted from GP.

GREENE, Francis, of Uffculme, chirurgeon, imprisoned in Devon Workhouse (DLD); presented at Exeter, March 1686, pardoned and dismissed (GD).

GREENE, Henry, of Crewkerne, 'rebel in Monmouth's army and not taken' (CP).

GREENE, Hugh, presented at Dorchester for publishing Monmouth's declaration, fined £1000, committed to prison till paid; to find sureties for good behaviour during life (JR).

GREENE, Richard, weaver, of Northleigh, imprisoned in the High Gaol, Devon (DLD); tried at Dorchester; transported for Nipho (JR) on the *Betty* from Weymouth, Nov. 25, to Barbados; sold to Christopher Williams (SL). Named on the 1689 petition (CSPD, W&M, I, 43).

GREENE, William, weaver, of Taunton St James, 'aiding' (CP); Blue Regt. (P). Excepted from GP.

GREENEHAM, Jeremiah, of Wilton, 'absent' (CP).

GREENEHAM, John, of West Chinnock, 'in the late rebellion' (CP).

GREENEHAM, Joseph, of Ruishton, 'absent' (CP).

GREENFIELD, Francis, presented at Dorchester; discharged for want of evidence (JR). [*See* Franklyn, James.]

GREENLAND, William, weaver, of Rode, 'in the rebellion' (CP), tried at Wells; transported for Howard (JR), Oct. 25, to Jamaica (SL).

GREENWAY, George, yeoman, of Thorverton, in the High Gaol, Devon (DLD); presented at Exeter, March 1686; pardoned and dismissed (GD).

GREENWAY, John, of Crewkerne, 'rebel in Monmouth's army and not taken' (CP); excepted from the GP, but pardoned, Feb. 22 and 26, 1686, 'in the late rebellious army, and having sold a horse to one of the rebels' (CSPD, J2, II, 179, 199).

GREENWAY, Thomas junior, weaver, of Colyton, imprisoned in the High Gaol, Devon (DLD); presented at Dorchester for levying war against the king; pleaded guilty but was 'humbly proposed for his Majesty's gracious pardon' (JR).

GREENWAY, William, (brother of Thomas – PR); aged 21, worsted comber, of Colyton, imprisoned in the High Gaol, Devon (DLD);

tried at Dorchester; transported for Nipho (JR) on the *Betty* from Weymouth on Nov. 25 towards Barbados; died at sea Dec. 25 (SL).

GREETE, John, of Berkley and Standerwick 'in the rebellion and not taken' (CP).

GREGORY, Thomas, tried at Dorchester; transported for Booth (JR) on the *Happy Return* from Weymouth, Sept. 25, to Barbados; sold to Capt. John Parnell (SL).

GREGORY, William, of Lydeard St Lawrence, 'absent' (CP).

GREY, Ford, Lord Grey of Wark, of Uppark, Sussex, came from Holland with Monmouth as Second in Command and Commander of the Cavalry; retired rather precipitately at Bridport and at Sedgemoor (W), but returned to fetch Monmouth; captured in Hampshire and taken to the Tower (CSPD, J2, I, 1212); excepted from GP; King's Evidence against Lord Delamere; pardoned and his outlawry reversed (CSPD, J2, II, 646). William III made him Earl of Tankerville and a Privy Councillor; and later 2nd Lord of the Treasury and then Lord Privy Seal. He died in 1707 and was buried in South Harting Church, Sussex.

GRIFFEN, Daniel, of Combe Florey, 'absent' (CP); 'taking up arms against the king, as we are credibly informed, and yet absent' (Som. QSR).

GRIFFEN, Henry, of Combe St Nicholas, 'absent and believed' (CP).

GRIFFEN, Nicholas, of Combe St Nicholas, 'absent and believed' (CP).

GRIFFEN, Nicholas, of Whitestaunton, 'in the rebellion and not come in' (CP).

GRIFFEN, Robert, of Stanton St Gabriel, 'suspected' (CP).

GRIFFEN, John Evans' man, of Bishop's Hull, 'absent' (CP); 'not taken' (CL).

GRIFFEN, a servant to Mallack, of Stoke St Mary, 'absent' (CP, CL).

GRIFFEN, William, presented at Wells and bound over (JR). He might be either of the above or an eighth Griffen.

GRIGG, James, weaver, of Taunton St Mary, 'aiding' (CP); Blue Regt. (P).

GRIGG, John, of Wootton Fitzpaine, 'suspected' (CP).

GRIGGS, John senior, tailor, of Lyme Regis, 'absent and supposed' (CP).

GRIGGS, William, shoemaker, of Lyme Regis, 'absent and supposed' (CP).

GRIMSTER, William, of Donyatt, 'out in the rebellion' (CP).

GRINHAM, Jonas, of Knowle St Giles, 'in the rebellion and not come in' (CP).

GRINHAM, Joseph, of Holford, 'absent' (CL).

GRINSLADE, John, hanged by Col. Kirke in Taunton on July 9 (P); buried there at St James's on July 10 (PR).

GRISE *see* Grace

GROODE, John, worsted comber, of Taunton St Mary, 'aiding' (CP); Blue Regt. (P).

GROVE, Abel, yeoman, of Axmouth, 'reported in arms' (CP); presented at Exeter but at large (JR).

GROVE, John, apothecary, of Taunton St Mary, 'aiding' (CP); Blue Regt. (P).

GROVE, William, presented at Dorchester for levying war against the king; pleaded guilty, but humbly proposed for his Majesty's gracious pardon' (GD & JR).

GROVES, Joseph, of Pitminster, 'absent' (CP).

GROVES, Simon, of Pitminster, 'absent' (CP).

GUDDRIDGE, Lawrence, junior, of North Curry, 'taking up arms against the king' (Som. QSR); 'mort' (CL). Killed at Sedgemoor or died of wounds (P).

GUDGE, Samuel, of Bridport, 'as informed, in the rebellion' (CP).

GULLEY, John, feltmaker, of Wincanton, 'actually in arms, as informed, and at large' (CP).

GULLEY, William, of Taunton St James, 'aiding' (CP); Blue Regt. (P).

GULLHAMPTON, Joseph, fuller, of Taunton St Mary, 'aiding' (CP); Blue Regt. (P).

GULLIVER, Abraham, husbandman, of Spaxton, 'absent . . . and believed, was aiding and assisting the rebels' (CP).

GUMMER, Roger, of Seavington St Mary, 'in the rebellion and not come in' (CP).

GUMMER, Samuel, of Seavington St Mary, 'in the rebellion and not come in' (CP).

GUNDRY, Nicholas, presented at Wells and bound over (JR).

GUNNER, John, of Chard, 'in the rebellion' (CP).

GUNSTONE, Arthur, fuller, of Taunton St Mary, 'aiding' (CP); Blue Regt. (P).

GUNT, George, of Ilminster, 'in the late rebellion' (CP).

GUPPY, Justinian, of Taunton, tried there and transported for Booth (JR) via Exeter and Bristol, Oct. 24, on the *John* towards Barbados; died at sea (SL).

GUPPY, Roger, tried at Taunton; hanged at Bridgwater (JR, JW).

GUPPY, William, woolcomber, of Axminster, 'supposed' (CP); wounded at Sedgemoor; imprisoned at Wells (DLD); presented at Exeter but 'at large'; tried at Wells and transported for Stapleton (JR) in the *Indeavour* from Bristol Oct. 20, to Nevis or St Kitts (SL).

GUPPY, William, of Charmouth, 'supposed' (CP); tried at Dorchester and transported for Nipho (JR) from Weymouth, Nov. 25, on the *Betty* towards Barbados; died at sea on Dec. 17, 1685 (SL).

GUY, Edward, weaver, of Rode, 'in the rebellion' (CP).

HACK *see* Hale.

HACKER, Joseph, yeoman, of Axmouth, 'in arms in the late rebellion' (CP); presented at Exeter but at large (JR).

HACKER, Solomon, yeoman, of Axmouth, 'in arms in the late rebellion' (CP); presented at Exeter but at large (JR).

HACKER, Timothy, yeoman, of Thorncombe, 'wanting from his habitation' (CP); presented at Exeter but at large (JR).

HACKER, Tobias, tried at Taunton, 'remaining in gaol till further order' (JR); transported from Wells by White, Nov. 12, on the *Constant Richard* to Jamaica (SL).

HACKER (Hackett), Walter, butcher, of West Woodlands, 'in the rebellion and in prison' (CP); tried at Taunton; to be transported for the Queen (JR) by John Rose of London, merchant, on Oct. 12, 1685 (SL).

HAGLEY, Lewis, tried at Taunton, remaining in gaol (JR); transported from Wells by White, Nov. 12, on the *Constant Richard* to Jamaica (SL).
*And see* Hogley.

HAIREY, Thomas, of Ashill, 'out in the rebellion' (CP).

HAKINS, John, of Durleigh, 'absent and not taken' (CP).

HALE (Hack), Benedict, yeoman, of Colyton, 'absent' (CP); presented at Exeter but at large (JR). As Benedict Hack excepted from GP.

HALES, Francis, tried at Wells; transported for Stapleton (JR) in the *Indeavour* from Bristol Oct. 20, to Nevis or St Kitts (SL).

HALFYARD (Halfyeard), George, of Sampford Arundel, 'absenting' (CP); tried at Wells; transported for Stapleton (JR) in the *Indeavour* from Bristol Oct. 20, to Nevis or St Kitts (SL).

HALL, Abraham, presented at Taunton for levying war, pleaded guilty, but was 'humbly proposed for pardon' (JR, GD).

HALL, Richard, aged 25, cordwainer, of Colyton, imprisoned in the High Gaol, Devon (DLD); 'absent' (CP); tried at Dorchester, Sept. 10; hanged at Sherborne, Sept. 15 (JR, NL). Also presented at Exeter and misreported at large (JR).

HALL, William, of Bampton, woolcomber, wounded at Sedgemoor, imprisoned at Wells (DLD). Did he die in prison?

HALL, William, of Chard, imprisoned at Bridgwater; tried at Taunton; transported for Booth (JR) via Bristol, Oct. 24, on the *John* to Barbados. Sold to Silas Marchant (SL).

HALLETT, Daniel, of Wilton, 'absent' (CP); tried at Taunton; remaining in gaol (JR); transported from Wells by White on the *Constant Richard* to Jamaica (SL).

HALLETT, George, of Thorncombe, yeoman, 'wanting from his habitation' (CP); presented at Exeter but at large; tried at Wells; transported for Howard (JR) Oct. 25, to Jamaica (SL).

HALLETT, Geoorge, presented at Exeter, March 1686, pardoned and dismissed (GD).

HALLETT, John, of Wilton, 'absent' (CP).

HALLETT, Joseph, husbandman, of Marshwood, 'suspected' (CP); tried at Dorchester; to be transported for Booth (JR) but died in prison. Land forfeit and for sale (TB) valued at £8 a year. Mary, his widow (with 5 children) petitioned the king to remit the forfeiture, 2 years' arrears, and a fine of £44 (TB, June 28, 1688).

HALLETT, Robert, of Corfe, 'absent, supposed' (CP).

HALLETT, Thomas, tried at Dorchester; transported for Booth (JR) on the *Happy Return* from Weymouth, Sept. 25, to Barbados; sold to Col. Samuel Titcombe (SL).

HALSEY, Edward, tried at Wells, transported thence for Bridgeman (JR) by White, Oct. 31, on the *Constant Richard* to Jamaica (SL).

HALSEY (Halesey), William, of Lillesdon, North Curry 'absent' (Som. QSR).

HALSEWELL, Edward, tried at Taunton; hanged at Keynsham (JR, JW).

HALSEWELL, Robert, of Thornfalcon, a sergeant (Som. QSR); of North Curry, 'out in the late rebellion and in prison' (CP); tried at Taunton; hanged at Crewkerne (JR, JW).

HALSON, Robert, yeoman, of Colyton, 'absent' (CP); presented at Dorchester, certificate allowed. Also presented at Exeter; reported at large (JR).

HAM, John, tried at Taunton, 'remaining in gaol' (JR); transported from Wells by White, Nov. 12, on the *Constant Richard* to Jamaica (SL).

HAM, Joseph, yeoman, of Upottery, 'absent' (CP); presented at Exeter but at large (JR).

HAMLYN (Hambler), John, yeoman, of Axminster, 'supposed' (CP); taken to prison (Pulman, *Book of the Axe*); presented at Exeter but 'at large' ('85) (JR); presented at Exeter, March '86, for High Treason; pardoned and dismissed (GD).

HAMLYN, Simon, tailor, of Pitminster (TB) presented at Taunton, Sept. 18, for levying war, pleaded not guilty (GD); hanged at Taunton, Sept. 21; (JR) buried at St Mary's, Sept. 22 (PR). A pardon came too late (CSPD, J2, II, 791). Land forfeit (TB) to the lord of the manor (CL).

HAMLYN, Simon junior, of Taunton St Mary, 'aiding' (CP); Blue Regt. (P); petition for pardon, 'concerned in the rebellion in the West,' June 1, 1686; pardon, July 18 (CSPD, J2, II, 617, 822).

HAMME, Edward, yeoman, of Luppitt, 'out in the rebellion' (CP); presented at Exeter but at large (JR).

HAMMETT (Hammond), Henry, of Wilton, 'absent' (CP); tried at Taunton; transported for Musgrave (JR) on the *Jamaica Merchant* from Weymouth to Jamaica; there by March 12 (SL).

HAMMOND (Hamwood), Edward, tried at Wells; originally entered as to be transported for Bridgeman but entry deleted; 'remaining in custody' (JR); 'humbly proposed for pardon' (JR2).

HAMMOND, Thomas, weaver, of Taunton St Mary, 'aiding' (CP); Blue Regt. (P).

HAMPTON, Robert, Monmouth's butler, 'in charge of the carriages'; presented at Taunton, 'remaining in gaol' (JR). 'Engaged in the late rebellion and sentenced to death' – pardon Sept. 22, 1687 (CSPD, J2, III, 368).

HANHAM, Robert, of Croscombe, 'in Scott's army and in prison' (CP); 'wounded at Norton [St Philip]: shot, bones broken to pieces'; taken to Ilchester gaol and treated by Dr Winter (WB); tried at Wells; transported for Stapleton (JR) in the *Indeavour* from Bristol Oct. 20, to Nevis or St Kitts (SL).

HANNING, John, of Chiselborough, 'in the late rebellion' (CP), tried at Wells; transported for Howard (JR), Oct. 25, to Jamaica (SL).

HANNON, James, sergemaker, of Taunton St Mary, 'aiding' (CP); Blue Regt. (P).

HAPPER, *see* Hooper.

HARBETT *see* Horne.

HARBOTTLE, James, chandler, of Beckington, 'in the rebellion, out of Beckington, at large' (CP).

HARCOMBE, John, sergemaker, of Taunton St Mary (married, 1682), 'aiding' (CP); Blue Regt. (P); tried at Wells; transported for Nipho (JR) on the *Betty* from Weymouth, Nov. 25, to Barbados; sold to John Smart (SL).

HARCOMBE, John, of South Trendle, Pitminster, 'a rebel' (CL).

HARD *see* Hurd

HARDING, George, tried at Wells; transported for Howard (JR), Oct. 25, to Jamaica (SL).

HARDMAN, John, of Martock, 'absent' (CP).

HARDMAN, John, weaver, of Thorncombe, 'wanting from his habitation' (CP); imprisoned in Wilts. (DLD); tried at Dorchester; transported for Booth (JR) on the *Happy Return* from Weymouth, Sept. 25, to Barbados; sold to John How (SL). Also presented at Exeter and misreported at large (JR).

HARDMAN, Nathaniel, yeoman, of Thorncombe, 'wanting' (CP); presented at Exeter but at large (JR).

HARDMAN, Thomas senior, of Trull, 'absent' (CP).

HARDMAN, Thomas junior, of Trull, 'absent' (CP).

HARDMAN, William, yeoman, of Thorncombe, 'wanting' (CP); clothier, in Bridgwater prison (DLD); tried at Dorchester, Sept. 10; hanged at Poole, Sept. 21 (JR, NL). Also presented at Exeter and misreported at large (JR).

HARDY, William, apothecary, of Lyme Regis, 'absent and supposed' (CP); after the action at Norton St Philip he removed the bullet from Thomas Coad's back at Shepton (CM); presented at Dorchester, certificate allowed (JR).

HARE, John, of West Monkton, 'out in the rebellion and at large' (CP).

HARE, William, of West Monkton, 'out in the rebellion and at large' (CP).

HARFORD *see* Hurford.

HARLE, Richard, of Kingston St Mary, 'for entertaining one Samuel Trottle, a rebel' (CP).

HARLEY *see* Hurley

HARMAN, James, tried at Wells; transported for Stapleton (JR) in the *Indeavour* from Bristol Oct. 20, to Nevis or St Kitts (SL).

HARMAN (Hurman), John, tried at Taunton; hanged at Bridgwater (JR, JW).

HARMAN, William, of Walton, 'absent' (CP).

HARPER, John, 'engaged in the late rebellion,' pardon 31 May 1687 (CSPD, J2, II, 1833).

HARRIS, Edward, tried at Wells; transported for Stapleton (JR) in the *Indeavour* from Bristol Oct. 20, to Nevis or St Kitts (SL).

HARRIS, John, of Huntspill, 'active soldier in the Duke of Monmouth's army' (Som. QSR); in prison at Bridgwater; tried at Taunton; transported for Booth (JR) via Bristol, Oct. 24, on the *John* to Barbados; sold to John Hethersell, Esq. (SL).

HARRIS, John junior, of Queen Charlton, 'absent and not returned' (CP).

HARRIS, Lewis (Luice), of Creech St Michael, 'took up arms against his Majesty' (Som. QSR); tried at Taunton; hanged at Keynsham (JR, JW).

HARRIS, Richard, of Huntspill, 'active soldier in the Duke of Monmouth's army' (Som. QSR), tried at Taunton; hanged at Bridgwater (JR, JW).

HARRIS, Robert, presented at Wells for levying war against the king; pleaded guilty (GD) but was recommended for pardon (JR).

HARRIS, Samuel, of Kingston St Mary, 'absent' (CP).

HARRIS, Thomas, of Barrington, 'in the rebellion and not come in' (CP).

HARRIS, Thomas, husbandman, of Rode, 'in the rebellion' (CP).

HARRIS, William, clothworker, of Rode, 'in the rebellion' (CP).

HARRIS, William, driller, of Membury, wounded at Sedgemoor, imprisoned at Wells (DLD) and tried there; transported for Howard (JR), Oct. 25 on the *Port Royal Merchant* to Jamaica (SL).

HARRISON, William, of Sidmouth, 'went to Monmouth' (CP).

HART, John, glazier, of Lyme Regis 'absent, supposed' (CP); present at Dorchester, continued in gaol, not indicted' (JR).

HARD, John, of Donyatt, 'out in the rebellion' (CP).

HART, John, of Wellington, 'absent' (CP); tried at Wells; to be transported for Howard (JR) but escaped from Sherborne prison on the way from Wells to Weymouth (SL).

HART, Josias, taken at Lyme Regis and sent to Dorchester gaol, July 14, (LRMB); tried at Taunton; transported for Musgrave (JR) on the *Jamaica Merchant* from Weymouth to Barbados; there by March 12 (SL).

HART, Thomas, porter, of Lyme Regis, 'absent and supposed' (CP).

HART, Thomas, tailor, of Lyme Regis, 'absent and supposed' (CP).

HART, William, tried at Dorchester, Sept. 10; hanged at Sherborne, Sept. 15 (JR, NL).

HARTE, Henry, of South Quarter, Exeter, 'absenting' (CP).

HARTLEY, John, tried at Dorchester, Sept. 10; hanged at Weymouth or Melcombe Regis, Sept. 15 (JR, NL).

HARVEY, John, yeoman, of Axminister, 'supposed'; presented at Exeter but at large; tried at Taunton; to be transported for the Queen (JR); on the list of John Rose of London, merchant (SL).

HARVEY, Richard, tried at Wells; hanged at Wincanton (JR, JW).

HARVEY, Roger, weaver, of Taunton St Mary, 'aiding' (CP); Blue Regt. (P).

HARVEY, Samuel, yeoman, of Axminster, 'supposed' (CP); presented at Exeter but at large; tried at Taunton; 'remaining in gaol' (JR); transported from Wells by White on the *Constant Richard*, Nov. 12, to Jamaica (SL).

HARVEY, Thomas, weaver, of Taunton St Mary, 'aiding' (CP); Blue Regt. (P).

HARVEY, Tristram, yeoman, of Axminster, 'supposed' (CP); presented at Exeter but at large (JR).

HARVEY, William, yeoman, of Axminster, 'supposed' (CP), presented at Exeter but at large (JR).

HARVEY, William senior, tinker, of Membury, 'wanting, dead (mort.)' (CP); killed at Sedgemoor (P) but presented at Exeter and reported at large (JR). Land forfeit and for sale (TB).

HARVEY, William junior, yeoman, of Membury, 'wanting; in prison' (CP); presented at Exeter and reported at large; tried at Taunton; transported for Booth (JR) from Bridgwater prison via Bristol, Oct. 24, on the *John* to Barbados; sold to Thomas Burke (SL). Named on the petition of 1689 (CSPD, W&M, I, 43).

HARWOOD, John, tried at Wells; transported Oct. 25, for Howard (JR) on the *Port Royal Merchant* to Jamaica (SL).

HARWOOD, Thomas, of Curland, 'out in the rebellion' (CP).

HASKINS, John, of Pitminster, 'supposed' (CL).

HASSELBURY, Nicholas, of Chardland, 'absent and believed' (CP).

HAWKER, Christopher, of Thurlbear, 'absent' (CP).

HAWKER, Edward, of Chaffcombe, 'in the rebellion and not come in' (CP).

HAWKER, Emanuel, yeoman, of Offwell, 'supposed' (CP); in Bridgwater prison (DLD); presented at Wells; pardoned by proclamation (GD).

HAWKER, Joseph, of Chard, 'in the late rebellion' (CP); tried at Wells; to be transported for Howard (JR) but escaped at Wells (SL); Thomas Coad took his place (CM).

HAWKER, Richard, of Chilton Polden, yeoman, pardon of all treasons, March 22, 1686 (CSPD, J2, II, 309).

HAWKER, Richard, of Thurlbear, 'absent' (CP).

HAWKER, Timothy, yeoman (DLD) of Thorncombe, 'wanting' (CP); imprisoned at Bridgwater; tried at Taunton; transported for Booth (JR) via Bristol, Oct. 24, on the *John* to Barbados; sold to Col. John Sampson (SL).

HAWKER, William junior, of Barrington, 'in the rebellion and not come in' (CP).

HAWKIER *see* Hawler.

HAWKINS, Joseph, of Chard, 'in the late rebellion' (CP).

HAWKINS, Nicholas, of Dowlishwake, 'in the rebellion and not come in' (CP).

HAWKINS, Simon, tried at Taunton; to be hanged at Minehead (JR, JW), where 3 of 6 so sentenced were hanged (NL).

HAWKINS, William, presented at Dorchester, remaining in custody (JR).

HAWKLAND, William, presented for High Treason at Exeter in March 1686; pardoned and dismissed (GD).

HAWLER (Hawkier), John, yeoman, of Colyton, 'absent' (CP); presented at Exeter but at large (JR). Aged 32, if son of John; 28, if son of Thomas (PR).

HAWLEY, Adam, tried at Dorchester, Sept. 10; hanged at Wareham, Sept. 22 (JR, NL).

HAWLSEY *see* Halsey.

HAYDON, Samuel, of Ashcott, 'carrying provisions to Monmouth's army' (CP). Local tradition reports him a fugitive near Hinton Blewett.

HAYES, James (John), came from Holland with Monmouth, in command of the powder ship, a captain in the Red Regiment (W); was against kingly government (L/Williams); captured after Sedgemoor and taken to London, Newgate, for interrogation (L/August 16); misnamed John in GD and JR; tried at Dorchester, Sept. 10; hanged at Lyme Regis, Sept. 12 (JR, NL, Br).

HAYES, William, tried at Taunton; transported for Musgrave (JR) on the *Jamaica Merchant* from Weymouth to Barbados; there by March 12 (SL).

HAYMAN, Robert, yeoman, of Colyton, 'absent' (CP); presented 1685 at Exeter but at large (JR); presented 1686 at Exeter; pardoned and dismissed (GD).

HAYNE (Heyne), John, of Broadwindsor, 'trained soldier and in the rebellion' (CP); tried at Dorchester; transported for Nipho (JR) on the *Betty* from Weymouth, Nov. 25, to Barbados; sold to Lt. Col. Richard Vinter (SL).

HAYNES, John, clerk, of Stoke sub Hamdon 'absent' (CP).

HAYNES, William, of Beckington, tried at Taunton; transported for Booth (JR) from Taunton Bridewell via Bristol, Oct. 24, on the *John* to Barbados; sold to Henry Quintyne, Esq. (SL).

HAYNES, William, yeoman, of Thorncombe, 'wanting from his habitation' (CP); tried at Dorchester; transported for Nipho (JR) on the *Betty* from Weymouth, Nov. 25, to Barbados; sold to Richard Walters (SL). Also presented at Exeter and misreported at large (JR).

HAYWARD, Robert, imprisoned at Wells and tried there; transported for Howard, Oct. 25 on the *Port Royal Merchant*, to Jamaica (JR, SL).

HAYWARD, Thomas, of Chewton, 'absenting' (CP); tried at Wells; hanged at Norton St Philip (JR, JW).

HAYWARD, Thomas, of Monkton Wyld, 'suspected' (CP).

HAYWARD, William, presented at Wells and bound over (JR).

HAZLE, Samuel, carpenter or 'hoste', of Taunton St Mary, 'aiding' (CP); Blue Regt. (P).

HEALE, James, of Chewton, 'absenting' (CP); tried at Wells; transported for Howard (JR), Oct. 25, to Jamaica (SL).

HEARLE, William, of Durleigh, 'absent and not taken' (CP).

HEARNE, Bartholomew, of Chard Town, 'absent and believed' (CP).

HEARNE, John junior, of Beaminster, 'wanting from his home' (CP).

HEARNE, John senior, of Creech St Michael, 'in the rebellion and taken' (CP).

HEARNE, Lewis, of Creech St Michael, 'in the rebellion and taken' (CP).

HEARNE, William, of Stockland, 'suspected' (CP).

HEARSE, Joseph, of Badgworth, excepted from GP; but pardoned October 2, 1686 (CSPD, J2, II, 1035).

HEATHFIELD, John, cordwainer, of Colyton, 'absent' (CP); tried at Dorchester; transported for Nipho (JR) on the *Betty* from Weymouth, Nov. 25, to Barbados; sold to Nicholas Maynard (SL). Also presented at Exeter and misreported at large (JR). Land forfeit and for sale (TB). Named on petition of 1689 (CSPD, W&M, I, 43).

HEBBETT, Nicholas, of North Curry, 'absent' (CP).

HEELES, Francis, of Mells, 'supposed in Monmouth's army' (CP).

HELLEN, Edward, shoemaker, of Lyme Regis, 'absent and supposed' (CP).

HELLEN, John senior, husbandman, of Lyme Regis, 'absent and supposed' (CP).

HELLEN, John junior, husbandman, of Lyme Regis, 'absent and supposed' (CP).

HELLER, Jonathan, shoemaker, of Lyme Regis, 'absent and supposed' (CP).

HELLIER, Edward, of Stoke Atrum, in Netherbury, suspected; (CP).

HELLIER, Francis, presented at Wells and bound over (JR).

HELLIER, John, tobacco cutter, of Lyme Regis, 'absent and supposed' (CP).

HELLIER, John, weaver, of Mark, a Quaker who 'took up arms in the late insurrection' and survived Sedgemoor (Som. Record Soc. 75, p. 37).

HELLIER, John, husbandman, of Weare; tried at Wells; hanged at Norton St Philip (JR, JW). Land forfeit and for sale (TB).

HELLIER, Nicholas, of Stoke Atrum, in Netherbury, 'suspected' (CP); presented at Dorchester; certificate allowed (JR).

HELLIER, Robert, tried at Dorchester; transported for Booth (JR) on the *Happy Return* from Weymouth, Sept. 25, to Barbados, sold to Col. Richard Williams (SL).

HELLIER, Samuel, of Marshwood, 'suspected' (CP).

HELLIER, Stephen, presented at Wells and bound over (JR).

HELLIER, Thomas, tried at Dorchester; transported for Booth (JR) on the *Happy Return* from Weymouth, Sept. 25, to Barbados; sold to Col. Richard Williams (SL).

HELLIER, William, presented at Wells for 'levying war against the king'; pleaded guilty, but was 'recommended for pardon' (GD, JR).

HELLYAR *see* Hillary.

HELMAN *see* Hillman, Holman

HELPS, John, tried at Wells; transported for Howard (JR), Oct. 25 on the *Port Royal Merchant* to Jamaica (SL).

HEMBOROUGH, Thomas, of Cheddon Fitzpaine, 'absent' (CP).

HEMBURY, Emanuel, of Taunton St Mary, 'aiding' (CP); Blue Regt. (P).

HENDY, John junior, of Isle Abbotts, 'out in the rebellion and not taken' (CP).

HENDY, Thomas, of Barrington, 'in the rebellion and not come in' (CP); tried at Taunton; transported for Musgrave (JR) from Weymouth on the *Jamaica Merchant* to Barbados; there by March 12 (SL).

HENLEY, William, seaman, of Lyme Regis, 'absent, supposed' (CP).

HENNING, Henry, tailor, of Taunton St Mary, 'aiding' (CP); Blue Regt. (P).

HENSLEY, John, wiredrawer, of Frome, 'with the rebels and at large' (CP); tried at Taunton; transported for Musgrave (JR) on the *Jamaica Merchant* from Weymouth to Barbados; there by March 12 (SL).

HENSLEY, Samuel, tried at Taunton; transported for Musgrave (JR) on the *Jamaica Merchant* from Weymouth to Barbados; there by March 12 (SL).

HENSON, John, of Pawlett (Som. QSR), North Petherton, 'in the rebellion and in prison' (CP); tried at Wells; transported for Stapleton (JR) on the *Indeavour* from Bristol Oct. 20, to Nevis or St Kitts (SL).

HENSON, Roger, carpenter, of Taunton St James, 'aiding' (CP); Blue Regt. (P).

HERD, Roger, of Chard, 'absent and believed' (CP).

HERRING (Hirren), Henry, tailor, of Taunton, excepted from GP, but pardoned, Oct. 2, 1686 (CSPD, J2, II, 1035).

HERRING, James, of Pitminster, 'absent' (CP); tried at Taunton, 'remaining in gaol' (JR); transported from Wells by White on the *Constant Richard*, Nov. 12, to Jamaica (SL).

HERRING, John, of Taunton, pardoned March 27 and July 18, 1686 (CSPD, J2, II, 356, 822).

HERRING, John, Captain (in Albermarle's list of 'commission' officers); tried at Taunton; hanged and quartered at Tower Hill, Stogursey on Nov. 1 (JR, JW, NL, PR).

HERRING, Samuel, of Pitminster, 'taking up arms against his Majesty' (Som. QSR).

HERRING, Thomas senior, of Pitminster, 'taking up arms against his Majesty' (Som. QSR). [*See below.*]

HERRING, Thomas junior, his son, of Pitminster, 'taking up arms against his Majesty' (Som. QSR). [*See* below.] One of these two was tried at Wells and transported for Stapleton (JR) in the *Indeavour* from Bristol Oct. 20, to Nevis or St Kitts (SL).

HERRING, William, of Pitminster, 'absent' (CP).

HEWES, John, yeoman, of Colyton, 'absent' (CP); presented at Exeter but at large (JR).

HEWES, Robert, of Wayford, 'rebel in Monmouth's army and not taken' (CP).

HEWLETT, John, presented at Wells and bound over (JR).

HEWLETT, Thomas, of Yetminster, 'suspected' (CP).

HEWLETT, William, presented at Wells and bound over (JR).

HEWLING, Benjamin, aged 22, student in Holland, came before Monmouth, arrested, put in Ilchester gaol, released by Monmouth's men, appointed Captain of Horse; sent to Minehead to collect cannon, so not at Sedgemoor; rode to Ilfracombe with Wade (W); surrendered July 8 and was sent to London, July 16 (CSPD, J2, I, 1236); tried at Taunton; hanged there on Sept. 30 (JR, JW); buried at St Mary's, Oct. 1 (PR). Last letter in BA.

HEWLING, William, aged 19, student in Holland, came with Monmouth, Lieut. in Red Regt. (W); at Sedgemoor, escaped with Wade, captured July 12, put in Exeter gaol, sent to London on the *Swan* (CSPD, J2, I, 1236), July 16; put in Newgate; tried at Dorchester, Sept. 10; hanged at Lyme Regis, Sept. 12 (JR, NL). Buried in the church yard there July 13 (T). Last letter in BA.

HEYDON, Thomas, comber, of Taunton St Mary, 'aiding' (CP); Blue Regt. (P).

HEYNE *see* Hayne.

HICKS, John, of Stawell 'out in the rebellion and at large' (CP).

HICKS, Rev. John, of 'Portmouth', Hants; Nonconformist minister, B.A. of Trinity College, Dublin; curate of Saltash; ejected 1661; joined Monmouth at Shepton Mallet; after Sedgemoor sought a night's lodging at Moyles Court, the home of Dame Alice Lisle; captured there; tried at Wells for 'aiding and assisting the rebels', pleaded guilty (GD); visited by Bishop Ken in prison (Plumptre's *Life of Ken*, ii. 302–3); hanged at Glastonbury (JR, JW). Last letter and written dying speech' in BA. Buried at Ken's request in 'Glastonbury church' (Plumptre); St John's (PR).

HICKWELL *see* Luckwill

HIGDEN, William, tried at Wells; transported for Stapleton (JR) in the *Indeavour* from Bristol Oct. 20, to Nevis or St Kitts (SL).

HIGG *see* Lugg.

HIGGANS *see* Huggins.

HIGWELL, Moses, tried at Wells; transported for Stapleton (JR) in the *Indeavour* from Bristol Oct. 20 to Nevis or St Kitts (SL).

HILL, George, of Mells, 'supposed' (CP).

HILL, Hannibal, of Wellington, 'absent' (CP).

HILL, John, of Bampton, 'supposed' (CP). [*See below.*]

HILL, John, of Ilminster, 'in the late rebellion' (CP). [*See below.*]

HILL, John, worsted comber, of Taunton St Mary, 'aiding' (CP); Blue Regt. (P). One of these three was tried at Wells; transported thence for Bridgeman (JR) by White, Oct. 31, on the *Constant Richard* to Jamaica (SL).

HILL, Richard, of Taunton St Mary, 'aiding' (CP); Blue Regt. (P).

HILL, Richard, of West Pennard, 'from home at the time of the rebellion' (CP). 'Munmouth Rebell in custody' (Som. QSR).

HILL, Robert, tried at Taunton; hanged at Crewkerne (JR, JW).

HILL, Thomas, of Wellington, 'absent' (CP); tried at Wells; transported for Stapleton (JR) in the *Indeavour* from Bristol Oct. 20, to Nevis or St Kitts (SL).

HILL, William, of Taunton St Mary, 'aiding' (CP); Blue Regt. (P).

HILLARD, Benjamin, weaver, of Wincanton, 'absent, and informed in Scott's army' (CP).

HILLARD, Henry, porter, of Taunton St Mary, 'aiding' (CP); Blue Regt. (P).
*And see* Carew; Gillard.

HILLIARD, Joseph, clothier, of Taunton, got away to Holland; making 'English' cloth there; pardoned of all treasons,parch 27, 1686, (CSPD, J2, II, 356) and returned to England.

HILLIARD, Samuel, tried at Dorchester, Sept. 5; pleaded not guilty (GD) hanged at Dorchester, Sept. 7 (JR, NL).

HILLARY, Thomas, tried at Wells; hanged at Axbridge (JR, JW).

HILLARY (Hellyar), Weston, soapboiler, of Hawkchurch, joined Monmouth at Chard; wounded at 'the last fight'; taken at Lyme Regis and examined July 13; named three companions; sent to Dorchester gaol, July 14 (LRMB) tried at Taunton; hanged at Ilminster (JR, JW).

HILLIER, John, of Coxley, Wells, 'supposed' (CP).

HILMAN (Holman), James, of Milverton (SL), tried at Taunton; transported for Booth (JR) from the Bridewell, Taunton, via Bristol, Oct. 24, on the *John* to Barbados; sold to R. Harwood, Esq. (SL).

HINCKS, Theophilus, wiredrawer, of Frome, 'in the rebellion and at large' (CP).

HINGSTON, William, presented at Exeter, March 1686, pardoned and dismissed. (GD).

HINDE *see* Hyne.

HIPPISLEY, George, of Melsbury, Wells, 'supposed' (CP).

HIPPISLEY, John, presented at Dorchester for levying war, pleaded guilty (GD) but was 'humbly proposed for his Majesty's gracious pardon' (JR).

HIPPISLEY, Thomas, of Burcott, Wells, supposed (CP).

HIRREN *see* Herring.

HITCHCOCK (Hedgecock), Humphrey, clothworker (DLD) of Thorncombe, 'wanting from his habitation' (CP); imprisoned at Bridgwater (DLD); presented at Exeter but 'at large'; tried at Taunton; hanged at Chard (JR, JW).

HITCHCOCK, John, yeoman, of Thorncombe, 'wanting' (CP); tried at Dorchester; transported for Nipho (JR) on the *Betty* from Weymouth Nov. 25, to Barbados; sold to Thomas Austin (SL). He had also been presented at Exeter and misreported at large (JR).

HITCHCOCK, John, of Chard Town, 'absent and believed' (CP).

HITT, James senior, yeoman, of Axminster, 'supposed' (CP); presented at Exeter but at large (JR).

HITT, James junior, yeoman, of Axminster, 'supposed' (CP); presented at Exeter but at large (JR); 'seen in Monmouth's camp' (LRMB).

HITT, Nathaniel, yeoman, of Axminster, 'supposed' (CP); presented at Exeter but at large (JR); 'seen in Monmouth's camp' (LRMB).

HOARE, Daniel, yeoman, of Musbury, 'in the rebellion' (CP); presented at Exeter (wrongly as of Axminster) but at large (JR).

HOARE, John, tried at Taunton; transported for Musgrave (JR) on the *Jamaica Merchant* from Weymouth to Barbados; there by March 12 (SL).

HOARE, Nicholas, tanner, of Colyton, 'absent' (CP); tried at Dorchester; hanged at Poole, Sept. 21 (JR, NL). Land forfeit and for sale (TB). Also presented at Exeter and misreported at large (JR).

HOARE, Nicholas, excepted from GP.

HOARE, Richard, of Beaminster, 'wanting' (CP); tried at Dorchester; transported for Nipho (JR) on the *Betty* from Weymouth, Nov. 25, to Barbados; sold to Matthew Chapman (SL).

HOARE, Richard senior, of Chillington, 'in the rebellion and not come in'. (CP).

HOARE, Richard, husbandman, of Hinton St George, tried at Wells; to be transported for Howard (JR); reprieved (JR2). Elias Holmes transported in his place to Jamaica (SL). Hoare's land forfeit and for sale (TB).

HOARE, Roger, mercer, of Bridgwater (TB); presented at Wells for aiding and assisting the rebels; pleaded guilty (GD); to be hanged at Bridgwater (JR) but reprieved (JR2) under the gallows (Lo). Pardon under the Great Seal, 24 Feb. 1686, but land forfeit and for sale (TB).

HOARE (Hore), Thomas, yeoman, of Uplyme, imprisoned in Wilts. (DLD); tried at Dorchester; transported for Booth (JR) on the *Happy Return* from Weymouth, Sept. 25, to Barbados; sold to Col. Richard Williams (SL).

HOBART, B. of Lillesdon, North Curry, 'absent' (Som. QSR).

HOBBES, Oliver, yeoman, of Musbury, 'in the rebellion' (CP); tried at Dorchester; transported for Nipho (JR) on the *Betty* from Weymouth, Nov. 25, to Barbados; sold to John Shahany (SL). Also presented at Exeter and misreported at large (JR).

HOBBES, Roger, tried at Dorchester; transported for Booth (JR) on the *Happy Return* from Weymouth, Sept. 25, to Barbados; sold to Capt. Robert Harrison (SL).

HOBBES, Thomas, presented at Exeter 'for proclaiming James Scott, late Duke of Monmouth, King,' Sept. 14; pleaded not guilty; verdict guilty (GD); hanged the same day at Crediton (JR, NL).

HOBLYN *see* Holbin.

HOCKADAY, Thomas, of Ilminster, 'in the rebellion' (CP).

HOCKER, William, shoemaker, of Lyme Regis, 'absent and supposed' (CP).

HOCOMBE, John, of Honiton, 'a rebel' (CP).

HODDER, John, of Axminster, 'seen in Monmouth's camp' (LRMB).

HODDER, William, of Stanton St Gabriel, 'suspected' (CP); of Whitechurch Canonicorum, of Morcombelake, said to have sent a horse and man to the rebels' army; sent to Dorchester gaol, July 14 (LRMB); presented at Dorchester; pleaded not guilty and found not guilty (GD).

HODGE (Hody), Humphrey, of Bradford on Tone, 'absent' (CP); tried at Wells; transported for Stapleton (JR) in the *Indeavour* from Bristol Oct. 20, to Nevis or St Kitts (SL).

HODGES, Giles, of Knowle St Giles, 'in the rebellion and not come in' (CP).

HODGES, Henry, presented at Taunton 'for levying war'; pleaded guilty, (GD) but 'humbly proposed for pardon' (JR).

HODGES, Robert, of Whatley, 'in the rebellion and not taken' (CP); convicted, pardoned and dismissed at Wells, 1686 (GD).

HODY, Edward, tried at Wells; transported thence for Bridgeman (JR) by White on the *Constant Richard* to Jamaica (SL).

HOELL, Edward, clothworker, of Rode, 'in the rebellion' (CP).

HOELL, John, tobacco pipe maker, of Rode, 'in the rebellion' (CP). *And see* Howell.

HOGLEY, Ambrose, of Langford Budville, 'supposed' (CP).

HOGLEY, Humphrey, of Langford Budville, 'supposed' (CP).

HOGLEY, John, of Langford Budville, 'supposed' (CP); presented at Taunton, certificate, allowed (JR). *And see* Hagley.

HOILE, Henry, of Creech St Michael, 'absent and not taken' (CP).

HOKEM, James, of Beaminster, 'absent at the time of the rebellion' (CP).

HOLBEN, Philip, of Tiverton, 'with the late Duke of Monmouth' (CP).

HOLBIN (Hoblyn), Christopher, aged 40, weaver (SL), tried at Taunton; transported for the Queen (JR) on the *Jamaica Merchant* to Barbados; there by March 12; sold to John Gray (SL).

HOLCOMBE, Andrew, tried at Wells; transported for Nipho (JR) on the *Betty* from Weymouth, Nov. 25, to Barbados; sold to Peter Flewilling (SL).

HOLDSWORTH, John, tried at Wells; hanged at Shepton Mallet (JR, JW).

HOLE, Antony, presented at Exeter, March 1686, pardoned and dismissed (GD).

HOLE, Arthur, of Bampton, 'supposed' (CP).

HOLE, Richard, yeoman, of East Woodlands, 'in the rebellion and at large' (CP).

HOLE, William, of Bampton, 'supposed' (CP).

HOLEMAN, Arthur, of Milverton, 'absenting' (CP).

HOLIDAY, Richard, presented at Dorchester, 'for conducting the Lord Gray from Gillingham to Ringwood after the fight at Weston'; to be whipped twice, fined a mark, and to find sureties for good behaviour for a year (JR). Presented at Dorchester in March 1686 and pardoned by Proclamation (GD).

HOLLADAY, John, yeoman, of Frome, 'with the rebels and at large' (CP).

HOLLADAY, John junior, feltmaker, of Frome, 'with the rebels and at large' (CP).

HOLLIDAY, Robert, yeoman, of Frome, 'with the rebels and at large' (CP).

HOLLAND, Hugh, husbandman, of South Petherton (TB), tried at Wells; hanged at Wincanton (JR, JW); land forfeit and for sale (TB).

HOLLAND, Thomas, tailor, of Lyme Regis, 'absent, supposed' (CP).

HOLLAND, William, husbandman, of South Petherton (TB); tried at Wells; hanged at Wincanton (JR, JW); land forfeit and for sale (TB).

HOLLAND, William, weaver, of Rode, 'in the rebellion' (CP).

HOLLETT, John, of Honiton, 'a rebel' (CP).

HOLLINGS, George, of Kittisford, 'absenting' (CP).

HOLLMAN, Thomas, of Charmouth, 'suspected' (CP).

HOLLOWAY, John, tobacconist, of Lyme Regis, 'absent, supposed' (CP); originally a member of Lyme defence force (Roberts, *Life of the Duke of Monmouth*, i. 226); laid down his arms one day too late (T); tried at Dorchester; hanged at Wareham (JR, NL) on Sept. 22.

HOLLOWAY, John, of Chardland, 'absent and believed' (CP), presented at Wells; pleaded not guilty and found not guilty (GD).

HOLLOWAY, John, tried at Wells; transported for Howard (JR), Oct. 25 on the *Port Royal Merchant* to Jamaica (SL).

HOLLWAY, William, of West Pennard, 'from home at the time of the rebellion' (CP).

HOLMAN, Elias, presented at Exeter; convicted of levying war; remaining in custody; reprieved (JR) but transported for Howard from Exeter gaol to Jamaica on the *Port Royal Merchant* Oct. 25 in place of Richard Hoare (SL).

HOLMAN, Stephen, weaver, of Rode, 'in the rebellion' (CP); tried at Taunton; remaining in gaol (JR); transported from Wells by White on the *Constant Richard* to Jamaica (SL).
*And see* Hillman.

HOLMES, Abraham, a Major in Cromwell's Army, under Monk in 1654 and 1659; a Baptist and a Republican; imprisoned at Windsor at the Restoration; escaped to Holland; came with Monmouth as Lieut Colonel of the Green Regiment (W); distinguished service at Norton St Philip (W), where he was shot in the arm; led the Green Regt. into action at Sedgemoor; captured and taken to Newgate, London; interrogated on July 20; mentioned only Foulkes and Venner (L); tried at Dorchester, Sept. 10; hanged at Lyme Regis, Sept. 12 (JR, NL). Dying speech and prayer for maintenance of the Protestant religion (BA).

HOLMES, son of Abraham, rode from London, a Captain in the Green Regt.; killed at Norton St Philip (W).

HOLMES, John senior, of Milverton, 'absenting' (CP). [*See below.*]

HOLMES, John junior, of Milverton, 'absenting' (CP). [*See below.*] One of these two was tried at Wells and transported for Stapleton (JR) in the *Indeavour* from Bristol Oct. 20, to Nevis or St Kitts (SL).

HOLMES, Joseph, clothier, of Ilminster, 'in the rebellion' (CP). He rode to Forde Abbey with others seeking arms, and on to Taunton next day, but returned with his servant. He wrote his 'defence' which could have been used as evidence against Edmund Prideaux (Dep.). Pardon, July 4 and 11, 1686 (CSPD, J2, II, 768, 822).

HOLWELL, Walter, presented at Exeter, March 1686; pardoned and dismissed (GD).

HONAN, Richard, of Wedmore, 'absent and in the rebellion' (CP).

HONE, John, of Burstock 'suspected' (CP).

HOOK, Nathaniel, studied at Dublin, Glasgow and Cambridge; Congregational minister; Monmouth's domestic chaplain; came with him from Holland; sent to London after Norton St Philip to urge Col. Danvers to start a rising there (W); excepted from the GP; in hiding until 1688, when he was pardoned and entered King James's service. He joined Dundee in 1689; fought in the Battle of the Boyne; was commissioned in the French Irish Regt. of Galway; turned Roman Catholic; rose to be a Brigadier; and twice fought against Marlborough (*Dictionary of National Biography*).

HOOKIER, Nicholas, of West Buckland, 'absent' (CP). His wife, Ann, was buried 6 March, 1686 (PR).

HOOPE alias Ellstone, William junior, cordwinder, of Dunster, 'in arms in the rebellion' (CP).

HOOPER, Edward, shuttlemaker, of Whitford; imprisoned at Taunton (DLD).

HOOPER, George, of Lopen, 'in the rebellion and not come in' (CP).

HOOPER, Henry, tried at Taunton; transported for Musgrave (JR) on the *Jamaica Merchant* from Weymouth to Barbados; there by 12 March, 1686 (SL).

HOOPER, James, rode from London to join Monmouth at Taunton. Warrant for his arrest July 16, 1685 (CSPD, J2, I, 1246). Excepted from GP, but pardoned of all treasons, Nov. 25, 1686 (CSPD, J2, II, 1186).

HOOPER (Happer), James, of Goathurst, 'took up arms against his Majesty' (Som. QSR); 'absent and not taken' (CP).

HOOPER, John, of Lyng, 'absent and not taken' (CP); tried at Taunton; transported for Musgrave (JR) on the *Jamaica Merchant* from Weymouth to Jamaica; there by March 12, 1686 (SL).

HOOPER, John, tried at Wells; transported for Nipho (JR) from Ilchester gaol to Barbados, Oct. 21, on the *Rebecca* (SL).

HOOPER, John (another), also tried at Wells and transported for Nipho (JR) from Ilchester gaol to Barbados, Oct. 21, on the *Rebecca* (SL).

HOOPER, Paul, of Bampton, 'supposed to be a rebel' (CP).

HOOPER, Richard, tried at Wells; to be transported for Howard (JR), Oct. 25, but escaped from Sherborne prison (SL).

HOOPER, Samuel, yeoman, of Axminister, 'supposed' (CP); presented at Exeter but at large (JR).

HOOPER, Thomas, of Crewkerne, 'rebel in Monmouth's army and not taken' (CP). Excepted from GP, but pardoned, Nov. 6, 1686, and his outlawry reversed on Dec. 2 (CSPD, J2, II, 1124, 1206).

HOOPER, Thomas, weaver, of Taunton St Mary, 'aiding' (CP); Blue Regt. (P); tried at Wells; transported for Stapleton (JR) in the *Indeavour* from Bristol Oct. 20, to Nevis or St Kitts (SL).

HOOPER, William, of Crewkerne, 'rebel and not taken' (CP); presented at Wells, March 1686, as from Taunton Bridewell, as 'convicted at the last Sessions'; pardoned and dismissed (GD).

HOOPER, William, of Huntspill, 'active soldier in the Duke of Monmouth's army' (Som. QSR).

HOOPER, William, comber, of Whitford; imprisoned at Taunton (DLD) and tried there; transported for Musgrave (JR) from Weymouth to Barbados (SL).
*And see* Bryant

HOPKINS, Edward, of West Buckland, 'absent' (CP).

HORE, George, presented for high treason at Exeter in March 1686; pardoned and dismissed (GD).

HORE, see Hoare

HORNE alias Harbett, Thomas, clothier, of Dunster, 'in arms in the rebellion of James Scott' (CP).

HORNE, William, of Wootton Fitzpaine, 'suspected' (CP).

HORSEY, Philip, of Ilminster, 'in the late rebellion' (CP).

HORSLEY, William, of St Martin-in-the-Fields, London, 'engaged in the late rebellion'; pardon May 31, 1687 (CSPD, J2, II, 1833).

HORTON, Peter, weaver, of East Woodlands, 'in the rebellion and at large' (CP).

HORWOOD, Henry, of Barrington, 'in the rebellion and not come in' (CP).

HOSKINS, John, of Beaminster, 'wanting from his home' (CP).

HOSKINS, John, of Pitminster, 'absent' (CP).

HOSKINS, Robert, of Monkton, 'suspected' (CP).

HOSKINS, Samuel, of Beaminster, 'wanting' (CP).

HOSSEY *see* Hussey

HOULD, ——, servant to Sir W. Young of Colyton, 'seen in Monmouth's camp' (LRMB).

HOUNDSELL, Andrew, of Marshwood, 'suspected' (CP).

HOUSE (Howse), Christopher, of Curload, Stoke St Gregory and Thornfalcon, 'absenting' (CP); a tenant, taking up arms against the King'; 'fled' (Som. QSR, CL).

HOUSE, Nathaniel junior, of Ilminster, 'in the late rebellion' (CP).

HOWARD, Andrew, yeoman, of South Molton, imprisoned in Wilts. (DLD); tried at Wells; transported for Stapleton (JR) in the *Indeavour* from Bristol Oct. 20, to Nevis or St Kitts (SL).

HOWARD, Edward, yeoman, of Axmouth, 'reported in arms' (CP); presented at Exeter but at large (JR).

HOWARD, John, of Chardland, 'absent, believed' (CP).

HOWARD, Josias, tried at Wells; transported for Stapleton (JR) in the *Indeavour* from Bristol Oct. 20, to Nevis or St Kitts (SL).

HOWDON, Robert, maltster, of Taunton St Mary, 'aiding' (CP); Blue Regt. (P).

HOWELL, John, yeoman, of Rode (TB), tried at Wells; hanged at Wincanton (JR, JW); land forfeit and for sale (TB). *See* Hoell.

HOWELL, Ralph, of Huntspill, 'a rebel in arms' (Som. QSR).

HOWELL, Thomas, tried at Taunton; transported for Musgrave (JR) on the *Jamaica Merchant* from Weymouth to Barbados; there by March 12 (SL).

*And see* Hoell

HOWELLS (Howills), Richard, tried at Wells; transported for Stapleton
   (JR) in the *Indeavour* from Bristol to Nevis or St Kitts (SL).

HOWSE, Nicholas, junior, of Creech St Michael, 'absent and not taken'
   (CP); 'took up arms against his Majesty' (Som. QSR).

HOYLE, Abraham, bricklayer, of Taunton St Mary, 'aiding' (CP); Blue
   Regt. (P).

HOYLE, Henry, of Creech St Michael, 'took up arms against his
   Majesty' (Som. QSR).

HOYLE, Ralph, of Huntspill, 'active soldier in the Duke of Monmouth's
   army' (Som. QSR).

HUBBARD, Richard, servant to the late Duke of Monmouth, pardon of
   all treasons, April 17, 1687, and warrant to pass freely (CSPD, J2,
   II, 417–8).

HUCKER, John, sergemaker, of Taunton St Mary, a Captain of Horse,
   entertained Monmouth and Grey in Taunton; wrongly suspected of
   firing his pistol near the Langmoor Rhine; brought his squadron
   intact back to Bridgwater; tried at Taunton and hanged there, Sept.
   30 (JR, JW). Land forfeit and for sale (TB). A Dissenter. Last letter
   in BA.

HUCKER, John junior, tried at Taunton, transported for Musgrave (JR)
   on the *Jamaica Merchant* from Weymouth to Barbados; there by
   Mar. 12 (SL).

HUCKER, Robert, son of John senior, gentleman (CP), woolcomber (in
   pardon), of Taunton St Mary, 'aiding' (CP); Captain in the Blue
   Regt. (Lo); excepted from the GP, but pardoned 31 May 1687
   (CSPD, J2, II, 1833).

HUCKER, William, of Puriton, 'active soldier in Duke of Monmouth's
   army' (Som. QSR).

HUDDON, Robert, of Chard, 'absent, believed' (CP).

HUDDY, John, of Chard Town, 'absent, believed' (CP).

HUGGINS (Higgans) John, yeoman, of Luppitt, 'out in the rebellion'
   (CP); presented at Exeter but at large (JR).

HUGGINS, Joseph, yeoman, of Luppitt, 'out in the rebellion' (CP);
   presented at Exeter but at large (JR).

HUGGINS, Richard, yeoman, of Luppitt, 'out in the rebellion' (CP);
   presented at Exeter but at large (JR).

HUGHES, Daniel, of Milverton, 'absenting' (CP).

HUISH, John, clerk to Mr Marshall (CP), yeoman (in pardon), of
   Taunton St Mary, 'aiding' (CP); Blue Regt. (P); excepted from GP,
   but pardoned 22 March 1687 (CSPD, J2, II, 311).

HULL, John, tried at Wells; transported for Stapleton (JR), in the
   *Indeavour* from Bristol Oct. 20, to Nevis or St Kitts (SL).

HULL, William, husbandman, of Ash Priors, 'absent' (CP).

HUMPHREY, Joseph, of Kingsbury Episcopi, 'absent, believed' (CP).

HUMPHREY (Humphreys), Thomas, of Kingsbury Episcopi, 'absent,
   believed' (CP), tried at Wells; transported for Stapleton (JR) in the
   *Indeavour* from Bristol Oct. 20, to Nevis or St Kitts (SL).

HUMPHREYS, John, tailor, of Marston Bigot, 'in the rebellion not taken' (CP); Monmouth rebel in custody (Som. QSR) tried at Wells; hanged at Frome (JR, JW). Land forfeit and for sale (TB).

HUNT, Abraham, yeoman, of Axmouth, 'reported in arms' (CP); tried at Exeter; transported for Nipho (JR) on the *Betty* from Weymouth Nov. 25, to Barbados; sold to Edward Henley (SL). Also misreported at large (JR).

HUNT, Henry, of Glastonbury, 'from home at the time of the rebellion' (CP); tried at Wells; transported for Howard (JR) Oct. 25 on the *Port Royal Merchant* from Weymouth to Jamaica (SL).

HUNT, Job, aged 26, carrier (SL), tried at Taunton; transported thence for the Queen (JR) on the *Jamaica Merchant* to Barbados; shipped Dec. 9; sold March 12 to George Harper (SL).

HUNT, William, of Bishop's Hull, 'absent' (CP), 'not taken' (CI.).

HURD, Edmund, tried at Wells; transported for Howard (JR), Oct. 25 on the *Port Royal Merchant* to Jamaica (SL).

HURD, James, husbandman, of Langport, 'absent' (CP); tried at Wells; transported for Howard (JR) Oct. 25 on the *Port Royal Merchant* to Jamaica (SL). Excepted from GP.

HURD, Jedidiah, husbandman, of Langport, 'absent' (CP); presented at Wells and bound over (JR).

HURD, John, of Chardland, 'absent, believed' (CP).

HURD, Robert, of Chardland, 'absent, believed' (CP).

HURD, Thomas, of Langport, tried at Wells; to be transported for Howard (JR) but escaped between Wells and Sherborne (SL). Excepted from GP.

HURDING, William, of Bryant's Puddle, militia soldier in Capt. Erle's company; 'departing from his Colours without leave' (CP).

HURFORD, Cornelius, of Wellington, 'in prison for rebellion' (CP); tried at Taunton; hanged at South Petherton (JR, JW).

HURFORD, Thomas, of Huntspill, 'active soldier in the Duke of Monmouth's army' (Som. QSR); tried at Taunton; hanged at Yeovil (JR, JW).

HURLEY, Andrew, of Churchstanton, 'suspected' (CP).

HURLEY, Christopher, comber, of Taunton St Mary, 'aiding' (CP); Blue Regt. (P).

HURLEY, Enoch, yeoman, of Axminister, 'supposed' (CP); presented at Exeter but at large (JR).

HURLEY, John, of Milverton, 'absenting' (CP); tried at Wells; transported for Howard (JR), Oct. 25 on the *Port Royal Merchant* to Jamaica (SL).

HURLEY (Hussey), Lawrence, of Wellington, 'in prison for rebellion' (CP); tried at Taunton; transported for Booth (JR) from Taunton Bridewell via Bristol, Oct. 24, on the *John* to Barbados; sold to William Slograve (SL).

HURMAN *see* Harman.

HURMAN, Thomas, feltmaker, of Wincanton, 'actually in arms, as informed and at large' (CP).

HUSSEY (Hossey), George junior, worsted comber, of Taunton St Mary, 'aiding' (CP); Blue Regt. (P); tried at Wells; hanged at Frome (JR, JW).

HUSSEY, John, clothworker, of Rode, 'in the rebellion, at large' (CP); tried at Wells; transported for Howard (JR) Oct. 25 on the *Port Royal Merchant* to Jamaica (SL).

HUSSEY, Simon, of Wellington, 'absent, in prison for rebellion' (CP); 'for marching in Monmouth's army till they were engaged' (Wilts. QSR); presented at Wells for levying war and pleaded guilty (GD), but 'recommended for the King's pardon' (JR).

HUSSEY, William, excepted from GP.

*And see* Hurley.

HUTCHINS, Arthur, of Cudworth, 'in the rebellion and not come in' (CP).

HUTCHINS, Humphrey, yeoman, of Musbury, 'in the rebellion' (CP); presented at Exeter (wrongly as of Axminster) but at large (JR).

HUTCHINS, Isaac, of Pitminster, 'absent' (CP); presented at Wells in March 1686 as 'convicted at the last Sessions'; pardoned and dismissed (GD).

HUTCHINS, John, of Chardland, 'absent, believed' (CP); tried at Dorchester; transported for Booth (JR) on the *Happy Return* from Weymouth, Sept. 25, to Barbados (SL). [*See below.*]

HUTCHINS, John (another), tried at Dorchester; transported for Booth (JR) on the *Happy Return* from Weymouth, Sept. 25, to Barbados (SL). One John Hutchins was sold to Capt. Tobias Frere; the other to John Haywood (SL).

HUTCHINS, Matthew, of Broadwindsor, 'being out in the horrid rebellion' (CP); tried at Dorchester; transported for Booth (JR) on the *Happy Return* from Weymouth, Sept. 25, to Barbados; sold to Thomas Hayse (SL).

HUTCHINS, Moses, weaver, of Taunton St Mary, 'aiding' (CP); Blue Regt. (P).

HUTCHINS, Richard, of Woolminstone, Crewkerne, 'rebel in Monmouth's army and not taken' (CP).

HUTCHINS, Simon, husbandman, of Taunton St James, 'aiding' (CP); Blue Regt. (P).

HUTCHINS, Thomas, husbandman, of Merriott (TB), tried at Wells; transported for Stapleton (JR) in the *Indeavour* from Bristol Oct. 20, to Nevis or St Kitts (SL). Land forfeit and for sale (TB).

HUTCHINS, Thomas, of Wilton, 'absent' (CP).

HUTCHINS, William, sergemaker, of Upottery, 'absent' (CP); imprisoned in Exeter (SL); tried at Taunton; transported for Booth (JR) via Bristol, Oct. 24, on the *John* towards Barbados, but died at sea (SL).

HYDON, Christopher, of Thurloxton, 'in the rebellion and in prison' (CP). As he was not brought to trial, perhaps he died in prison (P).

HYER (Hyne), Robert, weaver, of Taunton St Mary, 'aiding' (CP); Blue Regt. (P); tried at Taunton; hanged at Castle Cary (JR, JW).

ILES, Joseph, yeoman, of West Woodlands, 'in the rebellion and not taken' (CP).

INDOE (Judes), James, presented at Taunton, 'remaining in gaol'; marked 'run away' (JR).

INGRAM, Richard, of Thurloxton, 'in the rebellion and in prison;' (CP); tried at Taunton; hanged at Bridgwater (JR, JW).

IRELAND, Thomas, of Beaminster, 'absent at the time of the rebellion' (CP).

IRETON, Henry of Gray's Inn, supplied arms to Ford, Lord Grey; excepted from the GP, but pardoned April 19, 1686 (CSPD, J2, II, 422).

IRISH, Henry, yeoman, of Axminster, presented at Exeter but at large (JR).

IRISH, John, of Chard, 'in the late rebellion' (CP); presented at Taunton, certificate allowed (JR).

IRISH, Joseph, yeoman, of Axminster, 'supposed' (CP); presented at Exeter but at large (JR).

IRISH, Joseph, of Chardland, 'absent, believed' (CP); presented at Taunton; certificate allowed (JR).

IRISH, Richard junior, of Chard, 'in the late rebellion' (CP); presented at Taunton: certificate allowed (JR).

IRISH, Thomas, of Chard Town, 'absent, believed' (CP).

IRWELL *see* Jewell.

ISAACK, George, of Kingsbury Episcopi, 'absent, believed' (CP).

ISAACK, Thomas, of Kingsbury Episcopi, 'absent, believed' (CP).

JACKSON, Edward, of Sidbury, 'joined in the rebellion' (CP).

JACKSON, Leonard, blacksmith, of Lyme Regis, broke open the Town Hall door for Monmouth; taken to London, in Newgate, July 16 (CSPD, J2, I, 1249), tried at Dorchester, Sept. 10; hanged at Lyme Regis, Sept. 12 (JR, NL).

JACKSON, William, tried at Wells; transported for Stapleton (JR) in the *Indeavour* from Bristol Oct. 20, to Nevis or St Kitts (SL).

JACOB, Richard, comber, of Uffculme, imprisoned in Wilts. (DLD); tried at Wells; transported for Stapleton (JR) in the *Indeavour* from Bristol Oct. 20, to Nevis or St Kitts (SL).

JACOB, Thomas, worsted comber, of Taunton St Mary, 'aiding' (CP); Blue Regt. (P).

JAELL, William, of Combe St Nicholas, 'absent, believed' (CP).

JAMES, Henry junior, yeoman, of Axminster, 'supposed' (CP); presented at Exeter but at large (JR).

JAMES, John senior, of Cudworth, 'in the rebellion and not come in' (CP).

JAMES, John, yeoman, of Uplyme, imprisoned in Dorset (DLD); tried at Dorchester; transported for Musgrave (JR) on the *Jamaica Merchant* from Weymouth to Jamaica, there by 12 March 1686 (SL).

JAMES, Joseph, printmaker, of Lyme Regis, 'absent, supposed' (CP). Presented for High Treason at Exeter in March 1686; pardoned and dismissed (GD).

JAMES, Robert, yeoman, of Thorncombe, 'wanting from his home' (CP); presented at Exeter but at large (JR).

JAMES, Samuel, yeoman, of Thorncombe, 'wanting from his home' (CP); presented at Exeter but at large (JR).

JARVICE, ——, feltmaker, of Yeovil, 'a notorious fellow', captured near Somerton, hanged by Churchill near Pensford, June 26 (Dummer).

JARVICE, ——, brother of the feltmaker, killed in skirmish near Somerton (Dummer).

JARWISH, Thomas, of Combe St Nicholas, 'absent, believed' (CP).

JAY, Christopher, of Taunton St James, 'taking up arms against the king' (Som. QSR).

JEANS, John junior, worsted comber, of Taunton St Mary, 'aiding' (CP); Blue Regt. (P); tried at Taunton; hanged at Dunster (JR, JW).

JEANES, Joseph, of Kingsbury Episcopi, 'absent, believed' (CP).

JEANES, William senior, of Martock, 'absent' (CP).

JEFFERY, Henry, of Crewkerne, 'rebel in Monmouth's army and not taken' (CP).

JEFFERYES, Arthur, presented at Wells and bound over (JR).

JEFFERYES, Stephen, of Taunton St Mary, 'aiding' (CP); tried at Taunton; transported for the Queen (JR); on John Rose's receipt 12 Oct. (SL).

JENKINS, Edward, worsted comber, of Taunton St Mary, 'aiding' (CP); Blue Regt. (P); pardon 2 Oct. 1686 (CSPD, J2, II, 1035).

JENKINS, Robert, husbandman, of Broomfield (CP); 'in the rebellion and taken' (CP); tried at Taunton, 'remaining in gaol' (JR), attainted of treason (TB). Land valued at £30 in tenure of Joan Jenkins forfeit but not for sale; reversion to Brent, Loder and Clarke, pardon money to be kept by William Harrison (TB).

JENKINS, Thomas, tried at Dorchester; hanged at Poole, Sept. 21 (JR, NL).

JENKINS, William, of Wedmore, 'absent' (CP).

JENKYN, William, of London, son of a Nonconformist minister who died in Newgate; rode to join Monmouth; arrested on suspicion and put in Ilchester gaol; released by a party of Monmouth's soldiers, and joined him; captured and taken to London (CSPD, J2, I, 1236). At Dorchester Assize he was 'continued in gaol, not indicted'. Tried at Taunton and hanged there, Sept. 30 (JR, JW); buried at St Mary's, Oct. 1 (PR). Last letter to his mother: 'I die a martyr for the Protestant religion, and merely for doing my duty, in opposing that flood of Popery, which seemed to be just overwhelming the Church and interest of Christ in these nations' (BA).

JENNINGS, Edward. Warrant of April 2, 1686, to search the *Modena* now in the Thames and arrest Edward Jennings (CSPD, J2, II, 368).

JENNINGS, Francis, of Combwich, present at Wells Assize and bound over. At Quarter Sessions he was presented for 'informing the Duke of Monmouth's men for the preserving and securing of their arms' (Som. QSR).

JENNINGS, Mary, of Burton Pynsent, Curry Rivel, daughter of George Speke of Whitelackington, sent four horses to Monmouth's army; excepted from the GP; Oct. 2, 1686 petition for a pardon as she is of Burton, Somerset, whereas the person excepted was Mary Jennings of London (CSPD, J2, II, 1032). Feb. 18, 1687 pardon to George Speke, etc. and Mary Jennings his daughter of all treasons and of all indictments incurred by reason thereof (CSPD, J2, II, 1471). In 1689 the house of Mrs Mary Jennings at Curry Rivel was registered as a nonconformist meeting house.

JENNINGS, Maurice, of Curry Rivel, 'for letting out hacks for Scott' (CP).

JENNINGS alias Appledore, Robert, of Milverton, 'absenting'; tried at Wells; transported for Howard (JR), Oct. 25 on the *Port Royal Merchant* to Jamaica (SL).

JENNINGS, Thomas, locksmith, of Taunton St Mary, 'aiding' (CP); Blue Regt (P).

JENNINGS, Thomas (another), of Taunton St Mary, 'aiding', (CP); Blue Regt. (P).

JENNINGS, William, of Hillfarrance, 'absent' (CP); imprisoned in Wilts. 'being suspected to have run from his Colours and to be going over to the Rebels' (Wilts. QSR).

JERMAN (German), James, tried at Wells; transported for Stapleton (JR) in the *Indeavour* from Bristol Oct. 20, to Nevis or St Kitts (SL).

JERMYN, Joseph, tried at Wells; transported for Stapleton (JR) in the *Indeavour* from Bristol Oct. 20, to Nevis or St Kitts (SL).

JERVIS, Francis, of North Petherton, 'in the rebellion and in prison' (CP); presented at Taunton for levying war; pleaded guilty (GD) but was 'humbly proposed for pardon' (JR).

JERVIS, John, tried at Taunton; hanged at Chard (JR, JW).

JESSE, Edward, of Chard, 'absent, believed' (CP).

JESSE, George, of Churchstanton, 'on suspicion of absconding' (CP).

JESSE, John, of Beckington, clothier, 'in the rebellion, out of Beckington, at large' (CP); excepted from GP; a prisoner in Newgate, April 13 1686 (CSPD, J2, II, 396); petition for pardon: 'in arms in the late rebellion, repented and forsook the rebels before their defeat'; referred to the Lord Chancellor, April 30 (CSPD, J2, II, 473).
*And see* Joss.

JESSE, Marmaduke, of Curry Rivel, 'out in the rebellion and not taken' (CP).

JESSE, Robert, of Pitminster, 'absent' (CP).

JEUL, Richard, chirurgeon, of Dunster, 'in arms in the rebellion of James Scott' (CP).

JEW, James, yeoman, of Frome, 'in the rebellion and in prison' (CP).

JEW, Thomas, woodman, of Frome, 'for a riot and amongst the Clubmen, the 25 June last' (CP).

JEW, William junior, cardmaker, of Frome, 'in the rebellion and in prison (CP).

JEWELL (Irwell), Christopher, lacemaker (DLD) of Honiton, 'a rebel' (CP); in the High Gaol, Devon (DLD); tried at Dorchester; transported for Nipho (JR) on the *Betty* from Weymouth, Nov. 25, to Barbados; sold to Rebecca Beal (SL). Named on the 1689 petition (CSPD, W&M, I, 43).

JOBBINS, William, excepted from GP.

JOHN, servant to Thomas Warren or Waring, of Bishop's Hull, 'absent' (CP); 'not taken' (CL).

JOHNS, John, presented at Dorchester for levying war; pleaded and found not guilty (GD). Described as one of Monmouth's captains. Subsequently Muster Master of the City of London (BA, 186).

JOHNS, Samuel, presented at Dorchester for levying war; pleaded and found not guilty (GD).

JOHNSON, Archibald, tried at Taunton; hanged at Milborne Port (JR, JW).

JOHNSON, Henry, of Glastonbury, 'from home at the time of the rebellion' (CP).

JOHNSON, John, tried at Dorchester; transported for Booth (JR) on the *Happy Return* from Weymouth, Sept. 25, to Barbados; sold to John Hethersell, Esq. (SL).

JOHNSON, John, tried at Wells; transported for Nipho (JR). On Penne's receipt Sept. 26; shipped Oct. 21 on the *Rebecca* from Ilchester gaol to Barbados (SL).

JOHNSON, Thomas the elder, of Stepney, pardon authorised July 18, granted August 22 1686 (CSPD, J2, II, 822, 922).

JOHNSON, William, tried at Taunton; hanged at Yeovil (JR, JW).

JOHNSON, William, of Glastonbury, tried at Wells; transported for Stapleton (JR) in the *Indeavour* from Bristol Oct. 20, to Nevis or St Kitts (SL).

JOLLIFFE, John, tried at Wells; transported for Nipho (JR) from Ilchester gaol, Oct. 21, on the *Rebecca* to Barbados (SL).

JOLLIFFE, Thomas, presented at Wells and bound over (JR).

JONES, Arthur junior, cardmaker, of Frome, 'with the rebels and at large' (CP).

JONES, Charles, tried at Wells; transported for Stapleton (JR) in the *Indeavour* from Bristol Oct. 21, to Nevis or St Kitts (SL).

JONES, George, of Sutton Mallet, 'out in the rebellion' (CP). [*See* Thomas Jones *below*.]

JONES, George, imprisoned in Wilts, 'being taken at Hindon upon suspicion of going to join with the late Duke of Monmouth and other traitors against his Majesty' (Wilts. QSR).

JONES, John, cabinet-maker, of London, an old Ironside, rode down from London, Captain of Horse in Monmouth's army, fought Compton's patrol of the Blues for the Upper Plungeon at Sedgemoor, captured and sent to Newgate, interrogated Aug. 16, gave the names of his Lieut. (Burton) and his Cornet (Lloyd); at Wells Assize Jones was 'left in custody as a witness for the king' (JR); excepted from GP; bailed, June 3 1686; pardoned June 5 (CSPD, J2, II, 631, 638).

JONES, John, of Ilchester, 'in the late rebellion' (CP); tried at Wells; to be transported (JR). [*See below.*]

JONES, John, weaver, of Tiverton, imprisoned in Wilts. (DLD); tried at Wells; to be transported (JR). [*See below.*] One of these two was allotted to Howard (JR) and escaped between Wells and Sherborne (SL). The other was for Stapleton (JR), collected on Oct. 20 and sent on the *Indeavour* from Bristol to Nevis or St Kitts (SL).

JONES, Richard, imprisoned in the Workhouse, Exeter; presented at the 1686 Assize, pardoned and dismissed (GD).

JONES, alias Evans, Robert, tried at Taunton; hanged at Minehead (JR, JW) on Dec. 8 (NL, which says that 3 of 6 so sentenced were hanged there).

JONES, Robert, worsted comber, of Taunton St Mary, 'aiding' (CP); Blue Regt. (P). Petition for pardon, he 'being in a very mean and low condition'; report to Sunderland that he was not excepted from GP; July 10; pardon granted Aug. 2 (CSPD, J2, I, 791, 853, 862).

JONES, Thomas, weaver, of Milborne Port, 'in the late rebellion and at large' (CP).

JONES, Thomas, of Sutton Mallet, 'for concealing George Jones, out in the rebellion' (CP).

JORDAN, Christopher, of Wellington, 'absent' (CP).

JOSS, John, clothier, of Beckington, 'in the rebellion; out of Beckington; at large' (CP).
    *And see* Jesse.

JOURDAN, Edward, aged 20, serge weaver (SL); tried at Taunton; transported for the Queen (JR) on the *Jamaica Merchant* to Barbados (SL).

JOYCE, Robert, of Blagdon, 'supposed' (CL).
    JUDES *see* Indoe.

JUSTIN, Humphrey, aged 19, comber (SL), tried at Taunton; transported for the Queen (JR) on the *Jamaica Merchant*, Oct. 12 from Taunton, to Barbados, Dec. 9; sold to Archibald Johnson, March 12 (SL).

KAY *see* Key.

KEATE, Thomas junior, of Leigh (Dorset), 'supposed in the rebels' army' (CP).

KEATES, Richard, of Nether Compton, 'absent, suspected' (CP).

KEATES, Thomas, of Taunton St James, 'aiding' (CP); Blue Regt. (P).

KEECH, Edward, excepted from GP.

KEECH, Nicholas (in CP); Richard (in JR), of Chardland, 'absent, believed' (CP); tried at Dorchester; transported for Booth (JR) on the *Happy Return* from Weymouth, Sept. 25, to Barbados; sold to Richard Lintott (SL).

KEEL, George, husbandman, of Chilton Polden (TB), in Bridgwater prison, tried at Taunton; transported for Booth (JR) via Bristol, Oct. 24, on the *John* to Barbados; died at sea (SL). Land forfeit and for sale (TB).

KEEL (Kerle), John, of Chilton Polden, presented at Taunton for levying war; pleaded guilty but 'humbly proposed for pardon' (GD); transported for Booth (JR), via Bristol, Oct. 24, on the *John* to Barbados; died on shore before sale; certified Jan. 29 (SL).

KEENE, Edward, of Pitminster, 'absent' (CP); tried at Wells; hanged at Norton St Philip (JR, JW).

KEEPING, John, presented at Wells; 'left in custody as a witness for the King' (JR).

KEEPING, Philip, tried at Wells; transported for Stapleton (JR) in the *Indeavour* from Bristol Oct. 20, to Nevis or St Kitts (SL).

KELFORD, Nicholas, tried at Wells; transported for Howard (JR), Oct. 25 on the *Port Royal Merchant* to Jamaica (SL).

KELLAWAY, Joseph, of Clifton (Maybank), 'supposed in the rebels' army' (CP); tried at Taunton; hanged at Somerton (JR, JW). At Dorchester in March 1686 Anna Strode presented for entertaining Joseph Kelway, a rebel convicted, knowing him so to be; and was found not guilty (GD).

KEMPE, Edward, tried at Wells; transported for Howard (JR), Oct. 25 on the *Port Royal Merchant* to Jamaica (SL).

KEMPLYN (Scramplyn, SL), John, tried at Exeter; transported for Nipho (JR) on the *Betty* from Weymouth, Nov. 25, to Barbados; sold to Hester Foster (SL).

KEMPSON, James, of Ilminster, 'in the late rebellion' (CP).

KENT, Edward, aged 19, of Nailsbourne (CL), Kingston St Mary, 'absent' (CP); tried at Taunton; transported thence for the Queen (JR) on the *Jamaica Merchant* to Barbados; 'shipt' Dec. 9; sold to William Allamby (SL).

KENT, Peter, sergemaker, of Ottery St Mary, in the High Gaol, Devon (DLD); tried at Dorchester; transported for Nipho (JR) on the *Betty* from Weymouth, Nov. 25, to Barbados; sold to Thomas Prothers (SL). Named on the 1689 petition (CSPD, W&M, I. 43).

KERLE *see* Keel.

KERLE, Richard, of Othery, 'absent' (CP); in prison at Bridgwater, tried at Taunton; to be transported for Booth (JR), but not on SL.

KERRIDGE, John, mariner, of Lyme Regis, 'absent, supposed' (CP); excepted from GP. He was seized by Capt. Tily to be pilot to Bristol, but was taken to Spain and imprisoned there for 11 months; on his return to England he was imprisoned in the Marshalsea; petitioned the king for pardon and release; granted, Aug. 8 1686 (CSPD, J2, II, 876).

KERSWELL, Robert, of Trull, 'absent' (CP).

KEWER, Robert, of North Curry, 'absent' (CP); 'in the late rebellion'; killed at Norton St Philip (CL).

KEY (Kay), Alexander, clothier, of Ilminster, an erstwhile Quaker disowned by the Quakers for excessive drinking and 'playing at cards' (Som. Record Soc. 75, pp. 37, 169); tried at Wells for levying war; hanged at Wrington (JR, JW).

KEY, John, tried at Wells; transported thence for Bridgeman (JR) by White, Oct. 31, on the *Constant Richard* to Jamaica (SL).

KEY, Samuel, clothier, of Ilminster, went to Forde Abbey seeking arms (Dep); 'in the late rebellion' (CP); escaped to London; excepted from GP; Feb. 17 warrant to search for and arrest; offered free pardon if he would swear against Edmund Prideaux; refused (*House of Commons Journal*); pardon, July 4 1686 (CSPD, J2, II, 153, 768).

KEY, William, tried at Wells; transported for Stapleton (JR) in the *Indeavour* from Bristol Oct. 20, to Nevis or St Kitts (SL).

KIDD, John, gamekeeper at Longleat; NCO in militia; was in Holland buying horses; joined Monmouth who, later, knighted him; a Captain; imprisoned in Wilts. for 'marching in Monmouth's army till they were engaged' (Wilts. QSR); taken to Newgate and interrogated on Aug. 16 (L); tried at Dorchester Sept. 10; hanged at Lyme Regis Sept. 12 (JR, NL).

KIMBER, Daniel, of Othery, 'absent' (CP).

KING, Abraham, presented at Wells and bound over (JR).

KING, Jacob, tried at Taunton; transported for Musgrave (JR) on the *Jamaica Merchant* from Weymouth to Barbados; there by March 12 (SL).

KING, John, of Durleigh, 'absent, and not taken' (CP).

KING, John, of Kingsbury Episcopi, 'absent, believed' (CP).

KING, Richard, aged 18, plowman [carter] (SL), tried at Taunton; transported thence for the Queen (JR) to Barbados on the *Jamaica Merchant*; sold to John Bawden, Esq. (SL). 'Boatman'; friend of Enoch Gold; will 1717 (Barbados records).

KING, Stephen, glover, of Frome, 'in the rebellion and at large' (CP).

KING, Thomas, of Glastonbury, 'absent' (CP).

KINGMAN, Henry, clothier, of Frome, 'in the rebellion and at large' (CP).

KINGSTONE, Bartholomew, of Chardland, 'absent, believed' (CP).

KINGSTONE, Isaac, tried at Taunton; transported for Musgrave (JR) on the *Jamaica Merchant* from Weymouth to Barbados; there by Mar. 12 (SL).

KINGSTONE, John, bricklayer, of Taunton St Mary, 'aiding' (CP); Blue Regt. (P).

KIRKHAM, Richard senior, of Stogursey, 'for absenting himself from his parish church and for being very much concerned with the Duke of Monmouth and his men' (Som. QSR).

KITCH, *see* Rock.

KNIGHT, Christopher, cordwainer, of Honiton, 'a rebel' (CP), imprisoned in the High Gaol, Devon (DLD); tried at Taunton; transported for the Queen (JR); on John Rose's receipt, Oct. 12 (SL).

KNIGHT, Edward, of Honiton, 'a rebel' (CP).

KNIGHT, George junior, of South Petherton, 'in the rebellion and not come in' (CP); tried at Wells; hanged at Pensford (JR, JW).

KNIGHT, Henry, of Chardstock, 'suspected guilty' tried at Exeter; hanged at Honiton, Oct. 7 (JR, JW, NL). Land forfeit and for sale (TB).

KNIGHT, Henry, of Trull, 'absent' (CP).

KNIGHT, John, of Chardland, 'absent, believed' (CP). [*See below.*]

KNIGHT, John, of South Petherton, 'in the rebellion and not come in' (CP). [*See below.*]

KNIGHT, John, of Taunton St. James, 'aiding' (CP); Blue Regt. (P). [*See below.*] Of these three, two were tried at Taunton; one was hanged at Chard; the other transported for the Queen (JR) and on John Rose's receipt, Oct. 12 (SL).

KNIGHT, Roger, yeoman, of Somerset, pardon May 12, 1686 (CSPD, J2, II, 530).

KNIGHT, Samuel, tried at Wells; transported for Stapleton (JR) in the *Indeavour* from Bristol Oct. 20, to Nevis or St Kitts (SL).

KNIGHT, William, sergeweaver, of Ottery St Mary, imprisoned in the High Gaol, Devon (DLD); presented at Dorchester, certificate allowed (JR).

KNIGHT, William, of Stockland, 'suspected' (CP).

KNOTT, Ben, of Bishop's Hull, 'in prison' (CL).

KNOWLES, John, aged 39 (PR), yeoman, of Colyton, 'absent' (CP); tried at Exeter; hanged at Honiton (JR) on Oct. 7 (NL). Misreported at large (JR).

KNOWLES, Percival, yeoman, of Colyton, imprisoned at Taunton (DLD); presented at Exeter, reported at large (JR).

LACEY, Amos, presented at Dorchester for levying war, pleaded guilty (GD), but 'humbly proposed for pardon' (JR).

LACEY, Joseph, tried at Taunton; transported for Musgrave (JR) on the *Jamaica Merchant* from Weymouth to Barbados; there by March 12 (SL).

LACEY, Philip, tried at Wells; transported for Howard (JR), Oct. 25 on the *Port Royal Merchant* to Jamaica (SL).

LACEY, William, tried at Wells; transported for Howard (JR), Oct. 25, on the *Port Royal Merchant* to Jamaica (SL).

LACKE, John, of Stowell, 'absent' (CP. Name deleted).

LACKYS *see* Lucas.

LADER, William, of Wedmore, 'absent and in the late rebellion' (CP).

LAKE, John, of Milverton, 'absenting' (CP).

LAKE, Michael, of Whitelackington, yeoman, pardoned July 4 1686 (CSPD, J2, II, 768).

LAMBERT, Humphrey, yeoman, of Combe Raleigh, 'in the late rebellion and not yet taken' (CP); presented at Exeter but at large (JR).

LAMBERT, John junior, of Luppitt, 'out in the rebellion' (CP).

LAMBERT *see* Lumbard.

LANCASTER, William, of Allington, 'suspected' (CP); tried at Dorchester; hanged at Weymouth or Melcombe Regis, Sept. 15 (JR, NL).

LANCKTON *see* Larkham.

LANE, Benjamin, of Creech St Michael, 'absent and not taken' (CP).

LANE, Daniel, of Curry Rivel, 'out in the rebellion and not taken' (CP).

LANE, Edward, presented at Dorchester for levying war, pleaded guilty (GD), but 'humbly proposed for pardon' (JR).

LANE, Henry, presented at Exeter, March 1686, for High Treason; pardoned and dismissed (GD).

LANE, John, of Sidmouth, 'went to Monmouth' (CP).

LANE, John, of Stockland, 'suspected' (CP).

LANE, John, worsted comber, of Taunton St Mary, 'aiding' (CP); Blue Regt. (P).

LANE, Matthew, presented at Exeter, March 1686, for High Treason; pardoned and dismissed (GD).

LANE, Thomas, of Axminster, Ruling Elder of the Congregational Church, marched as far as Norton St Philip, and returned safely (Ecc).

LANE, Walter, of East Brent, 'absent' (CP).

LANE, William, tried at Wells; transported for Howard (JR) Oct. 25 to Jamaica (SL).

LANG, Richard, tried at Taunton; transported for Musgrave (JR) on the *Jamaica Merchant* from Weymouth to Barbados; there by March 12 (SL).

LANGBRIDGE, Francis, tried at Dorchester; transported for Booth (JR) on the *Happy Return* from Weymouth, Sept. 25, to Barbados; sold to Hester Foster (SL).

LANGFORD (Longford), John, tried at Wells; transported for Stapleton (JR) in the *Indeavour* from Bristol Oct. 20, to Nevis or St Kitts (SL).

LANGWILL, Daniel, of Bathealton, 'absenting' (CP).

LANGWILL, David, tried at Taunton; hanged at Ilchester (JR, JW).

LARKE, Sampson, Baptist minister (L), gentleman (DLD), of Combe Raleigh, 'in the rebellion and not yet taken, (CP); captured and sent to the Gatehouse, Westminster, July 16 (CSPD, J2, I, 1250); interrogated (L); tried at Dorchester, Sept. 10; hanged at Lyme Regis, Sept. 12 (JR, NL). Last letter and prayer in BA. Land forfeit and for sale (TB). Also presented at Exeter and misreported at large (JR).

LARKHAM (Lanckton), John, tried at Wells; transported for Stapleton (JR), Oct. 20, on the *Indeavour* from Bristol to Nevis or St Kitts (SL).

LARKUM, Elias, of Bath Forum, 'in Monmouth's army and not yet taken' (CP).

LASHLEY, William, tried at Taunton; hanged at Crewkerne (JR, JW).

LATCHAM, Richard, of Wedmore, 'absent and in the late rebellion' (CP).

LATHIE, Nicholas, of Monkton Wyld, 'suspected' (CP).

LAWRENCE, Henry, at Taunton Assize convicted of High Treason; to be hanged at Keynsham, but was reprieved (JR, JW). Land forfeit but not for sale: reversion to Brent, Loder and Clarke. Pardon money to be kept by David Trim (TB).

LAWRENCE, John, of Cheddon Fitzpaine, 'absent' (CP). [*See below.*]

LAWRENCE, John, of Merriott, 'rebel and not taken (CP). [*See below.*]

LAWRENCE, John. [*See below.*] One of these 3 was tried at Dorchester on Sept. 10 and hanged at Sherborne on Sept. 15 (JR, NL). Another, tried at Wells, was transported for Stapleton (JR) in the *Indeavour* from Bristol Oct. 20, to Nevis or St Kitts (SL). The third was tried at Wells and transported for Howard (JR), Oct. 25, to Jamaica (SL).

LAWRENCE, Samuel, tried at Dorchester; transported for Booth (JR) on the *Happy Return* from Weymouth, Sept. 25, to Barbados; sold to Col. Richard Williams (SL).

LAWRENCE alias Turke, Thomas, of Merriott, 'rebel and not taken' (CP). [*See below.*]

LAWRENCE, Thomas, of West Chinnock, 'in the late rebellion' (CP). [*See below.*] One of these two was tried at Wells and transported for Howard (JR), Oct. 25 on the *Port Royal Merchant* to Jamaica (SL).

LAWRENCE, Thomas, bailiff of a farm near Lyme Regis, from which three horses were commandeered for Monmouth (BA); presented at Dorchester; 'remaining in custody' (JR); threatened with hanging at Wareham; paid Loder £400 (BA); pardoned. Land forfeit but not for sale: reversion to Brent, Loder and Clarke. Money received by Loder 'under colour of obtaining the king's pardon' to be kept by Loder (TB).

LAVER, John, in Ilchester gaol; tried at Wells; transported for Howard (JR), Oct. 25, to Jamaica (SL).

LAVER, Thomas, tried at Wells; transported for Howard (JR), Oct. 25 on the *Port Royal Merchant* to Jamaica (SL).

LAVER, Samuel, of South Petherton, 'in the rebellion and not come in' (CP).

LAWRING, Aaron, of Chardland, 'absent, believed' (CP).

LAYTON, Thomas senior, yeoman, of Colyton, 'absent' (CP), presented at Exeter but at large (JR).

LEA, Oades, of Thornfalcon (CL), Stoke St Gregory, 'in arms, aiding and assisting James Scott in the time of the rebellion' (CP); 'dead' (CL).

LEA, Peter senior, of North Curry, 'wanting from his home and in the late Duke of Monmouth's service. Killed' (CL).

LEA, Samuel, of Stoke St Gregory, 'in arms' (CP), wounded (CL) at Sedgemoor.

LEA, Thomas, of Martock, 'absent' (CP).

LEACOTT, Richard, of Ottery St Mary, 'in the rebellion as supposed' (CP).

LEAKER, John junior, of Huntspill, 'active soldier in Monmouth's army' (CL); in Bridgwater prison; tried at Taunton; transported for Booth (JR) on the *John* from Bristol, Oct. 24, to Barbados; sold to Capt. W. Scott (SL).

LEAKEY, John, of Stoke St Gregory, 'absent' (CP).

LEAKEY, Richard junior, of Curload, Thornfalcon, (CL), Stoke St Gregory, 'in arms in the rebelli'n' (CP); 'no tenant; fled' (CL).

LEAKEY, Robert, of Stoke St Gregory, 'in arms in the rebellion' (CP); 'no tenant; fled' (CL).

LEAKEY, Thomas junior, of Stoke St Gregory, 'absent' (CP).

LEAKEY, William, of Taunton St Mary, 'aiding' (CP); Blue Regt. (P).

LEANE, Richard, of Stawell, 'out in the rebellion and at large' (CP).

LEASE alias Gamling, John, in Ilchester gaol; tried at Wells; transported for Howard (JR), Oct. 25 on the *Port Royal Merchant* to Jamaica (SL).

LEATHERMORE *see* Levermore

LEE, John, yeoman, of Buckerell, tried at Dorchester, Sept. 10; hanged at Bridport, Sept. 12 (JR, NL).

LEE, ?Aghn, of Bishop's Hull, 'absent, not taken' (CL).

LEE, Nicholas, of Honiton, 'a rebel, not taken,' (CP). [*See also* Leigh.]

LEETE (Sente), Robert, of Ilminster, 'in the late rebellion' (CP); tried at Taunton; transported for Booth (JR) from Taunton Bridewell via Bristol, Oct. 24, on the *John* to Barbados; sold to Henry Quintyne, Esq. (SL).

LEGG, George, of Sidmouth, 'went to Monmouth' (CP).

LEGG, George, of Wrington, captured, escaped; excepted from GP. At Exeter Assizes Daniel Gammon and John Brewer were presented for wilfully suffering George Legg to escape; they pleaded not guilty and were acquitted (GD), but Brewer was presented at Wells and bound over (JR).

LEGG, John, roper, of Axminster, Cornet of Horse, killed in skirmish at Ashill, June 19 (W).

LEGG, John, of Taunton St Mary, 'aiding' (CP); Blue Regt. (P).

LEGG, Mark, of Bishop's Hull, 'absent, not taken' (CL).

LEGGATT, Edward, tried at Dorchester; hanged at Weymouth or Melcombe Regis (JR, NL).

LEGGATT, John, tried at Dorchester; hanged at Sherborne (JR, NL).

LEIGH, William, aged 20 plowman [carter] (SL), tried at Taunton; transported for the Queen (JR) from Taunton on the *Jamaica Merchant* towards Barbados; died at sea, Dec. 9; 'thrown overboard' (SL).

LENNINGTON, Peter, of Hardington Mandeville, 'in the late rebellion' (CP).

LENNINGTON, Stephen, of Hardington Mandeville, 'in the late rebel·lion' (CP).

LEONARD, Anthony, of Paul, Cornwall, accused of high treason; warrant 'to arrest and bring to Lord Middleton', May 9, 1686 (CSPD, JR, II, 524).

LESTER *see* Pester

LEVERMORE (Leathermore), Philip, tanner, of Honiton (TB); imprisoned in Dorset (DLD); tried at Dorchester, Sept. 5; hanged there, Sept. 7 (JR, NL); land forfeit and for sale (TB).

LEVERSEDGE (Loversedge), Alleyn, of Rodden, 'in the rebellion and not taken' (CP); presented at Taunton for levying war and pleaded guilty (GD); 'designed to be executed but omitted from the warrant;' subsequently transported (JR2) probably by Heywood or White on the *Constant Richard* to Jamaica.

LEWIS, John, senior, of Axbridge (Axbridge Convocation Bk); disfranchised for 'bearing arms' Aug. 3 (Axbridge Convocation Bk.); tried at Wells; transported for Stapleton (JR) in the *Indeavour* from Bristol Oct. 20, to Nevis or St Kitts (SL).

LEWIS, John, of Babcary, 'absent and not returned' (CP); excepted from GP.

LEWIS, Thomas, of Babcary, 'absent and not returned' (CP); excepted from GP.

LEWIS, William, of Beercrocombe, 'out in the rebellion' (CP).

LEY, George, tried at Taunton; transported for Musgrave (JR) on the *Jamaica Merchant* from Weymouth to Barbados; there by March 12 (SL).

LEY, John, of Kingsbury Episcopi, 'absent, believed' (CP).

LEY, Marmaduke, weaver, of Taunton St Mary, 'aiding' (CP); Blue Regt. (P).

LEY, Peter, of West Buckland, 'absent' (CP).

LEY, Samuel, of Kingsbury Episcopi, 'absent, believed' (CP).

LIBBETT, Giles, imprisoned in the Workhouse, Exeter, presented there, March 1686, pardoned and dismissed (GD).

LIDDEN, John, of Axmouth, blacksmith, 'seen in Monmouth's camp' (LRMB); presented at Exeter, but at large (JR).
*And see* Lyddon.

LIGGENS, William, of Forde, excepted from GP.

LILLEY, Henry, cobbler, of Taunton St Mary, 'aiding' (CP); Blue Regt. (P).

LILLINGTON, ——, came from Holland with Monmouth; Lieut. in the Red Regt. commanded north flank guard at Bridport (W); killed at Sedgemoor (P).

LIMBERRY, John, yeoman, of Axmouth, 'reported in arms in the late rebellion' (CP); presented at Exeter but at large (JR).

LIMBERRY, Joseph, yeoman, of Axmouth, presented at Exeter but at large (JR).

LIMBERRY, William, yeoman, of Axmouth, 'reported in arms in the late rebellion' (CP); presented at Exeter but at large (JR).

LIMBERRY, William, glazier, of Lyme Regis, 'absent, supposed' (CP).

LINCOCK, Thomas, of South Petherton, 'in the rebellion and not come in' (CP).

LINCOLNE, Richard, miller, of Axminster, 'supposed' (CP); 'seen in Monmouth's camp' (LRMB); presented at Exeter but at large (JR).

LINDSEY, John, pedler, pardoned, Oct. 2, 1686 (CSPD, J2, II, 1035).

LINN (Lyne), Richard, clothworker, of Rode, 'in the rebellion' (CP); tried at Wells; transported for Howard (JR), Oct. 25 on the *Port Royal Merchant* to Jamaica (SL).

LISCOMBE (Riscombe, Ruscombe), William, of Wellington, 'in prison for rebellion' (CP); presented at Taunton; hanged as Ruscombe at Wiveliscombe (JR, JW).

[LISLE, Dame Alice, of Moyles Court, Hants, presented at Winchester for 'Treason in receiving, ayding, assisting and comforting Johem Hicks, being a rebel against the King'. Sentence: drawn to the gallows and burnt at the stake; commuted to beheading. Lands not for sale (GD, TB).]

LISLE, Henry, taken from Exeter to London, July 16 (CSPD, J2, I, 1236); tried at Taunton, Sept. 18; hanged there, Sept. 30; buried at St Mary's, Oct. 1 (JR, JW, PR).

LISSANT, George, fuller, of Taunton St James, 'aiding' (CP); Blue Regt. (P).

LISSANT, Thomas, tried at Taunton; hanged at Somerton (JR, JW).

LISSANT, William, weaver, of Taunton St James, 'aiding' (CP); Blue Regt. (P).
*And see* Nash.

LITTLE, John, of Burcott, Wells, 'supposed' (CP).

LITTLE, John, his son, of Cuthbert's, Wells, 'supposed' (CP).

LITTLEJOHN, John, aged 30, of Taunton St Mary, 'aiding' (CP); Blue Regt. (P).

LLOYD (Lyde), Edward, of Ilchester, 'in the late rebellion' (CP), tried at Taunton, transported for Booth (JR); 'rebel prisoner', transported to York River, Virginia, on the *Exchange* of Topsham (CSPC, xii. 442, SL).

LLOYD, John, of Taunton St James, 'aiding' (CP); Cornet in Capt. Jones's Troop of Horse (L 240); tried at Taunton; hanged at Dulverton, Dec. 8 (JR, JW, NL).

LOBB, Stephen, clerk, excepted from GP, but pardoned Dec. 23, 1686 (CSPD, J2, II, 1267).

LOCK, Antony, presented at Exeter, March 1686, pardoned and dismissed (GD).

LOCK, Arthur, of Wellington, 'absent' (CP).

LOCK, Christopher, butcher, of Taunton St Mary, 'aiding' (CP); Blue Regt. (P).

LOCK, John, taken at Lyme Regis and sent to Dorchester gaol (LRMB); tried there for levying war, pleaded not guilty, found guilty (GD); 'intended for execution but omitted from warrant' (BA); transported for Musgrave (JR) on the *Jamaica Merchant* from Weymouth to Barbados; there by March 12 (SL).

LOCK, John, of Extraportam tithing, Taunton, 'absent' (CL); tried at Wells; transported for Stapleton (JR) in the *Indeavour* from Bristol Oct. 20, to Nevis or St Kitts (SL). Lo says that John died in gaol before the rest were sent off.

LOCK, Joshua senior, got to Holland, making English cloth; pardoned May 16, 1686 (CSPD, J2, II, 546).

LOCK, Joshua junior, excepted from GP; reached Holland, making English cloth; pardoned, May 16, 1686 (CSPD, J2, II, 546).

LOCK, Nicholas, merchant of Great St Bartholomew's, London; gone to Norway with Manley (L 227). Warrant to arrest him and his son Nicholas, merchant, July 16 1685 (CSPD, J2, I, 1246; J2, II, 545).

LOCK, Richard, of Wellington, 'absent' (CP).

LOCK, Robert, of Ruishton 'absent' (CP, CL).

LOCK, William, brother of John, of Taunton above, arrested for visiting John in Westonzoyland Church (Lo); tried at Wells; transported for Stapleton (JR) in the *Indeavour* from Bristol to Nevis or St Kitts

(SL). Lo says he was pardoned at the request of Sir William Portman and brought up a large family in or near Taunton, one of whom was alive when he wrote.

LOCKBEARE (Loquier), Elias, aged 18, tanner (SL), of Milverton, 'absenting' (CP); tried at Taunton; transported for the Queen (JR) from Taunton on the *Jamaica Merchant*, Dec. 9, to Barbados. No note of sale (SL).

LOCKETT, John, late of Dorchester, 'absenting . . . and actually in the rebellion' (CP).

LOCKSTON, John, of Wilton, 'absent' (CP); tried at Taunton; hanged at Stogumber (JR, JW).

LOCKYER, John, of Stoke St Gregory, 'absenting' (CP).

LOCKYER, Nathaniel, presented at Wells and bound over (JR).

LOCKYER, Thomas, of Ilchester, 'in the late rebellion' (CP); presented at Wells and bound over (JR).

LOCKYER, Thomas, husbandman (TB), of Thornfalcon (Som. QSR), of Stoke St Gregory, 'in arms . . . in the rebellion' (CP); tried at Wells; transported thence for Bridgeman (JR) by White, Oct. 31, on the *Constant Richard* to Jamaica (SL). Land forfeit and for sale (TB).

LODER, John, of Northcote, Honiton, 'a rebel' (CP).

LODGE, James, yeoman, of Colyton, 'absent', (CP); presented at Exeter but at large (JR).

LODING, William, of Curry Mallet, 'in the late rebellion and at large' (CP).

LOMBARD, ——, of Cudworth, 'drew in' John Marders of Crewkerne (L). *And see* Lumbard

LONE *see* Love

LONG, Bernard, yeoman, of Membury, 'wanting' (CP); presented at Exeter but at large (JR).

LONG, John, of Alstone, Huntspill, 'in arms in the late rebellion' (CP). [*See below.*]

LONG, John, yeoman, of Axminster, 'supposed' (CP); presented at Exeter and reported or misreported at large (JR). [*See below.*] One of these two or another John was tried at Dorchester and transported for Booth (JR) on the *Happy Return* from Weymouth, Sept. 25, to Barbados; sold to Col. Richard Williams (SL).

LONG, Joseph, of Fivehead, 'out in the rebellion and not taken' (CP).

LONG, Matthew, presented at Dorchester, March 1686; pardoned by the king's Proclamation (GD).

LONG alias Baker, of Shaftesbury, inn-keeper, a Captain under the Duke in the Western Rebellion; at Sedgemoor, escaped to London, apprehended there on 19 Oct. and put in Newgate for high treason; hanged himself there on the 20th (Br, licensed by R.L.S. 22 Oct.)

LONG, Simon, of Stanton St Gabriel, 'suspected' (CP), at Wells Assizes left in custody as a witness for the king (JR).

LONG, Thomas, of Trull, 'absent' (CP), 'a rebel' (CL); in Exeter Workhouse and presented at Assizes, March 1686; pardoned and dismissed (GD).

LONG, William, yeoman, of Membury, 'wanting' (CP); presented at Exeter but at large (JR).

LOQUIER, John, of Milverton, 'absenting' (CP).
*And see* Lockbeare.

LORCOMB, Stephen, of Chardstock, 'suspected' (CP).

LORING, David, yeoman, of Combpyne, 'with Monmouth in the late rebellion' (CP); presented at Exeter but at large (JR).

LORING, William, yeoman, of Membury, 'wanting; killed' (CP); presented at Exeter and misreported at large (JR).

LOTT, David, of Combwich, 'for taking up arms against the king' (Som. QSR).

LOTT, Lawrence, tried at Wells; hanged at Frome (JR, JW).

LOTT, Richard, upholsterer, of Taunton St. Mary, 'aiding' (CP); Blue Regt. (P).

LOTT, Thomas, tried at Wells; hanged at Frome (JR, JW).

LOVE, John, yeoman, of Axminster, 'supposed' (CP); presented at Exeter but at large (JR).

LOVE alias Alexander, Thomas, of London, excepted from GP.

LOVEDALE, Thomas, of Taunton St Mary, 'aiding' (CP); Blue Regt. (P).

LOVELACE, John senior, of Pilsdon, 'suspected' (CP).

LOVELACE, John junior, of Pilsdon, 'suspected' (CP).

LOVERIDGE, Bernard, of Axminster, 'supposed' (CP); presented at Exeter but at large (JR).

LOVERIDGE, Bernard, yeoman, of Musbury, 'in the rebellion' (CP), presented at Exeter but at large (JR); pardoned May 12 1686 (CSPD, J2, II, 532).

LOVERIDGE, Bernard, aged 22, soapboiler (SL), chandler, of Uplyme, imprisoned at Taunton (DLD); tried there and transported for the Queen (JR) on the *Jamaica Merchant*, Dec. 9, to Barbados; sold to Capt. Thomas Morris (SL). Land forfeit and for sale (TB).

LOVERIDGE, Edward, of Wootton Fitzpaine, 'suspected' (CP).

LOVERIDGE, John, of Wootton Fitzpaine, 'suspected' (CP); tried at Dorchester; transported for Booth (JR) on the *Happy Return*, Sept. 25, from Weymouth to Barbados; sold to William Weaver (SL).

LOVERIDGE, Samuel, yeoman, of Musbury, 'in the rebellion' (CP); presented at Exeter (as of Axminster) but at large (JR).

LOVERIDGE, Thomas, yeoman, of Musbury, 'in the rebellion' (CP); presented at Dorchester and discharged for want of evidence (JR). Subsequently presented at Exeter and reported at large (JR).

LOVERIDGE, William, yeoman, of Musbury, 'in the rebellion' (CP); imprisoned at Ilchester (DLD); tried at Dorchester; to be transported for Booth (JR); not on SL. Also presented at Exeter and reported at large (JR).

LOVERSEDGE *see* Leversedge.

LOW, Roger, of Bishop's Hull, 'absent, not taken' (CL).

LOWDON, Arthur, presented at Wells and bound over (JR).

LOWMAN, Bernard, of Colyton, 'supposed' (CP); tried at Dorchester; transported for Nipho (JR) on the *Rebecca* to Barbados (SL).

LOWMAN, George, yeoman, of Luppitt, 'out in the rebellion' (CP); presented at Exeter but at large (JR).

LOWMAN, Philip, of Honiton, 'a rebel' (CP).

LOYD *see* Lyde.

LUCAS, Charles, imprisoned in Taunton Bridewell (SL); tried at Taunton; to be transported for Booth (JR). On Booth's receipt but not on SL, nor marked 'died at sea'.

LUCAS, John, of Stockland, 'suspected' (CP).

LUCAS, Richard, of Dulverton, 'engaged in the late rebellion', excepted from GP, but pardoned May 31 1687 (CSPD, J2, II, 1833).

LUCAS (Lackys), Robert, of Colyton, 'supposed' (CP).

LUCAS (Luckis), Robert, carpenter, of Seaton, imprisoned in the Devon Workhouse (DLD); tried at Taunton; hanged at Ilminster (JR, JW); land forfeit and for sale (TB).

LUCE, Edward, hellier, of Lyme Regis, 'absent, supposed' (CP).

LUCKES, Robert, of Bishop's Hull, 'absent, not taken' (CL).

LUCKWILL (Hickwell), Henry, carpenter, of Dunster, 'in arms' (CP); tried at Taunton; hanged at Dunster (JR, JW).

LUD, Michael, 'out in the rebellion' (CP).

LUGG (Higg), Edward or Edmund, of Wellington, 'in prison for rebellion' (CP); tried at Taunton; transported for Musgrave (JR) on the *Jamaica Merchant* from Weymouth to Barbados; there by March 12 (SL).

LUGG, John, husbandman, of Trent, 'in the late rebellion and at large' (CP).

LUGG, William, husbandman, of Trent, 'in the late rebellion and at large' (CP).

LUGG, William, of Aller, 'in the rebellion and not come home' (CP).

LUKER, Henry, of Huish Episcopi, 'absent, believed' (CP).

LUKER (Luckis), Robert, carpenter, of Seaton, imprisoned in the Devon Workhouse (DLD); tried at Taunton; hanged at Ilminster (JR, JW); land forfeit and for sale (TB).

LUMBARD, George, of Chard, 'in the late rebellion' (CP); presented at Taunton: certificate allowed (JR).

LUMBARD, John, of Chaffcombe, 'in the rebellion and not come in' (CP).

LUMBARD, John, of Cudworth, 'in the rebellion and not come in' (CP).

LUMBARD, Joseph, of Chard, 'absent, believed' (CP).

LUMBARD, Richard junior, of Chard, 'absent believed' (CP).

LUMBARD (Lambert), Robert, tried at Dorchester; transported for Booth (JR) on the *Happy Return* from Weymouth, Sept. 25, to Barbados; sold to Richard Adamson (SL).

LUMBARD, Thomas, presented at Taunton; certificate allowed (JR). *And see* Lombard.

LUMDAR, John, tanner, of Taunton St Mary, 'aiding' (CP); Blue Regt. (P).

LUNDON, Richard junior, of Milverton, 'absenting' (CP).

LUPPINCOTT, Thomas, of Sidbury, 'joined in the rebellion' (CP).

LUSH, Arthur, of Bridport, 'in the rebellion, as informed' (CP), tried at Dorchester; transported for Booth (JR) on the *Happy Return* from

Weymouth, Sept. 25, to Barbados; sold in Dec. to Col. Richard Williams (SL).

LUSH, John, tried at Wells; transported for Howard (JR), Oct. 25 on the *Port Royal Merchant* to Jamaica (SL).

LUSH, William, of Bridport, 'in the rebellion as informed' (CP); tried at Dorchester; transported for Musgrave (JR) on the *Jamaica Merchant* from Weymouth to Barbados; there by March 12 (SL).

LUSH, William, presented at Wells and bound over (JR).

LUTHER, Edward, of Bridport, 'in the rebellion as informed' (CP); tried at Dorchester; transported for Booth (JR) on the *Happy Return* from Weymouth, Sept. 25, to Barbados; sold in Dec. to Col. John Sampson (SL).

LUTLEY, David, of Hillfarrance, 'taking up arms against his Majesty' (Som. QSR).

LUTLEY, Dionisius, in the Workhouse at Exeter; presented there in March 1686: pardoned and dismissed (GD).

LUTTLEY, Bernard, of Pitminster, 'absent' (CP).

LYDDON, Gabriel, of North Curry, 'taking up arms against the king' (Som. QSR).

LYDDON, John, yeoman, of Axminster, 'supposed' (CP); presented at Exeter but at large (JR).

LYDDON, John, of Axmouth, yeoman, 'reported in arms' (CP); presented at Exeter but at large (JR).
*And see* Lidden.

LYDE, Edward, of Sidmouth, 'went to Monmouth'; tried at Taunton; transported for Booth (JR) from Taunton Bridewell. On Booth's receipt, but not on SL.

LYDE, John, presented at Wells and bound over (JR).

LYDE (Loyd), Silvester, aged 27, butcher (SL); tried at Taunton; transported for the Queen (JR) from Taunton to Barbados on the *Jamaica Merchant*, Dec. 9; sold to Francis Young, Mar. 12 (SL).
*And see* Lloyd.

LYE, George, of Wedmore, 'absent and in the rebellion' (CP).

LYE, William, of Wedmore, 'absent and in the rebellion' (CP).

LYNE *see* Linn.

LYNEING, William, tried at Wells; to be transported for Howard (JR), Oct. 25, but escaped between Wells and Sherborne (SL).

MABER, Joseph, worsted comber, of Taunton St James, 'aiding' (CP); Blue Regt. (P).

MACEY, George, aged 30 (PR), yeoman, of Colyton, imprisoned in Dorset (DLD); tried at Dorchester; transported for Booth (JR) on the *Happy Return* from Weymouth, Sept. 25, to Barbados; sold to Capt. Walter Scott (SL). Named on the 1689 petition (CSPD), W&M, I, 43).

MACEY, John, of West Monkton, 'out in the rebellion and at large' (CP).

MACEY, Thomas, shoemaker, of Taunton St Mary, 'aiding' (CP); Blue Regt. (P).

MACHELL (Mitchell), Robert, yeoman, of Thorncombe, 'wanting' (CP); tried at Dorchester, Sept. 10; hanged at Lyme, Sept. 12 (JR, NL). Also presented at Exeter and reported at large (JR).

MADDERS *see* Marders.

MADER, William, carpenter, of Colyford, imprisoned in the High Gaol, Devon (DLD).

MAFFY, George, James, and John. All three presented at Exeter in March 1686 for high treason; all three pardoned and dismissed, (GD).

MALE, Tristram, presented at Wells and bound over (JR).

MALER, John, of Dorchester, 'absenting . . . and actually in the rebellion' (CP).

MALLACK, Malachi, clothier, of Axminster, 'supposed' (CP); 'seen in Monmouth's camp' (LRMB); was with Thomas Dare at Forde Abbey; tried at Dorchester, Sept. 10 (JR); was to be hanged at Bridport on Sept. 12 (Br) but turned King's Evidence against Edmund Prideaux, respited (CSPD, J2, I, 1629); taken out of Penne's custody 'for a witness' (SL). Interrogated (L). Pardon under Great Seal Oct. 15 1685 (BA. Also *House of Commons Journal* May 1 1689 and Dec. 26 1690). Land forfeit and for sale (TB).

[MALLET, Stephen, listed with those hanged at Shepton Mallet in Thomas Salmon's *Proceedings and Trials against State Prisoners*, 1741; and in Locke, 1782. None of the original documents mentions him. Probably a mistake of a copying clerk.]

MAN, Robert, tried at Wells; hanged at Frome (JR, JW).

MANDER, Robert, of Ashill, 'out in the rebellion' (CP).

MANDWORTH, Luser (?Lewis), of Durston, North Petherton, 'in arms against his Majesty' (Som. QSR).

MANGELL, William, Col. Matthews' servant, presented at Wells, pleaded not guilty, found guilty (GD); hanged there the same day (JR, JW, BA).

MANLEY, John, Major of Horse, came from Holland with Monmouth; in the cavalry skirmish at Bridport; sent from Bridgwater to London to expedite a rising there (W and L); escaped to Holland; interested in the manufacture of English cloth at Groningen (PE). Excepted from GP of 1686 and 1688.

MANLEY, Issac, son of John above, rode down from London; went to London with his father (W). Excepted from both GP.

MANLY, John, of Chardstock, 'suspected guilty' (CP).

MANNING, Anthony, presented at Wells and bound over (JR).

MANNING, Daniel, aged 20 (PR), blacksmith's apprentice at Shoreditch, lived at Stoke St Mary, 'absent' (CP); conscripted by Monmouth's officers; marched with them to Bridgwater where he gave them the slip; enlisted in Col. Kirke's regiment (the Queen Dowager's) and marched with them to Westonzoyland; having no weapons he was not allowed into the battle; marched to Taunton and was there discharged with a certificate of service from Capt. Thomas St John, which twice saved him from arrest. He sought work in

London and was kidnapped on to the *Golden Lyon* to serve John
Peirson in Barbados. There he petitioned the Lieutenant Governor
Edwyn Stede, who sent duplicate papers to the Colonial Office
(PRO, CO1/59/75–6 and CSPC xii, 561).

MANNING, John, in prison in Dorchester; tried there; transported for
Booth (JR) on the *Happy Return* from Weymouth, Sept. 25, to
Barbados; sold to Nicholas Prideaux (SL).

MANNING, Thomas, presented for high treason at Exeter in March
1686; pardoned and dismissed (GD).

MANNING, William, of Cudworth, 'in the rebellion and not come in'
(CP); excepted from GP.

MANSTON *see* Mounstone.

MARCHANT (Merchant), Emanuel, aged 20, plowman [carter] (SL), of
Honiton, imprisoned at Taunton (DLD), tried there; transported
thence for the Queen (JR) on the *Jamaica Merchant*, Dec. 9, to
Barbados; sold on March 12 to Major Abel Allen (SL). Named on
the 1689 petition (CSPD, W&M, I, 43).

MARCHANT, Richard, of Honiton, 'a rebel' (CP).

MARCHANT, William, of Honiton, 'a rebel' (CP), tried at Taunton;
transported thence for the Queen (JR). On John Rose's list, Oct. 12,
but not on SL.

MARDERS, John, constable of Crewkerne, 'drawn in . . . for the
maintenance of the protestant religion' (L); Captain in the Green
Regt. captured and sent to the Gatehouse, Westminster, for interrogation, July 20; named some who sent money or horses; admitted
'he did sometimes go to hear conventicle preachers' (L); tried at
Dorchester, Sept. 10; described as 'a good Protestant', Jeffreys
replying 'You mean Presbyterian' (Lo); hanged at Lyme, Sept. 12
(NL). Last prayer in BA.

MARDERS, John junior, mercer, of Crewkerne, 'rebel in Monmouth's
army and not taken' (CP); tried at Dorchester; transported for Booth
(JR) on the *Happy Return* from Weymouth, Sept. 25, to Barbados;
sold in Dec. to Richard Lintott (SL). Friends obtained a pardon on
July 4 1686, repeated on May 31 1687 (CSPD, J2, II, 768, 1833).
Died (will) Barbados 1705 (Barbados records).

MARKS alias Staple, Gabriel, of North Curry, 'absent' (CP); 'taking up
arms against the king' (Som. QSR).

MARKS, John, tried at Dorchester; to be transported for Booth (JR). One
of 10 not shipped on the *Happy Return* (SL).

MARKS, John, presented at Wells and bound over (JR).

MARKS, Peter, presented for high treason at Exeter in March 1686;
pardoned and dismissed (GD).

MARKS, Thomas, tried at Taunton; transported for Musgrave (JR) from
Weymouth on the *Jamaica Merchant* to Barbados (SL).

MARRY, John, of Catcott, 'out in the rebellion and not taken' (CP).

MARSH, Edward, tried at Dorchester; transported for Nipho (JR) on the
*Betty* from Weymouth, Nov. 25, to Barbados; sold to Thomas
Beresford (SL).

MARSHALL, John, of West Dowlish, 'in the rebellion and at large' (CP).

MARSHALL, Thomas, tried at Dorchester; transported for Booth (JR) on the *Happy Return* from Weymouth, Sept. 25, to Barbados; sold to John Burston (SL).

MARSHALL, William, of Ilminster, 'Monmouth rebel in custody' (Som. QSR).

MARSHMAN, Thomas, wiredrawer, of Frome, 'for a riot and amongst the Clubmen' (CP).

MARTHERS, William, aged 28 (PR), carpenter, of Colyton, tried at Dorchester; transported for Nipho (JR) on the *Betty* from Weymouth, Nov. 25, to Barbados; died after arrival but before sale, Jan. 1686 (SL).

MARTIN, John, of Ruishton, 'absent' (CP); pardon March 26 and April 14 (CSPD, J2, II, 351, 403).

MARTIN, John, of Broadwindsor, 'being out in the horrid rebellion' (CP).

MARTIN, William, of Goathurst, 'in the rebellion and taken (CP); tried at Taunton, 'remaining in gaol' (JR); transported from Wells, Nov. 12, by White on the *Constant Richard* to Jamaica (SL).

MARTIN, William, of Honiton, 'a rebel' (CP); a potter, imprisoned in Devon Workhouse (DLD); tried at Dorchester, Sept. 10; hanged at Poole, Sept. 21 (JR, NL).

MARWOOD, John, yeoman, of Colyton, 'absent' (CP); presented at Exeter but at large (JR). Died in 1710 (PR).

MARWOOD, John, of Tiverton, 'with the late Duke of Monmouth' (CP); tried at Taunton; to be transported for the Queen (JR); on John Rose's receipt of Oct. 12 but not on SL.

MASON, Charles, of Chard, 'absent, believed' (CP); tried at Wells; to be transported for Howard (JR) on Oct. 25, but escaped between Wells and Sherborne (SL).

MASON, Ezekiel, of Cannington, 'taking up arms against the king' (Som. QSR).

MASON, Robert, currier, of Taunton St Mary, 'aiding' (CP); Blue Regt. (P).

MASON, Thomas, of Taunton St Mary, 'aiding' (CP); Blue Regt. (P).

MASTERS, Christopher, of West Hatch, 'in the rebellion and in prison' (CL); tried at Wells; transported for Howard (JR) Oct. 25 on the *Port Royal Merchant* to Jamaica (SL).

MASTERS, John, a customary tenant (CL) of West Hatch, 'in the rebellion and in prison' (CP); tried at Wells; hanged at Ilchester (JR, JW); 'convicted, condemned and executed' (CL).

MASTERS, Richard, of Taunton, 'conscripted by king's men'; wounded in cheek and jaw at Bridport; treated at Ilchester by Dr Winter; joined Monmouth (WB), Blue Regt. (P); captured after Sedgemoor; tried at Taunton; transported for Musgrave (JR) on the *Jamaica Merchant* from Weymouth to Barbados; there by March 12 (SL).

MATTHEWS, Arthur, Captain of Foot (Lo), 'a rebel taken' to Newgate, July 16; (CSPD, J2, I, 1249); tried at Taunton; hanged there Sept. 30 (JR, JW); dying speech in BA.

MATTHEWS, Edward, Esq. of Lincoln's Inn, sometime a Captain in the Guards, rode down from London, Colonel of the Yellow Regt. at Sedgemoor (W); escaped to Holland; excepted from GP of 1686 and 1688; estate forfeited for treason (CSPD, J2, III, 1246); a Lt. Col. in William III's army (CSPD, W&M, I, 95, 144, 159, 406).

MATTHEWS, Nicholas, yeoman, of Axminster, 'supposed' (CP); presented at Exeter but at large (JR).

MATTHEWS, Thomas, of Chideock, in the Bridewell (SL), Taunton; tried there; transported for Booth (JR) via Bristol, Oct. 24, on the *John* to Barbados; sold to John Alchorne (SL).

MAUNDERY, Humphrey, of Combe St Nicholas, 'absent, believed' (CP); tried at Wells; to be transported for Howard (JR), Oct. 25, but escaped between Wells and Sherborne (SL).

MAUNDERY, John, of Combe St Nicholas, 'absent, believed' (CP).

MAXEY (Moxey), Thomas, yeoman, of Colyton, 'absent' (CP); presented at Exeter but at large (JR).

MAXWELL, James, a Scot who joined Monmouth in Holland (family T); tried at Taunton; hanged at Milborne Port (JR, JW).

MAYDER, William, yeoman, of Colyton, 'absent' (CP); presented at Exeter but at large (JR).

MAILARD, William, of Whitelackington, 'concerned in the rebellion and gone out of the country' (SRO, D/D/Ppb).

MAYNARD, James, aged 22, plowman [carter] (SL), of Whatley, 'in the rebellion and not taken' (CP); tried at Taunton; transported thence for the Queen (JR) on the *Jamaica Merchant*, Dec. 9, to Barbados; there by March 12; sold to Nicholas Prideaux (SL).

MAYNARD, Jonathan, sergeweaver, of Taunton St Mary, 'aiding' (CP); Blue Regt. (P).

MAYNARD, Richard, weaver, of Mells, 'supposed' (CP).

MAYS, John, of Extraportam tithing, Taunton, 'absent' (CL).

MAYS, William, of Extraportam tithing, Taunton, 'absent' (CL).

MEACHAM, Roger, of Crewkerne, 'rebel in Monmouth's army and not taken' (CP).

MEADE, Edward, of Curry Rivel, 'out in the rebellion and not taken' (CP).

MEADE, Francis, of Fivehead, 'out in the rebellion and not taken' (CP).

MEADE, George, worsted comber, of Taunton St Mary, 'aiding' (CP); Blue Regt. (P).

MEADE, Henry, comber, of Taunton St Mary, 'aiding' (CP); Blue Regt. (P).

MEADE, John, presented at Taunton; 'remaining in gaol' (JR); transported for Peter Heywood by Thomas Heywood, Nov. 12, on the *Constant Richard* to Jamaica (SL). A Devon man, named on the petition of 1689 (CSPD, W&M, I, 43). [*See below.*]

MEADE, John, tried at Wells; transported for Nipho (JR); on Penne's list, Sept. 26, but from Ilchester gaol Oct. 21 on the *Rebecca* to Barbados (SL). [*See below.*]

MEADE, John, presented at Wells and bound over (JR). [*See below.*] One John Meade was reprieved (JR2), perhaps too late.

MEADE, Matthew, Clerk, Nonconformist minister in Stepney and later in Amsterdam, disapproved of ungodly leaders (PE); pardon of all treasons, March 19, 1687 (CSPD, J2, II, 1599).

MEADE, Robert, tried at Taunton; transported for Musgrave (JR) on the *Jamaica Merchant* from Weymouth to Barbados; there by March 12 (SL).

MEADE, Thomas, aged 22, glover (SL), of Honiton, 'a rebel' (CP); fellmonger, imprisoned in the Devon Workhouse (DLD); tried at Taunton; transported thence for the Queen (JR) on the *Jamaica Merchant*, Dec. 9, to Barbados; there by March 12; sold to Thomas Colleton (SL). Named on the petition of 1689 (CSPD, W&M, I, 43).

MEADE, William, tailor, of Bridgwater (TB), tried at Wells; hanged at Glastonbury (JR, JW). Land forfeit and for sale (TB).

MEADE, William, of Chilton Polden, 'out in the rebellion and at large' (CP); in Bridgwater prison; tried at Taunton; transported for Booth (JR) from Bristol, Oct. 24, on the *John* to Barbados. Died at sea (SL).

MEADE, William, glover, tried at Wells and hanged there (JR, JW).

MEARE *see* Moore.

MEECH, Richard, of Beaminster, 'wanting' (CP).

MELLARD, John, of Tiverton, 'with the late Duke of Monmouth'(CP).

MELLDROM, John, presented at Wells and bound over (JR).

MELLINER, William, maltster, of Taunton, pardoned July 4, 1686 (CSPD, J2, II, 768).

MEMBERRY, William, of Cudworth, 'in the rebellion and not come in' (CP).

MERCER, Hugh, comber, of Taunton St Mary, 'aiding' (CP); Blue Regt. (P).

MERCHANT *see* Marchant.

MERCEY, George, of Wellington, 'absent' (CP).

MERCY, James, of Wellington, 'absent' (CP).

MERCY, John, of Wellington, 'absent' (CP).

MERREFEILD, Robert, of Woolminstone, Crewkerne, 'rebel in Monmouth's army and not taken' (CP).

MERRICK, Edward, of Glastonbury, 'from home at the time of the rebellion' (CP); tried at Wells; 'designed for execution, yet omitted in the warrant' (JR); transported from Wells gaol for Nipho in place of Walter Teape (SL).

MERRICK, Thomas, worsted comber, of Taunton St Mary, 'aiding' (CP); Blue Regt. (P).

MERRICK, William, tried at Wells; transported for Howard (JR), Oct. 25, on the *Port Royal Merchant* to Jamaica (SL).

MERRIWEATHER, Thomas, weaver, of East Woodlands, 'in the rebellion and at large' (CP).

METYARD (Weatyard), John, of Bishop's Hull, 'absent' (CP); tried at Taunton; transported for Musgrave (JR) on the *Jamaica Merchant* from Weymouth to Jamaica; there by March 12 (SL).

*And see* Moatyard.

MEW alias Seller, Thomas, of Woolavington, 'out in the rebellion and at large' (CP).

MEY, John, of Crediton, 'absent' (CP).

MEYER (Mico), Henry, of Bridgwater, in the Bridewell, Taunton; tried there; transported thence for Booth (JR) via Bristol, Oct. 24, on the *John* to Barbados; sold to Dr Battyn (SL).

MICELL *see* Mihill.

MICHELL *see* Mitchell.

MICHO, John, of Bishop's Hull, 'absent' (CP), 'not taken' (CL).

MICO *see* Meyer.

MICRE, James, comber, of Taunton St Mary, 'aiding' (CP); Blue Regt. (P).

MICRE, Thomas, worsted comber, of Taunton St Mary, 'aiding' (CP); Blue Regt. (P).

MIDDLETON, Eli senior, tailor, of Taunton St Mary, 'aiding' (CP); Blue Regt. (P).

MIDDLETON, John, yeoman, of Luppitt, 'out in the rebellion' (CP); presented at Exeter but at large (JR).

MIDDLETON, Ralph, of Donyatt, 'out in the rebellion' (CP); tried at Wells; transported for Howard (JR), Oct. 25, on the *Port Royal Merchant* to Jamaica (SL).

MIDDLETON, Thomas, of Taunton, in the Bridewell there (SL); tried at Taunton; transported for Booth (JR) via Bristol on the *John*, Oct. 24, to Barbados; sold to Richard Harwood, Esq. (SL).

MIDDLETON, William, tinker, of Taunton St Mary, 'aiding' (CP); Blue Regt. (P).

MIHILL (Micell, Mitchell), George, of Bridgwater, in prison there (SL); tried at Taunton; transported for Booth (JR) via Bristol on the *John* Oct. 24, towards Barbados but died at sea (SL).

MILES, Matthew, of Wilton, 'absent' (CP).

MILLARD, Robert, weaver, of West Woodlands, 'in the rebellion, at large' (CP); tried at Wells; transported for Howard (JR) Oct. 25 on the *Port Royal Merchant* to Jamaica (SL).

MILLER, George, husbandman, of Whitelackington (TB); tried at Taunton; 'although designed to be executed, omitted in the warrant' (JR); transported from Wells by White on the *Constant Richard* to Jamaica (SL). Land forfeit and for sale (TB).

MILLER, Hezekiah, tailor, of Lyme Regis, 'absent, supposed' (CP).

MILLER, John, aged 35, plowman [carter] (SL), of Hewish, Crewkerne, 'rebel and not taken' (CP); tried at Taunton; transported for the Queen (JR) on the *Jamaica Merchant*, Dec. 9, to Barbados; there by March 12; sold to Francis Bond, Esq. (SL).

MILLER, John, husbandman, of Uplyme, 'being in the late rebellion, a notorious rebel', entertained by John Trall of Uplyme on Jan. 21; apprehended in John Wyatt's house on Feb. 4 (LRMB).

MILLER, John, comber, of Taunton St Mary, 'aiding' (CP); Blue Regt. (P).

MILLER, Richard, tried at Wells; to be transported, Oct. 25, for Howard (JR) to Jamaica but escaped between Wells and Sherborne (SL).

MILLER, Thomas, tallow chandler, of Hewish, Crewkerne, 'rebel in Monmouth's army and not taken' (CP). Baptist preacher at Yeovil, North Perrott and 'Lashe', Dorset (OR); trustee of Chard Baptist Chapel, 1700, 'commonly called Captain Miller from his being an officer both in Cromwell's and Monmouth's army' (MS. list of officers and trustees, viii).

MILLER, William, of Westonzoyland, 'absent' (CP).

MILLS, Henry senior, of Taunton St Mary, 'aiding' (CP); Blue Regt. (P); tried at Wells; transported for Howard (JR) Oct. 25, on the *Port Royal Merchant* to Jamaica (SL).

MILLS, Robert, of Combe St Nicholas, 'absent, believed' (CP).

MILLS, Thomas, tried at Wells; transported for Howard (JR), Oct. 25, on the *Port Royal Merchant* to Jamaica (SL).

MILLS, William, of Pitminster, 'absent' (CP), 'a rebel' (CL).

MILTON, Amos, of Milverton, 'absenting' (CP).

MILTON, Henry junior, of Milverton, 'absenting' (CP).

MILTON, Henry, weaver, of Taunton St Mary, 'aiding' (CP); Blue Regt. (P).

MILTON, John, of Milverton, 'absenting' (CP).

MILWARD, Richard, presented at Wells: 'remaining in custody for want of evidence' (JR).

MINIFIE, James, sergemaker, of Taunton St James, 'aiding' (CP); Blue Regt. (P).

MINIFIE, John, shoemaker, of Honiton, 'a rebel' (CP); imprisoned in Wilts. (DLD), tried at Dorchester; to be transported for Booth (JR); on Booth's receipt Sept. 25, but one of 10 not on the *Happy Return* (SL), one of the 10 is marked 'died in prison' (SL). Land forfeit and for sale (TB).

MINIFIE, John, presented at Dorchester and 'humbly proposed for pardon' (JR).

MINIFIE, John, sergemaker, of Taunton St James, 'aiding' (CP); Blue Regt. (P).

MITCHELL (Michell), Lieutenant, came from Holland with Monmouth, Lieut, in the Red Regt., led the vanguard at Bridport (W); probably killed at Sedgemoor (P).

MITCHELL, Aaron, presented at Dorchester, March 1686; pardoned by the king's Proclamation (GD).

MITCHELL, Edward, in prison in Wilts. 'confessing that he was in arms in the late rebellion' (Wilts. QSR); tried at Wells; transported for Howard (JR) Oct. 25, on the *Port Royal Merchant* to Jamaica (SL).

MITCHELL, George, of Ilminster, 'in the late rebellion' (CP).

MITCHELL, Humphrey, aged 27 (PR), yeoman, of Colyton, 'absent' (CP); presented at Exeter but at large (JR); imprisoned at Taunton (DLD) and tried there; hanged at Nether Stowey (JR, JW). His widow, Elizabeth, died in February 1686 leaving 3 children under 6 (PR).

MITCHELL, Humphrey, presented at Exeter, March 1686, pardoned and dismissed (GD).
MITCHELL, James, of Merriott, 'rebel . . . and not taken' (CP).
MITCHELL, John, of Merriott, 'rebel . . . and not taken '(CP); 'proposed for pardon, 12 Jan. 1686 (TB).
MITCHELL, John, yeoman, of Membury, tried at Dorchester; transported for Booth (JR) on the *Happy Return* from Weymouth, Sept. 25, to Barbados; sold to Capt. John Parnell (SL). Also presented at Exeter and misreported at large (JR).
MITCHELL, John, gentleman, of near Sidmouth, who by tradition fed rebel fugitives in the caves, presented at Dorchester and discharged for want of evidence (JR). He is entered twice in JR, but not in GD.
MITCHELL, John, yeoman, of Thorncombe, 'wanting from home' (CP); in Exeter prison; tried at Taunton; transported for Booth (JR) via Bristol, Oct. 24, on the *John* to Barbados; sold to Col. John Sampson (SL).
MITCHELL, John, fuller, of Taunton St Mary, 'aiding' (CP); Blue Regt. (P).
MITCHELL, John, of Bishop's Hull, 'absent' (CP), 'not taken' (CL). One of these two, or the John from Merriott, or yet another John, was presented at Wells and bound over (JR). Another John was presented at Exeter in March 1686 for high treason, pardoned and dismissed (GD).
MITCHELL, Michael, yeoman, of Membury, presented at Exeter but at large (CP).
MITCHELL, Nicholas, of Membury, 'wanting from home' (CP). 'Killed' has been added in the margin (CP).
MITCHELL, Peter, of Merriott, 'rebel . . . and not taken' (CP); 'proposed for pardon' (JR2).
MITCHELL *see* Machell.
MITCHELL, Robert, of Ilton, tried at Taunton; transported for Booth from Taunton Bridewell (JR) via Bristol, Oct. 24, on the *John* to Barbados; sold to Capt. W. Scott (SL).
MITCHELL, Thomas, tried at Wells; transported for Howard (JR), Oct. 25 on the *Port Royal Merchant* to Jamaica (SL).
MITCHELL, William, of Isle Abbotts, 'out in the rebellion and not taken' (CP).
*And see* Mihill.
MOATYARD, Thomas, of Sampford Arundel, 'absenting' (CP).
*And see* Meryard.
MOGRIDGE, Ames, of Pitminster, 'taking up arms against the king' (Som. QSR).
MOGRIDGE, Charles, of Pitminster, 'taking up arms against the king' (Som. QSR).
MOGRIDGE, John senior, of Pitminster, 'taking up arms against the king' (Som. QSR).
MOGRIDGE, John junior, aged 23, weaver (SL) of Pitminster, taking up arms against the king' (Som. QSR); tried at Taunton; transported

thence for the Queen (JR) on the *Jamaica Merchant*, Dec. 9, to
Barbados; sold on March 12 to Matthew Gray (SL).

MOGRIDGE (Moggridge), John, yeoman, of Colyton, imprisoned in the
High Gaol, Devon, (DLD); tried at Dorchester; transported for
Nipho (JR) on the *Betty* from Weymouth, Nov. 25, to Barbados;
sold to Elizabeth Foster (SL).

MOGRIDGE (Moggeridge), Timothy, chandler (DLD), of Honiton, 'a
rebel' (CP); pardoned by proclamation at Wells Assize (GD).

MOGRIDGE (Moggeridge), William, of Chard, 'absent and believed'
(CP); tried at Taunton; hanged at Bridgwater (JR, JW).

MOGRIDGE (Moggeridge), William, of Pitminster, 'absent' (CP); 'I
suppose he was in rebellion' (CL); presented at Taunton and
proposed for pardon (JR).

MOLTON (Moulton), Humphrey, tried at Dorchester; transported for
Booth (JR) on the *Happy Return* from Weymouth, Sept. 25, to
Barbados; sold to Capt. Walter Scott (SL).

MOODY, James, tried at Wells; to be transported for Howard (JR), Oct.
25, but escaped between Wells and Sherborne (SL).

MOORE, George, of Chilton Polden, 'out in the rebellion and at large'
(CP).

MOORE, George, of Fivehead, 'out in the rebellion and not taken' (CP).

MOORE, James, of Kingsbury Episcopi, 'absent and believed' (CP). [*See
below.*]

MOORE, James, of Staple Fitzpaine, 'out in the rebellion' (CP). One of
these two was tried at Wells and transported for Howard (JR) on
Oct. 25 on the *Port Royal Merchant* to Jamaica (SL).

MOORE, John junior, of Ilminster, 'in the rebellion' (CP); presented at
Wells. [*See below.*]

MOORE, John, of Symondsbury, 'suspected' (CP); presented at Wells
[*See below.*] One of these two was recommended for pardon; the
other was bound over (JR).

MOORE, John (or Robert), of Hawkchurch, excepted from GP.

MOORE, Moses, of Leigh on Mendip, 'supposed' (CP); tried at Wells;
transported thence for Bridgeman (JR) by White, Oct. 31, on the
*Constant Richard* to Jamaica (SL).

MOORE (Moor), Nathaniel junior, of Bridport, 'in the rebellion, as
informed' (CP).

MOORE, Nicholas, weaver, of Axminster, 'supposed' (CP); in
Bridgwater prison (DLD); presented at Exeter but at large (JR).

MOORE, Robert, of Merriott, 'rebel . . . and not taken' (CP); 'slain in
King's Sedgemoor, being in the Duke's service' (PRO Chancery
Suit, Moore v Harvey, printed *Som. and Dors. Notes and Queries* xix,
515–16).

MOORE, Thomas, shoemaker, of Lyme Regis, 'absent, supposed' (CP);
presented at Dorchester; proposed for pardon (JR).

MOORE, Thomas, sergeweaver, of West Sandford, Crediton (DLD); of
Milverton, 'absenting' (CP) imprisoned in the High Gaol, Devon
(DLD); tried at Taunton; transported for the Queen (JR); on John

Rose's receipt of Oct. 12, but not shipped on the *Jamaica Merchant* (SL).

MOORE, William, of Ruishton, 'absent' (CP).
*And see* Morre, Morse.

MORLEY, John, tried at Wells; transported for Howard (JR), Oct. 25, on the *Port Royal Merchant* to Jamaica (SL).

MORLEY, Shadreck, in Ilchester gaol; tried at Wells; transported for Howard (JR), Oct. 25, on the *Port Royal Merchant* to Jamaica (SL).

MORRE, James, weaver, of Taunton St Mary, 'aiding' (CP); Blue Regt. (P).
*And see* Moore.

MORREN (Morris), Pearce, tried at Taunton and hanged there, Sept. 30; buried at St James's, Oct. 1 (JR, JW, NL). Petition, Dec. 20 1686, from Castillian Morris: his father was hanged, drawn and quartered; he prays for an allowance to meet the great expense of his government post (TB).

MORRIS, James, of Milverton, 'absenting' (CP).

MORRIS, John, yeoman, of Thorncombe, 'wanting from his habitation' (CP); presented at Exeter but at large (JR).

MORRIS, Robert, shoemaker, of Lyme Regis, 'absent, supposed' (CP).

MORRIS, Samuel, barber, of Lyme Regis, 'absent, supposed' (CP).

MORRIS, Thomas, of Mells, 'supposed' (CP).
*And see* Morren.

MORSE, John, tried at Taunton; transported for the Queen (JR). On John Rose's receipt of Oct. 12, but not shipped on the *Jamaica Merchant* (SL).

MORSE (Moore), Paul, tried at Wells; transported for Stapleton (JR) in the *Indeavour* from Bristol Oct. 20 to Nevis or St Kitts (SL).

MORSE, William, of Chiselborough, 'in the late rebellion' (CP).

MORTIMER, Roger, tried at Wells; transported for Howard (JR), Oct. 25, on the *Port Royal Merchant* to Jamaica (SL).

MORTIMORE, John, of North Petherton, 'in the rebellion and in prison' (CP); tried at Taunton; hanged at Ilchester (JR, JW).

MORTIMORE, Robert, of Trull, 'absent' (CP).

MORTON, Edward, tried at Dorchester; transported for Booth (JR) on the *Happy Return* from Weymouth, Sept. 25, to Barbados; sold to Capt. William Marshall (SL).

MOULTON *see* Molton.

MOUNSEIR, Thomas, weaver, of Frome, 'in the rebellion and at large' (CP).

MOUNSTONE (Manston), Richard, of South Trendle tithing, Pitminster, 'a rebel' (CL); 'absent' (CP).

MOUNTSTEPHEN, Samuel, of Pitminster, 'absent' (CP); tried at Taunton; transported for the Queen (JR); on John Rose's receipt of Oct. 12 but not shipped on the *Jamaica Merchant* (SL).

MOXEY *see* Maxey.

MOXHIDGE, Richard, carrier, of Lyme Regis, 'absent, supposed' (CP).

MUDFORD *see* Mumford.

MULLENS, Edward, weaver, of Taunton St Mary, 'aiding' (CP); Blue Regt. (P).

MULLENS, George senior, of Taunton (CSPD, J2, II, 1833), in the Bridewell there, tried there; transported thence for Booth (JR) via Bristol, Oct. 24, on the *John* to Barbados; sold to Richard Harwood, Esq. (SL). Pardoned 31 May 1687 (CSPD, J2, II, 1833).

MULLENS, Joseph, tried at Wells; transported for Howard (JR) Oct. 25 on the *Port Royal Merchant* to Jamaica (SL).

MULLENS, Robert, of Sidmouth, 'went to Monmouth' (CP); tried at Dorchester; transported for Nipho (JR) on the *Betty* from Weymouth, Nov. 25, to Barbados; sold to Michael Child (SL).

MULLINS, William junior, yeoman, of Colyton, 'absent' (CP); presented at Exeter but at large (JR).

MUMFORD (Mudford, Munford), Robert, of Chard, 'absent, believed' (CP), tried at Wells; transported thence for Bridgeman (JR) by White, Oct. 31, on the *Constant Richard* to Jamaica (SL).

MUNDAY, Thomas, tried at Wells; hanged at Axbridge (JR, JW).

MUSGRAVE, Nathaniel, tried at Taunton; transported for Musgrave (JR) on the *Jamaica Merchant* from Weymouth to Jamaica; there by March 12 (SL).

MUTTLEBURY, John, tried at Wells; transported for Howard (JR) Oct. 25, on the *Port Royal Merchant* to Jamaica (SL).

MUXWORTHY, John, of Bampton, 'supposed to be a rebel' (CP).

NABRICK, Andrew, tried at Taunton; transported for Musgrave (JR) on the *Jamaica Merchant* from Weymouth, to Barbados; there by March 12 (SL).

NAPPER, Richard, presented at Wells; 'recommended for pardon' (JR).

NAPPER, Thomas, presented at Wells; 'recommended for pardon' (JR).

NASH, Francis, weaver, of Rode, 'in the rebellion' (CP).

NASH alias Lissant, Richard, tried at Wells; transported for Nipho (JR) on the *Betty* from Weymouth, Nov. 25, to Barbados; sold to Rebecca Beal (SL).

NASHION, Thomas, tried at Wells; transported thence for Bridgeman (JR) by White, Oct. 31, on the *Constant Richard* to Jamaica (SL).

NATION, John, of North Petherton, 'absconded' (CP); 'taking up arms against the king' (Som. QSR).

NATION, Robert, of Ash Priors, 'absent' (CP).

NEEDS, John, tried at Taunton; transported for the Queen (JR); on John Rose's receipt of Oct. 12 but not on the *Jamaica Merchant* (SL).

NELTHORPE, Richard, barrister, of Gray's Inn, outlawed after the Rye House Plot; came from Holland with the Duke; a captain in his army; escaped from Sedgemoor with the Revd. J. Hicks; captured and hanged in London (DNB).

NEW, Thomas, worsted comber, of Taunton St Mary, 'aiding' (CP); Blue Regt. (P).

NEWBERRY, John, yeoman, of Membury, 'wanting' (CP); presented at
  Exeter but at large (JR). [*See below.*]
NEWBERRY, John (another), of Membury, 'wanting' (CP). [*See below.*]
NEWBERRY, John, of Stockland, 'suspected' (CP). [*See below.*]
NEWBERRY, John, yeoman, of Yarcombe, 'wanting' (CP); presented at
  Exeter but at large (JR). [*See below.*] One John Newberry was in
  March 1686 presented at Exeter, pardoned and dismissed (GD).
NEWBERRY, Joseph, yeoman, of Yarcombe, 'wanting' (CP); presented
  at Exeter but at large; brought from Exeter prison to be tried at
  Taunton; to be transported for Booth (JR); on Booth's receipt dated
  Dorchester, Oct. 24, but not shipped or sold (SL); reprieved (JR2).
  A Joseph Newberry, 'a rebel', was buried on Nov. 20 at Taunton St
  Mary's (PR).
NEWBERRY, Samuel, yeoman, of Membury, 'wanting' (CP); 'seen in
  Monmouth's camp' (LRMB); presented at Exeter but at large (JR);
  presented at Taunton; certificate allowed (JR).
NEWBERRY, Samuel, yeoman, of Yarcombe, 'wanting' (CP); presented
  at Exeter but at large (CP); 'seen in Monmouth's camp' (LRMB);
  pardoned March 26, 1686 (CSPD, J2, II, 351).
NEWELL, Richard, yeoman, of Combpyne, 'with Monmouth in the late
  rebellion' (CP); presented at Exeter but at large (JR); in the
  Workhouse at Exeter; presented there 23 March 1686; pardoned and
  dismissed (GD).
NEWMAN, Samuel, of Taunton St Mary, 'aiding' (CP); Blue Regt. (P).
NEWMAN, Stephen, of Pitminster, 'taking up arms against his Majesty'
  (Som. QSR); tried at Taunton; hanged at Ilminster (JR, JW).
NEWTON, John, probably aged 33 and brother of Philip (PR);
  yeoman, of Colyton, 'absent' (CP); presented at Exeter but at large
  (JR).
NEWTON, Peter, fuller, of Taunton St Mary, 'aiding' (CP); Blue Regt.
  (P).
NEWTON, Philip, aged 29 (PR), yeoman, of Colyton, 'absent' (CP);
  presented at Exeter but at large (JR).
NEWTON, Thomas, tailor, of Lyme Regis, 'absent, supposed' (CP).
NEWTON, Thomas, of Taunton, pardon of all treasons, March 27, 1686
  (CSPD, J2, II, 356).
NEWTON, William, yeoman, of Axminister, 'supposed' (CP); presented
  at Exeter but at large (JR).
  *And see* Godfrey, Benjamin.
NICHOLAS, Oliver, of Ashill, 'out in the rebellion' (CP).
NICHOLLS, John, of Bruton, 'in James Scott's army and not yet taken'
  (CP).
NICHOLLS, Richard, husbandman, of Taunton St James, 'aiding' (CP);
  Blue Regt. (P).
NIPE, George, of Cheddar, excepted from GP.
NIPPERETT, Andrew, yeoman, of East Woodlands, 'in the rebellion
  and in prison' (CP). Not presented at the Assize. Did he die in
  prison or, just possibly, escape?

NOLSTON, Nathaniel, yeoman, of Upottery, presented at Exeter but at large (JR).

NOON, Henry, of Axminster Congregational church, a pious and lively Christian who marched forth with the [rebel] Army; was slain at Norton St Philip (Ecc).

NOONE, Henry, tried at Wells; transported thence for Bridgeman (JR), Oct. 31, by White on the *Constant Richard* to Jamaica (SL).

NORCOTT, Adrian, shoemaker, married 1680 (PR), of Taunton St Mary 'aiding' (CP); Blue Regt. (P).

NORCOTT, Daniel, yeoman, of Cullompton, imprisoned at Taunton (DLD); presented there and proposed for pardon (JR).

NORMAN, James, presented at Taunton; certificate allowed (JR).

NORMAN, James, presented at Wells; 'remaining in custody' (JR).

NORMAN, John, of Wellington, 'in prison for rebellion' (CP).

NORMAN, Thomas, of Creech St Michael, 'took up arms against his Majesty' (Som. QSR); 'absent, and not taken' (CP).

NORMAN, William, of Wellington, 'in prison for rebellion' (CP); tried at Taunton; transported for Musgrave (JR) on the *Jamaica Merchant* from Weymouth to Barbados; there by 12 March 1686 (SL).

NORRIS, Giles, of Wayford, 'a rebel and not taken' (CP).

NORRIS, Thomas, transported on the *Jamaica Merchant* from Weymouth to Barbados (PRO CO 1/59, f. 149). Was he a rebel or a felon?

NORSEY, George, of Chilton Polden, 'out in the rebellion and at large' (CP).

NORTH, John senior, of Chaffcombe, 'in the rebellion and not come in' (CP).

NORTH, John junior, of Chaffcombe, 'in the rebellion and not come in' (CP).

NORTH, William, of Donyatt, 'out in the rebellion' (CP).

NORTHAN, John, of Wellington, 'in prison for rebellion' (CP); presented at Taunton; 'remaining in gaol' (JR).

NORTON, Edward, brother of Sir George Norton, baronet, 'unfortunately drawn into the late conspiracy, but was never in arms'; pardon approved, May 1686; granted June 10; outlawry reversed, Nov. 12 (CSPD, J2, II, 615, 653, 1143). NL of Dec. 11 records his pardon and return from Holland.

NORTON, alias Norden, mariner, Jan. 27, 1686, warrant to arrest, 'accused of assisting escape of rebels' (CSPD, J2, II, 83).

NORTON, Henry, of Taunton St James, 'aiding' (CP); Blue Regt. (P); presented at Wells: 'recommended for pardon' (JR).

NORTON, John junior, of Bishop's Hull, 'absent' (CP), 'not taken' (CL).

NORTON, Robert, tried at Wells; transported for Howard (JR), Oct. 25, on the *Port Royal Merchant* to Jamaica (SL).

NORTON, Thomas, of Coleford, 'absenting' (CP); tried at Wells; transported for Howard (JR), Oct. 25, on the *Port Royal Merchant* to Jamaica (SL). His wife and children chargeable to the parish for poverty, his father being charged 2s. 6d. a week (Som. QSR).

NORVELL, William, weaver, of Wincanton, 'actually in arms in the rebellion, as informed, and at large' (CP).

NORVILLE, James, tried at Wells; transported for Howard (JR), Oct. 25, on the *Port Royal Merchant* to Jamaica (SL).

NORVILLE, James (another) presented at Wells and bound over (JR).

NOSS, Peter, of Taunton St James, 'aiding' (CP); Blue Regt. (P).

NOTT, Benjamin, of Bishop's Hull, 'absent' (CP); presented at Taunton and 'proposed for pardon' (JR).

NOWELL, George, of Taunton, in the Bridewell there (SL); tried there; transported for Booth (JR) via Bristol, Oct. 24, on the *John* to Barbados; sold to Ann Gallop (SL).

NOWIS, Percival, hatter, aged 23, imprisoned in Taunton (SL) and tried there; transported for the Queen (JR) on the *Jamaica Merchant* to Barbados; sold on March 12 to Joseph Jones (SL).

NURTON, Henry, mason, of Taunton St Mary, 'aiding' (CP); Blue Regt. (P).

NURTON, William, of Wellington, 'absent' (CP).

OAKEY, William, presented at Wells and bound over (JR). Perhaps a Bridgwater Quaker and weaver.

OAKLY, Rowland, presented at Wells and bound over (JR).

OAKSHAVE, John, carpenter, of Lyme Regis, 'absent, supposed' (CP).

OASTLER (Walter) (JR2), William senior, tried at Wells; 'designed for execution yet omitted in the warrant for execution'; bound over (JR). In Jeffreys' later report in TB, Nov. 12, Oastler is 'humbly proposed for his Majesty's gracious pardon'. Land confiscated and granted to the lawyers. Pardon money to be kept by Morgan Harbin (TB).

OATEWAY, Daniel, worsted comber, of Taunton St Mary, 'aiding' (CP); Blue Regt. (P).

OATEWAY, Jacob, worsted comber, of Taunton St Mary, 'aiding' (CP); Blue Regt. (P).

OATEWAY (Wottway), Thomas, of Creech St Michael, 'in arms against his Majesty' (Som. QSR); 'absent and not taken' (CP).

ODAMS, Nicholas, of Taunton St James, 'aiding', (CP); Blue Regt. (P).

ODSEY (Ordrey), John, of North Curry, 'absent' (CP); 'fled' (CL); 'taking up arms against the king' (Som. QSR).

OKE, Nathaniel, of Staplegrove, 'taking up arms against the king' (Som. QSR).

OLAND, John, silkweaver, of Taunton St Mary, 'aiding' (CP); Blue Regt. (P).

OLD, Walter, of Curry Rivel, 'out in the rebellion and not taken' (CP).

OLD, William, presented at Wells and bound over (JR).

OLIVER, John, yeoman, of Axminster, 'supposed' (CP); presented at Exeter, Sept. 14, reported at large (JR), but *see below*.

OLIVER, John, yeoman, of Axmouth, 'reported to be in arms' (CP); presented at Exeter, Sept. 14, reported at large (JR) but *see below*. One of these two was sentenced on Sept. 14 to be hanged, and was hanged on Oct. 7 at Honiton (JR, NL).

OLIVER, Robert, yeoman, of Axminster, 'supposed' (CP); presented at Exeter but at large (JR).

OLIVER, William, aged 26, a Cornishman, medical student at Leyden; came with Monmouth as surgeon; left Sedgemoor with Monmouth, advising him to make for Uphill. Oliver reached Bristol and thence London and Holland. Excepted from GP. Returned with William of Orange as a combatant officer. Completed his L.C.P. London, 1692. Surgeon to the Red Squadron, R.N. Physician at Chatham and then at Greenwich. Retired to Bath. Memorial tablet in Bath Abbey, 1716 (Oldmixon and the tablet).

OLLVARD, Thomas, presented at Wells and bound over (JR).

ONWIN, Richard, of Milverton, 'absenting' (CP).

ONWYNS, Henry senior, of Milverton, 'absenting' (CP).

ONWYNS, Henry junior, of Milverton, 'absenting' (CP).

ORAM (Worne), John, woolcomber, of Worminster, Wells, 'supposed' (CP); excepted from GP; 'engaged in the late rebellion'; tried at Wells; transported for Howard (JR), Oct. 25 on the *Port Royal Merchant* to Jamaica (SL). Pardoned July 4, 1686 and May 31, 1687 (CSPD, J2, II, 768, 1833).

ORAM (Cram, Worne), Thomas, woolcomber, of Worminster, Wells, 'supposed' (CP); excepted from GP, pardoned July 4, 1686 (CSPD, J2, II, 768).

ORCHARD, James, yeoman, of Whitechurch Canonicorum (DLD); of Marshwood, 'supposed' (CP); 'went into Monmouth's camp with Matthew Bowditch'; taken Jan. 5 at Lyme Regis and sent to Dorchester gaol; presented March 1686 at Dorchester and pardoned by proclamation (LRMB, GD).

ORCHARD, John, of Knowle St Giles, 'in the rebellion and not come in' (CP).

ORCHARD, Robert, at Dorchester Assize 'continued in gaol, not indicted' (JR).

ORCHARD, Thomas, tried at Wells; transported for Howard (JR), Oct. 25 on the *Port Royal Merchant* to Jamaica (SL).

ORCHARD, William, yeoman, of Abbotts Wootton, 'supposed' (CP); 'a rebel, went into Monmouth's camp and marched with them'; taken at Lyme Regis about Jan. 5; sent to Dorchester gaol (LRMB); in March presented at Dorchester and pardoned by proclamation (GD).

ORDREY see Odsey.

OSBORNE, Alexander, of Merriott, 'rebel and not taken' (CP).

OSBORNE, Christopher, of Butleigh, 'absent and in custody' (CP). Not presented at Assize. Did he die? or was the evidence insufficient?

OSBORNE, Moses, tried at Taunton; to be transported for the Queen (JR); on John Rose's receipt of Oct. 12, but not shipped on *Jamaica Merchant*.

OSBORNE, Walter, dyer, of Crewkerne, a Quaker, tried at Dorchester; to be transported for Nipho (JR); on Penne's list but not on the *Betty*. On Jeffrey's later list of Nov. 12 in TB, Osborne was proposed for pardon, which was authorised on July 4, 1686 (CSPD, J2, II, 768). Land forfeit and for sale, July 17 (TB), but CSPD, J2, II, 1798 reports a petition citing a circuit pardon for Dorset, and praying a pardon for the forfeiture (TB).

OSBORNE, William, husbandman, of Wittington in co. [blank]. Land forfeit and for sale (TB).

OSMANS, James, of North Curry, 'taking up arms against the king' (Som. QSR).

OSMANS, William, of North Curry, 'taking up arms against the king' (Som. QSR).

OSMOND, Christopher, presented at Wells and bound over (JR).

OSMOND alias Seward, Phillipe, of North Curry, 'took up arms against the king' (Som. QSR).

OSMOND (Osnance), Stephen, of Hillfarrance, 'absent' (CP); 'taking up arms against the king' (Som. QSR).

OSTLER, John, of Kingsbury Episcopi, 'absent, believed' (CP).

OUSELEY, Andrew, presented at Wells and bound over (JR). Perhaps a Quaker of Long Sutton.

OWIN *see* Onwin.

PACEY (Parry), John, of West Monkton, 'out in the rebellion and at large' (CP); tried at Taunton; 'designed to be executed' (JR); escaped from prison at Taunton but returned the same evening (NL); omitted in the warrant for execution; proposed for pardon in Jeffreys' second report (TB) Nov. 12; pardoned under the Privy Seal, Dec. 7 (CSPD, J2, I, 2025).

PACKE, Samuel, presented at Wells and bound over (JR).

PACKER, John, presented at Wells and bound over (JR).

PAGE, Edward, of Ashill, 'out in the rebellion' (CP).

PAGE, Francis, of Donyatt, 'out in the rebellion' (CP).

PAGE, William senior, of Chardland, 'absent, believed' (CP). [*See below.*]

PAGE, William junior, of Chardland, 'absent, believed' (CP). [*See below.*] One of these two was tried at Taunton; transported for Musgrave (JR) on the *Jamaica Merchant* from Weymouth to Jamaica, March 12 (SL).

PAINE, James, tried at Wells; to be transported for Howard (JR) but escaped between Wells and Sherborne (SL).

PAINE, John, of Alstone, Huntspill, 'being in arms' (CP); 'active soldier in the Duke of Monmouth's army' (Som. QSR).

PALE, Simon, of Durston, 'in arms against his Majesty' (Som. QSR).

PALFREY, Matthew, yeoman, of Upottery, 'absent' (CP); presented at Exeter but at large (JR).

PALFREY, Sampson, yeoman, of Upottery, 'absent' (CP); presented at Exeter but at large (JR); represented in March; pardoned and dismissed (GD).

PALMER, Andrew, tried at Wells; transported for Howard (JR) Oct. 25 on the *Port Royal Merchant* to Jamaica (SL).

PALMER, George, in the GD Book for Wells but no further note. Did he die before sentence?

PALMER, Henry, fuller, of Taunton St Mary, 'aiding' (CP); Blue Regt. (P).

PALMER, John, of Chard, 'in the late rebellion' (CP); tried at Wells; transported for Howard (JR), Oct. 25 on the *Port Royal Merchant* to Jamaica (SL).

PALMER, John junior, of Martock, 'absent' (CP); tried at Wells; transported for Howard (JR), Oct. 25 on the *Port Royal Merchant* to Jamaica (SL).

PALMER, John, of Bridgwater, excepted from GP; June 28 petition for pardon as 'compelled to guide the rebels'; pardoned July 11 1686 (CSPD, J2, II, 742, 795).

PALMER, Matthew, of North Petherton, 'absconded' (CP).

PALMER, Nicholas, of Hawkchurch, 'seen in Monmouth's camp' (LRMB); tried at Dorchester; transported for Booth (JR) on the *Happy Return* from Weymouth Sept. 25, to Barbados; sold to Capt. George Terwight (SL).

PALMER, Roger, of Crewkerne, 'rebel and not taken' (CP).

PALMER, Thomas, of Alstone, Huntspill, 'being in arms in the late rebellion' (CP); of Puriton, 'active soldier in Monmouth's army' (Som. QSR); presented in March 1686 at Dorchester, pardoned by proclamation (GD).

PARBURY, Thomas, at Dorchester Assize 'continued in gaol, not indicted' (JR).

PARBURY, William, mariner, of Lyme Regis, 'absent, supposed' (CP); excepted from GP.

PARDOE, William, excepted from GP.

PARKER, Baldwin, of Chiselborough, 'in the late rebellion' (CP); tried at Wells; transported for Howard (JR), Oct. 25 on the *Port Royal Merchant* to Jamaica (SL).

PARKER, Daniel, tried at Dorchester; transported for Nipho (JR) on the *Betty* from Weymouth, Nov. 25, to Barbados; sold to Michael Child (SL).

PARKER, James, of Chewton, 'absenting' (CP); tried at Wells; transported for Howard (JR), Oct. 25 on the *Port Royal Merchant* to Jamaica (SL).

PARKER, John, of Honiton, 'a rebel' (CP).

PARKER, Richard, tried at Dorchester; transported for Nipho (JR) on the *Betty* from Weymouth, Nov. 25, to Barbados; sold to John Chace (SL). Named on the petition of 1689 (CSPD, W&M, I, 43).

PARKER, Walter, weaver, of East Woodlands, 'in the rebellion and at large' (CP).

PARKER, William, of Taunton, in the Bridewell there (SL); tried there; transported for Booth (JR) via Bristol, Oct. 24, on the *John* to Barbados; sold to Ann Gallop (SL).

PARR, Thomas, weaver, of Taunton St James, 'aiding' (CP); Blue Regt. (P).

PARRICK, Francis junior, yeoman, of Axminster, 'supposed' (CP); presented at Exeter but at large (JR).

PARRICKE (Parris), John, of Hawkchurch, 'seen in Monmouth's camp' (LRMB); presented at Dorchester in March 1686 and pardoned by proclamation (GD).

PARRISH, Thomas, of Chardstock, 'suspected guilty' (CP).

PARRETT *see* Perrot.

PARRIS *see* Parricke.

PARRY *see* Pacey, Perry.

PARSONS, Arthur, yeoman, of Bishop's Hull, pardon of all treasons, March 22 1686 (CSPD, J2, II, 310).

PARSONS, Edward, of Beer or Seaton, 'supposed' (CP).

PARSONS, Edward junior, of Beer or Seaton, 'supposed' (CP).

PARSONS, Edward, of Taunton St Mary, 'aiding' (CP); Blue Regt. (P).

PARSONS, George, presented at Wells and bound over (JR).

PARSONS, Henry, presented for high treason at Exeter in March 1686; pardoned and dismissed (GD).

PARSONS, John, yeoman, of Babcary, excepted from GP; land forfeit and for sale (TB). Was he killed at Sedgemoor?

PARSONS, John, of Beer or Seaton, 'supposed' (CP). [*See below.*]

PARSONS, John, of Charmouth, 'suspected' (CP). [*See below.*]

PARSONS, John, of Ilminster, 'in the late rebellion' (CP); wounded at Norton St Philip, arm badly broken, set by Dr Winter in Ilchester gaol; 'is yet in prison and very poor' (WB). [*See below.*]

PARSONS, John, of Milverton, 'absenting' (CP). [*See below.*]

PARSONS, John, weaver, of Taunton St Mary, 'aiding' (CP); Blue Regt. (P). [*See below.*]

PARSONS, John, of Wellington, 'in prison for rebellion' (CP). [*See below.*]

PARSONS, John and William, 'idle persons and wandering up and down the country and suspected for being in James Scott's, late Duke of Monmouth's army' (Som. QSR). These may be the Charmouth pair. [*See below.*] Of these six or seven John Parsons, two, tried at Taunton, were hanged, one at Ilminster, one at South Petherton (JR, JW). Another, tried at Taunton, was to be transported for the Queen (JR); he is on John Rose's receipt of Oct. 12 but was not on the *Jamaica Merchant* (SL). Two others were tried at Wells and both transported thence for Bridgeman (JR) Oct. 31 by White on the *Constant Richard* to Jamaica (SL).

PARSONS, Robert, of Cheddon, 'absent' (CP).

PARSONS, Robert, Major, came from Holland; Second-in-command, Green Regt.; deserted at Frome with Venner (W); excepted from GP of 1686 and 1688.

PARSONS, Thomas, yeoman, of Membury, 'wanting from his habitation' (CP); 'a free willed Baptist', an old Cromwellian soldier, made a captain (CSPD, 1683 (ii), 217–18); presented at Exeter but at large (JR). [*See below.*]

PARSONS, Thomas, worsted comber, of Taunton St James, 'aiding' (CP); Blue Regt. (P); tried at Taunton; 'remaining in gaol' (JR) till Nov. 12; then transported by White on the *Constant Richard* to Jamaica (SL).

PARSONS, Thomas senior, of Charmouth, 'suspected' (CP). [*See below.*]

PARSONS, Thomas junior, of Charmouth, 'suspected' (CP). [*See below.*] One of these two was tried at Dorchester and transported for Booth (JR) on the *Happy Return* from Weymouth, Sept. 25, to Barbados; sold to Capt. John Parnell (SL).

PARSONS, William, husbandman, of Charmouth, 'suspected' (CP). [*See* John Parsons of Charmouth.] William was tried at Exeter and hanged in October at Ottery St Mary (JR, NL). Land at 'Shint [?Shute], co. Devon' forfeit and for sale (TB).

PARTRIDGE, Henry, tried at Wells; hanged at Norton St Philip (JR, JW).

PARTRIDGE, John, tried at Wells; transported thence for Bridgeman (JR) by White Oct. 31 on the *Constant Richard* to Jamaica (SL).

PARVUNCLE, John, of Creech St Michael, took up arms against his Majesty (Som. QSR).

PARYS, Aaron, of Whitestaunton, 'in the rebellion and not come in' (CP).

PASMORE, Samuel, of Langford Budville, 'absenting' (CP).

PASS, Henry, tailor, of Lyme Regis, 'absent, supposed' (CP).

PATCH, Edward, of Meare, 'from home at the time of the rebellion' (CP).

PATCHELL, ——, came from Holland, a captain in the Green Regt.; killed at Norton St Philip (W).

PATCHER, Thomas, of Taunton St Mary, 'aiding' (CP); Blue Regt. (P).

PATIL, Arthur, of Wellington, 'absent' (CP).

PATTEN, James, husbandman, of South Petherton, tried at Taunton; transported for the Queen (JR); on John Rose's receipt of Oct. 12 but not on the *Jamaica Merchant* (SL). Land forfeit and for sale (TB).

PATTEN, John, of Ruishton, 'absent' (CL); presented at Wells; 'recommended for pardon' but bound over (JR).

PATTEN, Robert senior, of Southarp, South Petherton, 'in the rebellion and not come in' (CP).

PATTERUM, John, worsted comber, of Taunton St Mary, 'aiding' (CP); Blue Regt. (P); tried at Taunton, Sept. 19; hanged there Sept. 30 (JR, JW, NL).

PAULL, Arthur, of Stocklinch, 'suspected' (CP).

PAULL, George, of Ilminster, 'in the late rebellion' (CP).

PAULL, John, of Ilminster, 'in the late rebellion' (CP).

PAULL, Joseph, tried at Dorchester; transported for Booth (JR) on the *Happy Return* from Weymouth, Sept. 25, to Barbados; sold to Capt. John Parnell (SL).

PAULL, Maurice, of Winsham, 'absent, believed' (CP).

PAULL, Richard, tried at Dorchester; transported for Booth (JR) on the *Happy Return* from Weymouth, Sept. 25, to Barbados; sold to Capt. John Parnell (SL).

PAULL, Robert, of Ilton, in the Bridewell at Taunton; tried at Taunton transported for Booth (JR) via Bristol, Oct. 24, on the *John* towards Barbados; died at sea (SL).

PAULL, Robert, of Lopen, 'in the rebellion and not come in' (CP).

PAULL, Samuel, tried at Dorchester; pleaded not guilty (GD); transported for Musgrave (JR) on the *Jamaica Merchant* from Weymouth to Barbados; there by March 12 (SL).

PAULL, Thomas, of Barrington, 'in the rebellion and not come in' (CP).

PAULL, Thomas, of Ilminster, sergemaker, a Quaker, upwards of 60 years old (JB/JD), 'in the late rebellion' (CP); tried at Taunton; hanged at Frome JR, JW).

PAULL, William, of Ilminster, 'in the late rebellion' (CP).

PAVIOR, George, blacksmith, of Langport, tried at Wells; hanged at Shepton Mallet (JR, JW). Land forfeit and for sale (TB).

PAVIOR, George, blacksmith, of Langport, 'concerned in the rebellion in the West,' excepted from GP. Petition for pardon, June 1 1686; pardon granted August 2, and again May 31 1687 (CSPD, J2, II, 617, 862, 1833).

PAWLEY, John, weaver, of Taunton St Mary, 'aiding' (CP); Blue Regt. (P).

PAYLE, John, of Creech St Michael, 'absent and not taken' (CP).

PAYNE, John junior, broadweaver, of Frome, 'in the rebellion and at large' (CP).

PAYNE, Jonathan, yeoman, of Colyton, 'absent' (CP); presented at Exeter but at large (JR).

PAYNE, William, weaver, of Rode, 'in the rebellion' (CP).

PEADON *see* Peddon

PEARCE, Charles, of Milverton, 'absenting' (CP).

PEARCE, Humphrey, of Milverton, 'absenting' (CP); tried at Taunton; hanged at Langport (JR, JW).

PEARCE, James, of Berkley and Standerwick, 'in the rebellion and in prison' (CP); tried at Wells; to be transported for Howard, Oct. 25, but escaped between Wells and Sherborne (SL).

PEARCE, Joseph, of Milverton, 'absenting' (CP).

PEARCE, Richard, cordwainer, of Chard Town, 'absent, believed' (CP); tried at Wells; to be hanged [*see below*] (JR); land forfeit and for sale (TB).

PEARCE, Richard, of Tiverton, 'with the late Duke of Monmouth' (CP); tried at Wells; to be hanged [*see below*] (JR). One Richard Pierce was hanged at Glastonbury (JR, JW). A Pierce was hanged at Pensford (JR, JW), his name given as William, but this would seem to have been a clerk's copying error.

PEARCE, Robert, aged 25, clothier (SL); tried at Taunton; transported thence for the Queen (JR) on the *Jamaica Merchant* to Barbados; sold to Archibald Johnson (SL).

PEARCE, Robert, tried at Wells; 'transported for Nipho' (JR) on the *Betty* from Weymouth, Nov. 25, to Barbados; sold to Thomas Holeman (SL).

PEARCE, Thomas, of North Bradley, Wilts. (TB), tried at Wells; hanged at Norton St Philip (JR, JW). Land forfeit and for sale (TB).

PEARCE, Thomas, sergeweaver, of West Sandford, Crediton, imprisoned at Taunton (DLD) and tried there; hanged at Wiveliscombe (JR, JW).

PEARCE, William, of Whitechurch Canonicorum, 'suspected' (CP).

PEARD, John, in the Workhouse, Exeter, presented at Assize, March 1686, pardoned and dismissed (GD).

PEASE, James, yeoman, of Colyton, 'absent' (CP); presented at Exeter but at large (JR).

PEATHER, William, bricklayer, of Taunton St Mary, 'aiding' (CP); Blue Regt. (P); tried at Taunton; hanged at Crewkerne (JR, JW).

PECKETT see Perritt.

PEDDON (Peadon), Humphrey, of Chard, 'absent and believed' (CP); tried at Wells; hanged at Bruton (JR, JW).

PEDDON, John, of Chard, 'absent, believed' (CP).

PEDDON, Joseph, of Chard, 'absent, believed' (CP).

PEDDON, Richard, of Chard, 'absent, believed' (CP).

PEETERS, James, of Wellington, 'absent' (CP).

PEIRCY, John, tried at Wells; transported for Howard (JR), Oct. 25 on the *Port Royal Merchant* to Jamaica (SL).

PEIRCY, Richard, aged 20, comber (SL), tried at Taunton; transported thence for the Queen (JR) on the *Jamaica Merchant* to Barbados; sold to John Hethersell, Esq. (SL).

PENDER, Thomas, weaver, of Frome, 'in the rebellion and at large' (CP).

PENNY, Robert, of Shepton Mallet, excepted from GP.

PENNY, William, of Ashcott, 'absent' (CP).

PEPPIN see Pippen.

PERIAM, Bernard, tried at Taunton; transported for Musgrave (JR) on the *Jamaica Merchant* from Weymouth to Barbados; there by March 12 (SL).

PERKINS, John, yeoman, of Sidbury, 'joined in the rebellion' (CP); in the High Gaol, Devon (DLD); presented at Dorchester; certificate allowed (JR).

PERKINS, Richard, of Milverton, 'absenting' (CP); tried at Taunton; transported for Musgrave (JR) on the *Jamaica Merchant* from Weymouth to Barbados; there by March 12 (SL).

PERNISCOMBE see Brinscombe.

PERRITT (Peckett), William, of Bishop's Hull, 'absent, not taken' (CL); 'absent' (CP).

PERROT, Robert, silk dyer, of London, a Lieutenant under Harrison in Cromwell's army, an Anabaptist and Fifth Monarchy Man; assistant to Col. Blood in the theft of the Crown; pardoned 1671; Major in Monmouth's Yellow Regt. and Second-in-command after Keynsham; captured after Sedgemoor and taken to the Gatehouse, Westminster, July 16, for interrogation (L 238, CSPD, J2, I,

1250); tried at Taunton, Sept. 19, and hanged there Sept. 30 (JR, JW).

PERROTT, ——, of Dulverton, presented 'for harbouring rebels' (CP).

PERRY, James, of Glastonbury, 'from home at the time of the rebellion' (CP).

PERRY, James, of Pitminster, 'absent' (CP).

PERRY, John, of Croscombe, 'in Scott's army and not taken' (CP).

PERRY, John, sergemaker (in CP); worsted comber (in pardon); of Taunton St James, 'aiding' (CP); Blue Regt. (P); escaped to Holland, where concerned in manufacture of English cloth; pardon, June 2, 1686, 'if he return from abroad with his goods and effects within 2 calendar months' (CSPD, J2, II, 625).

PERRY (Terry), Peter, gentleman (in CP); mercer (in pardon); of Taunton St James, 'aiding' (CP); Blue Regt. (P); excepted from the GP. Warrant for pardon, Jan. 29 1686; petition for group pardon, June 1; group pardon, 'if they return etc. within 2 months'. (CSPD, J2, II, 89, 617, 625, 682, 791).

PERRY, William, of Yeovil, 'absent . . . and not returned' (CP).

PESTER (Lester), Thomas, tried at Dorchester; transported for Nipho (JR) on the *Betty* from Weymouth, Nov. 25, to Barbados; sold to Rebecca Beal (SL). Named on the 1689 petition (CSPD, W&M, I, 43).

PETHER *see* Peather, Petter

PETTARD, William, shoemaker, of Taunton St Mary, 'aiding' (CP); Blue Regt. (P).
*And see* Pittard.

PETTER, George, tried at Wells; hanged at Norton St Philip (JR, JW).

PHEERE, *see* Plaice.

PHELPS, Daniel, yeoman, of Thorncombe, 'wanting from his habitation' (CP); presented at Exeter but at large (JR).

PHELPS, Humphrey, of Winsham, 'absent, believed' (CP); presented at Dorchester but 'proposed for pardon' (JR).

PHELPS, John, of Merriott, 'rebel, and not taken' (CP).

PHELPS, John, of Taunton St James, 'aiding' (CP); Blue Regt. (P).

PHELPS, Joseph, of Whitechurch, wounded in elbow and shoulder at Norton St Philip; taken at Ilchester gaol and treated by Dr Winter (WB); presented at Dorchester and 'proposed for pardon' (JR).

PHILAMORE, Thomas, of Tiverton, imprisoned in Wilts, 'for the late rebellion; dead' (DLD).

PHILDREY, John, tried at Taunton; hanged at Keynsham (JR, JW).

PHILIP *see* Servis

PHILLIPS, Silas, tried at Wells; to be transported for Howard (JR) to Jamaica, Oct. 25, but escaped between Wells and Sherborne (SL).

PHILLIPS, Thomas, of Cudworth, 'in the rebellion and not come in' (CP).

PHILLIPS, Walter, tried at Taunton; transported for Musgrave (JR) on the *Jamaica Merchant* from Weymouth to Barbados (SL).

PHILLIPS, Walter, presented from the Workhouse, Exeter, in March 1686, pardoned and dismissed (GD).

PHILLIPS, William, aged 26, plowman [carter] (SL), tried at Taunton; transported for the Queen (JR) on the *Jamaica Merchant* to Barbados; sold to Nicholas Prideaux (SL).

PHILLY, Robert, yeoman, of Thorncombe, 'wanting from his habitation' (CP); presented at Exeter but at large (JR).

PHIPPEN, Francis, presented at Wells and bound over (JR).

PHIPPEN, Richard, of Chardstock, 'suspected guilty' (CP).

PHIPPEN, William, yeoman, of Axminster, 'supposed' (CP); of Hawkchurch (SL); dyer, wounded at Sedgemoor, imprisoned at Wells (DLD); presented at Exeter and misreported at large (JR); in Bridgwater prison; tried at Taunton; transported for Booth (JR) via Bristol, Oct. 24, on the *John* to Barbados; sold to Samuel Smart (SL).

PHIPPETT, Geoffrey, presented at Wells and bound over (JR).

PHIPPETT, William, at Assize at Wells: 'remaining in custody for want of evidence' (JR).

PHINIMORE *see* Finnimore.

PHINNIER, *see* Fineere.

PHOOCE, PHOOKS, *see* Plaice.

PHORTON, William, of Donyatt, 'out in the rebellion' (CP).

PICCARD (Pickard), George, haberdasher, of Rode, 'in the rebellion' (CP); pardon May 31, 1687 (CSPD, J2, II, 1833).

PICK, Edward, of Lying, 'absent and not taken' (CP); 'took up arms against the king' (Som. QSR).

PICK, Stephen, of Street, 'absent' (CP).

PICKMAN, George, of Chard, 'in the late rebellion' (CP).

PIKE *see* Pyke.

PILL, Abraham, husbandman, of Chilton Polden (TB), tried at Taunton; hanged at Chard (JR, JW); land forfeit and for sale (TB).

PILLICK, Philip, of Othery, 'absent' (CP).

PILLING, William, of Honiton, 'a rebel' (CP).

PINE (Pyne), Alexander, of Combe St Nicholas, 'absent and believed' (CP).

PINE, Cornelius junior, of Wellington, 'absent' (CP).

PINE, Edward, cordwinder, of Taunton St Mary, 'aiding' (CP); Blue Regt. (P).

PINE, Richard, of Northcote, Honiton, 'a rebel' (CP); tried at Dorchester; transported for Nipho (JR) on the *Betty* from Weymouth, Nov. 25, to Barbados; sold to Capt. John Gibbs (SL). Named on the 1689 petition (CSPD, W&M, I, 43).

PINE, William, of Creech St Michael, 'in the rebellion and taken' (CP).

PINNELL, Abel, yeoman, of Combpyne, imprisoned in Wilts. (DLD); presented at Dorchester and 'proposed for pardon' (JR).

PINNEY, Abraham, of Trull, 'absent' (CP); hanged in Taunton on July 9 by Col. Kirke (P); buried at St James's as 'a rebel soldier' on July 10 (PR).

PINNEY, Alexander, at Wells Assize 'remaining in custody for want of evidence' (JR).

PINNEY, Azariah, yeoman, a young married man, of Axminster, 'supposed' (CP), got to London after Sedgemoor, arrested and sent to Dorchester for trial; at first to be hanged at Bridport (Br); but then to be transported for Nipho (JR); his sister Hester paid £65 for a ransom (PP); 'taken out of my custody, sent away to Bristol' (G. Penne on SL); his brother Nathaniel paid his passage to Nevis, £5; clothes and other equipment, including a Bible, £15; and £15 to start him in Nevis (PP), where he set up as a factor. He became a Lieutenant. His pardon was approved on 31 May 1687 (CSPD, J2, II, 1833) in the Defence Force, a Member of the Assembly, and Treasurer of the Island. He visited England twice, dying in London in 1719 (University of Bristol, Pinney Papers). He had been presented at Exeter and misreported at large (JR).

PINNEY, George, of Chardstock, 'suspected guilty' (CP).

PINNEY, John, of Chardstock, 'suspected guilty' (CP); tried at Dorchester; transported for Booth (JR) on the *Happy Return* from Weymouth, Sept. 25, to Barbados; sold to Capt. George Terwight (SL).

PINNEY, John, of Wellington, 'absent' (CP).

PINNEY, Nathaniel, of Isle Abbots, son of the vicar, the Revd. Robert Pinney. Local written tradition says 'involved in the Monmouth Rebellion.'

PINNEY, Robert, clothworker, of Thorncombe, imprisoned in Dorset (DLD); tried at Dorchester, Sept. 5; pleaded not guilty; hanged at Dorchester, Sept. 7 (JR, NL).

PINSENT (Pinson), Samuel, of Honiton, 'a rebel' (CP); tried at Dorchester; transported for Nipho (JR) from Dorchester gaol via Weymouth, Nov. 25, on the *Betty* to Barbados; sold to Peter Flewilling (SL). Named on the 1689 petition (CSPD, W&M, I, 43).

PIPPEN (Peppin), George, gentleman, yeoman, of Dulverton, excepted from GP; presented at Wells in March 1686 for 'persuading diverse subjects to join with Monmouth, and concealing traitors and direction them to escape'; pleaded and found not guilty (GD); petition, 'falsely accused concerning the late rebellion' Aug. 2, 1686; pardon of all treasons Oct. 18 (CPSD, J2, II, 861, 1078).

PITCHER, Amos, of Merriott, 'rebel and not taken' (CP).

PITCHER, George, tried at Taunton; hanged at Yeovil (JR, JW).

PITCHER, John, of Creech St Michael, 'absent and not taken' (CP).

PITCHER, Joseph, of Chardland, 'absent, believed' (CP).

PITCHER, Richard, of Ilminster, 'in the late rebellion' (CP).

PITMAN, Henry, chirurgeon, of Yeovil, of Quaker family, doctored wounded of both sides, captured and robbed on his way home from Sedgemoor; imprisoned at Ilchester; tried at Wells; transported for Nipho (JR) on the *Betty* from Weymouth to Barbados on Nov. 25 (SL). In spite of ransom money paid, he was sold to, and badly treated by, Robert Bishop. He organised the escape of six rebels and two debtors, first to Tortuga, and thence to England. Pardon dated 31 May 1687 (CSPD, J2, II, 1833). He published an account of the

escape in 1689 (Pitman, *A Relation of the Great Sufferings*, etc.);
returned to Barbados in 1691 and died there in 1693 (*Letters of John
Pinney*, 1679–99, ed. G.F. Nuttall).

PITMAN, William, of Sandford Orcas, brother of Henry, tried at Wells;
transported for Nipho (JR) to Barbados and sold there to John Bishop:
Buried 1687 (BMi). Pardon, May 31 1687 (CSPD, J2, II, 1833).

PITT, Francis, of Puriton, 'active soldier in the Duke of Monmouth's
army' (Som. QSR).

PITT, Joseph, yeoman, of Colyton, 'absent' (CP); presented at Exeter but
at large (JR).

PITT, Robert, of Tiverton, 'with the late Duke of Monmouth' (CP).

PITT, Thomas, worsted comber, of Tiverton, imprisoned in the High
Gaol, Devon (DLD).

PITT, William, aged 28, woolcomber (SL), of Bishop's Hull, 'absent'
(CP); tried at Taunton; transported for the Queen (JR) on the
*Jamaica Merchant* to Barbados; sold to Capt. John Sutton (SL).

PITTARD, George, of Kingsbury Episcopi, 'absent, believed' (CP).

PITTARD, Robert, of Kingsbury Episcopi, 'absent, believed' (CP).

PITTARD, Thomas, of Kingsbury Episcopi, 'absent, believed' (CP);
tried at Wells; transported for Howard (JR) on Oct. 25 in the *Port
Royal Merchant* to Jamaica (SL).

PITTARD, William, aged 28, woolcomber (SL) of Kingsbury Episcopi,
'absent, believed' (CP); tried at Taunton; transported thence for the
Queen (JR) on the *Jamaica Merchant* to Barbados; sold to Capt.
John Sutton (SL).

PITTMAN, John, of Bishop's Hull, 'absent' (CP); 'dead' (CL).

PITTMAN, John, of Stalbridge, 'absconding, suspected' (CP).

PITTS, James, mercer, of Lyme Regis, 'absent, supposed' (CP);
presented at Dorchester; certificate allowed (JR); member of Lyme
Corporation (LRCB).

PITTS, James junior, presented at Wells; 'recommended for pardon'
(JR).

PITTS, James, presented at Wells and bound over (JR).

PITTS, John, of Chard, 'absent, believed' (CP). [*See below.*]

PITTS, John, of Chardland, 'absent, believed' (CP). [*See below.*]

PITTS, John, of Knowle St Giles, 'in the rebellion and not come in' (CP).
One of these three, or another John Pitts, was tried at Dorchester;
and transported for Booth (JR) on the *Happy Return* from
Weymouth, Sept. 25, to Barbados; sold to Col. Richard Williams
(SL). Another was presented at Wells: his certificate allowed (JR).

PITTS, Jonathan, of Knowle St Giles, 'in the rebellion and not come in'
(CP).

PLAICE, Thomas, sergemaker, of Edington, a Quaker, 'out in the
rebellion and at large' (CP); leader of the Clubmen; disowned by
Quakers (FQMN); excepted from the GP; arrested in London; tried
at Wells, March 21 1687, to be hanged on April 15 (GD); stay of
execution, April 11; pardon May 31 (CSPD, J2, II, 1667, 1833).
Land forfeit and for sale (TB). Petition for remission of forfeiture

(TB 1973). [Name has been misread as Pheere, Phooce, and Phooks.]

PLATT, Richard, at Dorchester Assize 'continued in gaol,' not indicted (JR).

PLATT, William, at Dorchester Assize 'continued in gaol, not indicted' (JR).

PLOMER, Francis, tried at Wells; transported for Howard (JR) on Oct. 25 in the *Port Royal Merchant* to Jamaica (SL).

PLUMLEY, George, tried at Dorchester; transported for Booth (JR) on the *Happy Return* from Weymouth, Sept. 25, to Barbados; sold to Nicholas Prideaux (SL).

PLUMLEY, William, lord of the manor of Locking; reached home after Sedgemoor and hid; his dog unwittingly revealed his hiding place (T); tried at Wells and hanged there (JR, JW); land forfeit but not for sale; granted to his son Francis, John Vyner, and Edward Hancock (TB). The manor, the advowson and lands were valued at £130 19s (TB).

POCOCK, George senior, of Curry Rivel, 'out in the rebellion and not taken' (CP). [*See below.*]

POCOCK, George junior, of Curry Rivel, 'out in the rebellion and not taken' (CP). [*See below.*] One of these two was presented at the Somerset Assize on August 9 1686 for speaking seditious words; pleaded not guilty; found guilty; to stand in the pillory at Langport (GD).

POCOCK, John, of Swell, 'being in the late rebellion and at large' (CP).

POCOCK, William, tried at Taunton; hanged at Somerton (JR, JW).

PODDINGTON, Richard, yeoman, of Sawley, imprisoned in the High Gaol, Devon (DLD).

POLE, Simon, of Creech St Michael, 'in the rebellion and taken' (CP).

POLLARD, Abraham, of Chardland, 'absent, believed' (CP); in Bridgwater prison, tried at Taunton; transported for Booth (JR) via Bristol, Oct. 24, on the *John* to Barbados; sold to William Marchant (SL).

POLLARD, John, brewer, of Taunton St Mary, 'aiding' (CP); Blue Regt. (P).

POLLING *see* Dolling.

POMEROY (Pumrey), Daniel, of Taunton, in the Bridewell there, tried there; transported for Booth (JR) via Bristol, Oct. 24, on the *John* to Barbados; sold to John Denner (SL). Pardon May 31 1687 (CSPD, J2, II, 1833).

POMEROY, James, yeoman, of Uplyme, imprisoned in Wilts (DLD), tried at Dorchester; transported for Booth (JR) on the *Happy Return* from Weymouth, Sept. 25, to Barbados; sold to Capt. William Marshall (SL).

POMFRETT (Pumphrey), Thomas, tried at Taunton; to be transported for the Queen (JR); on John Rose's receipt of Oct. 12, but not on the *Jamaica Merchant* (SL). Late of Worcester, 'engaged in the late rebellion', was pardoned May 31 1687 (CSPD, J2, II, 1833).

POOKE, Richard, carpenter, of Lyme Regis, 'absent, supposed' (CP).

POOKE, Richard (another), carpenter, of Lyme Regis, 'absent, supposed' (CP).

POOLE, Edward senior, of West Buckland, 'absent' (CP).

POOLE, Edward, comber, of Taunton St Mary, 'aiding' (CP); Blue Regt. (P).

POOLE, Henry, cooper, of Taunton St James, 'aiding' (CP); Blue Regt. (P).

POOLE, Jeremiah, aged 30, clothier (SL), 'in Scott's army and not taken' (CP), tried at Taunton; transported thence for the Queen (JR) on the *Jamaica Merchant* Dec. 9, to Barbados; sold on March 12 to Major Abel Allen (SL).

POOLE, John, in the Bridewell, Taunton; tried at Taunton; transported thence for Booth (JR); on his receipt of Oct. 24 but not on the *John* (SL).

POOLE, Simon, of Beaminster (SL), in Bridgwater prison, tried at Taunton; transported for Booth (JR) via Bristol, Oct. 24, on the *John* towards Barbados; died at sea (SL).

POOLE, Sylvester, aged 24, butcher (SL), of Milverton, 'absenting' (CP); tried at Taunton; transported thence for the Queen (JR) on the *Jamaica Merchant*, Dec. 9, to Barbados; sold on March 12 to Major George Lillington (SL).

POOLE, William, of Exeter, 'absenting' (CP).

POOLE, William, of Taunton St James, 'aiding' (CP); Blue Regt. (P).

POPE, Benjamin, of Ilminster, 'in the late rebellion' (CP).

POPE, Henry junior, of Ilminster, 'in the late rebellion' (CP).

POPE, Humphrey, of Taunton, in the Bridewell there, tried there; transported for Booth (JR) via Bristol, Oct. 24, on the *John* to Barbados; sold to John Burston (SL).

POPE, James, weaver, of East Woodlands, 'in the rebellion and at large' (CP).

POPE, John, of Trull, 'absent' (CP), tried at Taunton; transported for Musgrave (JR) on the *Jamaica Merchant* from Weymouth to Barbados; there by March 12 (SL).

POPE, John, tried at Wells; transported for Howard (JR), Oct. 25 on the *Port Royal Merchant* to Jamaica (SL).

POPE, William, yeoman, of Frome, 'for a riot and amongst the Clubmen' (CP).

POPLE, Charles, tried at Wells; transported for Howard (JR), Oct. 25 on the *Port Royal Merchant* to Jamaica (SL).

PORTER, Frank, presented in March 1686 for high treason at Exeter; pardoned and dismissed (GD).

PORTER, Henry, locksmith, of Taunton St Mary, 'aiding' (CP); Blue Regt. (P).

PORTER, Luke, aged 20, shoemaker (SL); tried at Taunton; transported thence for the Queen (JR) on the *Jamaica Merchant*, Dec. 9, to Barbados; sold on March 12 to Benjamin Middleton (SL).

PORTER, Matthew, tried at Dorchester; transported for Booth (JR) on the *Happy Return* from Weymouth, Sept. 25, to Barbados; sold to Nicholas Prideaux (SL).

PORTLOCK, Robert, presented at Wells and bound over (JR).

PORTNELL, John, tried at Wells; transported for Howard (JR), Oct. 25 on the *Port Royal Merchant* to Jamaica (SL).

POTTER, John, presented at Wells and bound over (JR).

POTTLE, Nathaniel, sergeweaver, of Bradninch, Cullompton, imprisoned at Taunton (DLD); tried there (as Matthew); transported for Musgrave (JR) on the *Jamaica Merchant* from Weymouth to Jamaica; there by March 12 (SL).

POTTS, Samuel, tried at Exeter (JR); hanged at Honiton Oct. 7 or 14 (NL). Locke says he was about 20 and a surgeon.

POUND, Francis, shoemaker, of Taunton St James, 'aiding' (CP); Blue Regt. (P).

POVEY, Francis, clothworker, of Beckington, 'in the rebellion, out of Beckington; at large' (CP).

POWELL, Isaac senior (CL), of Stoke St Gregory, 'absent' (CP); of Thornfalcon, 'took up arms against the king' (Som. QSR).

POWELL, Isaac junior, of Stoke St Gregory, 'absenting' (CP).

POWELL, Jacob, tried at Taunton; to be transported for the Queen (JR). On John Rose's receipt of Oct. 12 but not on the *Jamaica Merchant* (SL).

POWELL, Michael, of Neath, in Bridgwater prison (SL); tried at Taunton; transported for Booth (JR) via Bristol, Oct. 24, on the *John* to Barbados; sold to Capt. Walter Scott (SL).

POWELL, Oliver, tried at Taunton; hanged at Yeovil (JR, JW).

POWELL, Thomas, of Thornfalcon, 'absent' (CP).

POWELL, William, of Stoke St Gregory, 'in arms aiding and assisting James Scott in the time of the rebellion' (CP); tried at Wells; transported thence for Bridgman (JR) by White on the *Constant Richard* to Jamaica (SL).

POWNELL, James, presented at Wells and bound over (JR).

POWSLAND, Samuel, from the Workhouse, Exeter, presented there, March 1686, pardoned and dismissed (GD).

POYNTER, Richard, feltmaker, of Wincanton, 'actually in arms in the rebellion, as informed, and at large' (CP).

POYNTINGTON, John, weaver, of Taunton St Mary, 'aiding' (CP); Blue Regt. (P). Married and a father (PR).

PRANCE, Roger, tried at Taunton; hanged at Chewton Mendip (JR, JW).

PREIST, Francis, of Pitminster, tried at Taunton; hanged at Wellington (JR, JW) on Oct. 1 (NL).

PREIST, Henry, aged 22, plowman [carter] (SL), of Puriton, 'active soldier in the Duke of Monmouth's army' (Som. QSR); tried at Taunton; transported thence for the Queen (JR) on the *Jamaica Merchant*, Dec. 9, to Barbados; sold on March 12 to Robert Kelly (SL).

PREIST, James, of Pitminster, 'absent' (CP).

PREIST, Lawrence, tried at Taunton; to be transported for the Queen (JR). On John Rose's receipt of Oct. 12, but not on the *Jamaica Merchant* (SL).

PREIST, Thomas, aged 20, sergemaker (SL), of Pitminster, 'absent' (CP), tried at Taunton; transported thence for the Queen (JR) on the *Jamaica Merchant*, Dec. 9, to Barbados, there by March 12; sold to Col. Thomas Colleton (SL).

PREIST, William, tried at Wells; transported for Howard (JR), Oct. 25 on the *Port Royal Merchant* to Jamaica (SL).

PREW, Abraham, of Martock, 'absent' (CP).

PREW (Price), John, yeoman, of Crewkerne, imprisoned in the High Gaol, Devon, (DLD); tried at Dorchester; transported for Nipho (JR) on the *Betty* from Weymouth, Nov. 25, to Barbados; sold to Peter Flewilling (SL).

PRICE, James, of Glastonbury, 'from home at the time of the rebellion' (CP); tried at Wells; 'designed for execution yet omitted in the warrant' (JR).

PRICKMAN, John, presented at Taunton; certificate allowed (JR).

PRIDDY, Richard, of Milverton, 'absenting' (CP).

PRIDEAUX, Edmund, of Forde Abbey, suspected of sending horses and £500 to Monmouth; in the Tower from July to March; 'given' by the king to Lord Chief Justice Jeffreys; ransomed by Mrs Prideaux for £15,000 less £240 for cash payment. Pardon March 12, 1686 (CSPD, J2, II, 265).

PRIGG, Thomas, dyer, of Taunton St Mary, 'aiding' (CP); Blue Regt. (P).

PRINCE, James, porter, of Lyme Regis, 'absent, supposed' (CP).

PRING, Benjamin, of Milverton, 'absenting' (CP).

PRING, William, of MIlverton, 'absenting' (CP).

PRIST, John junior, of Martock, 'absent' (CP).

PROWSE (Prusson), Samuel, currier, of Honiton, imprisoned in the High Gaol, Devon (DLD); presented at Wells and bound over (JR).

PROWSE, William, tried at Wells; transported for Howard (JR); Oct. 25 in the *Port Royal Merchant* to Jamaica (SL).

PROWSE, William, tried at Wells; transported thence Oct. 31 for Bridgeman (JR) by White on the *Constant Richard* to Jamaica (SL).

PRUSSON *see* Prowse.

PRYOR, Edward, weaver, of Rode, 'in the rebellion' (CP).

PRYOR, Isaac, tried at Wells; transported for Howard (JR), Oct. 25 on the *Port Royal Merchant* to Jamaica (SL).

PRYOR, John, husbandman, of Stoke sub Hamdon, 'absent' (CP). [*See below.*]

PRYOR, John, of Huntspill, 'absent and in the late rebellion' (CP). [*See below.*] One of these two was tried at Dorchester; transported for Booth (JR) on the *Happy Return* from Weymouth, Sept. 25, to Barbados; sold there to Col. Richard Williams in December (SL).

PRYOR, Matthew, tried at Wells; to be transported for Howard to Jamaica but escaped between Wells and Sherborne (JR, SL):

PRYOR, William, presented at Wells and bound over (JR).

PUCKER *see* Packer.

PUCKERIDGE, George, the elder, of North Petherton, 'took up arms against the king' (Som. QSR); tried at Dorchester, Sept. 10; hanged at Sherborne, Sept. 15 (JR, NL).

PUCKETT, Francis, of Bridport, 'in the rebellion, as we are informed' (CP); tried at Dorchester; pleaded not guilty (GD); transported for Musgrave (JR) from Weymouth on the *Jamaica Merchant* to Barbados; there by March 12 (SL). Named on the petition of 1689 (CSPD, W&M, I, 43).

PULLEN, Edward, of Ruishton, 'absent' (CP).

PULLING, John, tried at Dorchester, Sept. 10; hanged at Poole, Sept. 21 (JR, NL).

PULLMAN, James, of Chard, 'in the late rebellion' (CP). [*See below.*]

PULLMAN, James, of Chardland, 'absent and believed' (CP). [*See below.*] One of these two was tried at Wells; was to be transported for Howard (JR) but escaped from Sherborne prison (SL).

PULMAN, Thomas junior, of Luppitt, 'supposed' (CP).

PUMPHREY *see* Pomfrett.

PURCELL, John, of Taunton St Mary, 'aiding' (CP); Blue Regt. (P).

PURCHAS, Francis, yeoman, of Colyton, 'absent' (CP); presented at Exeter but at large (JR).

PURDY, Bartholomew, worsted comber, of Taunton St James, 'aiding' (CP); Blue Regt. (P).

PURDY, William, worsted comber, of Taunton St James, 'aiding' (CP); Blue Regt. (P).

PURKIS, Thomas, comb maker, of Taunton St Mary, 'aiding' (CP); Blue Regt. (P).

PUSSEY *see* Brassey.

PYES, James, carpenter, of Colyton, wounded at Sedgemoor, imprisoned at Wells (DLD), tried there and hanged at Glastonbury (JR, JW).

PYKE, Hugh, of Dowlishwake, 'in the rebellion and not come in' (CP(.

PYKE, John, of Dowlishwake, 'in the rebellion and not come in' (CP).

PYKE, John junior, of Dowlishwake, 'in the rebellion and not come in' (CP).

PYKES, Roger, of Sidmouth, 'went to Monmouth' (CP).

PYNE see *Pine*.


QUANT, Henry, of Taunton, imprisoned in the Bridewell there; tried at Taunton; transported thence for Booth (JR) via Bristol, Oct. 24, on the *John* to Barbados; sold to Capt. Walter Scott (SL).

QUESTION, Augustine, of Carhampton, 'in the late rebellion' (CP).

QUICK, Henry senior, husbandman, of Upottery, 'absent' (CP); presented at Exeter but at large (JR). [*See below.*]

QUICK, Henry junior, yeoman, of Upottery, 'absent' (CP); presented at Exeter but at large (JR). [*See below.*] One of these two was tried at

Wells and transported, Oct. 20, for Stapleton (JR) in the *Indeavour* from Bristol to Nevis or St Kitts (SL). One was excepted from GP; his land forfeit and for sale. Was the father killed at Sedgemoor, or died of wounds, and the son transported?

QUICK, John, yeoman, of Axmouth, 'reported to be in arms' (CP); presented at Exeter but at large; tried at Wells; transported, Oct. 31, for Bridgeman (JR) by White on the *Constant Richard* to Jamaica (SL).

QUICK, Robert senior, yeoman, of Axmouth, 'reported' (CP); presented at Exeter but at large (JR).

QUICK, Robert junior, yeoman, of Axmouth, 'reported' (CP); presented at Exeter but at large (JR).

QUICK, Thomas, yeoman, of Luppitt, 'out in the rebellion' (CP); in Dorchester gaol, tried at Dorchester; transported for Nipho (JR) from Weymouth, Nov. 25, on the *Betty* to Barbados; sold to Ralph Lane (SL). Also misreported presented at Exeter and at large (JR). [*See below.*]

QUICK, Thomas, silkweaver, of Membury, imprisoned in the High Gaol, Devon (DLD). [*See below.*] One of these two was named on the petition of 1689 (CSPD, W&M, I, 43).

QUICK, William, yeoman, of Axmouth, reported (CP); presented at Exeter but at large (JR).

QUICK, William, yeoman, of Upottery, wounded at Sedgemoor; imprisoned at Wells (DLD).

QUINTON, Thomas, tried at Exeter (JR), hanged at Ottery St Mary in Oct. (NL).

QUINTON alias Frear, William yeoman, of Shute, imprisoned in Wilts. (DLD); tried at Dorchester, Sept. 10 (JR); hanged at Bridport, Sept. 12 (NL). Land forfeit and for sale (TB).

QUIRE, Joseph, presented at Taunton; certificate allowed (JR).

QUIRE, Raymond, presented at Taunton; certificate allowed (JR).

RADD, Thomas, of Combe St Nicholas, 'absent, believed' (CP).

RADDLE *see* Ruddle.

RADFORD, Cornelius, aged 20, broadweaver, imprisoned at Taunton (DLD); tried there and transported thence for the Queen (JR) on the *Jamaica Merchant*, Dec. 9, to Barbados, sold there on March 12 to George Harper (SL).

RADWAY, Thomas junior, wiredrawer, of Frome, 'in the rebellion and at large' (CP).
*And see* Rodway.

RALPH, Edward, of Wellington, 'absent' (CP).

RALPH, George, of Wellington, 'absent' (CP).

RALPH, Richard, of North Petherton, 'absconded' (CP).

RAND, Richard senior, chirurgeon, of Dunster, 'bearing arms under the Duke of Monmouth' (Som. QSR).

RANDALL, Bartholomew, of West Coker, in the Bridewell at Taunton (Som. QSR); tried at Taunton and transported thence for Booth (JR) via Bristol, Oct. 24, on the *John* to Barbados; sold to Capt. Stoaks (SL).

RANDALL, Edward, of Hardington, 'in the late rebellion' (CP).

RANDALL, Henry, tried at Taunton; to be transported for the Queen (JR); on John Rose's receipt, Oct. 12, but not on the *Jamaica Merchant* (SL).

RANSOME (Rempson), Samuel, yeoman, of Axminster, member of the Congregational church (Ecc); 'supposed' (CP); in Monmouth's Horse; 'seen in his camp' (LRMB); mortally wounded at Ashill on June 19 or 20 (Ecc). Presented at Exeter and misreported at large (JR).

RAPSON, Andrew, of Clapton, Crewkerne, 'rebel and not taken' (CP); tried at Dorchester; transported for Booth (JR) on the *Happy Return* from Weymouth, Sept. 25, to Barbados; sold there in December to John Hethersell, Esq. (SL).

RAPSON, Robert, of Over Compton, 'absconding, and suspected' (CP).

RAWBONE, Edward, tried at Wells; transported thence for Bridgeman (JR) Oct. 31, by White on the *Constant Richard* to Jamaica (SL).

RAWE, Richard, clerk to Mr Marshall, of Taunton St Mary, 'aiding' (CP); Blue Regt. (P). Excepted from GP.

RAWE, Robert, presented at Wells and bound over (JR).

RAWLINS (Rawlings), George, of Combe St Nicholas, 'absent, believed' (CP).

RAWLINS, John, of Seavington St Mary, 'in the rebellion and not come in' (CP).

RAWLINS, Richard, of Taunton St Mary, 'aiding' (CP); Blue Regt. (P).

RAWLINS, Thomas, of Llangarran, Hereford, pardon of all treasons, rebellions, etc. June 14, 1686 (CSPD, J2, II, 680, 696).

RAWLINS, William, of Chard, 'in the late rebellion' (CP).

RAY, George, of Chard, 'absent, believed' (CP).

RAYMOND, Arthur, ploughman [carter], of Axminster, 'seen in Monmouth's camp' (LRMB); 'not in arms but followed his plough [cart]' (DLD).

RAYMOND, George, of Ilchester, 'in the late rebellion' (CP); presented at Wells and bound over (JR).

RAYMOND, William, of Northover, 'in the late rebellion' (CP); presented at Wells and bound over (JR).

RAYSE, Thomas, of Barrington, 'in the rebellion and not come in' (CP).

RAYSON, Thomas, husbandman, of Stoke sub Hamdon, 'absent' (CP). *And see* Reason.

REA, William, of Curry Rivel, 'out in the rebellion and not taken' (CP).

READ, David, yeoman, of Axminster, 'supposed' (CP); presented at Exeter but at large (JR).

READ, Osmund, of Taunton, imprisoned in the Bridewell there (Som. QSR); tried at Taunton; transported for Booth (JR) via Bristol, Oct. 24, on the *John* to Barbados; sold to John Burston (SL).

READ, Robert senior, of Taunton St Mary, 'aiding' (CP); Blue Regt. (P).

READ, Robert junior, of Wellington, 'in prison for rebellion' (CP); tried at Taunton; hanged at Wellington, Oct. 1 (JR, NL).

READ, William, husbandman, of North Bradley, Wilts., tried at Wells; transported for Howard (JR), Oct. 25 on the *Port Royal Merchant* to Jamaica (SL). Land forfeit and for sale (TB).

REASON, John, tried at Dorchester; transported for Booth (JR) on the *Happy Return* from Weymouth, Sept. 25, to Barbados; sold as Thomas Reason (? Thomas Rayson above) to Col. John Sampson (SL).

RECKETT (Rickett), William, of North Petherton, 'taking up arms against the king' (Som. QSR), 'absconded' (CP).

REDBEARD, William, tried at Wells; transported thence for Bridgeman (JR) by White, Oct. 31, on the *Constant Richard* to Jamaica (SL).

REDD, Arthur, of Bampton, 'supposed to be a rebel' (CP).

REDD, Laurence, of Bampton, 'supposed to be a rebel' (CP).

REDWAY, Stephen, of West Woodlands, 'in prison for the late rebellion' (CP). Did he die there?

REDWOOD, Henry, of Northcote, Honiton, 'a rebel' (CP).

REDWOOD, John, of Gittisham, 'a trained soldier and went to Monmouth and is yet in rebellion' (CP).

REDWOOD, Philip, of Ditcheat, 'being in arms in Scott's army and not taken' (CP).

REDWOOD, Thomas, of Gittisham, 'went to Monmouth and is yet in rebellion' (CP); tried at Taunton; 'designed to be executed but omitted in the warrant' (JR); transported by Capt. Heywood on the *Constant Richard*, Nov. 12, to Jamaica (SL).

REEKEMAN, John, of Wareham, 'absent' (CP).

REEVE, Henry, of Glastonbury, 'from home at the time of the rebellion' (CP); presented at Taunton but 'proposed for pardon' (JR).

REEVE, John, of Street, 'absent' (CP); tried at Wells; transported for Nipho (JR) on the *Betty* from Weymouth, Nov. 25, to Barbados; sold to John Smart (SL).

REEVE, Robert, of Crediton, 'absent' (CP); tried at Wells; transported for Howard (JR), Oct. 25 on the *Port Royal Merchant* to Jamaica (SL).

REEVE, Robert, cardmaker, of West Woodlands, 'in prison for the late rebellion' (CP); tried at Wells; transported for Howard, Oct. 25 on the *Port Royal Merchant* to Jamaica (SL).

REEVE, Stephen, of Glastonbury, 'from home at the time of the rebellion' (CP).

REEVE, Thomas, of Street, 'absent' (CP). [*See below.*]

REEVE, Thomas, worsted carder, of Taunton St Mary, 'aiding' (CP). [*See below.*] One of these two was presented at Taunton and proposed for pardon (JR).

REEVES, William, of Taunton, sergemaker, confessed to having been in Monmouth's army; committed to prison in Exeter City Sessions 14 Aug. 1685 (Exeter City Sessions Bk.).

REEVE (Reives), a Lieutenant on Albemarle's list.

REIVES, William, at Taunton Assize 'remaining in gaol till further order' (JR). Reprieved (JR2).

REMAN, John, scrivener, of Rode, 'in the rebellion' (CP).

REMAN *see* Beman.

RENDON, Laurence, of Croscombe, 'in Scott's army and not taken' (CP).

RENWAY, William, of Axminster, 'supposed' (CP).

RESDON, John, worsted comber, of Taunton St James, 'aiding' (CP); Blue Regt. (P).

RESTORICK, Joseph, of Colyton, husbandman, aged about 30; married in 1677 (PR); tried at Dorchester, Sept. 10 (JR); hanged at Poole, Sept. 21 (NL). Land forfeit and for sale (TB).

REW, John, of North Petherton, 'taking up arms against the king' (Som. QSR).

REWELL, Stephen, presented at Exeter, March 1686; pardoned and dismissed (GD).

REYNOLDS, John, tried at Wells; to be transported for Howard (JR), Oct. 25 on the *Port Royal Merchant* to Jamaica, but escaped between Wells and Sherborne (SL).

REYNOLDS, Richard, cardmaker, of Beckington, 'in the rebellion, out of Beckington, at large' (CP); presented at Taunton; 'proposed for pardon' (JR).

REYNOLDS, Roger, husbandman, of Dunster, 'in arms in the rebellion of James Scott' (CP).

REYNOLDS, James, of Northcote, Honiton, 'a rebel' (CP).

RICH, George, of Crewkerne, 'a rebel and not taken' (CP).

RICHARDS, Christopher, of Witham Friary, 'in the rebellion and not taken' (CP); tried at Wells; transported for Howard (JR), Oct. 25 on the *Port Royal Merchant* to Jamaica (SL).

RICHARDS, Francis, of Milverton, 'absenting' (CP).

RICHARDS, Henry, of Coleford, 'absenting' (CP).

RICHARDS, James, of Milverton, 'absenting' (CP).

RICHARDS, John, of Marston Bigot, husbandman, 'in the rebellion, not taken'; (CP); tried at Wells; hanged at Norton St Philip (JR, JW). Land forfeit and for sale (TB).

RICHARDS, John, of Bradford on Tone, 'absent' (CP). [*See below.*]

RICHARDS, John, of Milverton, 'absenting' (CP). [*See below.*] One of these two at Wells pleaded and was found not guilty (JR). The other was presented at Exeter in March 1686, was pardoned and dismissed (GD).

RICHARDS, Robert, aged 28, tailor, of Cullompton (DLD), imprisoned at Taunton (Som. QSR), tried there; transported thence for the Queen (JR), Dec. 9 on the *Jamaica Merchant* to Barbados; sold there on March 12 to Francis Bond, Esq. (SL).

RICHMOND, George, 'engaged in late rebellion'; pardon 13 May 1687 (CSPD, J2, II, 1833).

RICKETT *see* Reckett.

RICKMAN, George, presented at Dorchester for sending a horse to the rebels; certificate allowed, but he died in prison (JR).

RICKMAN, Giles, of Sherborne, 'absconding' (CP).

RIDGE, John, of Taunton St Mary, Extraportam tithing (CL), 'aiding' (CP); Blue Regt. (P).

RIDLEY, Samuel, of Taunton St Mary, 'aiding' (CP); Blue Regt. (P).

RING, William, of St Clement Danes, convicted of treason at Old Bailey in Oct. 1685; reprieved by Royal Warrant Oct. 23; pardon Jan. 17 1686 (CSPD, J2, II, 43).

RISCOMBE *see* Liscombe.

ROBBINS, James, fuller, of Taunton St Mary, 'aiding' (CP); Blue Regt. (P).

ROBBINS, John, tried at Dorchester, Sept. 10; hanged at Weymouth or Melcombe Regis, Sept. 15 (JR, NL).

ROBBINS, John, of Stoke St Gregory (CP), of Thornfalcon (Som.QSR), 'in arms' (CP); tried at Taunton; to be transported for the Queen (JR); on John Rose's receipt of Oct. 12 but not on *Jamaica Merchant* (SL).

ROBBINS, Joseph, tried at Wells; transported for Howard (JR) Oct. 25 on the *Port Royal Merchant* to Jamaica (SL).

ROBBINS, Samuel, of Charmouth, 'taken at Lyme Regis and sent to Dorchester gaol', July 14 (LRMB); tried at Dorchester Sept. 10; hanged at Wareham Sept. 22 (JR, NL). He sold fish to Monmouth at sea and so landed with him. A copy of the Solemn League and Covenant found in his house (BA).

ROBBINS, Thomas, of North Petherton, 'absconded' (CP); 'took up arms against the king' (Som. QSR).

ROBENS, Philip, of Ilminster, 'in the late rebellion' (CP).

ROBERTS, Francis, yeoman, of Colyton, 'absent' (CP); presented at Exeter but at large (JR).

ROBERTS, Francis, brewer, of Taunton St Mary, 'aiding' (CP); Blue Regt. (P).

ROBERTSON (Robinson, DLD, SL), George, broadweaver, of Colyton, imprisoned at Taunton (DLD); tried there; transported for Musgrave (JR) on the *Jamaica Merchant* from Weymouth to Jamaica, there by March 12. (SL).

ROBINSON, Alexander, tried at Wells; transported for Howard (JR) Oct. 25 on the *Port Royal Merchant* to Jamaica (SL).

ROBERTON *see* Rotherton.

ROBJOUNT, Edward, yeoman, of Upottery, 'absent' (CP); presented at Exeter but at large (JR).

ROCK, William, tried at Taunton; hanged at Ilminster (JR, JW). [Misread and spelt Kitch in the warrant.]

ROCKETT, Aaron, fuller, of Lyme Regis, 'absent' (CP).

ROCKETT or Wakely, Matthew, of Wootton Fitzpaine, 'suspected' (CP).

ROCKETT, Philip, yeoman, of Axminster, 'supposed' (CP); presented at Exeter but at large (JR).

ROCKETT, Robert, yeoman, of Musbury, 'in the rebellion' (CP); presented as of Axminster in BL. Add. MS. 30077 at Exeter, and at large (JR).

ROCKETT, Solomon, of Monkton Wyld, 'suspected' (CP).

RODBEARD, Thomas, tried at Wells; transported for Howard (JR), Oct. 25 on the *Port Royal Merchant* to Jamaica (SL).

RODWAY, Stephen, of Frome, in Bridgwater prison (SL); tried at Taunton; transported for Booth (JR) via Bristol, Oct. 24, on the *John* to Barbados; sold to Ann Gallop (SL).
*And see* Radway.

ROE *see* Rowe.

ROGERS, Christopher, yeoman, of Luppitt, 'absent' (CP); presented at Exeter but at large (JR).

ROGERS, Edward, of Banwell, excepted from GP.

ROGERS, Francis, wiredrawer, of Frome, 'in the rebellion and at large' (CP).

ROGERS, John, of Banwell, presented at Wells and bound over (JR); but excepted from GP.

ROGERS, John, of Whitelackington, in the Bridewell, Taunton (SL); tried at Taunton; transported thence for Booth (JR) via Bristol on the *John*, Oct. 24, to Barbados; sold to Major Johnson (SL).

ROGERS, John, aged 38, clothworker, of West Woodlands, 'in prison for the late rebellion' (CP); imprisoned at Taunton (SL), tried there; transported thence for the Queen (JR) on the *Jamaica Merchant*, Dec. 9, to Barbados; sold there on March 12 to John Summers (SL).

ROOKE, George, of North Curry, 'in arms against the king' (Som. QSR).

ROOKES, Henry, of Tiverton, comber's salter and apprentice, imprisoned in Wilts. (DLD); tried at Wells; transported for Howard (JR) Oct. 25 on the *Port Royal Merchant* to Jamaica (SL).

ROOST *see* Rust.

ROPER, Henry, tried at Wells; transported for Howard (JR), Oct. 25 on the *Port Royal Merchant* to Jamaica (SL).

ROPER, Hugh, of Burnham, tried at Taunton; to be hanged at Bridgwater (JR, JW), reprieved 'under the gallows' and released (JR2, NL). Land forfeit but not for sale; reversion to Brent, Loder and Clarke; pardon money to be kept by Oxburgh (TB).

ROPER, John, of Combe St Nicholas, 'absent, believed'. (CP).

ROPER, John, of Marshwood, 'suspected' (CP); presented at Dorchester: certificate allowed (JR).

ROPER, William senior, of Marshwood, 'suspected' (CP). [*See below.*]

ROPER, William junior, of Marshwood, 'suspected' (CP). [*See below.*] One of these two was presented at Dorchester: his certificate allowed (JR).

ROPER, William, of Exeter St Davids, 'absenting' (CP).

ROSE (Rosse), John, came from Holland with the Dukœ artilleryman, captured; tried at Exeter; hanged at Axminster, Oct. 14 (W, JR, NL).

ROSE, Richard, of North Petherton, 'took up arms against the king' (Som. QSR).

ROSE, Theodore, of North Petherton, 'absconded' (CP); 'took up arms against the king' (Som. QSR).

ROSEWELL, Robert, of Stoke St Gregory, 'absenting' (CP).

ROSSITER, Charles, soaper, of Taunton St James, 'aiding' (CP); Blue Regt. (P).

ROSSITER, John, miller, of Bishop's Sutton, tried at Taunton; 'designed to be executed but omitted from the warrant'; transported in place of James Baker (JR) by Heywood on the *Constant Richard* to Jamaica (SL).

ROSSITER, Matthias, worsted comber, of Taunton St Mary, 'aiding' (CP); Blue Regt. (P); pardoned, July 18, 1686 (CSPD, J2, II, 832).

ROSSITER, Richard junior, weaver, of East Woodlands, 'in the rebellion and at large' (CP); at Wells Assizes a witness for the king, left in custody (GD).

ROSTER, Richard, of Leigh on Mendip, 'supposed' (CP).

ROTHERTON, John, tried at Wells; 'remaining in custody' deleted; his name added to Bridgeman's list in place of E. Hammond (JR); transported from Wells by White, Oct. 31, to Jamaica on the *Constant Richard* (SL).

ROW, Christopher, aged 38, serge weaver, of Cullompton, imprisoned at Taunton; tried there; transported thence for the Queen (JR) on the *Jamaica Merchant*, Dec. 9, to Barbados; sold there on March 12 to Col. Thomas Colleton (SL).

ROWE, Francis, of Taunton St Mary, 'aiding' (CP); Blue Regt. (P).

ROWE, Henry, of Chardstock, 'supposed guilty' (CP); tried at Dorchester, Sept. 10; hanged at Sherborne, Sept. 15 (JR, NL).

ROWE, John, of Thurloxton, 'absconded' (CP).

ROWE, Nathaniel, taken to prison (ACWA), presented for high treason at Exeter in March 1686; pardoned and dismissed (GD).

ROWE, Peter, weaver, of Tavistock, imprisoned in Wilts. (DLD); tried at Dorchester; transported for Booth (JR) on the *Happy Return* from Weymouth, Sept. 25, to Barbados; sold to Hester Foster (SL).

ROWE, Thomas, weaver, of Taunton St Mary, 'aiding' (CP); Blue Regt. (P).

ROWE, William, of Axminster, 'supposed' (CP); tried at Taunton; transported for Musgrave (JR) on the *Jamaica Merchant* from Weymouth to Barbados; there by March 12 1686 (SL).

ROWLACE, ——, tailor, in Long Acre, 'in the rebellion'. Interrogation of John Kidd (L 1152A).

ROWLAND, John, of Trull, 'absent' (CP).

ROWLAND, Richard, sergemaker, of Taunton St Mary, 'aiding' (CP); Blue Regt. (P).

ROWNSELL, Andrew, tried at Taunton; hanged at Keynsham (JR, JW).

ROWSELL, George, aged 30, woolcomber, 'a rebel', imprisoned at Taunton (SL); tried there; transported thence for the Queen (JR) on the *Jamaica Merchant*, Dec. 9, to Barbados; sold to Archibald Johnson (SL).

ROWSELL, James, presented at Wells and bound over (JR).

ROWSELL, John, yeoman, of Colyton, 'absent' (CP); presented at Exeter but at large; presented at Wells and bound over (JR).

ROWSELL, John, weaver, of Trent, 'in the late rebellion and at large' (CP).

ROWSEWELL, Thomas, tried at Taunton; to be transported for the Queen (JR); on John Rose's receipt, Oct. 12, but not on the *Jamaica Merchant* (SL).

ROY, John, carpenter, of Frome, 'for a riot and amongst the Clubmen' (CP).

RUDDLE (Raddle), Samuel, tried at Wells; transported thence for Bridgeman (JR) by White, Oct. 31, on the *Constant Richard* to Jamaica (SL).

RUDDON, Edward, committed to gaol in Dorset 'upon suspicion of going to join with the late Duke of Monmouth and other traitors against his Majesty' (Wilts. QSR).

RUGG, John, of Wellington, 'in prison for rebellion. Dead' (CP). He had married Mary Grave of Milverton in 1684 (PR).

RUGG, Richard, of Milverton, 'absenting' (CP). He had married Elizabeth Thomas at Milverton in 1670 (PR).

RUGG, Robert senior, of Milverton, 'absenting' (CP). Exempted from Hearth Tax at Milverton 1670–74 (E. Dwelly, *Hearth Tax Exemptions*).

RUGG, Robert junior, of Milverton, 'absenting' (CP). He married Mary Morrish at Milverton in 1685 (PR).

RUSCOMBE *see* Liscombe.

RUSHELL, Abraham, of Street, Winsham, 'in the rebellion and not come in' (CP).

RUSSELL, George, tried at Wells; transported for Howard (JR) Oct. 25 to Jamaica (SL).

RUSSELL *see* Rowsell.

RUSSELL, Henry, tried at Wells; hanged at Pensford (JR, JW).

RUSSELL, James, at Wells Assize 'remaining in custody for want of evidence' (JR).

RUSSELL, William senior, of Cheddon Fitzpaine, 'absent' (CP). [*See below.*]

RUSSELLL, William junior, of Cheddon Fitzpaine, 'absent' (CP). [*See below.*]

RUSSELL, William, of Mells, 'supposed' (CP). [*See below.*]

RUSSELL, William, of West Bradley, 'from home at the time of the rebellion' (CP). [*See below.*] One of these four was tried at Wells and 'remaining in custody' (JR); then transported by T. Heywood on the *Constant Richard* to Jamaica (SL).

RUST, Argentine, aged 21 (PR), weaver, of Colyton, wounded at Sedgemoor, imprisoned at Wells (DLD); tried there; transported for Howard (JR) Oct. 25, to Jamaica (SL). Named on petition of 1689 (CSPD, W&M, I, 43).

RUTT, John, of West Bradley, 'from home at the time of the rebellion' (CP).

RUTTER, Daniel, aged 20, sergeweaver, of Wellington, 'in prison for rebellion' (CP); tried at Taunton; transported thence for the Queen (JR) on the *Jamaica Merchant*, Dec. 9, to Barbados; sold there on March 12 to Edward Jourdan (SL).

RUTTER, Thomas, of Wellington, 'in prison for rebellion' (CP).

SACHELL *see* Satchell

SALISBURY, John, yeoman, of Axminster, 'supposed' (CP); presented at Exeter but at large (JR).

SALISBURY, Thomas of Ilchester; 'in the rebellion' (CP); tried at Wells; transported for Howard (JR), Oct. 25 on the *Port Royal Merchant* to Jamaica (SL).

SALTER, George, yeoman, of Sarum Wells, Whitechurch Canonicorum 'suspected'; (CP); 'went to Monmouth's camp and drove one of the great guns to Philip's Norton'; in hiding for 23 weeks; captured at Wootton Fitzpaine in December; in Dorchester gaol Dec. 5; pardoned at Dorchester Assize in March 1686 (LRMB, GD).

SALTER, James, yeoman, of Musbury, 'in the rebellion' (CP); imprisoned at Ilchester (DLD); tried at Dorchester; transported for Booth (JR) on the *Happy Return* from Weymouth, Sept. 25, to Barbados; sold there in December to Agnes Fenton (SL). Also presented at Exeter and misreported at large (JR).

SALTER, Nicholas, husbandman, of Upottery, 'absent' (CP); imprisoned in the High Gaol, Devon (DLD); tried at Dorchester; transported for Nipho (JR) from Dorchester gaol via Weymouth, Nov. 25, on the *Betty* to Barbados; sold to Ralph Lane (SL). Land forfeit and for sale. Also presented at Exeter and misreported at large (JR). Named on the petition of 1689 (CSPD, W&M, I, 43).

SALTER, Robert, serge weaver, of Upottery, 'absent' (CP); in Bridgwater prison (DLD); tried at Dorchester, Sept. 10; hanged at Poole, Sept. 21 (JR, NL). Land forfeit and for sale. Also presented at Exeter and misreported at large (JR).

SALTER, Thomas, presented at Exeter in March 1686 for 'levying war, being a captain'; pleaded and found not guilty (GD).

SALWAY (or Sallaway), Arthur, tried at Wells; hanged at Pensford (JR, JW).

SALWAY, Nathaniel, burgess, of Axbridge; disfranchised for 'bearing arms', Aug. 3 1685 (Axbridge Convocation Bk.).

SAM, John, tried at Dorchester; transported for Nipho (JR) on the *Betty* from Weymouth, Nov. 25, to Barbados; sold to Thomas Beresford (SL).

SAMERHAYES *see* Somerhaies.

SAMPSON, John, of Charmouth, 'suspected' (CP); John Sansome of Hawkchurch 'seen in Monmouth's camp' by Weston Hillary (LRMB).

SAMPSON, William, of Kingsbury Episcopi, 'absent, believed' (CP).

SAMPSON, William, weaver, of Taunton St Mary, 'aiding' (CP); Blue Regt. (P).

SAMSON, Richard, taken to prison (Pulman, *Book of the Axe*).

SAMSON, Stephen, of Bishop's Hull, 'in prison' (CL).

SAMS, Richard, clothier, of Stoke St Gregory, pardoned March 24, 1686 (CSPD, J2, II, 332).

SAMUEL, servant to Mrs Mullens (or Muller) of Bishop's Hull, 'absent' (CP).

SANDFORD, Benjamin, husbandman, of Combpyne, imprisoned in Wilts. (DLD); tried at Dorchester Sept. 10; hanged at Bridport Sept. 12. Short dying speech (JR, NL). Land forfeit and for sale (TB).

SANDFORD, Benjamin, yeoman, of Lyme Regis, 'absent' (CP).

SANDS, Robert, yeoman, of Somerset, presented at Wells and bound over (JR); pardoned May 12, 1686 (CSPD, J2, II, 530).

SANDS (Sandy, Sandway), Robert, of Colyton, husbandman; 'absent' (CP); badly wounded (two sabre cuts on head) at Norton St Philip; taken to Ilchester gaol and treated by Dr Winter (WB); tried at Dorchester; transported for Nipho (JR) on the *Betty* from Weymouth, Nov. 25, to Barbados; sold to John Goldingham (SL). Land forfeit and for sale. Also presented at Exeter and misreported at large (JR).

SANFORD, Mr, came from Holland with the Duke, Ensign in the Red Regt. (W); probably killed at Sedgemoor (P).

SANSOME *see* Sampson.

SATCHELL (Sachell), Henry, presented at Wells and bound over (JR).

SATCHELL, John, yeoman, of Stoke St Mary, 'absent' (CP).

SATCHELL, John, yeoman, of Taunton St Mary, 'aiding' (CP); Blue Regt. (P); tried at Taunton; 'designed to be executed but omitted in the warrant' (JR), 'remaining in gaol; proposed for pardon' (JR2); transported by Thomas Heywood on the *Constant Richard* to Jamaica (SL). Land forfeit and for sale.

SATCHELL, Roger, cordwainer, yeoman, of Colyton, 'absent' (CP); 'seen in Monmouth's camp' (LRMB); captured at Chard; imprisoned at Ilchester (DLD); tried at Dorchester Sept. 10; hanged at Weymouth Sept. 15. Short dying speech (JR, NL). Estate worth £20 a year seized and for sale. Also presented at Exeter and misreported at large (JR).

SATCHELL, Thomas, presented at Wells and bound over (JR).

SATCHELL, William, tried at Taunton; hanged there on Sept. 30; buried at St James's on Oct. 1 (JR, PR).

SAUNDERS, George, chandler, of Frome, 'for a riot and amongst the Clubmen' (CP).

SAUNDERS, Humphrey, tried at Taunton; transported for Musgrave (JR) on the *Jamaica Merchant* from Weymouth to Jamaica; there by March 12 (SL).

SAUNDERS, John, carpenter, of Compton Peverell, imprisoned in Wilts. (DLD); tried at Wells; transported for Howard (JR), Oct. 25 on the *Port Royal Merchant* to Jamaica (SL).

SAUNDERS, Richard, hosier, of West Woodlands, 'in the rebellion and not taken' (CP).

SAUNDERS, Thomas, of Milverton, 'absenting' (CP); tried at Wells; transported thence for Bridgeman (JR) by White, Oct. 31, on the *Constant Richard* to Jamaica (SL).

SAUNDERS, William, yeoman, of Combe Raleigh, 'in the rebellion and not yet taken' (CP); tried at Dorchester; transported for Booth (JR) on the *Happy Return* from Weymouth, Sept. 25, to Barbados; sold in Dec. to Col. John Sampson (SL). Also presented at Exeter and misreported at large (JR).

SAUNDERS, William, aged 19, clothier, of Milverton, 'absenting' (CP); tried at Taunton; transported thence for the Queen (JR) on the *Jamaica Merchant*, Dec. 9, to Barbados; sold there on March 12 to Thomas Estwicke (SL). Buried 1688 St John's, Barbados (BJo).

SAUNDERS, William, presented at Dorchester for 'levying war against the king'; pleaded and found not guilty (GD).

SAUNDERS, William, presented at Taunton; 'humbly proposed for his Majesty's gracious pardon' (JR).

SAUNDERS, William, presented at Wells and bound over (JR).

SAUNDERS, William, presented at Exeter on March 23, 1686, pardoned and dismissed (GD).

SAUNDY, ——, 'servant to Sir Walter Young', 'seen in Monmouth's camp' (LRMB).

SAVAGE, Francis, tried at Wells; transported for Howard (JR), Oct. 25 on the *Port Royal Merchant* to Jamaica (SL).

SAVAGE, John, of Colyton, yeoman, 'absent' (CP); tailor, imprisoned in the High Gaol, Devon (DLD); tried at Dorchester, Sept. 10; hanged at Sherborne, Sept. 15 (JR, NL). Also presented at Exeter and misreported at large (JR).

SAVAGE, John, worsted comber, of Taunton St Mary (CP); Extraportam tithing, 'absent' (CL); 'aiding' (CP); Blue Regt. (P). Married in 1679 (PR).

SAVAGE, John, of West Monkton, 'out in the rebellion and at large' (CP).

SAVAGE, John, son of William [*below*], of Taunton St Mary (CP); of Extraportam tithing (CL); 'aiding' (CP); Blue Regt. (P); tried at Taunton; hanged there, Sept. 30; buried at St Mary's, Oct. 1 (JR, PR).

SAVAGE, Robert senior, weaver, of Taunton St Mary, 'aiding' (CP); Blue Regt. (P).

SAVAGE, William, innholder of the *Red Lion*, Taunton St Mary; released from the Bridewell by Monmouth's men (Axe); 'aiding' (CP); Lieut. of Horse under Hucker; tried to rally the Horse at Sedgemoor (Hist. MSS. Comm. Stopford-Sackville MSS. 28); excepted from GP, but pardoned 31 May 1687 (CSPD, J2, II, 1833).

SAVIDGE *see* Savage.

SAVORY, Andrew, tailor, of Taunton St Mary, 'aiding' (CP); Blue Regt. (P).

SAVORY, George, of Chardstock, 'suspected guilty' (CP).

SAXBEE, Samuel, tried at Taunton; transported for Musgrave (JR) on the *Jamaica Merchant* from Weymouth to Barbados; there by March 12 (SL).

SAXON, Thomas, excepted from GP.

SAY, John, tried at Wells; transported for Howard (JR), Oct. 25 on the *Port Royal Merchant* to Jamaica (SL).

SAY, Jonas, tried at Wells; transported for Howard (JR), Oct. 25 on the *Port Royal Merchant* to Jamaica (SL).

SAYER, Simon, hanged at Taunton by Col. Kirke on July 9; buried at St James's, July 10 (PR).

SAYES, Robert, of Staplegrove, 'absent' (CP); 'a rebel, for which he lieth now under condemnation' (CL).

SCADDING, George, presented at Exeter in March 1686, pardoned and dismissed (GD).

SCADDING, Nicholas, of Blagdon Green, Pitminster, 'absent' (CP); 'supposed' (CL). Pardoned May 31, 1687 (CSPD, J2, II, 1833).

SCADDING, Richard, sergemaker, of Taunton St Mary, 'aiding' (CP); Blue Regt. (P). Pardon March 26 and April 14, 1686 (CSPD, J2, II, 351, 403).

SCADDON (Scading), John, of Pitminster, 'absent, supposed' (CP).

SCHILY, John, confessed 'that he landed at Lyme with the Rebels as servant to one Bruce and ran away from Bridgwater on Monday last' (Wilts. QSR).

SCOTT, Francis, husbandman, of Hambridge, Curry Rivel, Quaker, sold horses to Monmouth and marched with them to Sedgemoor; captured there and imprisoned in Westonzoyland church; got out of the 'little north door while the guard slept, and going by night and lying in corn by day' made his way home and lay about till the GP. Brother-in-law of John Whiting, Quaker, whose autobiography, *Persecution Exposed* (1715) tells the story.

SCOTT, John, presented at Dorchester, March 3, 1686; pardoned by proclamation (GD).

SCRAMPLYN *see* Kemplyn.

SCRIVEN, George, of Street, Winsham, 'in the rebellion and not come in' (CP).

SCRIVEN, James, of Donyatt, 'out in the rebellion' (CP).

SCRIVEN, Thomas, of Winsham, 'absent, believed' (CP).

SCRIVEN, William, of Chard Town, 'absent, believed' (CP).

SCROOP, John, son of Thomas, 'said to have been in Monmouth's army'; similar warrants and pardon.

SCROOP (Scrope), Thomas, merchant, of Bristol, warrant to arrest, July 13, 1685 (CSPD, J2, I, 1218); pardon of all treasons, and for not coming to church, March 22, 1686 (CSPD, J2, II, 308, 354).

SCURRIER (Currier), William, aged 22, weaver, tried at Taunton; transported thence for the Queen (JR) via Weymouth on the *Jamaica Merchant*, Dec. 9, to Barbados; sold there on March 12 to George Hannay, Esq. (SL).

SEABY, William, of Taunton St Mary, 'aiding' (CP); Blue Regt. (P).

SEABY, William (another), of Taunton St Mary, 'aiding' (CP); Blue Regt. (P).

SEAGARD, Robert, presented at Wells and bound over (JR).

SEALY *see* Seley.

SEAMAN, Henry, comber, of Taunton St Mary, 'aiding' (CP); Blue Regt. (P); married in 1666 (PR).

SEAMAN, John, comber, of Taunton St Mary, 'aiding' (CP); Blue Regt. (P).

SEAMAN, Robert (or George), of Taunton, imprisoned in the Bridewell there; tried at Taunton; transported thence for Booth (SL, JR) via Bristol, Oct. 24, on the *John* to Barbados; sold (as George Seaman) to Ann Gallop (SL).

SEARLE (Serle), Edward, of Sidbury, 'joined in the rebellion' (CP).

SEARLE, George, yeoman, of Axminster, 'supposed' (CP); presented at Exeter but at large (JR); imprisoned in Wilts. (DLD); tried at Wells; transported for Howard (JR), Oct. 25 on the *Port Royal Merchant* to Jamaica (SL).

SEARLE, John, of Chardstock, 'suspected guilty' (CP).

SEARLE (Serle), John, of Combe Raleigh, yeoman, 'in the late rebellion and not yet taken' (CP); presented at Exeter but at large (JR).

SEARLE, Jonathan, pardoned July 18, 1686 (CSPD, J2, II, 822).

SEARLE, Robert, presented at Exeter, March 23, 1686; pardoned and dismissed (GD).

SEARLE, Thomas, sergeweaver, of Sidbury, in the High Gaol, Devon (DLD).

SEARLE, William, presented at Exeter, March 23, 1686; pardoned and dismissed (GD).

SEARLE, William, husbandman, of Whitford, imprisoned at Taunton (DLD); tried there; remaining in gaol till further order (JR); transported from Wells by White, Nov. 12, on the *Constant Richard* to Jamaica (SL). Land forfeit and for sale (TB).

SEAWARD (Seward, Selwood), George, aged 42, of Colyton, yeoman, 'absent' (CP); imprisoned in Dorset (DLD); tried at Dorchester, Sept. 5; pleaded not guilty; hanged at Dorchester, Sept. 7 (JR, NL). Also presented at Exeter and misreported at large (JR).

SEAWARD, William, yeoman, of Colyton, 'absent' (CP); presented at Exeter but at large (JR).
*And see* Seward.

SEDGEMORE, Arthur, of Stockland, 'suspected' (CP).

SELEY, Nicholas, of Street, ploughman [carter], 'conscripted by rebels to drive baggage'; taken under guard to Wells Assizes but not called by Jeffreys. A Nicholas Sealy was buried at Street in 1724 (SRO, Street churchwardens' account and family tradition).

SELFE, William, clothworker, of Beckington, 'in the rebellion, out of Beckington, at large' (CP); tried at Wells; transported for Howard (JR), Oct. 25 on the *Port Royal Merchant* to Jamaica (SL).

SELLER (Siller), Henry, of Gittisham, 'trained soldier, went to Monmouth and yet in rebellion' (CP).

SELLER, Peter, yeoman, of Colyton, 'absent' (CP); presented at Exeter but at large (JR). Died Feb. 1686 (PR).

SELLER, William junior, presented at Exeter for 'levying war against the king'; convicted, 'remaining in custody' (JR) reprieved (JR2).

SELLICK, Christopher, of Rich's Holford, Lydeard St Lawrence, 'absent' (CP).

SELLICK, Thomas, of Ruishton, 'absent' (CP).

SELWARD (Sellward), Andrew, of Chard, 'absent, believed' (CP).

SELLWARD, Austin, of Chard Town, 'absent, believed' (CP).

SELLWARD, Henry junior, of Chard, 'absent, believed' (CP).

SELLWOOD, Abraham junior, of Chard, 'absent, believed' (CP). In 1706 he registered his house as a nonconformist meeting house (SRO).

SELLWOOD, Augustine, smith, of Taunton St Mary, 'aiding' (CP); Blue Regt. (P).

SELLWOOD, Clement, of Chard, 'in the late rebellion' (CP).

SELLWOOD, Henry, of Taunton St Mary, 'aiding' (CP); Blue Regt. (P).

SELLWOOD, John, tried at Taunton; hanged at Langport (JR, JW).

SELLWOOD, Joseph, clothier, of Lyme Regis, 'absent, supposed' (CP).

SELLWOOD, Richard, woollen weaver, of Axminster, wounded at Sedgemoor, imprisoned at Wells (DLD); tried there; transported for Howard (JR), Oct. 25 on the *Port Royal Merchant* to Jamaica (SL).

SELLWOOD, William, clothier, of Chard, 'absent, believed' (CP); tried at Dorchester; transported for Musgrave (JR) from Weymouth on the *Jamaica Merchant* to Barbados; there by March 12 (SL). Land forfeit and for sale.
*And see* Seaward.

SELWAY, John, of Shute, 'Monmouth rebel in custody, mortally wounded; died' (Devon. QSR).

SERGEANT, Thomas, of Beaminster, 'wanting from his home' (CP).

SERLE *see* Searle

SERVIS, Philip, servant to Aldred Millett, clothier, of Dunster, 'in arms in the rebellion' (CP).

SEWARD, David, John, Richard, Richard, William. All yeoman of Axminster, 'supposed to be in the rebellion'; presented at Exeter, but at large (CP). Definitely two Richards.
*And See* Seaward.

SEXTON, John *see* Randall Furnivall.

SEYMORE, John, of Chilton 'Seamer', in Bridgwater prison (SL); tried at Taunton; transported for Booth (JR) via Bristol, Oct. 24, on the *John* to Barbados; sold to Col. John Farmer (SL).

SHALE, Robert, yeoman, of Uplyme, imprisoned in Wilts. (DLD); tried at Dorchester; to be transported for Booth (JR); on Booth's receipt but not on the *Happy Return* (SL).

SHARE, Henry, of Merriott, 'rebel in Monmouth's army and not taken' (CP).

SHARPE, Abraham, of Taunton St Mary, 'aiding' (CP); Blue Regt. (P).

SHARPE, John, tried at Taunton; hanged there Sept. 30 (JR, JW).

SHARPE, William, hanged at Taunton by Col. Kirke on July 9; buried at St James's that day (PR).

SHAVE, Samuel, coachman, of Lyme Regis, 'absent, supposed' (CP).

SHAVE, William, of Charmouth, 'suspected' (CP).

SHAW, William, husbandman, of Trent, 'in the late rebellion and at large' (CP).

SHEIRE, John, presented at Wells and bound over (JR).

SHEPPARD; James, tried at Wells; transported for Howard (JR), Oct. 25 on the *Port Royal Merchant* to Jamaica (SL).

SHEPPARD, John, of Bampton, 'supposed to be a rebel' (CP).

SHEPPARD, John, of Compton Dando, husbandman, tried at Wells; to be hanged (JR) but marched off with Howard transportees; recaptured between Shepton Mallet and Castle Cary (CM); hanged at Wells (NL, JW). Land forfeit and for sale (TB).

SHEPPARD, John, of Crewkerne, 'rebel and not taken' (CP).

SHEPPARD, John, of Luppitt, yeoman, 'absent' (CP); presented at Exeter but at large (JR).

SHEPPARD, Samuel, presented at Wells and bound over (JR).

SHEPPARD, Thomas, of Bampton, 'supposed to be a rebel' (CP).

SHEPPARD, William, tried at Wells, transported for Howard (JR), Oct. 25 on the *Port Royal Merchant* to Jamaica (SL).

SHERBORNE, William, clothier, of Frome, 'in the rebellion and in prison' (CP); tried at Taunton; 'designed to be executed but omitted in the warrant' (JR); transported from Taunton and shipped on the *Constant Richard*, Nov. 12, to Jamaica (SL).

SHERBROOKE, John, of Trull, 'absent' (CP).

SHERBROOKE, William, of Dipford, Trull, 'a rebel' (CL).

SHERRY, William, tried at Wells; transported for Howard (JR), Oct. 25 on the *Port Royal Merchant* to Jamaica (SL).

SHERWARD, Hugh, of Cricket Malherbie, 'being in the late rebellion and at large' (CP).

SHIER, Philip junior, miller, of Lyme Regis, 'absent, supposed' (CP).

SHINDLER (Shingler), Thomas, of Chardland, 'absent, believed' (CP), presented at Dorchester; not sentenced (JR). 'Proposed for pardon' (JR2).

SHINDLER, William, of Chardland, 'absent, believed' (CP); presented at Wells and bound over (JR).

SHINLER, John, presented at Wells and bound over (JR).

SHINLER, John, tried at Dorchester; transported for Musgrave (JR) from Weymouth to Barbados on the *Jamaica Merchant*; there by March 12 (SL).

SHOALE, William, of Dowlishwake, 'in the rebellion and not come in' (CP).

SHOELITH, Francis, yeoman, of Burlescombe, in the High Gaol, Devon (DLD).

SHOESMITH, Robert, tried at Taunton; transported for Musgrave (JR) on the *Jamaica Merchant* from Weymouth to Jamaica; there by March 12 (SL).

SHORE, John, comber, of Lyng, got away to Holland, engaged in the manufacture of English cloth; pardon June 2, 1686 'if he return from abroad with his goods and effects within two calendar months' (CSPD, J2, II, 626).

SHORLAND, Peter, of Staplegrove, 'absent' (CP); 'taking up arms against the king' (Som. QSR); tried at Taunton; transported for Musgrave (JR) on the *Jamaica Merchant* from Weymouth to Jamaica, March 12 (SL).

SHORT, Benjamin, of Westbury, 'in the rebellion as we are informed' (Wilts. QSR); presented at Wells and bound over (JR).

SHORT, John, worsted comber, of Taunton St Mary, 'aiding' (CP); Blue Regt. (P).

SHORT, Samuel, of Taunton St James, 'aiding' (CP); Blue Regt. (P).

SHOWERS, John and Phineas, late of London. At least one came from Holland with the Duke and became an Ensign (H). Both were pardoned of all treasons, Nov. 5, 1686 (CSPD, J2, II, 1119).

SHRAPNILL, Henry, committed 'for entertaining Thomas Garridge and Stephen Curle of Taunton, actually rebels in arms against his Majesty' (Wilts. QSR).

SIBLEY, Edward, of Kingsbury Episcopi, 'absent, believed' (CP).

SILLER *see* Seller.

SIMON, John, tried at Wells; transported for Howard (JR), Oct. 25 on the *Port Royal Merchant* to Jamaica (SL).

SIMONS, Roger, of Taunton St James, 'aiding' (CP), Blue Regt. (P). *And see* Symons.

SIMPKINS, Joseph, presented at Wells and bound over (JR).

SIMS (Symes), Henry, of Bathpool, was in arms (Burton's evidence in BL. Lansdowne MS. 1152 A); tried at Dorchester; transported for Nipho (JR) on the *Betty* from Weymouth, Nov. 25, to Barbados; sold to Richard Cheesman (SL). *And see* Symes.

SKIFFES, John, aged 22 (PR), yeoman, of Colyton, 'absent' (CP); shoemaker; wounded at Sedgemoor, imprisoned at Wells (DLD); presented at Exeter but at large; tried at Wells; transported for Howard (JR) Oct. 25 on the *Port Royal Merchant* to Jamaica (SL). Named on the 1689 petition (CSPD, W&M, I, 43). Returned and had children baptised in 1694 and 1697 (PR).

SKINNER, Francis senior, of Chard Town, 'absent, believed' (CP); tried at Dorchester, Sept. 10; hanged at Sherborne Sept. 15 (JR, NL).

SKINNER, John, cordwainer, of Honiton, in the High Gaol, Devon (DLD); tried at Dorchester; 'remaining in custody' deleted; 'proposed for pardon' (JR). Land forfeit and for sale (TB).

SKINNER, John junior, of Honiton, 'a rebel' (CP).

SKINNER, Richard, of Chard, 'absent, believed'; presented at Wells and bound over (JR).

SKINNER, Thomas, Esquire, of Dawlish, excepted from GP.

SLADE, Edward, yeoman, of Axminster, 'supposed' (CP); presented at Exeter but at large (JR).

SLADE, Humphrey senior, of Honiton, 'a rebel' (CP). [*See below.*]

SLADE, Humphrey junior, of Honiton, 'a rebel' (CP). [*See below.*] One of these two, a lacemaker, was imprisoned at Taunton (DLD), tried there and transported for Musgrave (JR) on the *Jamaica Merchant* from Weymouth to Barbados; there by March 12 (SL). His release was requested on the petition of 1689 (CSPD, W&M, I, 43).

SLADE, John, aged 25, sergeweaver, of Bampton, 'supposed' (CP); imprisoned at Taunton (DLD), tried there and transported thence for the Queen (JR) on the *Jamaica Merchant*, Dec. 9, to Barbados; sold there on March 12 to Edward Jourdan (SL).

SLADE, John and William, father and son, of Ilminster, 'taken for spies at Wincanton'; tortured by burning by Kirke's 'Lambs'; treated by Dr Winter in Ilchester gaol; poor (WB).

SLADE, Richard, of Combe St Nicholas, 'absent, believed' (CP).

SLADE, Robert, of Crewkerne, 'rebel, and not taken' (CP); tried at Dorchester Sept. 10; hanged Sept. 15 at Weymouth or Melcombe Regis (GR, NL).

SLADE, Thomas, yeoman, of Thorncombe, 'wanting from his habitation' (CP); presented at Exeter but at large (JR).

SLAPE, James, of Chard, 'absent, believed' (CP).

SLAPE, Peter, of Taunton St James, 'aiding' (CP); Blue Regt. (P); pardoned March 27, 1686 (CSPD, J2, II, 356).

SLAPE, Richard, gentleman (son of Army officer), of Taunton St James, 'aiding' (CP); Captain in Red Regt. (W); excepted from GP, but pardoned Oct. 2, 1686 (CSPD, J2, II, 1035).

SLATER, John, of Chard, 'absent, believed' (CP).

SLEY (Slye), Robert, of Croscombe, 'in Scott's army'; 'in prison' (CP); tried at Wells; transported for Howard (JR), Oct. 25 on the *Port Royal Merchant* to Jamaica (SL).

SMALL (Smale), Robert, of Milverton, 'absenting' (CP); presented at Exeter in March 1686, pardoned and dismissed (GD).

SMALLCRONE, Samuel, of Chard, 'in the late rebellion' (CP).

SMART, Gabriel, of Witham Friary, 'in the rebellion and not taken' (CP); tried at Wells; transported for Howard (JR), Oct. 25 on the *Port Royal Merchant* to Jamaica (SL).

SMART, John, of Long Sutton, 'in the late rebellion and not come home' (CP).

SMART, Thomas senior, weaver, of East Woodlands, 'in the rebellion and in prison' (CP). Land in Marston Bigot forfeit and for sale (TB).

SMIRNEY, John, of Chard, 'absent, believed' (CP).

SMIRNEY, John junior, of Chard, 'absent, believed' (CP); presented at Taunton; certificate allowed (JR).

SMIRNEY, Joseph, of Chard, 'in the late rebellion' (CP); presented at Taunton; certificate allowed (JR).

SMIRNEY, Thomas, of Chard, 'in the late rebellion' (CP); presented at Taunton; certificate allowed (JR).

SMITH, Aaron, gent., of London, Whig, messenger or conspirator (W); excepted from GP.

SMITH, Aaron, yeoman, of Musbury, 'in the rebellion' (CP); presented at Exeter but at large (JR). Wrongly 'of Axminster' in BL. Add. MS. 90337.

SMITH, Aaron, tucker, of Taunton St Mary, 'aiding' (CP); Blue Regt. (P).

SMITH, Aaron, of Haselbury Plucknett, 'in the late rebellion' (CP).

SMITH, Abram, of Haselbury Plucknett, 'in the late rebellion' (CP).

SMITH, Adam, tried at Wells; transported for Howard (JR) Oct. 25 on the *Port Royal Merchant* to Jamaica (SL).

SMITH, Christopher, cooper, of Lyme Regis, 'absent, supposed' (CP).

SMITH, Edward, of Beaminster, 'absent at the time of the rebellion' (CP).

SMITH, Edward, yeoman, of Upottery, 'absent' (CP); presented at Exeter but at large (JR).

SMITH, Francis, of Honiton, 'a rebel' (CP); worsted comber; in the High Gaol, Devon (DLD); tried at Dorchester; transported for Nipho (JR) on the *Betty* from Weymouth, Nov. 25, to Barbados; sold to Major George Bushell. Named on the 1689 petition (CSPD, W&M, I, 43).

SMITH, Francis, tried at Wells; hanged at Frome (JR, JW).

SMITH, George, tried at Dorchester, Sept. 10; hanged at Weymouth or Melcombe Regis, Sept. 15 (JR, NL). [*See below.*]

SMITH, George, tried at Taunton, transported for Musgrave (JR) on the *Jamaica Merchant* from Weymouth to Barbados; there by March 12 (SL). One of these two came from Northover, presented as 'in the late rebellion' (CP).

SMITH, George, presented at Wells and bound over (JR).

SMITH, James, clothworker, of West Woodlands or Frome, 'in prison for the late rebellion' (CP); tried at Taunton; 'designed to be executed but omitted in the warrant for execution'; presented at Wells and transported thence for Howard (JR), Oct. 25 on the *Port Royal Merchant* to Jamaica (SL). Land forfeit and for sale (TB).

SMITH, James, yeoman, of Upottery, 'absent' (CP); presented at Exeter but at large (JR).

SMITH, John, of Beckington, broadweaver, 'in the rebellion, out of Beckington, at large' (CP). [*See below.*]

SMITH, John of Chard, 'absent, believed' (CP). [*See below.*]

SMITH, John, of Honiton, imprisoned in Exeter, tried at Taunton; transported for Booth (JR) via Bristol Oct. 24 on the *John* to Barbados; sold, Jan. 28, to R. Harwood, Esq. (SL).

SMITH, John, of South Petherton, 'in the rebellion and not come in' (CP). [*See below.*]

SMITH, John, tucker, of Taunton St Mary, 'aiding' (CP), Blue Regt. (P). [*See below.*]

SMITH, John, another, as above.

SMITH, John, yeoman, of Upottery, 'absent' (CP), presented at Exeter but at large (JR); in Bridgwater prison, tried at Taunton; to be transported for Booth (JR); on his receipt though not on SL. Named on 1689 petition for return (CSPD, W&M, I, 43).

SMITH, John, of Wedmore, 'absent and in the late rebellion' (CP). [*See below.*] Of the above John Smiths one was presented at Dorchester (JR) but may have died before sentence, which is not recorded. Another was tried at Taunton and transported for Musgrave (JR) on the *Jamaica Merchant* to Jamaica (SL). Two were presented at Wells, one being hanged at Norton St Philip (JR, JW); the other remaining in custody as King's Evidence (JR).

SMITH, Joseph, miller, of Chard, 'absent, believed' (CP); tried at Wells; hanged at Shepton Mallet (JR, JW). Land forfeit and for sale (TB).

SMITH, Nicholas, of Bridport, 'as we are informed, in the rebellion under James Scott, late Duke of Monmouth' (CP); tried at Dorchester; transported for Booth (JR) on the *Happy Return* from Weymouth, Sept. 25, to Barbados; sold in Dec. to Hugh Williams (SL).

SMITH, Nicholas, excepted from GP.

SMITH, Philip, of Chardland, 'absent, believed' (CP); tried at Wells; transported thence for Bridgeman (JR) by White, Oct. 31, on the *Constant Richard* to Jamaica (SL).

SMITH, Ralph, presented at Wells and bound over (JR).

SMITH, Richard, yeoman, of Axminster, 'supposed' (CP); presented at Exeter but at large (JR).

SMITH, Richard, of Ilminster, 'in the late rebellion' (CP).

SMITH, Richard, yeoman, of Thorncombe, 'wanting from his habitation' (CP); presented at Exeter but at large (JR).

SMITH, Robert senior, of Haselbury Plucknett, 'in the late rebellion' (CP). [*See below.*]

SMITH, Robert junior, of Haselbury Plucknett, 'in the late rebellion' (CP). [*See below.*]

SMITH, Robert, of Ilminster, 'in the late rebellion' (CP). [*See below.*]

SMITH, Robert, of Pilsdon, 'suspected' (CP). [*See below.*]

SMITH, Robert, of Stoford, 'in the late rebellion' (CP). [*See below.*]

SMITH, Robert, of Taunton St Mary, 'aiding' (CP); Blue Regt. (P). [*See below.*]

SMITH, Robert junior, of Taunton St Mary, 'aiding' (CP); Blue Regt. (P). [*See below.*] One of these seven was tried at Wells and transported for Howard (JR), Oct. 25 on the *Port Royal Merchant* to Jamaica (SL).

SMITH, Thomas, husbandman, of Chard or Chardland, member of the Axminster congregation, 'absent' 'believed' (CP); 'taken' on his way home from Norton St Philip; tried at Wells; to be hanged at Shepton Mallet (JR, JW) but 'another prisoner standing forth in his name', Smith continued in prison; he then escaped, but wandering and weak, died within a few weeks (Ecc). Land forfeit and for sale (TB).

SMITH, Thomas, husbandman, constable of Chardstock, tried at Dorchester, Sept. 5; hanged there Sept. 7 (JR, NL). Land forfeit and for sale (TB). Argument with LCJ Jeffreys and his dying speech reported in BA.

SMITH, Thomas, of Frome, Captain, 'for plundering Constable Somers' house' (CP).

SMITH, Thomas, of Rode, weaver, 'in the rebellion' (CP).

SMITH, Thomas, of Wedmore, 'absent, in the late rebellion' (CP). One Thomas Smith was reprieved (JR2).

SMITH, alias Woolfridge, William, of Lyme Regis, fuller, 'absent, supposed' (CP).

SMITH, William, of Rode, weaver, 'in the rebellion', in Bridgwater prison (SL); tried at Taunton; transported for Booth (JR) via Bristol Oct. 24, on the *John* to Barbados; sold to Capt. Walter Scott (SL).

SMITH, William junior, of Upottery, yeoman, 'absent', presented at Exeter and misreported at large; from Exeter to Taunton for trial; transported for Booth (JR) towards Barbados but died at sea (SL).

SMITH, William, of Frome, feltmaker, 'in the rebellion and at large' (CP). [*See below.*]

SMITH, William, of Trull, 'absent' (CP). [*See below.*] One of these two was tried at Wells and transported for Howard (JR), Oct. 25 on the *Port Royal Merchant* to Jamaica (SL).
    *And see* Cragg.

SMITHIER, Richard, presented at Wells and bound over (JR).

SNOOKE, Henry, of Marshwood, 'supposed' (CP); tried at Wells; transported for Howard (JR), Oct. 25 on the *Port Royal Merchant* to Jamaica (SL).

SNOOKE, Richard, of Colford, Wilts, 'absenting' (CP); tried at Wells; transported thence for Bridgeman (JR) by White, Oct. 31, on the *Constant Richard* to Jamaica (SL).

SNOOKE, Richard, of Lyme Regis, merchant, 'absent, supposed' (CP); member of Lyme Corporation (LRCB).

SNOOKE, Thomas, of Marshwood, Whitechurch Canonicorum, labourer, 'supposed' (CP); tried at Wells; transported for Howard (JR), Oct. 25, to Jamaica (SL). Land forfeit and for sale (TB).

SNOW, George, aged 19, of Tiverton, comber, 'with the Duke of Monmouth' (CP); tried at Taunton; transported thence for the Queen (JR) on the *Jamaica Merchant*, Dec. 9, to Barbados; sold there on March 12 to George Hannay, Esq. (SL).

SNOW, Thomas, of North Curry, Thornfalcon, 'absent' (CP); 'in arms. Fled' (CL).

SOMERS, Richard, of Midsomer Norton, 'absenting' (CP).

SOMERHAIES (Samerhayes), Richard, yeoman, constable of Yarcombe, 'a rebel, wanting' (CP); presented at Exeter but at large (JR).

SOMERTON, William, of Chiselborough, 'in the late rebellion' (CP); tried at Wells; hanged at Ilchester (JR, JW).

SOPER, James, tried at Taunton; transported for Musgrave (JR) on the *Jamaica Merchant* from Weymouth to Barbados; there by March 12 (SL).

SOPER, Robert, of Stoke St Gregory, 'absenting' (CP); of North Curry; killed at Sedgemoor; 'no tenant' (CL).

SOUNDY, servant to Sir W. Young of Colyton, 'seen in Monmouth's camp' (LRMB).

SOUTHEY, Robert, yeoman, of Wellington, 'drew his sword in the rebellion' so stated his great-grandson, Robert Southey, the poet. A Dissenter.

SPARKE, Benjamin, of Mells, 'supposed' (CP); tried at Taunton; transported for Musgrave (JR) on the *Jamaica Merchant* from Weymouth to Barbados; there by March 12 (SL).

SPARKE, Roger, yeoman, of Upottery, 'absent' (CP); presented at Exeter but at large (JR).

SPARROW, Randolph, 'engaged in the late rebellion'; pardon April 17 1687 (CSPD, J2, II, 417).

SPEARING (Spiring), John, of Axminster Congregational church, tried at Dorchester; transported for Booth (JR) on the *Happy Return* from Weymouth, Sept. 25, to Barbados; sold in December to Major George Lillington (SL); ransomed by members of the church but drowned in shipwreck on the way home (Ecc).

SPEED, Andrew senior, of Oake, 'absent' (CP). [*See below.*]

SPEED, Andrew junior, of Oake, 'absent' (CP). [*See below.*] One of these two 'engaged in the late rebellion', was pardoned on May 31 1687 (CSPD, J2, II, 1833).

SPEED, John, of Chard, 'absent, believed' (CP).

SPEED, John, of Chardstock, 'suspected guilty' (CP).

SPEED, Joseph, aged 40+, of Colyton, shoemaker, cordwainer, 'absent' (CP); imprisoned in Dorset (DLD); tried at Dorchester, Sept. 5; hanged there, Sept. 7. Dying speech: 'to fight for the Protestant Religion', (JR, BA). Also presented at Exeter and misreported at large (JR).

SPEED, Joshua, of Oake, 'absent' (CP).

SPEED, Philip, of Crewkerne, mercer, 'rebel, not taken' (CP); pardoned April 19 1687 (CSPD, J2, II, 423).

SPEED, Thomas, of Chard, 'absent, believed' (CP); tried at Wells; transported for Howard (JR), Oct. 25 on the *Port Royal Merchant* to Jamaica (SL).

SPEEDWELL, Andrew 'late rebel in West' convicted at Wells Assizes, Oct. 2, 1686: petition for grant of estate (TB, viii. 919).

SPEKE, Charles, of Whitelackington, gentleman, 'fileser' (filed legal documents) in London 'for marching in the late Duke of Monmouth's army' (Wilts. QSR); tried at Wells 'for aiding and assisting the rebels against the king'; refused to swear against Edmund Prideaux; hanged at Ilminster, a reprieve arriving too late (JR, *House of Commons Journal*, NL).

SPEKE, John, Esq. of Ilminster, 'in the late rebellion' (CP); joined Monmouth at Chard 'with a company of ragged horse'; became their colonel (W); said to have left the army at Frome (Goodenough in L); excepted from the GP. Pardon Feb. 18 1687 (CSPD, J2, II, 1471). M.P. for Taunton 1695. Son-in-law of Edmund Prideaux.

SPENCE, James (or John), tried at Dorchester; transported for Booth (JR) on the *Happy Return* from Weymouth, Sept. 25, to Barbados; sold to Capt. John Parnell (SL).

SPENCER (Spurrier), Lancelot, of Dunster, glazier, 'in arms in the rebellion of James Scott' (CP), 'bearing arms against his Majesty (Som. QSR).

SPENDER, John, presented at Wells and bound over (JR).

SPILLER, George, of Colyton, yeoman, 'absent' (CP); presented at Exeter but at large (JR).

SPILLER alias Dodridge, John, of Ottery St Mary, 'in the rebellion, as supposed' (CP).

SPILLER, John, of Stockland, 'suspected' (CP).

SPILLER, Richard, of Chardstock, 'suspected guilty' (CP); tried at Wells; transported for Howard (JR), on Oct. 25 on the *Port Royal Merchant* to Jamaica (SL).

SPILLER, Thomas junior, of Trull, 'absent' (CP).

SPIRING *see* Spearing.

SPORE, John, tried at Taunton; hanged at Crewkerne (JR, JW).

SPRAKE (Spragg, Sprague), Charles, of Lyme Regis, 'absent, supposed' (CP).

SPRAKE, Edward, of Membury, yeoman, 'absent' (CP); presented at Exeter but at large (JR).

SPRAKE, James, of Lyme Regis, cobb mason, 'absent, supposed' (CP).

SPRAKE, John, of Colyton, yeoman, a married man with children (PR), 'absent' (CP); tried at Exeter; hanged at Colyton (JR) in October. Dying speech: 'Protestantism being in danger' (BA). Also presented at Exeter and misreported at large (JR).

SPRAKE, John, of Axminster, clothworker, imprisoned in Wilts. (DLD).

SPRAKE, John, of Lyme Regis, fuller, a married man with children (PR), 'absent, supposed' (CP); taken near Salisbury; tried at Dorchester; originally to be hanged at Bridport and so reported on the Broadsheet of 1686, but transported for Musgrave on the *Jamaica Merchant* from Weymouth to Barbados; there by March 12 (SL).

SPRAKE, John, of Thorncombe, yeoman, 'wanting from his habitation' (CP); presented at Exeter but at large (JR).

SPRAKE, John, of Winsham, mason, 'absent, believed' (CP); tried at Wells; transported thence for Bridgeman (JR) by White, Oct. 31, on the *Constant Richard* to Jamaica (SL). Land forfeit and for sale (TB).

SPRAKE, Thomas senior, of Axminister, 'supposed' (CP).

SPRAKE, Thomas junior, of Axminister, yeoman, presented at Exeter but at large (JR).

SPREATE, William, tried at Taunton; transported for Musgrave (JR) on the *Jamaica Merchant* from Weymouth to Barbados; there by March 12 (SL).

SPREET (Spratt, Spright, Streete), Gabriel, of Ash Priors, of Combe Florey (CP), of Holford (CL), husbandman, 'absent' (CP); 'in arms against the king' (CL); excepted from GP. Pardoned Oct. 2 1686 (CSPD, J2, II, 1035).

SPRING, William, of Pitminster, 'absent' (CP).

SPURRIER *see* Spencer.

SPURWAY, Robert, of Axminster, yeoman, 'supposed' (CP); clothworker, imprisoned in Wilts. (DLD); tried at Dorchester; transported for Booth (JR) on the *Happy Return* from Weymouth, Sept. 25, to Barbados; sold in Dec. to Col. John Farmer (SL). Also presented at Exeter and misreported at large (JR). Named on petition for return 1689 (CSPD, W&M, I, 40).

SQUIBB, Henry, of Taunton St Mary, 'aiding' (CP); Blue Regt. (P).

SQUIRE, Andrew, presented for high treason, Exeter, March 1686; pardoned and dismissed (GD).

SQUIRE, George, weaver, of Taunton St Mary, 'aiding' (CP); Blue Regt. (P).

SQUIRE, Joseph, of Chard, 'absent, believed' (CP).

SQUIRE, Nicholas, of Chardland, 'absent, believed' (CP).

SQUIRE, Raymond, of Chard, 'absent, believed' (CP).

SQUIRE, Sebastian, barber, of Taunton St Mary, 'aiding' (CP); Blue Regt. (P).

SQUIRE, Stephen, of Chardland, 'absent, believed' (CP).

STACEY, John, of Taunton St James, 'aiding' (CP); Blue Regt. (P), laid down arms and claimed pardon (CP).

STACEY, Joseph, pardoned May 12 1686 (CSPD, J2, II, 531).

STACEY, Simon senior, of Taunton, pardon for him and sons Simon and Joseph [*below and above*], May 12 1686 (CSPD, J2, II, 531).

STACEY, Simon junior, of Taunton St James, 'aiding' (CP); Blue Regt. (P). 'Today appeared and pleaded benefit of the pardon proclaimed'. (CP).

STADITH, John, of Colyton, yeoman, 'absent' (CP); presented at Exeter but at large (JR).

STAGG, John, of Taunton St Mary, weaver, 'aiding' (CP); Blue Regt. (P).

STALEY, Andrew, tried at Wells; transported for Howard (JR), Oct. 25 on the *Port Royal Merchant* to Jamaica (SL).

STAMP, Malachi, of Upottery, yeoman, 'aiding' (CP); Blue Regt. (P).

STANDARD, James, presented at Wells, 'for the king's pardon' (JR).

STANDERWICK, Joseph, of Ilminster, sergemaker, 'in the late rebellion' (CP); went to Forde Abbey for arms (Dep); warrant for arrest (in London) 'for having been in the late rebellion', Feb. 21 (CSPD, J2, II, 174); refused to swear against Prideaux (*House of Commons Journal*); excepted from GP pardoned July 4 (CSPD, J2, II, 768).

STANDERWICK, Joseph, of Musbury, yeoman, pardoned May 12 1686 (CSPD, J2, II, 532).

STANDERWICK, Nathaniel, of Combe St Nicholas, 'absent, believed' (CP); tried at Wells; transported for Nipho (JR) on the *Betty* from Weymouth, Nov. 25, to Barbados; sold to Thomas Beresford (SL).

STANDFAST, Joseph, of Glastonbury, 'from home at the time of the rebellion' (CP).

STANDFAST, William, of Glastonbury, 'from home at the time of the rebellion' (CP).

STANNINGS, William junior, of Taunton St Mary, 'aiding' (CP); Blue Regt. (P).

STAPLE, Edward, of Lyme Regis, baker, 'absent, supposed' (CP); taken at Lyme Regis and sent to Dorchester gaol 14 July (LRMB); presented at Dorchester and discharged for want of evidence (JR).

STAPLE, James, of Thorncombe, 'wanting from his habitation' (CP).

STAPLE, John, of Buckland St Mary, 'out in the rebellion and not taken' (CP).

STAPLE, John, of Chardstock, 'suspected guilty' (CP).

STAPLE, John, of Stoke St Gregory, husbandman, tried at Wells; hanged at Norton St Philip (JR, JW). Land forfeit and for sale (TB).

STAPLE, John, of Thorncombe, yeoman, 'wanting from his habitation' (CP); presented at Exeter but at large (JR).

STAPLE, Leonard senior, of Combe St Nicholas, 'absent, believed' (CP).

STAPLE, Leonard, aged 20, plowman [carter], tried at Taunton; transported thence for the Queen (JR) on the *Jamaica Merchant*, Dec. 9, to Barbados; sold there on March 12 to Archibald Johnson (SL).

STAPLE, Matthew, of Lyme Regis, tobacconist, 'absent, supposed' (CP).

STAPLE, Matthew, of Thorncombe, 'absent, supposed' (CP); presented at Exeter, March 1686, pardoned and dismissed (GD).

STAPLE, Nathaniel, of Thorncombe, yeoman, presented at Exeter but at large (JR). It is possible that these two are the same man, 'Math' having been misread as 'Nath' in BL. Add. MS. 90337.

STAPLE, Samuel, of Thorncombe, yeoman, 'absent, supposed' (CP), presented at Exeter but at large (JR); presented at Exeter in March 1686, pardoned and dismissed (GD).
*And see* Marks.

STARKE, Hugh, tried at Taunton; to be hanged at Minehead on Dec. 8, when 3 out of 6 were hanged (JR, NL).

STARR (Starcke), John, aged 19 (PR) of Colyton, yeoman, imprisoned in Dorset (DLD); tried at Wells; hanged at Pensford (JR, JW).

STAUNTON, William, tried at Wells; transported for Howard (JR), Oct. 25 on the *Port Royal Merchant* to Jamaica (SL).

STEER, Richard, presented at Wells and bound over (JR).

STEPHENS, Christopher, tried at Taunton; hanged at Somerton (JR, JW).

STEPHENS, Elias, of Lyme Regis, joiner, 'absent, supposed' (CP); tried at Dorchester; transported for Booth (JR) on the *Happy Return* from Weymouth, Sept. 25, to Barbados; sold in Dec. to Capt. John Stewart (SL).

STEPHENS, John, of Wilton, 'absent' (CP); tried at Taunton; hanged at Ilchester (JR, JW).

STEPHENS, Richard, of Taunton St Mary, fuller, 'aiding' (CP); Blue Regt. (P).

STEPHENS, Richard, of Wrantage, North Curry, 'out in the late rebellion and in prison' (CP); in Bridgwater prison, 'executed' (CL); tried at Taunton; hanged at Crewkerne (JR, JW).

STEPHENS, Richard, of North Curry, 'out in the late rebellion and in prison' (CP, Som. QSR); tried at Taunton; transported for Booth (JR) from Taunton Bridewell, via Bristol, Oct. 24, on the *John* to Barbados; sold to John and William Holder (SL). One of these two was a cordwinder (CP).

STEPHENS, William, of Creech St Michael late servant to Mr Seage, 'absent and not taken' (CP).

STEVENS *see* Stephens.

STEPHENSON, Colonel, came from Holland (H).

STIBBS, George, worsted comber, of Taunton St Mary, 'aiding' (CP); Blue Regt. (P).

STIBBS, James, carpenter, of Taunton St Mary, 'aiding' (CP); Blue Regt. (P).

STOCKDALE, William weaver, of Ottery St Mary imprisoned in the High Gaol, Devon (DLD).

STOCKER, William, of Taunton St Mary, fuller, 'aiding' (CP); Blue Regt. (P). Probably killed at Sedgemoor, as his son, born in March 1686, was brought up fatherless in Cornwall by his mother or grandmother who came from Colyton (Family tradition).

STOCKS (Stoakes, Stokes), George, of Combpyne, husbandman, 'with Monmouth in the rebellion' (CP); presented at Exeter but at large (JR); at Lyme Regis Henry Scriven, husbandman, of Axmouth, swore that 'Stokes joined Monmouth at Lyme and served under his command' (LRMB Feb. 6–8); sent to Dorchester gaol; presented at Dorchester Assize, March 1686; pardoned by proclamation (GD).

STODGELL, Nicholas, of North Petherton, 'taking up arms against the king' (Som. QSR); tried at Taunton; hanged at Bridgwater (JR, JW).

STONE, Arthur, of Bishop's Hull, 'in prison' (CL).

STONE, George, of Taunton St James, 'aiding' (CP); Blue Regt. (P).

STONE, John, of Bradford Abbas, 'absent, suspected' (CP).

STONE, John, of Rode, weaver, 'in the rebellion' (CP); tried at Wells; transported for Howard (JR), Oct. 25 on the *Port Royal Merchant* to Jamaica (SL).

STONE, John. 'We present John Stone for setting forth his son with horse and arms in the late rebellion' (CL).

STONE, Richard, of Lyme Regis, seaman, 'absent, supposed' (CP); presented at Dorchester; certificate allowed (JR).

STONE, Thomas, of Plymtree, worsted comber, in the High Gaol, Devon (DLD).

STONE, Thomas, of Wrantage, North Curry, 'absent' (CP); 'in arms, fled' (CL).

STONE, William, of Blackford, 'absent' (CP).

STOODLEY, John, of Thorncombe, yeoman, 'wanting from his habitation' (CP); presented at Exeter but at large (JR).

STOODLEY, John, of Trent, tried at Taunton; transported for Booth (JR) from Taunton Bridewell via Bristol on Oct. 24, on the *John* to Barbados; sold to Capt. Walter Scott (SL).

STOODLEY, Samuel, presented at Dorchester: certificate allowed (JR).

STOODLEY, William, of Ashill, 'out in the rebellion' (CP).

STOODLEY, William, of Broadwindsor, 'being out in the horrid rebellion' (CP).

STOREY, Samuel, a Scot, came with Monmouth from Holland; a Captain and Commissary General; fetched Taunton councillors to the proclamation of Monmouth as king (Hist. MSS. Comm. Stopford-Sackville MSS, I, 24–6); exacted protection money at Wells (Hist. MSS. Comm. Dean and Chapter MSS, I, 460); at Wells Assizes he was left in custody as a witness for the king; (JR) excepted from GP.

STOWER, John, tried at Wells; transported for Howard (JR) on Oct. 25 on the *Port Royal Merchant* to Jamaica (SL).

STRABRIDGE *see* Trowbridge.

STREET *see* Spreet.

STREET, Hugh, of Axminster, 'seen in Monmouth's camp' (LRMB).

STREET, John, of Chard, mason, 'absent, believed' (CP).

STREET, Richard, of Chardland, 'absent, believed' (CP).

STREET, William, of Chardland, 'absent, believed' (CP).

STREET, William, of Wilton, 'absent' (CP).

- STRICKLAND, John, tailor, of Taunton St Mary, 'aiding' (CP); Blue Regt. (P).

STRICKLAND, William, of Martock, 'absent' (CP).

STRIDE, John, of Chewton, 'absenting' (CP).

STRODE, Edward, of Downside near Shepton Mallet, sheltered Monmouth, Grey and Buyse on the night of July 6; pardon of all treasons March 12 1686 (CSPD, J2, II, 266).

STRODE, William, of Barrington and Street, 'sent horses and money to Monmouth' (according to John Madder, L 240); excepted from the GP, but pardoned of all treasons, June 12 1686 (CSPD, J2, II, 659).

STRONG, Charles senior, of Beaminster, 'wanting from his home' (CP).

STRONG, Charles junior, of Beaminster, 'wanting' (CP); tried at Dorchester; transported for Booth (JR) on the *Happy Return* from Weymouth on Sept. 25 to Barbados; sold to Col. John Sampson (SL).

STRONG, John, at Dorchester Assize discharged for want of evidence (JR).

STRONG, Joseph, of Beaminster, 'wanting from his home'; at Wells Assizes 'left in custody as a witness for the king' (JR).

STRONG, Peter, of Pitminster, 'absent' (CP); 'a rebel' (Som. QSR).

STRONG, Richard, at Dorchester Assizes discharged for want of evidence (JR).

STRONG, Stephen, of Marnhull, 'absent' (CP).

STROUD, James, of Axminster, yeoman, 'supposed' (CP); presented at Exeter but at large (JR).

STUCKEY, George, of Whitelackington, 'out in the rebellion' (CP); went to Forde Abbey for arms; presented at Dorchester but 'humbly proposed for pardon'; excepted from the GP (Dep.; JR).

STUCKEY, Henry, of Kingsbury Episcopi, 'absent, believed' (CP).

STUCKEY, Pasche, tried at Wells; transported for Howard (JR) on Oct. 25 on the *Port Royal Merchant* to Jamaica (SL).

STUCKEY, Robert, tried at Wells; transported for Howard (JR) on Oct. 25 on the *Port Royal Merchant* to Jamaica (SL).

STUCKEY, William, of Street, Winsham, 'in the rebellion and not come in' (CP).

STUCKEY, William, of Taunton St Mary, worsted comber, 'aiding' (CP); Blue Regt. (P).

STUCKLEY, William, of Chard, 'in the late rebellion' (CP).

STURRICK, John, tried at Dorchester; transported for Musgrave (JR) from Weymouth on the *Jamaica Merchant* to Barbados, March 12 (SL).

STUTT, John, of Milverton, 'absenting' (CP).

SULLEY, Joshua, tried at Wells; transported for Howard (JR) on Oct. 25 on the *Port Royal Merchant* to Jamaica (SL).

SULLY, William, tried at Taunton; hanged at Dunster (JR, JW) in Nov. or Dec. (NL).

SURFILL, Arthur, of West Buckland, 'absent' (CP).

SUSTON, Christopher, of Chard, 'absent, believed' (CP).

SUTTON, Jonathan, tried at Wells; transported for Howard (JR) on Oct. 25 on the *Port Royal Merchant* to Jamaica (SL).

SWAFFEILD, Nathaniel, of Thorncombe, tailor, imprisoned in Wilts. (DLD); presented at Dorchester but 'proposed for pardon' (JR).

SWAINE, John, of Lyme Regis, fuller, 'absent, supposed' (CP); 'took up arms with Monmouth when he landed', and marched to Axminster, Chard and Taunton; 'from Taunton he returned home, and hath ever since laid hidden for fear'; taken at Lyme Regis, Jan. 27; to Dorchester gaol, Feb. 1 (LRMB); presented at Dorchester, March 1686 and pardoned by proclamation (GD).

SWAINE, John, of Shapwick (T) reached home after Sedgemoor, arrested by militia, escaped near Loxley Wood by triple jump, now marked by stones (Tradition; but no Swaines in that PR).

SWAYNE, John, of Seavington St Mary, 'in the rebellion and not come in' (CP).

SWEATLAND, John, of Axminster, yeoman, 'supposed' (CP); presented at Exeter but at large (JR); taken to prison (Pulman, Book of the Axe). *And see* Sweetland.

SWEET, William, tried at Wells; transported thence for Bridgeman (JR), by White, Oct. 31, on the *Constant Richard* to Jamaica (SL).

SWEETE, Richard, of Taunton St James, fuller, 'aiding' (CP); Blue Regt. (P); tried at Taunton; to be hanged at Minehead (JR, JW) where 3 of 6 so sentenced were hanged (NL of Dec. 8). Not on Broadsheet list of those hanged. Pardon authorised, March 27; granted April 14 (CSPD, J2, II, 356, 403). Land forfeit and for sale (TB).

SWEETE, Robert junior, tried at Wells; transported thence for Bridgeman (JR) by White, Oct. 31, on the *Constant Richard* to Jamaica (SL).

SWEETE, Thomas junior, of Chard, 'absent, believed' (CP).

SWEETING, Samuel, tried at Taunton; to be transported for the Queen. (JR but not on SL).

SWEETLAND, Dionisius, of Combe Raleigh, yeoman, 'in the rebellion and not yet taken' (CP); presented at Exeter but at large (JR).

SWEETLAND, George, of Yarcombe, yeoman, 'wanting from his habitation during the rebellion of James Scott' (CP); presented at Exeter but at large (JR).

SWETNAM, George, of Trull, 'absent, supposed' (CP).

SWETNAM, James, of Yeovil, 'absent and not returned' (CP).

SWINBORNE, ——, 'recommended for pardon' (JR2).

SWINNEY, John, presented at Wells and bound over (JR). Entered twice.

SYBLY, Peter, of Martock, 'absent' (CP).

SYLE, Edward, of Wellington, 'absent' (CP).

SYMES, Henry, of Frome, yeoman, 'in the rebellion and in prison' (CP); tried at Wells; transported for Howard (JR), Oct. 25 on the *Port Royal Merchant* to Jamaica (SL).

SYMES, Hugh, of Wilton, 'absent' (CP).

SYMES, John, of Bridport, 'in the rebellion, as we are informed' (CP).

SYMES, John, of South Petherton, 'in the rebellion and not come in' (CP).

SYMES, John, of Stoke Atrum, Netherbury, 'suspected' (CP).

SYMES, Richard, tried at Wells; transported for Howard (JR), Oct. 25 on the *Port Royal Merchant* to Jamaica (SL).

SYMES, Thomas, of Bridport, 'in the rebellion as informed' (CP). *And see* Sims.

SYMON *see* Simon.

SYMONDS, Joseph, of Martock, 'absent' (CP).

SYMONS, Benedict, of Taunton St James, 'taking up arms against the king' (Som. QSR).

SYMONS, Richard, aged 23, weaver, tried at Taunton, transported thence for the Queen (JR) on the *Jamaica Merchant*, Dec. 9, to Barbados; sold to Major Abel Allen (SL). *And see* Simons.

TALBOTT, Maximilian junior, apprentice worsted comber, of Taunton St Mary, 'aiding' (CP); Private in the Blue Regt. March 6 certificate in his favour signed by Major and 3 aldermen; April 19 a note added 'No presentment, and not excepted from GP'; June 1 petition for pardon: Sir Henry Tulse's kinsman, 'concerned in the rebellion in the West'. August 1 certificate in favour read at the Committee; Aug. 2 1686. Pardon granted (CSPD, J2, II, 234, 617, 862).

TALBOTT, Robert, of Staplegrove, yeoman, pardon March 22 (CSPD, J2, II, 310).

TALLIS, Nicholas, of Charmouth, 'suspected' (CP).

TAMSON *see* Thompson.

TANNER, John, of Axmouth, yeoman, 'reported to be in arms in the late rebellion' (CP); presented at Exeter but at large (JR).

TANNER, Richard, of Frome, cooper, 'in the rebellion and in prison' (CP); at Wells Assizes entered as 'witness for the king, remaining in custody'; this was deleted and 'bound over' substituted (JR).

TANNER, William, of Axmouth, yeoman, indicted for high treason at Exeter but at large (GD, JR).

TAPLEY, John, of Taunton St Mary, weaver, 'aiding' (CP); Blue Regt. (P).

TAPPELL, William, of Seavington St Mary, 'in the rebellion and not come in' (CP).

TAPPER, Andrew, of Durleigh, 'absent and not taken' (CP); presented at Wells and bound over (JR).

TAPPER, Richard, tried at Wells, transported for Howard (JR), Oct. 25 on the *Port Royal Merchant* to Jamaica (SL).

TAPPER, Thomas, of Chardland, 'absent, believed' (CP).

TAPSCOTT, William, of Culmstock, sergeweaver, imprisoned at Taunton (DLD); tried there; transported for Musgrave (JR) from Weymouth on the *Jamaica Merchant* to Jamaica; there by March 12 (SL).

TARR, William, presented at Wells and bound over (JR).

TARRELL, Robert, of Yeovil, 'absent and not returned' (CP).

TAYLOR, Blase, of Kingsbury Episcopi, 'absent, believed' (CP).

TAYLOR, Christopher, of Taunton St Mary, 'aiding' (CP); Blue Regt. (P); 'today appeared and pleaded benefit of the pardon proclaimed' entered on CP.

TAYLOR, Henry, of Taunton, 'a poor convict', pardoned Oct. 4 1686 (CSPD, J2, II, 1045).

TAYLOR, Humphrey, of Corfe, 'absent, supposed' (CP).

TAYLOR, James, of Axminster, yeoman, 'supposed;' presented at Exeter but at large (JR).

TAYLOR, Jasper, presented at Exeter, March 1686; pardoned and dismissed (GD).

TAYLOR, John, presented at Wells and bound over (JR).

TAYLOR, Lieutentant, came from Holland with the Duke (W); almost certainly killed at Sedgemoor (P).

TAYLOR, Marmaduke, of Isle Brewers, 'in the rebellion and not taken' (CP).

TAYLOR, Robert, of Stawell; 'out in the rebellion and at large' (CP).

TAYLOR, Robert junior, of Taunton St Mary, comber, 'aiding' (CP); Blue Regt. (P). He was married in 1673 (PR).

TAYLOR, Robert, of Wellington, 'absent' (CP).

TAYLOR, Robert, tallow chandler, pardoned 21 August 1686 (CSPD, J2, II, 916). He might be one of the above.

TAYLOR, Samuel, of Sarum Wells, Whitechurch Canonicorum, 'suspected' (CP).

TAYLOR, Thomas, presented at Wells and bound over (JR).

TAYLOR, William, of Ashcott, 'for carrying provisions to Monmouth's army' (CP).

TAYLOR, William, of Wedmore, 'absent, and in the late rebellion' (CP).

TEAPE, Robert, of Bridgwater, in prison in Exeter (SL); tried at Taunton; transported for Booth (JR) via Bristol, Oct. 24, on the *John* to Barbados; sold to Hugh Williams (SL).

TEAPE, Robert, of Colyton, cordwainer, in Bridgwater prison (DLD).

TEAPE, Thomas, of Colyton, yeoman, 'absent' (CP); presented at Exeter but at large (JR). Born 1656 or 1664; died 1721 (PR).

TEAPE, Walter, of Axmouth, yeoman, 'reported to be in arms in the late rebellion' (CP); tried at Exeter; to be transported for Nipho (JR); JR2 has 'reprieved': Edward Merrick in Wells Gaol to be transported in the place of Walter Teape. MS misreports him at large (JR).

TELLIER, John, an ex-officer, arrested in Holland and imprisoned on board ship to prevent him informing; was offered and accepted a captain's commission; interrogated in London after Sedgemoor (L). Excepted from GP, but apparently not indicted. Sick while a prisoner in Newgate; his wife, Mary, to have access, April 2 (CSPD, J2, II, 369).

TEMPLE, Benjamin, chirurgeon, of Nottingham but in Holland and joined the Duke 'for an expedition to the West Indies,' he said, in his dying speech (BA), but Kidd heard Dr Temple speak of his intention to come over (L). 'Taken' at Honiton, imprisoned at Exeter, tried at Dorchester, Sept. 10; hanged at Lyme, Sept. 12 (JR, NL).

TEMPLE, Joseph, chandler, of Frome, 'for a riot and amongst the Clubmen' (CP).

TEMPLEMAN, John, of Merriott, 'rebel in Monmouth's army and not taken' (CP); proposed for pardon; rick of wheat confiscated Jan. 12 (TB); pardon of all treasons, April 14 1686 (CSPD, J2, II, 404).

TEMPLEMAN, Nicholas, of West Chinnock, 'in the late rebellion and not taken' (CP).

TEMPLEMAN, Richard, of Merriott, 'rebel in Monmouth's army and not taken' (CP).

TEMPLEMAN, Thomas, of Merriott, 'rebel in Monmouth's army and not taken' (CP).

TERRY, Andrew, of Taunton St Mary, worsted comber, 'aiding' (CP); Blue Regt. (P).
*And see* Perry.

THATCHER, Barnard, of Stoke St Gregory, 'in the rebellion and in prison' (CP); tried at Taunton for concealing Bovett; hanged at Yeovil (JR, NL). CL has of 'Thornfalcon, North Curry, executed'.

THATCHER, Robert, chirurgeon, of Wedmore, tried at Wells; 'remaining in custody' deleted and his name added (in another hand) to those to be executed for high treason. No place of execution named on any list. Land forfeit and for sale (TB).

THATCHER, William, of Whatley, 'in the rebellion and not taken' (CP).

THEADROCK, John, of Tiverton, sergeweaver, wounded at Sedgemoor, imprisoned at Wells (DLD).

THICK, John, of Wincanton, yeoman, 'actually in arms in the rebellion, as informed, and at large' (CP).

THIMBLETON, Walter, excepted from GP.

THOMAS, Abraham, of Honiton, barber (DLD), 'a rebel' (CP); imprisoned and tried at Dorchester; transported for Nipho (JR) from Weymouth, Nov. 25, on the *Betty* to Barbados; sold to Ralph Lane (SL). Land forfeit and for sale. Named on the 1689 petition for release (CSPD, W&M, I, 43).

THOMAS, David, tried at Wells, transported thence for Bridgeman (JR) by White, Oct. 31, on the *Constant Richard* to Jamaica (SL).

THOMAS, Griffen, of Bishop's Hull, 'absent, not taken' (CP).

THOMAS, Howell, tried at Taunton; hanged at Keynsham (JR, JW).

THOMAS, James, presented at Wells and bound over (JR).

THOMAS, Martin, of Chardland, 'absent, believed' (CP).

THOMAS, Merricke (CP) or Mayrick (DLD), of Cullompton, tailor, imprisoned at Taunton (DLD); tried there; hanged at Nether Stowey (JR, JW).

THOMAS, Miles, of West Buckland, 'absent' (CP).

THOMAS, Moses, of Luppitt, yeoman, 'out in the rebellion' (CP); presented at Exeter but at large (JR).

THOMAS, Philip, of Luppitt, yeoman, 'out in the rebellion' (CP), presented at Exeter but at large (JR).

THOMAS, Samuel, of Northcote, Honiton, 'a rebel' (CP).

THOMAS, Thomas, of Northcote, Honiton, 'a rebel' (CP).

THOMAS alias Bisse, Walter, of Shaftesbury, 'in the rebellious army of James, Duke of Monmouth, as reported' (CP); presented at Wells and bound over (JR).

THOMPSON, George, of Taunton St Mary, weaver, 'aiding' (CP); Blue Regt. (P).

THOMPSON, Henry, tried at Taunton; to be hanged at Dulverton (JR, JW) where on Dec. 8 2 of the 3 condemned were hanged (NL).

THOMPSON, John, of Duddlestone, Pitminster, 'absent' (CP); 'I suppose they were in rebellion' (CL).

THOMPSON, John, of Taunton St James, 'aiding' (CP); Blue Regt. (P). One of these two was presented at Wells and bound over (JR).

THOMPSON, Nicholas, of Colyton, doctor, 'absent' (CP); presented at Exeter but at large – entered twice (JR). Pardon, as 'yeoman – of Somerset', May 12 1686 (CSPD, J2, II, 530).

THOMPSON (Tamson), Richard, of Axminster, yeoman, 'supposed' (CP); presented at Exeter but at large (JR). Presented for high treason at Exeter, March 1686, pardoned and dismissed (GD).

THOMPSON, Stephen, of Bishop's Hull, 'absent' (CP); presented at Wells and bound over (JR).

THOMPSON, Lieutenant, was in Holland, probably of an English regiment in the Dutch Service; came with Monmouth and was commissioned as 3rd Captain in the Red Regt.; commanded 100 musketeers at the Bridport skirmish (W). Probably killed at Sedgemoor.

THOMPSON, William, of London, milliner, linen draper or haberdasher, Captain in the Blue Regt. (W); commanded the Scythemen;
after Sedgemoor rode to Ilfracombe with Wade; excepted from GP
but was offered his life and £500 if he would swear that Prideaux sent
Monmouth £500 (L); pardoned August 21 (CSPD, J2, I, 916).

THORNE, Robert, of Colyton, yeoman, 'absent' (CP); presented at
Exeter but at large (JR).

THORNE, Simon, of Wilton, 'absent' (CP).

THORNE, Thomas, of Chilton Polden, 'out in the rebellion and at large'
(CP).

THORNE, Thomas, of Lopen, 'in the rebellion and not come in' (CP).

THORNE, William, of Wilton, 'absent' (CP).

TIBBS, Abraham senior, of South Petherton, 'in the rebellion and not
come in (CP).

TIBBS, George, of Combe St Nicholas, 'absent, believed' (CP).

TIBBS, William, of Kingsbury Episcopi, 'absent, believed' (CP).

TICKEN (Titchen, Tricker), Peter, aged 33, of Colyton, yeoman,
'absent' (CP); scrivener, imprisoned in Dorset (DLD); tried at
Dorchester; transported for Nipho (JR) on the *Rebecca*, Oct. 21, to
Barbados (SL). Also presented at Exeter and misreported at large
(JR). Married in 1680 (PR).

TIDBALL, William, presented at Exeter, March 1686; pardoned and
dismissed (GD).

TIGGINS, William, of Thorncombe, yeoman, 'wanting from his habitation' (CP); presented at Exeter but at large (JR).

TILY (Tyley), Joseph, of Bristol, came from Holland with Monmouth,
Captain in the Red Regt.; seized John Kerridge to be pilot to Bristol;
read the proclamation of Monmouth as king in Taunton; repaired
the bridge of Keynsham (W); in Newgate, Nov. 2 (CSPD, J2, II,
1852); escaped to Holland and took leading part in scheme to
manufacture English cloth there (PE); excepted from GP but
pardoned on condition of returning with gear.

TILLEY, John, of Glastonbury, 'from home at the time of the rebellion'
(CP); tried at Wells; transported for Howard (JR), Oct. 25 on the
*Port Royal Merchant* to Jamaica (SL).

TILLEY, Jude, of Glastonbury, 'from home at the time of the rebellion'
(CP).

TILLMAN, David, blacksmith, of Lyme Regis, 'absent, supposed' (CP).

TIMEWELL, William, of Wellington, 'absent' (CP).

TIMOTHY, John, aged 29, of Exeter, silk ribbon weaver, wounded at
Sedgemoor, imprisoned at Wells, then at Taunton (DLD); tried at
Taunton; transported for the Queen (JR) on the *Jamaica Merchant*
Dec. 9, to Barbados; sold there, March 12, to Ann Walters (SL).

TINCKNELL, John, tried at Wells; to be hanged on Redcliffe Hill,
Bristol (JR) on Oct. 13. Either hanged or died of smallpox (NL).

TIPPETT, Edward, tried at Wells; to be hanged on Redcliffe Hill, Bristol
(JR, JW); on Oct. 13. Either hanged or died of smallpox (NL).

TIRRILL, Richard, bailed at Taunton Assize (JR).

TITCHEN *see* Ticken.

TIVERTON, William, of Bridgwater, imprisoned there, tried at Taunton; transported for Booth (JR) via Bristol, Oct. 24, on the *John* to Barbados; sold to John and William Holder (SL).

TIZARD, Henry, no note of trial but named on 1689 petition for return (CSPD, W&M, I, 43).

TOLE, David, of Kingsbury, 'absent, believed' (CP). At Wells Assizes a witness for the king; left in custody (JR).

TOLEMAN, Nicholas, of Wellington, 'absent' (CP).

TOLEMAN, Timothy, of Kingsbury Episcopi, 'absent, believed' (CP); tried at Wells; transported for Howard (JR), Oct. 25 on the *Port Royal Merchant* to Jamaica (SL).

TOOGOOD, Henry, of North Curry, 'absent' (CP).

TOOGOOD, John senior, of Colyton, yeoman, 'absent' (CP); presented at Exeter but at large (JR).

TOOGOOD, John junior, of Colyton, yeoman, 'absent' (CP); presented at Exeter but at large (JR).

TOOGOOD (Towgood), Stephen, Congregational minister, Axminster, marched with Monmouth as far as Norton St Philip; then returned to his church (Ecc.).

TOOKER, Matthew senior, of Bampton, 'supposed' (CP).

TOOKER, Matthew junior, of Bampton, 'supposed' (CP).

TOOPE, Daniel, of Colyton, yeoman, 'absent' (CP); presented at Exeter but at large (JR).

TOTTLE, Samuel, of Wellington (CP), of Cullompton, sergeweaver, in prison at Taunton for rebellion (DLD); tried at Taunton; transported for Musgrave (JR) from Weymouth on the *Jamaica Merchant* to Barbados; there by March 12 (SL).

TOYE *see* Trye.

TOWGOOD *see* Toogood.

TOWELL, Edward, of Ilminster, comber; land forfeit and for sale (TB). Probably killed at Sedgemoor (P).

TOWILLS, Edward, presented at Dorchester, 'humbly proposed for pardon' (JR).

TOWNSEND (Townsell), Alexander, of Otterford (CL), tried at Taunton; transported for Musgrave (JR) from Weymouth on the *Jamaica Merchant* to Barbados; there by March 12 (SL).

TOWNSEND, John, presented at Wells and bound over (JR).

TOWNSEND, Robert, tried at Taunton; to be hanged at Ilchester (JR, JW) where 8 of 12 so sentenced were hanged (Whiting).

TOWNSEND, Samuel, of Ilminster, 'in the late rebellion' (CP); excepted from GP.

TOWNSEND, Thomas, tried at Dorchester; transported for Booth (GR) from Weymouth, Sept. 25, on the *Happy Return* to Barbados; sold in Dec. to Capt. Tobias Frere (SL).

TOYE *see* Trye.

TOZER, Andrew, tried at Dorchester; Sept. 10; hanged at Poole, Sept. 21 (JR, NL).

TRACEY, George, of Hillfarrance, 'absent' (CP); 'taking up arms against the king' (Som. QSR).

TRASK, Benjamin, of Stoford, 'in the late rebellion' (CP); tried at Wells; transported thence for Bridgeman (JR) by White, Oct. 31, on the *Constant Richard* to Jamaica (SL).

TRATT, John, of Sidbury, 'joined in the rebellion' (CP).

TRATTLE (Trottle), John, of Whitechurch Canonicorum, 'suspected' (CP); presented at Dorchester but 'proposed for pardon' (JR).

TRATTLE, Samuel, of Whitechurch Canonicorum, 'suspected' (CP).

TRAVERS, William, of Donyatt, 'out in the rebellion' (CP).

TREBY, Andrew, presented at Exeter in March 1686, pardoned and dismissed (GD).

TRECKEY, John, tried at Taunton; hanged there Sept. 30; buried, Oct. 2, at St James's (JR, JW, NL, PR).

TREHORNE, William, cardmaker, of Frome, 'with the rebels, at large' (CP).

TRENCHER, John, of Thorncombe, yeoman, 'wanting from his habitation' (CP); presented at Exeter but at large (JR).

TRENT, Samuel, of Ilchester, 'in the late rebellion' (CP); presented at Wells and bound over (JR).

TRESANE, John junior, of Ilminster, 'in the late rebellion' (CP).

TRESHAM, Robert junior, of Ilminster, 'in the late rebellion' (CP).

TREVETT, Samuel, of Allington, Bridport, 'suspected' (CP).

TREVITT (Trewett), Edward, of Musbury, yeoman, 'in the rebellion' (CP); presented at Exeter but at large (JR).

TREVITT, George, of Chardland, 'absent, believed' (CP).

TREVITT, John, of Chardland, 'absent, believed' (CP).

TREWEN, William, of Lyme Regis, hellier, 'absent, supposed' (CP).

TREWETT *see* Trevitt.

TRICKER *see* Ticken.

TRICKEY, Thomas, of Taunton, yeoman; lands forfeit and for sale (TB). Is he John Treckey?

TRICKS, Lewis, of Exeter, comber, imprisoned in Wilts. (DLD); tried at Wells; to be transported for Howard (JR), Oct. 25, but escaped between Wells and Sherborne (SL).

TRIM, Peter, of Stockland, 'suspected' (CP).

TRIPP, Jacob, aged about 21, of Shipham, tried at Wells; to be hanged at Axbridge (JR, JW), but 'being unconscious and dying of gaol fever', he was hanged in Wells Market Place (JB/JD).

TRIPP, John, of Shipham, brother of Jacob, excepted from GP.

TROCK, Thomas, of Wellington, 'in prison for rebellion' (CP); tried at Taunton; hanged at Ilminster (JR, JW). [Also entered in error as hanged at Keynsham – on one copy of JW.]

TROOD, John, of Northcote, Honiton, 'a rebel' (CP).

TROTE, Peter, of Chardland, 'absent, believed' (CP).

TROTT, Christopher senior, of Taunton St James, 'taking up arms against the king' (Som. QSR).

TROTT, Christopher junior, comber of Taunton St James, 'aiding' (CP); Blue Regt. (P).

TROTT, John, of North Petherton, 'in arms against the king' (Som. QSR); tried at Taunton; hanged at Bridgwater (JR, JW).

TROTT, Thomas, tried at Wells; transported thence for Bridgeman (JR) by White, Oct. 31, on the *Constant Richard* to Jamaica (SL).

TROTTLE *see* Trattle.

TROTTLE, Samuel, of Kingston St Mary, 'a rebel' (CP).

TROUBRIDGE (Strabridge), Moses, of Upottery, yeoman, 'absent' (CP); presented at Exeter but at large (CP).

TRUBBS (Scrubs), George, aged 28, plowman [carter], tried at Taunton; transported thence for the Queen (JR), Dec. 9, on the *Jamaica Merchant* to Barbados; sold there to Archibald Johnson (SL).

TRUMPE, Humphrey, blacksmith (DLD), of (West) Sandford, Devon, imprisoned in Taunton Bridewell (DLD); tried at Taunton; transported thence for Booth (JR) via Bristol, Oct. 24, on the *John* to Barbados; sold to Col. John Hallett (SL).

TRUREN (Trewron, Truen), John, of Colyton, worsted comber, imprisoned in the Devon Workhouse (DLD), tried at Dorchester; to be transported for Booth to Barbados (JR) but 'John Truen and his wife died in Dorchester gaol'; buried Jan. 20 (PR). Omitted from SL and sale. Land forfeit and for sale (TB).

TRYE (Toye), John, of West Buckland, 'absent' (CP).

TRYE, William, of West Buckland, 'absent' (CP).

TUCK, Benjamin, presented at Dorchester in March 1686 and pardoned (GD).

TUCKER, David, presented at Wells and bound over (JR).

TUCKER, Edward, of Donyatt, 'out in the rebellion' (CP).

TUCKER, Henry, of Donyatt, 'out in the rebellion' (CP).

TUCKER, Henry, of Bishop's Hull, 'absent' (CP); 'not taken' (CL).

TUCKER, James, of Pitminster, 'absent' (CP) 'a rebel' (CL), a captain excepted from GP; arrested Aug. 6 1686 (NL, CSPD, J2, II, 874).

TUCKER, James (son of Julian), of Lyme Regis, 'absent, supposed' (CP).

TUCKER, John, of Allington, 'suspected' (CP); tried at Wells; hanged at Wincanton (JR, JW).

TUCKER, John, of Angersleigh, 'taking up arms against the king' (Som. QSR).

TUCKER, John, of Shepton Mallet, excepted from GP.

TUCKER *see* Glover.

TUCKER, Matthew senior, presented at Wells and bound over (JR); presented at Exeter in March 1686, pardoned and dismissed (GD).

TUCKER, Matthew junior, presented at Exeter in March 1686, pardoned and dismissed (GD).

TUCKER, Reginald, of Long Sutton, yeoman, 'being in the late rebellion and not come home' (CP); a Captain of Horse; his house ransacked and his barn burnt by troops under Churchill (Whiting); excepted from GP; arrested in London and put in Newgate, Aug. 1686; stay of execution issued Feb. 23 1687; tried at Wells in March; to be hanged on April 15 but pardoned (CSPD, J2, II, 886, 1452 1483). Land confiscated but not for sale (TB); held by Theophilus Oglethorpe until 1688 but recovered in 1695 (*VCH Somerset* iii. 158).

TUCKER, Richard, of Bishop's Hull, 'absent' (CP), 'not taken' (CL); excepted from GP.

TUCKER, Richard, of Taunton St Mary, weaver, 'aiding' (CP), Blue Regt. (P).

TUCKER, Thomas, of Cheddon, 'absent' (CP).

TUCKER, Thomas, of Taunton St Mary, blacksmith, 'aiding' (CP), Blue Regt. (P).

TUCKER, William, of Allington, Bridport, weaver, 'suspected' (CP); tried at Dorchester; transported for Booth (JR) on the *Happy Return* from Weymouth, Sept. 25, to Barbados; sold to Richard Lintott (SL). Land forfeit and for sale (TB).

TUCKEY (Turkey), Thomas, tried at Wells; transported for Howard (JR), Oct. 25 on the *Port Royal Merchant* to Jamaica (SL).

TUCKWILL *see* Luckwill.

TUGGIE, Robert, broadweaver, of Beckington, 'in the rebellion, out of Beckington, at large' (CP).

TURBER *see* Furber.

TURKE *see* Lawrence.

TURLE, James and John, both tried at Taunton, 'remaining in gaol till further order' (JR); both transported by Heywood on the *Constant Richard* Nov. 12, to Jamaica (SL).

TURNER, Christopher, of Ruishton, 'absent' (CP).

TURNER, George, of Colyton, yeoman, in Bridgwater prison (DLD); at Dorchester Assizes discharged for want of evidence (JR). Died 1701 (PR).

TURNER, Henry, presented at Wells and bound over (JR).

TURNER, Jacob, of Ottery St Mary, 'in the late rebellion as supposed' (CP).

TURNER, John, of Alstone, Huntspill, 'being in arms in the late rebellion' (CP).

TURNER, John, of Colyton, yeoman, 'absent' (CP); presented at Exeter but at large (JR). Died either in 1691 or 1699 (PR).

TURNER, John, of Ilminster, 'in the late rebellion' (CP).

TURNER, John, of Lyme Regis, tailor, 'absent, supposed' (CP).

TURNER, John, of Oathill, Wayford, 'rebel in Monmouth's army and not taken' (CP).

TURNER, Joshua, of Offwell, 'supposed' (CP).

TURNER, Richard, of Coleford, 'absenting' (CP). [*See below.*]

TURNER, Richard, of Lyme Regis, 'absent, supposed' (CP). [*See below.*] One of these two was tried at Wells and transported for Howard (JR) Oct. 25 on the *Port Royal Merchant* to Jamaica (SL).

TURNER, Sachrill, of Cricket Malherbie, 'being in the late rebellion and at large' (CP).

TURNER, Samuel, of Ilminster, 'in the late rebellion' (CP).

TURNER, William, of Coleford, 'absenting' (CP); presented at Exeter in March 1686, pardoned and dismissed (GD).

TURNER, William, Lord Grey's henchman, appears to have been at and survived Sedgemoor. Pardon for all treasons committed by him, Dec. 10 1686 (CSPD, J2, II, 1230).

TUTCHER, Henry, tried at Dorchester; transported for Booth (JR) on the *Happy Return* from Weymouth, Sept. 25, to Barbados; sold to John Hethersell, Esq. (SL).

TUTCHER, Robert, of Durleigh, 'absent and not taken' (CP).

TUTT, Andrew, of Taunton St James, 'aiding' (CP); Blue Regt. (P).

TUTT, William, of Corfe, 'absent' (CP).

TUTTWELL, John, of Taunton St James, 'aiding' (CP); Blue Regt. (P).

TYLER, Edward junior, of Crewkerne, 'rebel and not taken' (CP).

TYLER, Thomas, of Bristol, mercer, a Lieut. in the Red Regt. who 'behaved himself very stoutly to the last' (BA); tried at Dorchester Sept. 10; hanged at Wareham Sept. 22 (JR, NL). Sarah, his widow, petitioned for power to receive his debts for the relief of herself and five children (CSPD, J2, II, 1724).

TYLEY *see* Tily.


UNWEN, Robert, of Combe St Nicholas, 'absent, believed' (CP).

UPCOTT, Robert, at Wells Assize among the 'prisoners for the king's pardon' (JR).

UPHAM, Thomas, of Milverton, 'absenting' (CP).

USHER, Benjamin, of Frome, cardmaker, 'in the rebellion and at large' (CP).

USHER, Philip, of North Bradley, Wilts., deputy tithingman, tried at Wells; hanged at Frome (JR, JW). Land forfeit and for sale. (TB).


VAGG, Edward, tried at Wells; transported for Howard (JR), Oct. 25 on the *Port Royal Merchant* on Jamaica (SL).

VARIARD *see* Verrier.

VAUTER (Vater, Vawter), Robert, of Sidmouth, woolcomber, 'went to Monmouth' (CP); wounded at Sedgemoor, imprisoned at Wells (DLD); tried at Dorchester; transported for Nipho (JR) from Weymouth, Nov. 25, on the *Betty* towards Barbados; died at sea Dec. 21 (SL).

VAUGHAN, Francis, Esq. of Christon, 'in Newgate for the rebellion in the west'; two certificates of loyalty (CSPD, J2, II, 468, 469; 503); indicated as a rebel and acquitted, yet excepted from GP (CSPD, J2, II, 764); pardon approved June 26; granted July 11, 1686 (CSPD, J2, II, 726, 795).

VENN (Wenn), Edward, of Colyton, yeoman or cordwainer, aged 50+, married in Feb. 1655/6 (PR), 'absent' (CP); tried at Dorchester; transported for Nipho (JR) on the *Betty* from Weymouth, Nov. 25, towards Barbados but died at sea 19 Dec. (SL). Land forfeit and for sale (TB). Also presented at Exeter and misreported at large (JR).

VENNER, Gustavus, of Somerset, yeoman, pardoned May 5 1686 (CSPD, J2, II, 513).

VENNER, Samuel, of Corfe, 'absent' (CP).

VENNER, Samuel, of London and Holland, wine merchant, a Fifth Monarchy Man, an ex-captain, came with Monmouth, Lt. Col. of the Red Regt.; wounded at Bridport, command of the Regt. devolving on Major Wade; Venner being chief military adviser to the Duke, very cautious, and at Frome advised abandonment of the army; went off with Major Parsons (W); excepted from GP of 1686 and 1688. A Lt. Col. Samuel Venner was commissioned in King William's Army in 1691 (CSPD, W&M, II, 403).

VENNER, Thomas, tried at Wells; transported for Nipho (JR) on the *Betty* from Weymouth, Nov. 25, towards Barbados; died at sea Dec. 16 (SL).

VENTING, Nicholas, tried at Taunton; hanged at Langport (JR, JW).

VENTING, William, tried at Taunton; transported for Musgrave (JR) on the *Jamaica Merchant* from Weymouth to Barbados; there by Mar. 12 (SL).

VERNCOMB, Hugh junior, of West Buckland, 'absent' (CP).

VERNCOMBE (Derncombe, Fornecombe), Hugh, of Pitminster, 'absent' (CP); 'supposed' (CL); taking up arms against his Majesty (Som. QSR).

VERRIER (Variard, Verryard), John, of Axminster, yeoman, 'supposed' (CP); presented at Exeter but at large (JR); 'taken to prison' (Pulman, *Book of the Axe*).

VERRIER, Richard, of North Curry, 'absent' (CP); 'in arms against the king' (Som. QSR).

VERRIER, Robert, of Taunton St Mary, carpenter, 'aiding' (CP); Blue Regt. (P); recently married (PR).

VERRIER, Thomas, of North Curry, 'absent' (CP); 'in arms against the king' (Som. QSR).

VERRIER (Verryard), William, aged 17, of North Curry, carpenter, 'out in the rebellion and in prison' (CP); 'now in prison' (Som. QSR); tried at Taunton; transported for the Queen (JR), Dec. 9, on the *Jamaica Merchant* to Barbados; sold on March 12 to Archibald Johnson (SL).

VERTUE, Nicholas, of Milverton, 'absenting' (CP).

VERTUE, William, of Milverton, 'absenting' (CP).

VICKERY, John, of Taunton St Mary, labourer, 'aiding' (CP); Blue Regt. (P). Married in 1678 (PR).

VIGGOR, John, of Hemington, 'absenting' (CP).

VIDDY (Vildue), Edward, of Membury, in prison, 'wanting from his habitation' (CP); imprisoned at Exeter; tried at Taunton; transported for Booth (JR) via Bristol, Oct. 24, on the *John* to Barbados; sold to Capt. Walter Scott. Named on the 1689 petition (CSPD, W&M, I, 43).

VILE, Edward, tried at Wells; transported for Howard (JR), Oct. 25 on the *Port Royal Merchant* to Jamaica (SL).

VILE (Oil, Vill), Samuel, tried at Wells; hanged at Frome (JR, JW).

VILE, Thomas, tried at Wells; transported thence for Bridgeman (JR) by White, Oct. 31, on the *Constant Richard* to Jamaica (SL).

VILES, Thomas, also tried at Wells; transported thence for Bridgeman (JR) by White, Oct. 31, on the *Constant Richard* to Jamaica (SL).

VINCENT, Francis, pardon of all treasons, June 26 and July 11 (CSPD, J2, II, 726).

VINCENT, John, came from Holland, Ensign in the Red Regt. (W) As Captain Vincent commanded 50 musketeers at the barricade at Norton St Philip (W); tried at Dorchester; transported for Nipho (JR) on the *Betty* from Weymouth, Nov. 25, to Barbados; sold to Capt. John King (SL).

VINCENT, John or Joshua, Nonconformist minister, released from prison in Taunton, helped to seize weapons stored in St Mary Magdalene's; warrant for high treason, Jan. 26, arrested in Exeter in Feb., imprisoned in Devon Workhouse (DLD); taken to Newgate (CSPD, J2, II, 77, 124). Excepted from GP.

VINCENT, Joseph, of Taunton St Mary, fuller, 'aiding' (CP); Blue Regt. (P). Taken January 1686 from Exeter to Sherborne (Axminster Constables' Accounts, Devon Record Office); presumably released under GP.

VINCENT, Nicholas, of Taunton St Mary, worsted comber, 'aiding' (CP); Blue Regt. (P).

VINCENT, Robert, of Stratton on the Fosse, 'in the rebellion and not come in' (CP).

VINCENT, William, of Cheddon Fitzpaine, 'absent' (CP).

VINICOT, Joseph, of Bridgwater, imprisoned there, tried at Taunton; transported for Booth (JR) via Bristol, Oct. 24, on the *John* to Barbados; sold to John Summers (SL).

VIRGIN, Henry, presented at Wells and bound over (JR).

VOSSE *see* Furze.

VOYE, John, of Dipford, Trull, 'a rebel' (CL).

VYNING, Ambrose, of Wincanton, weaver, 'actually in arms in the rebellion, as informed, and at large' (CP); tried at Wells and transported for Howard (JR), Oct. 25 on the *Port Royal Merchant* to Jamaica (SL).

VYNING, John, of Wincanton, weaver, 'absent, and informed in Scott's army' (CP).

VYNING, Simon, of Wincanton, worsted weaver, 'actually in arms, as informed, and at large' (CP).

WADDAMS, Nicholas, of Taunton St James, 'aiding' (CP); Blue Regt. (P).

WADE, Nathaniel, born 1646, lawyer, of Bristol and London, member of Castle Hill Independent church, Bristol; on the fringe of Rye House Plot; escaped to Switzerland; joined Monmouth in Holland; Major and second-in-command Red Regt.; brought the Foot back from Bridport; given command of Red Regt.; fought in all the skirmishes except Ashill; commanded Red Regt. at Norton St Philip and Sedgemoor, from which he marched 150 men back to Bridgwater; rode to Ilfracombe; was sheltered at Brendon; wounded and captured there; taken to Windsor and thence to Newgate; drafted or dictated his 'confession' half in each prison; King's Evidence against Lord Delamere but had only 'hearsay' evidence, so Delamere was acquitted. Wade was excepted from GP, but was pardoned on May 25 1686 (CSPD, J2, II, 600) and appointed Town Clerk of Bristol. He died in 1718. [*DNB* wrongly dates Wade's birth in 1666. He, aged 70, made his will in 1716.]

WADFORD, Joel, of Chard, 'absent, believed' (CP).

WADFORD, William, of Chard, 'absent, believed' (CP); tried at Dorchester; transported for Booth (JR) on the *Happy Return* from Weymouth Sept. 25, to Barbados; sold in Dec. to Richard Lintott (SL).

WADHAM, Richard, of Uplowman (DLD), Frome (CP); yeoman, imprisoned at Bridgwater, tried at Taunton; transported for Booth (JR) via Bristol, Oct. 24, on the *John* to Barbados; sold to Col. John Sampson (SL).

WAGGOTT, Thomas, tried at Wells; transported for Howard (JR), Oct. 25 on the *Port Royal Merchant* to Jamaica (SL).

WAGSTAFFE, Moses, one of Monmouth's servants, who 'attended on the carriages'; presented at Taunton, 'remaining in gaol till further order (JR); not excepted from GP, July 10; petition for pardon, 'being in a very mean and low condition'; pardon approved August 2 (CSPD, J2, II, 791, 853, 862).

WAKE, James, of Bradford Abbas, 'absent' (CP); tried at Wells; transported for Howard (JR), Oct. 25 on the *Port Royal Merchant* to Jamaica (SL).

WAKELY (Wakeford), John, of Thorncombe, worsted comber, imprisoned at Taunton (DLD); 'wanting from his habitation' (CP); presented at Exeter but at large (JR).

WAKELY, Nicholas, of Thorncombe, yeoman, 'wanting from his habitation' (CP); presented at Exeter but at large (CP).

WAKELY, Richard, presented for High Treason at Exeter in March 1686; pardoned and dismissed (GD).

WAKELY, Robert, of Thorncombe, yeoman, 'wanting from his habitation' (CP); presented at Exeter but at large (CP).

*And see* Rockett.

WALCH, William, of Wedmore, 'absent' (CP).

WALCH, William, of London, 'concerned in the rebellion in the West', petition for pardon, June 1; not excepted from GP June 10; pardon granted August 2 (CSPD, J2, I, 617, 791, 822).

*And see* Welch.

WALDRON, Samuel, of Sidbury, 'joined in the rebellion' (CP); tried at Dorchester, Sept. 10; hanged at Poole, Sept. 21 (JR, NL).

WALDROND, John, of Ilminster, 'in the late rebellion' (CP); tried at Taunton; to be hanged at Ilchester (JR) where 8 of the 12 so sentenced were hanged (NL, Whiting).

WALE, Edward, of Wootton Fitzpaine, 'suspected' (CP); presented at Dorchester; 'remaining in custody' (JR); presented again at Dorchester in March 1686 and pardoned (GD).

WALKER, Thomas senior, of Chard Town, 'absent, believed' (CP). *And see* Walter.

WALL, Edward, of Fivehead, 'out in the rebellion and not taken' (CP).

WALL, John, of Bridgwater, imprisoned there; tried at Taunton; transported for Booth (JR) via Bristol; Oct. 24, on the *John* to Barbados; sold to John and William Holder (SL).

WALLEN, William, tried at Taunton; hanged at Ilminster (JR, JW).

WALLIN, John junior, of Frome, cardmaker, 'with the rebels and at large' (CP).

WALLIS, Jasper, of Long Sutton, 'being in the late rebellion and not come home' (CP).

WALLIS, Peter, tried at Wells; transported for Howard (JR), Oct. 25 on the *Port Royal Merchant* to Jamaica (SL).

WALSH, Stephen, tried at Wells; transported for Howard (JR), Oct. 25 on the *Port Royal Merchant* to Jamaica (SL).

WALSH (Welch), Thomas, of Chard, yeoman, 'in the late rebellion' (CP); pardoned March 22, 1686 (CSPD, J2, II, 311).

WALTER, John, of Taunton, imprisoned in the Bridewell there, tried there; transported for Booth (JR) via Bristol, Oct. 24, on the *John* to Barbados; sold to Ann Gallop (SL). Pardon approved July 18 1686 (CSPD, J2, II, 822).

WALTER, Mark, of Croscombe, 'in Scott's army and not taken' (CP).

WALTER (Walker), Robert, of North Curry, 'absent' (CP); 'in arms against the king' (Som. QSR); 'fled' (CL).

WALTER, Thomas, tried at Wells; transported for Howard (JR), Oct. 25 on the *Port Royal Merchant* to Jamaica (SL).

WALTER, William, of Membury, imprisoned at Exeter, tried at Taunton; transported for Booth (JR) via Bristol, Oct. 24, on the *John* to Barbados; sold to Samuel Warner (SL). *And see* Oastler.

WALTERS, Henry, of Wellington, 'absent' (CP); 'Monmouth rebel in custody' (Som. QSR).

WALTERS, Richard, presented at Wells and bound over (JR). *And see* Woolters.

WANSEY, Arthur, of Merriott, 'being in Monmouth's army and not taken' (CP).

WANSEY, Joseph, of Merriott, 'being in Monmouth's army and not taken' (CP).

WANSTEY, Robert, presented at Wells and bound over (JR).

WARD, William, late soldier in Capt. Johnson's Company of Grenadiers in the Queen Consort's Regt. of Foot commanded by Col. Charles Trelawney, condemned to death at Exeter Assize 1686 for deserting his Colours; pardon approved, Feb. 25 1687, without transportation (CSPD, J2, II, 1495).

WARD, Zachariah, of Upottery, yeoman, 'absent' (CP); presented at Exeter but at large (JR).

WARE, William, of Ottery St Mary, 'in the late rebellion as supposed' (CP).

WARMOUTH, John, of Taunton St James, pipe-maker, 'aiding' (CP); Blue Regt. (P).

WARNER *see* Verrier.

WARNER, William, of Cheddon, 'absent' (CP).

WARNER, William, of North Petherton, 'absconded' (CP).

WARR (Ware), Thomas, tried at Wells; hanged at Frome (JR, JW).

WARREN, Edward, of Sidbury, 'joined in the rebellion' (CP). [*See below*.]

WARREN, Edward, of Taunton St Mary, comber, 'aiding' (CP); Blue Regt. (P). One of these two, probably the Taunton man, was tried at Taunton, and hanged at Chard (JR).

WARREN, George senior, of Milverton, 'absenting' (CP); imprisoned in the Bridewell at Taunton; tried there; transported thence for Booth (JR) via Bristol, Oct. 24, on the *John* to Barbados; sold to Ann Gallop (SL).

WARREN, James, of Upottery, yeoman, 'absent' (CP); presented at Exeter but at large (JR).

WARREN, John senior, of Upottery, yeoman, 'absent' (CP); presented at Exeter but at large (CP).

WARREN, John junior, of Upottery, yeoman, 'absent' (CP); presented at Exeter but at large (JR).

WARREN, John, of Thurloxton, 'absconded' (CP).

WARREN, John, of Milverton, 'absenting' (CP), imprisoned in the Bridewell at Taunton; tried there; transported thence for Booth (JR) via Bristol, Oct. 24, on the *John* to Barbados; sold to Ann Gallop (SL).

WARREN, Joseph, of Wellington, 'in prison for rebellion' (CP); tried at Wells; transported for Howard (JR), Oct. 25 on the *Port Royal Merchant* to Jamaica (SL).

WARREN, Nicholas, of Colyton, yeoman, imprisoned at Ilchester (DLD), tried at Dorchester; to be transported for Booth (JR); one of ten omitted from SL and sale.

WARREN, Peter, of Bishop's Hull, 'absent' (CP); 'in prison' (CL); tried at Taunton; to be hanged at Minehead (JR) in Nov. or Dec. where 3 of 6 so sentenced were hanged (NL).

WARREN, Richard of Crewkerne, 'rebel and not taken' (CP).

WARREN, Thomas, of Axminster, yeoman, 'supposed' (CP); presented at Exeter but at large (JR).

WARREN, William, of North Petherton, 'in arms against the king' (Som. QSR).

WARREN, William, of Trull, 'absent' (CP), tried at Wells; transported for Howard (JR), Oct. 25 on the *Port Royal Merchant* to Jamaica (SL).

WASH, Edward, of Taunton St Mary, tailor, 'aiding' (CP); Blue Regt. (P).

WASH, Thomas, of Taunton St Mary, baker, 'aiding' (CP); Blue Regt. (P).

WASON, William, of Glastonbury, 'from home' (CP).

WATERMAN, John, of Taunton St Mary, comber, 'aiding' (CP); Blue Regt. (P).

WATERS, Gabriel, of Milverton, 'absenting' (CP).

WATKINS, William, tried at Taunton; hanged at Chewton Mendip (JR, JW).

WATTS, Edward, of Wrantage, North Curry, 'absent' (CP), 'in arms against the king' (Som. QSR).

WATTS, George, of Bradford on Tone, 'absent' (CP).

WATTS, Henry, of Whitechurch Canonicorum (TB), tried at Dorchester Sept. 10; hanged at Lyme Regis, Sept. 12 (JR, NL); in list of lands forfeited but his estate was granted to Mary, his widow (TB).

WATTS, John, of Dulverton, 'being in the late rebellion' (CP); tried at Wells; to be transported for Howard (JR) but escaped between Wells and Sherborne (SL).

WATTS, John, presented at Wells and bound over (JR).

WATTS, Robert, of Over Compton, 'absconding, suspected' (CP).

WAY, Alexander, of West Buckland, 'absent' (CP).

WAY, Edward, of Trull (CL), tried at Taunton; 'omitted in the warrant for execution, altho' designed to be executed' (JR); transported by Heywood, Nov. 12, on the *Constant Richard* to Jamaica (SL).

WAY, John, of Taunton St Mary, tailor, 'aiding' (CP); Blue Regt. (P). He was married in 1670 (PR).

WAY, Joseph, of Bridport; 'as we are informed, in the rebellion under James Scott late Duke of Monmouth' (CP).

WAY, Moses, of Combe Raleigh, yeoman, 'in the late rebellion and not yet taken' (CL); presented at Exeter but at large (JR).

WAY, Richard, of Carhampton, 'in the late rebellion' (CP); presented at Exeter in March 1686, pardoned and dismissed (GD).

WAY, William, of Combe St Nicholas, 'absent, believed' (CP). In May 1685 he told the County Coroner that Monmouth was coming (Axe). Excepted from GP, but pardoned, May 31 1687 (CSPD, J2, II, 1833).

WAYMOUTH, Israel, of Buckland St Mary, 'out in the rebellion and not taken' (CP).

WAYMOUTH, Philip, of Cricket Malherbie, 'being in the late rebellion and at large' (CP).

WEALE, Nathaniel, tried at Wells; transported for Howard (JR), Oct. 25 on the *Port Royal Merchant* to Jamaica (SL).

WEAR, Richard, of Milverton, 'absenting himself' (CP).

WEATHAM, John, of Bishop's Hull, 'absent' (CP).

WEATYARD *see* Metyard.

WEAVER, Jasper, of Taunton St Mary, smith, 'aiding' (CP); Blue Regt. (P).

WEAVER, John, of Knowle St Giles, 'in the rebellion and not come in' (CP).

WEAVER, Samuel, tried at Wells; transported for Nipho (JR) on the *Betty* from Weymouth, Nov. 25, to Barbados; sold to Michael Child (SL).

WEAVER, William, of Wellington, 'absent' (CP).

WEBB, Daniel, of Frome, blacksmith, 'for a riot and amongst the Clubmen' (CP).

WEBB, Henry, tried at Taunton; 'omitted in the warrant for execution, altho' designed to be executed' (JR); transported by Heywood, Nov. 12, on the *Constant Richard* to Jamaica (SL).

WEBB, James, aged 18, husbandman, imprisoned at Taunton, tried there, and transported thence for the Queen (JR) on the *Jamaica Merchant* to Barbados; sold to John Bawden, Esq. (SL).

WEBB, John, of Shepton Mallet, 'in prison for rebellion' (CP); tried at Wells; transported for Howard (JR), Oct. 25 on the *Port Royal Merchant* to Jamaica (SL).

WEBB, John, of Taunton St Mary, 'aiding' (CP); Blue Regt. (P).

WEBB, John, of Thorncombe, 'wanting from his habitation' (CP).

WEBB, Roger, of Taunton St Mary, worsted comber 'aiding' (CP); Blue Regt. (P).

WEBBER, John, of Bridgwater, excepted from GP; petition for pardon, June 28; pardon for all treasons, July 11 1686 (CSPD, J2, II, 738, 795).

WEBBER, John, of Taunton St Mary, glover, 'aiding' (CP); Blue Regt. (P).

WEBBER, Nathaniel, of Marshwood, 'suspected' (CP); tried at Dorchester; transported for Booth (JR) on the *Happy Return* from Weymouth, Sept. 25, to Barbados; sold to William Weaver (SL). Buried 1687 (BMi).

WEBBER, Nicholas, of Monkton Wyld, 'suspected' (CP).

WEBBER, Richard, of Charmouth, 'suspected' (CP).

WEBBER, Robert, of Stoke St Gregory, 'absenting' (CP).

WEBBER, Robert, of Taunton St James, 'aiding' (CP); Blue Regt. (P).

WEECH, John, tried at Wells; to be transported for Howard (JR) but escaped between Wells and Sherborne (SL).

WEETON, Daniel, presented at Wells and bound over (JR).

WELCH, George, of Lyme Regis, thatcher, 'absent, supposed' (CP); entertained by John Trall of Uplyme, Jan. 21, 'being in the late rebellion' (LRMB).

WELCH, Thomas, of Bridport, carrier, 'in the rebellion as we are informed' (CP); tried at Dorchester, Sept. 5; pleaded not guilty; hanged at Dorchester, Sept. 7 (JR, NL). Land forfeit and for sale (TB).
*And see* Walch, Walsh.

WELLMAN, John, of Broadwindsor, 'out in the horrid rebellion' (CP); presented at Dorchester and 'proposed for pardon' (JR).

WELLMOUTH (Willmouth), John, of Trull, 'absent' (CP, CL).

WELLS, George, of Stoke Canon, yeoman, imprisoned in Dorset (DLD); tried at Taunton; 'remaining in gaol till further order' (JR); transported, Nov. 12, by Heywood on the *Constant Richard* to Jamaica (SL).

WENN *see* Venn.

WENSLEY, William, of North Curry, 'wanting' [from home] and 'in the late Duke of Monmouth's service; killed'. No tenant (CL).

WERNELL, Christopher, presented in Gaol Delivery at Wells and 'recommended for the king's favour', but his name seems to be omitted in JR. His name and favour are shown in BA.

WEST, Abraham junior, of Frome, wiredrawer, in the rebellion and at large' (CP).

WEST, Richard junior, of West Woodlands, mercer, 'in prison for the late rebellion' (CP); tried at Wells; transported for Howard (JR), Oct. 25 on the *Port Royal Merchant* to Jamaica (SL).

WEST, Robert, barrister in the Middle Temple, pardon for all treasons Dec. 5 1685 (CSPD, J2, I, 2011).

WESTCOMBE, John, of Stockland, 'suspected' (CP).

WESTCOTT, James, presented at Wells, and bound over (JR).

WESTCOTT, John, of Pitminster, 'absent' (CP).

WESTCOTT, Richard, of Pitminster, 'a rebel' (CL).

WESTCOTT, Samuel, of Martock, 'absent' (CP).

WESTLAKE, John, of Taunton St James, weaver, 'aiding' (CP); Blue Regt. (P); tried at Wells; transported thence for Bridgeman (JR) by White, Oct. 31, on the *Constant Richard* to Jamaica (SL).

WESTLY, William, of Nether Compton, 'suspected' (CP).

WESTOVER, Samuel, of Taunton St Mary, feltmaker, 'aiding' (CP); Blue Regt. (P).

WETHERELL, Joseph, tried at Wells; transported for Bridgeman (JR) by White, Oct. 31, on the *Constant Richard* to Jamaica (SL).

WHAITES, William, a prisoner bailed at Taunton (JR).

WHELER, Jeremiah, of Westbury, 'in the rebellion as we are informed' (Wilts. QSR).

WHELLIER, William, of Bruton, 'being in James Scott's army and not yet taken' (CP).

WHETHAM, James, of Bishop's Hull, maltster, 'in prison' (CL); tried at Taunton and hanged there, Sept. 30 (JR, JW); buried at St Mary's, Oct. 28 (PR). Land forfeit and for sale (TB).

WHETHAM, Joseph, of Taunton, yeoman, pardon Mar. 22 1686 (CSPD, J2, II, 311).

WHETHAM, William, of Thorncombe, yeoman, 'wanting from his habitation' (CP); presented at Exeter but at large (JR).

WHETTCOMBE (Whitcombe), Josias, of Taunton St Mary, comber, 'aiding' (CP); Blue Regt. (P). Presumably Capt. Whitcombe of Albemarle's list, and presumably killed at or after Sedgemoor.

WHICH, George, of Langport, husbandman, 'absent' (CP).

WHICH, John, of Langport, husbandman, 'absent' (CP).

WHICKER, Benjamin, aged 19, of Colyton, clothier, imprisoned at Bridgwater (DLD); tried at Dorchester; transported for Nipho (JR) on the *Betty* from Weymouth, Nov. 25, to Barbados; sold to Barnabas Chater (SL). Named on the 1689 petition for return (CSPD, W&M, I, 43).

WHICKER, John, Benjamin's father (PR), of Colyton, yeoman, 'absent' (CP); joiner, in Bridgwater prison (DLD); tried at Dorchester; transported for Nipho (JR) on the *Betty* from Weymouth, Nov. 25, to Barbados; sold to Charles Thomas & Co. (SL) escaped with Dr Pitman and returned to London. He wrote part of Pitman's *Relation*. He had been presented at Exeter and misreported at large (JR).

WHICKER, Samuel, senior, of Colyton, yeoman, 'absent' (CP); presented at Exeter, but at large (JR). He had a daughter christened in 1691; and he died in March 1714/5 (PR).

WHIFFEN, Lionel, at Dorchester Assizes he was continued in gaol, not indicted, 1685 (JR); at Dorchester Assizes in March 1686 he was pardoned by Proclamation (GD).

WHINNELL, William, excepted from GP.

WHITCHER, James, rick of wheat confiscated, Jan. 8 1686 (TB).

WHITE, Edward, of East Brent, 'absent' (CP).

WHITE, Henry, of Lyme Regis, hellier, 'absent, supposed' (CP).

WHITE, John, of Axmouth, yeoman, 'reported to be in arms in the late rebellion' (CP); tried at Dorchester; transported for Booth (JR) on the *Happy Return* from Weymouth, Sept. 25, to Barbados; sold either to Richard Adamson or to Richard Lintott (SL). Also presented at Exeter and misreported at large (JR).

WHITE, John, of Honiton, 'a rebel' (CP); cordwainer, imprisoned in the Devon Workhouse (DLD); tried at Dorchester; transported for Booth (JR) on the *Happy Return* from Weymouth, Sept. 25, to Barbados; sold either to Richard Lintott or to Richard Adamson (SL). One of these two was named on the 1689 petition for return (CSPD, W&M, I, 43).

WHITE, John, of Kilmington, yeoman, imprisoned in Wilts. (DLD).

WHITE, John, of East Brent, 'absent' (CP).

WHITE, Nicholas, of Wincanton, feltmaker, 'actually in arms in the rebellion, as informed, and at large' (CP).

WHITE, Peter, of Thurloxton, 'absconded' (CP). [*See below.*]

WHITE, Peter, of Trull, 'absent' (CP). [*See below.*] One of these two was presented at Wells and bound over (JR).

WHITE, Richard junior, of Wellow, 'in the late rebellion and not returned' (CP).

WHITE, Robert, tried at Dorchester; transported for Musgrave (JR) from Weymouth on the *Jamaica Merchant* to Barbados; there by March 12 (SL).

WHITE, Thomas, of Ilminster, 'being in arms in the late rebellion' (CP).

WHITE, Thomas, of Wincanton, weaver, 'actually in arms in the rebellion, as informed, and at large' (CP).

WHITE, William, of Lyme Regis, 'absent, supposed' (CP); presented at Dorchester, certificate allowed (JR). The certificate is in Dorset QSR.

WHITE, William, presented at Wells and bound over, 1685; also presented at Dorchester, March 1686, and pardoned by Proclamation (GD).

WHITEHEAD, Edward, late of Bridgwater, pardon for high treason, Dec. 5 1685 (CSPD, J2, I, 2009).

WHITEROW, George, of Street, Winsham, 'in the rebellion and not come in' (CP).

WHITTLE, Giles, of Merriott, husbandman, tried at Wells; transported for Howard (JR), Oct. 25 on the *Port Royal Merchant* to Jamaica (SL). Land forfeit and for sale (TB).

WHITTLEY, Richard, of Taunton St Mary, husbandman, 'aiding' (CP); Blue Regt. (P).

WHITTOCK, John, of Rode, clothworker, 'in the rebellion' (CP).

WHITTOCK, Thomas, of Frome, tailor, 'for a riot and among the Clubmen' (CP).

WHITTROW, James, of Cudworth, 'in the rebellion and not come in' (CP).

WHITTY, Thomas, of Frome Selwood, clothworker, 'in the rebellion and in prison,' (CP); tried at Taunton; transported for Musgrave (JR) on the *Jamaica Merchant* from Weymouth to Barbados; there by March 12 (SL). Land forfeit and for sale (TB).

WHORWOOD, Robert, of Honiton, cordwainer, 'a rebel' (CP), imprisoned in the High Gaol, Devon (DLD); tried at Dorchester, Sept. 10; hanged at Sherborne, Sept. 15 (JR, NL).

WHYTYE, Richard, of Lyme Regis, worsted comber, 'absent, supposed' (CP).

WICKHAM, Joseph, of Burnham, butcher (CP), imprisoned in Bridgwater, tried at Taunton; to be transported for Booth (JR) via Bristol, Oct. 24, but died on board ship in Kingsroad; buried in Bristol (SL).

WICKHAM, Nicholas, 'taken at Hindon upon suspicion that he was going to join with the late Duke of Monmouth and other traitors against his Majesty' (Wilts. QSR).

WICKHAM, Richard, of Stogursey, butcher, 'absent and believed aiding and assisting the rebels' (CP).

WICKS, Samuel, of Lyme Regis, tailor, 'absent, supposed' (CP).

WILKINS, Robert, tried at Wells; transported for Howard (JR), Oct. 25 in the *Port Royal Merchant* to Jamaica (SL).

WILKINS, Thomas, of Westonzoyland, 'out in the rebellion and at large'; 'taken' (added later) (CP); presented at Wells and bound over (JR).
*And see* Willkins.

WILKINS, William, of Rode, husbandman, 'in the rebellion' (CP).

WILLCOCKS, John, of East Brent, 'absent' (CP).

WILLCOX, Aaron, of Crewkerne, 'rebel and not taken' (CP).

WILLCOX, John, of Crewkerne, 'rebel and not taken' (CP).

WILLCOX, Peter, of Musbury, yeoman, 'in the rebellion' (CP); presented at Exeter but at large (JR). In BL. Add. MS. 90337 mistakenly 'of Axminster'.

WILLCOX, Philip, of Luppitt, yeoman, 'out in the rebellion' (CP); presented at Exeter but at large (JR).

WILLCOX, Richard, of West Horrington, 'supposed' (CP); tried at Wells; transported for Howard (JR), Oct. 25 on the *Port Royal Merchant* to Jamaica (SL).

WILLES, Thomas, of Clapton, Crewkerne, 'rebel in Monmouth's army and not taken' (CP); presented for high treason at Exeter, March 1686, pardoned and dismissed (GD).

WILLEY, George, of Kingsbury Episcopi, 'absent, believed' (CP).

WILLEY, John, of Kingsbury Episcopi, 'absent, believed' (CP); presented at Wells (JR). [*See below.*]

WILLEY, John, of Seavington St Michael, 'in the rebellion and not come in' (CP); presented at Wells (JR). [*See below.*] One of these two had his certificate allowed; the other remained in custody (both JR).

WILLIAMS, Arthur, of Extraportam tithing, Taunton, 'absent' (CL); tried at Taunton; hanged at Stogumber (JR, JW).

WILLIAMS, Giles, of Wayford, 'rebel and not taken' (CP).

WILLIAMS, Henry, of Taunton St Mary, comber, 'aiding' (CP); Blue Regt. (P).

WILLIAMS, John, of Axminster, 'supposed' (CP); tried to Taunton and hanged there on Sept. 30 (JR, JW).

WILLIAMS, John senior and junior, both of Axminster, yeomen, presented at Exeter, misreported at large; both tried at Wells and transported for Howard (JR) Oct. 25 on the *Port Royal Merchant* to Jamaica (SL).

WILLIAMS, John the elder and younger, both of Extraportam tithing, Taunton, 'absent' (CL).

WILLIAMS, Robert, of Axminster, 'supposed' (CP); presented at Exeter but at large (JR).

WILLIAMS, Seth, of Bampton, 'supposed' (CP).

WILLIAMS, Thomas, tried at Dorchester; transported for Booth (JR) on the *Happy Return* from Weymouth, Sept. 25, to Barbados; sold to Nicholas Prideaux (SL).

WILLIAMS, Thomas, of Minehead, tailor, 'in the late rebellion' (CP); presented at Wells and bound over (JR). He was married in Sept. 1686 (PR).

WILLIAMS, William, Monmouth's steward; came with him from Holland; at Sedgemoor gave the Duke 100 guineas before being captured by Major Hope, who found about 300 guineas on him; taken to the Gatehouse, Westminster, July 16 (CSPD, J2, I, 1250); interrogated (L. 1152A 237f); at Wells Assizes a witness for the king and left in custody (JR); on April 17 he, 'having been engaged in the late rebellion', was pardoned of all treasons (CSPD, J2, II, 417).

WILLIAMS, William, of Durleigh, 'absent and not taken' (CP); tried at Taunton; hanged at Chard (JR, JW). [Missing the Durleigh connexion, Locke thought this was Monmouth's Steward.]

WILLIAMS, William, of Axminster, clothmaker, imprisoned in the High Gaol, Devon (DLD); tried at Dorchester; transported for Booth (JR) on the *Happy Return* from Weymouth, Sept. 25, to Barbados; sold to Major John Johnson (SL).

WILLIS, John, of Rode, weaver, 'in the rebellion' (CP). [*See below.*]

WILLIS, John, of Taunton St Mary, weaver, 'aiding' (CP); Blue Regt. (P). One of these two was tried at Wells; transported for Nipho (JR) on the *Betty* from Weymouth, Nov. 25, towards Barbados but died at sea, 18 Dec. 1685 (SL).

WILLIS, Robert, of Rode, weaver, 'in the rebellion' (CP); tried at Wells; transported for Howard (JR), Oct. 25, to Jamaica (SL).

WILLIS, Thomas, of Chardstock, 'suspected' (CP); presented for high treason at Exeter, March 1686, pardoned and dismissed (GD).

WILLKINS, James, of Taunton St Mary, worsted comber, 'aiding' (CP); Blue Regt. (P).

WILLKINS, Taverner junior, of Taunton St James, weaver, 'aiding' (CP); Blue Regt. (P).

WILLKINS, Thomas, of Chillington, 'in the rebellion and not come in' (CP).

WILMOTT, Edward, tried at Dorchester; transported for Booth (JR) on the *Happy Return* from Weymouth, Sept. 25, to Barbados; sold to Peter Flewilling (SL).

WILMOTT, Edward, tried at Wells; transported for Howard (JR), Oct. 25 on the *Port Royal Merchant* to Jamaica (SL).

WILMOTT, George, tried at Dorchester Sept. 10; hanged at Weymouth or Melcombe Regis, Sept. 15 (JR, NL).

WILMOTT, Hugh, tried at Dorchester; transported for Booth (JR) on the *Happy Return* from Weymouth, Sept. 25, to Barbados; sold to John Burston (SL).

WILMOTT, John, of Ilminster, 'out in the rebellion' (CP).

WILMOTT, Odes, of Stoke St Gregory, 'not coming to church for a month, and for assisting one of the rebels in stealing of a mare' (Som. QSR).

WILMOTT (Wilmouth), Richard, of Colyton, mason, imprisoned at Ilchester (DLD); tried at Wells; transported for Howard (JR), Oct. 25 on the *Port Royal Merchant* to Jamaica (SL).

WILLMOUTH see Wellmouth.

WILLS, Henry, of Lopen, 'in the rebellion and not come in' (CP).

WILLS, John, of Broadwindsor, 'trained soldier and in the rebellion' (CP); tried at Dorchester, Sept. 5; pleaded not guilty; hanged there Sept. 7 (JR, NL).

WILLS *see* Willis.

WILLS, William, tried at Dorchester; transported for Booth (JR) on the *Happy Return* from Weymouth, Sept. 25, to Barbados; sold to Capt. William Kershall (SL).

WILLSMAN, William, of Colyton, yeoman, 'absent' (CP); presented at Exeter but at large (JR).

WILSHER, Walter, of Rode, weaver, 'in the rebellion' (CP).

WILSON, David, of Lyme Regis, seaman, 'absent, supposed' (CP).

WILSON, John, tried at Dorchester; transported for Booth (JR) on the *Happy Return* from Weymouth, Sept. 25, to Barbados; sold to Stephen Gibbs (SL).

WILTSHIRE, John, of North Petherton, 'absconded' (CP); 'in arms against the king' (Som. QSR).

WILTSHIRE, William, at Wells a witness for the king, left in custody (JR).

WINDHAM, Senticle (Senty), of Bishop's Hull, 'absent' (CP); 'dead' (CL).

WINDSOR, John, of Crewkerne, 'rebel and not taken' (CP).

WINIFEE *see* Minifee.

WINN (Wine), Robert, of Kingsbury Episcopi, 'absent, believed' (CP); tried at Wells; hanged at Pensford (JR, JW).

WINTER, Ambrose, of West Buckland (SL); 'in prison for rebellion' (CP) in Taunton Bridewell; tried at Taunton; transported for Booth (JR) via Bristol, Oct. 24, on the *John* to Barbados; sold to John and William Holder (SL).

WINTER, Christopher, of Wellington, 'absent' (CP).

WINTER, John, of Wellington, 'in prison for rebellion' (CP); tried at Taunton; hanged at Keynsham (JR, JW).

WINTER, John, of Langford Budville, 'absenting' (CP).

WINTER, Richard, of Wellington, 'absent' (CP).

WISE, Gabriel, presented at Dorchester; discharged for want of evidence (JR).

WISEMAN, John, of Curry Rivel, 'out in the rebellion and not taken' (CP).

WISEMAN, Richard, of Curland, 'absent, believed' (CP); tried at Wells; transported thence for Bridgeman (JR) by White, Oct. 31, on the *Constant Richard* to Jamaica (SL).

WITHYMAN, John junior, tried at Wells; transported thence for Bridgeman (JR) by White, Oct. 31, on the *Constant Richard* to Jamaica (SL).

WITTINGTON, William, of East Woodlands, weaver, 'in the rebellion and at large' (CP).

WOOD, John, of Axmouth, 'reported to be in arms in the late rebellion' (CP); presented at Exeter but at large; presented at Taunton (JR) but no note of sentence; was he absent ill? Presented in March 1686 at Exeter, pardoned and dismissed (GD).
*And see* Baker.

WOODALL, John, of Taunton St Mary, weaver, 'aiding' (CP); Blue Regt. (P).

WOODCOCKE, William, aged 19, comber, imprisoned at Taunton, tried there; transported thence for the Queen (JR) on the *Jamaica Archant*, Dec. 9, to Barbados; sold there to the dealers, Charles Thomas and Thomas Sadler, March 12 (SL). Escaped with Dr Pitman (PW).

WOODFORD, Henry, presented at Wells and bound over (JR).

WOODFORD, Thomas, of Wellington, 'absent' (CP).

WOODHEAD, Philip, of Thurloxton, 'absconded' (CP).

WOODLAND, Matthew, tried at Wells; transported for Howard (JR), Oct. 25 on the *Port Royal Merchant* to Jamaica (SL).

WOODLAND, Nathaniel, of Merriott, 'rebel and not taken' (CP).

WOODLAND, Robert, of Merriott, 'rebel and not taken' (CP).

WOODROFFE, John, of Luppitt, yeoman, 'out in the rebellion' (CP); presented at Exeter but at large (JR).

WOODROW, Anthony, tried at Wells; transported for Howard (JR), Oct. 25 on the *Port Royal Merchant* to Jamaica (SL).

WOODROW, John, tried at Wells; transported for Howard (JR), Oct. 25 on the *Port Royal Merchant* to Jamaica (SL).

WOODVINE, John, of Taunton St James, 'aiding' (CP); Blue Regt. (P).

WOODWARD, John, tried at Dorchester; transported for Musgrave (JR) on the *Jamaica Merchant* from Weymouth to Jamaica, there by March 12 (SL).

WOOLAVINGTON, Edward, of Taunton St Mary, smith, 'aiding' (SP); Blue Regt. (P).

WOOLCOTT, George, of West Monkton, 'out in the rebellion and at large' (CP).

WOOLCOTT, James, of Norton Fitzwarren, 'absent' (CP).

WOOLCOTT, Robert, of Taunton St Mary, tailor, 'aiding' (CP); Blue Regt. (P); pardon July 18 1686 (CSPD, J2, II, 822). He was married in 1662 (PR).

WOOLDRIDGE, William, of Tiverton, sergeweaver, wounded at Sedgemoor, imprisoned at Wells (DLD), then at Bridgwater; tried at Taunton transported for Booth (JR) via Bristol, Oct. 24, on the *John* to Barbados; sold to John Browne (SL). Buried 1686 (BMi).

WOOLFRIDGE *see* Smith.

WOOLMINGTON, Aaron, of Chardland, 'absent, believed' (CP).

WOOLMINGTON, John, aged 24, of Colyton, weaver, wounded at Sedgemoor, imprisoned at Wells (DLD), presented there and 'recommended for the king's pardon' (JR).

WOOLTERS (Walters), John, a pilot, came from Holland with Monmouth, excepted from GP; pardoned 'though engaged in the late rebellion', May 31 1687 (CSPD, J2, II, 1833).

WOOTTEN, Samuel, of Ilminster, 'out in the rebellion' (CP).

WORMEWOOD, James, of Bishop's Hull, 'absent' (CP); 'not taken' (CL).

WORNE *see* Oram.

WORRALL, John, tried at Wells; transported for Howard (JR), Oct. 25 on the *Port Royal Merchant* to Jamaica (SL).

WORRELL, Roger, of Taunton St Mary, labourer, 'aiding' (CP); Blue Regt. (P).

WORRELL, Stephen, of Leigh on Mendip, 'absent' (CP).

WORRELL, Thomas, presented at Taunton and 'proposed for pardon' (JR).

WORTHELL, John, of Northcote, Honiton, 'a rebel' (CP).

WORTHELL, Thomas, of Northcote, Honiton, 'a rebel' (CP); o Honiton, lace maker, imprisoned at Taunton (DLD).

WORTON, James, of Ashill, 'out in the rebellion and not taken' (CP).

WOTTWAY *see* Oateway.

WRENTMORE, Henry, tried at Taunton; transported for Musgrave (JR) on the *Jamaica Merchant* from Weymouth to Barbados; there by March 12 (SL).

WRIGHT, John, of Dunster, clothier, 'in arms in the rebellion of James Scott' (CP).

WRITT, Rawsin, of Chardland, 'absent, believed' (CP).

WRYARD, John, of Axminster, 'supposed' CP).

WYATT, Henry, of Lyme Regis, shoemaker, 'absent, supposed' (CP).

WYATT, John the elder, of Uplyme, weaver, sheltered his son, William Collins, and/or John Miller; taken at his house on Feb. 4; taken to Dorchester gaol, Feb. 8; pardoned by proclamation at the Assizes, March 1686 (LRMB, GD).

WYATT, John the younger, of Uplyme, husbandman, on Feb. 3 he and John Miller, pursued by 2 officers, escaped to his father's house; taken Feb. 4, interrogated Feb. 5; 'had been in Monmouth's camp'; to Dorchester gaol Feb. 8 (LRMB); pardoned by proclamation 1686 (GD).

WYATT, Thomas, of Wilton, 'absent' (CP).

WYATT, William, of Axminster, yeoman, 'supposed' (CP); presented at Exeter but at large (JR).

WYATT, Zachary, of Wilton, a captain, brought Taunton magistrates at sword point to hear Monmouth proclaimed king (Hist. MSS. Comm. Stopford-Sackville MSS. 25); pardoned March 27, April 14 1686 (CSPD, J2, II, 356, 403).

WYNE, John, of South Petherton, 'in the rebellion and not come in' (CP).

WYTHELL, Thomas, of Thorncombe, yeoman, 'wanting from his habitation during the greatest part of the rebellion' (CP); presented at Exeter but at large (JR).

WYTHERELL, Joseph, transported from Wells by Sir Richard White (SL).

WYTHIMAN *see* Withiman.

YELVERTON, Samuel, of South Petherton, 'in the rebellion and not come in' (CP).

YANDALL, George, of West Buckland, 'absent' (CP); presented at Exeter in March 1686 for high treason, pardoned and dismissed (GD).

YENDALL, James, tailor, of Bampton, 'supposed' (CP); imprisoned in Devon workhouse (DLD).

YENDALL, John, presented at Exeter in March 1686 for high treason, pardoned and dismissed (GD).

YENDALL, Robert, of West Buckland, presented at Exeter in March 1686 for high treason, pardoned and dismissed (GD).

YENDALL, William, of West Buckland, presented at Exeter in March 1686 for high treason, pardoned and dismissed (GD).

YENDE, James, junior, of Taunton St Mary, Extraportam tithing, 'aiding' (CP); 'absent' (CL); Blue Regt. (P).

YEO, John, of Wellington, 'absent' (CP).

YORKE, John, of Upottery, cordwainer, in Bridgwater prison (DLD); presented at Wells and bound over (JR).

YOUNG, John, of Fivehead, 'out in the rebellion and not taken' (CP).

YOUNG, John, of North Curry, 'absent' (CP); 'fled' (CL).

YOUNG, Richard, tried at Wells; transported for Howard (JR), Oct. 25 on the *Port Royal Merchant* to Jamaica (SL).

YOUNG, Robert, of Charmouth, 'suspected in the rebellion' (CP).

# INDEX OF PLACES OF ORIGIN OF THE REBELS

Lane, Thos
Legg, John
Lincole, Ric
Long, John
Love, John
Loveridge, Bernard
Lyddon, John
Mallack, Malachi
Matthews, Nic
Moore, Nic
Newton, Wm
Noon, Hen
Oliver, John
Oliver, Rob
Parrick, Fras, jun
Phippen, Wm
Pinney, Azariah
Quinton, Wm (Shute)
Ransome (Rempson), Sam
Raymond, Arth
Read, David
Renway, Wm
Rockett, Phil
Rowe, Wm
Salisbury, John
Searle, Geo
Sellwood, Ric
Selway, John (Shute)
Seward, David
Seward, John
Seward, Ric
Seward, Ric
Seward, Wm
Slade, Edw
Smith, Ric
Spearing (Spiring), John
Sprake, John
Sprake, Thos, sen
Sprake, Thos, jun
Spurway, Rob
Street, Hugh
Stroud, Jas
Sweatland, John
Taylor, Jas
Thompson, Ric
Toogood, Stephen
Verrier, John
Warren, Thos
Williams, John
williams, John, sen
Williams, John, jun
Williams, Rob
Williams, Wm
Wryard, John
Wyatt, Wm

AXMOUTH, DEVON
Baker, Bart
Bartlett, Josiah

Bowditch, Nat
Bragg, Caleb
Browne, Wm
Browne, Wm, jun
Clarke, John, sen
Clarke, John, jun
Coade, Geo
Coleman, John
Coleman, Jos
Cox, Jas
Cox, John
Cox, Rob
Deeme, John,
Ford, John
Gaitch, Ben
Gaitch, Jos
Gape, Wal
Grove, Abel
Hacker, Jos
Hacker, Solomon
Howard, Edw
Hunt, Abr
Lidden, John
Limberry, John
Limberry, Jos
Limberry, Wm
Lyddon, John
Oliver, John
Quick, John
Quick, Rob, sen
Quick, Rob, jun
Quick, Wm
Tanner, John
Tanner, Wm
Teape, Wal
White, John
Wood, John

AYLESBEARE, DEVON
Bennett, John

BABCARY, SOMERSET
Lewis, Thos
Parsons, John

BADGWORTH, SOMERSET
Hearse, Jos

BAMPTON, DEVON
Badcock, John
Berry, John
Bowden, Thos
Carnell, John, jun
Davis, Isaiah
Fudge, Ric
Hall, Wm
Hill, John
Hole, Art
Hole, Wm

Bowden, Geo
Coleman, Ric
Creed, Geo
Crocker, John
Crooker, And
Cross, Hugh, sen
Dyer, Thos
Edwards, John, jun
Ford, Art
Fry, Thos
Fuell, Wm
Griffen
Hunt, Wm
John
Knott, Ben
Lee, Aghn
Legg, Mark
Lower, Rog
Luckes, Rob
Metyard, John
Micho, John
Mitchell, John
Norton, John, jun
Nott, Ben
Parsons, Art
Perritt, Wm
Pitt, Wm
Pittman, John
Samson, Steph
Samson, Sam
Stone, Art
Thomas, Griffen
Thompson, Steph
Tucker, Hen
Tucker, Ric
Warren, Peter
Weatham, John
Whetham, Jas
Windham, Senticle
Wormewood, Jas

BISHOP SUTTON, SOMERSET
Rossiter, John

BLACKFORD, SOMERSET
Stone, Wm

BLAGDON *see* PITMINSTER

BRADFORD ABBAS, DORSET
Stone, John
Wake, Jas

BRADFORD ON TONE, SOMERSET
Banfield, Thos, jun
Burford, John
Hodge, Humph
Richards, John
Watts, Geo

BRADLEY, NORTH, WILTSHIRE
Cruise, Edw
Pearce, Thos
Read, Wm
Usher, Phil

BRADLEY, WEST, SOMERSET
Russell, Wm
Rutt, John

BRADNINCH, DEVON
Pottle, Nat

BRENT, EAST, SOMERSET
Dodd, Wm
Edwards, David
Lane, Wal
White, Edw
White, John
Willcocks, John

BRIDGWATER, SOMERSET
Carrow, Geo
Coleman, Wm
Condick, Geo, jun
Cooper, Wm
Dennis, Thos
Drew, Wm
Hoare, Rog
Meade, Wm
Meyer (Mico), Hen
Mihill, Geo
Palmer, John
Teape, Rob
Tiverton, Wm
Vinicot, Jos
Wall, John
Webber, John
Whitehead, Edw

BRIDPORT, DORSET
Billen, Dan
Bishop, Thos
Bond, Nat
Burten, John
Davys, Wm
Downe, John
England, Thos
Gale, Jos
Gray, Ben
Gudge, Sam
Lancaster, Wm (Allington)
Lush, Art
Lush, Wm
Luther, Edw
Moor, Nat, jun
Puckett, Fras
Smith, Nic

## CHARD, SOMERSET

Atkins, Jos
Barrett, Giles
Barrett, John
Batten, Rob
Baunton, Alex
Bellis, Thos
Bond, John
Bond, Rob
Brane, John
Brewer, Peter
Brewer, Wm
Bullman, Jas
Burrage, Ric
Burrage, Wm
Carter, Wm
Caslin (Castland), Jeffery
Channing, John
Channing, Rob
Channing, Thos, jun
Chapman, John
Chapman, Wm
Clarke, John
Collender, Ferdinand
Collins, Hen
Collins, John
Cooke, John
Dalley, John
Deane, Abr
Dudderidge, John
Dunn, Rob
Easton, Chris
Easton, John
England, John
Fort, Edm or Edw
French, Joshua
Fry, John
Gill, Ric
Gouge, Stephen
Gunner, John
Hall, Wm
Hawker, Jos
Hawkins, Jos
Herd, Rog
Huddon, Rob
Irish, John
Irish, Ric, jun
Jesse, Edw
Lumbard, Geo
Lumbard, Jos
Lumbard, Ric, jun
Mason, Chas
Moggeridge, Wm
Mumford, Rob
Palmer, John
Peddon, Humph
Peddon, John
Peddon, Jos
Peddon, Ric

Pickman, Geo
Pitts, John
Pullman, Jas
Rawlins, Wm
Ray, Geo
Selward, And
Sellward, Hen, jun
Sellwood, Abr, jun
Sellwood, Clement
Sellwood, Wm
Skinner, Ric
Slape, Jas
Slater, John
Smallcrone, Sam
Smirney, John
Smirney, John, jun
Smirney, Jos
Smirney, Thos
Smith, John
Smith, Jos
Smith, ?Thos
Speed, John
Speed, Joshua
Speed, Thos
Squire, Jos
Squire, Raymond
Street, John
Stuckley, Wm
Suston, Chris
Sweete, Thos, jun
Wadford, Joel
Wadford, Wm
Walsh, Thos

## CHARD TOWN TITHING, SOMERSET

French, Laur
Hearne, Bart
Hitchcock, John
Huddy, John
Irish, Thos
Pearce, Ric
Scriven, Wm
Sellward, Austin
Skinner, Fras, sen
Walker, Thos, sen

## CHARDLAND TITHING, SOMERSET

Atkins, John
Barnes, Ralph
Baunton, Gamaliel
Beavis, Preston
Bennett, Wm
Bond, Abr
Burridge, Geo
Chambers, Ralph
Chapman, Jos
Collins, Nic, sen
Collins, Nic, jun
Collins, Phil

Cookesley, Wm
Dawe, John
Dawe, Rob
Deane, Fras
Deane, John
Deane, Rob
Edmonds, Rob
England, John
England, Sam
Fort, Thos
Freke, Peter
Gooden, Abr
Graves, John, sen
Graves, John, jun
Hasselbury, Nic
Holloway, John
Howard, John
Hurd, John
Hurd, Rob
Hutchins, John
Irish, Jos
Keech, Ric or Nic
Kingstone, Bart
Knight, John
Lawring, Aaron
Page, Wm, sen
Page, Wm, jun
Pitcher, Jos
Pitts, John
Pollard, Abr
Pullman, Jas
Shindler, Thos
Shindler, Wm
Smith, Phil
Smith, ?Thos
Squire, Nic
Squire, Stephen
Street, Ric
Street, Wm
Tapper, Thos
Thomas, Martin
Trevitt, Geo
Trevitt, John
Trote, Peter
Woolmington, Aaron
Writt, Rawsin

**CHARDSTOCK, DEVON**
Browne, Thos
Budge, John
Chapman, Thos
Clode, Edw
Collier, Rob
Dabinett, John
Gillett, Nic
Knight, Hen
Lorcomb, Stephen
Manly, John
Parrish, Thos

Phippen, Ric
Pinney, Geo
Pinney, John
Rowe, Hen
Savory, Geo
Searle, John
Smith, Thos
Speed, John
Spiller, Ric
Staple, John
Willis, Thos

**CHARMOUTH, DORSET**
Birdle, John
Buffett, Thos
Burrowe, Jos
Follett, Geo
Guppy, Wm
Hollman, Thos
Parsons, John
Parsons, Thos, sen
Parsons, Thos, jun
Parsons, Wm
Robbins, Sam
Sampson, John
Shave, Wm
Tallis, Nic
Webber, Ric
Young, Rob

**CHEDDAR, SOMERSET**
Nipe, Geo

**CHEDDON FITZPAINE, SOMERSET**
Gold, John
Hemborough, Thos
Lawrence, John
Parsons, Rob
Russell, Wm, sen
Russell, Wm, jun
Tucker, Thos
Vincent, Wm
Warner, Wm

**CHEDZOY, SOMERSET**
Godfrey alias Newman, Ric

**CHETNOLE, DORSET**
Cox, Thos

**CHEWTON MENDIP, SOMERSET**
Hayward, Thos
Heale, Jas
Parker, Jas
Stride, John

**CHICHESTER, SUSSEX**
Covert, Nic

CHIDEOCK, DORSET
Matthews, Thos

CHILLINGTON, SOMERSET
Hoare, Ric, sen
Wilkins, Thos

CHILTON POLDEN, SOMERSET
Carver, Dan
Carver, John
Gilling, John
Godfrey, Wm
Hawker, Ric
Keel, Geo
Keel, John
Meade, Wm
Moore, Geo
Norsey, Geo
Pill, Abr
Seamer, John
Thorne, Thos

CHINNOCK, WEST, SOMERSET
Camp, Joshua
Eastwood, John
Greeneham, John
Lawrence, Thos
Templeman, Nic

CHISELBOROUGH, SOMERSET
Hanning, John
Morse, Wm
Parker, Baldwin
Somerton, Wm

CHRISTON, SOMERSET
Vaughan, Fras

CHURCHSTANTON, SOMERSET
Bishop, Wm
Channon, Caleb
Hurley, And
Jesse, Geo

CLAPTON *see* CREWKERNE

CLIFTON MAYBANK, DORSET
Kellaway, Jos

COKER, WEST, SOMERSET
Randall, Bart

COLEFORD, SOMERSET
Dennis, Sam
Norton, Thos
Richards, Hen
Snooke, Ric
Turner, Ric
Turner, Wm

COLYFORD, DEVON
Grace, John
Mader, Wm

COLYTON, DEVON
Abrahams, Isaac
Abrahams, John
Bagwell, Amos
Bagwell, Fras
Bagwell, John
Bagwell, Peter
Bagwell, Wal
Bagwell, Wm
Barber, Edw
Barnard, Wm
Barrett, Osmond
Basleigh, Rob
Battins, Jas
Blackmore, Wm, sen
Blackmore, Wm, jun
Butcher, John
Butter, Bart
Butter, John
Clapp, John
Clegg, Wm
Cooke, Joshua
Cooke, Rob
Cox, Phil
Cox, Thos
Daniel, Ambr
Daniel, Ric
Dare, John
Davy, Miles, jun
Drover, Isaac
Drover, Zachary
Duce, John
Dyer, Rob
Facey, John
Farrant, Geo, jun
French, Dan
French, John
French, Rog
Greenway, Thos, jun
Greenway, Wm
Hale, Benedict
Hall, Ric
Halson, Rob
Hawler (Hawkier), John
Hayman, Rob
Heathfield, John
Hewes, John
Hoare, Nic
Knowles, John
Knowles, Percival
Layton, Thos, sen
Lodge, Jas
Lowman, Bernard
Lucas, Rob
Macey, Geo

Marthers, Wm
Marwood, John
Maxey, Thos
Mayder, Wm
Mitchell, Humph
Moggridge, John
Mullins, Wm, jun
Newton, John
Newton, Phil
Payne, Jonathan
Pease, Jas
Pitt, Jos
Purchas, Fras
Pyes, Jas
Restorick, Jos
Roberts, Fras
Robertson, Geo
Rowsell, John
Rust, Argentine
Sands, Rob
Satchell, Rog
Savage, John
Seaward, Geo
Seaward, Wm
Seller, Wm
Skiffes, John
Soundy, ——
Speed, Jos
Spiller, Geo
Sprake, John
Stadith, John
Starr, John
Teape, Rob
Teape, Thos
Thompson, Nic
Thorne, Rob
Ticken, Peter
Toogood, John, sen
Toogood, John, jun
Toope, Dan
Truren, John
Turner, Geo
Turner, John
Venn, Edw
Warren, Nic
Whicker, Ben
Whicker, John
Whicker, Sam, sen
Wilmott, Ric
Willsman, Wm
Woolmington, John

COMBE FLOREY, SOMERSET
Griffen, Dan
Spright, Gabriel

COMBE RALEIGH, DEVON
Lambert, Humph
Larke, Sampson

Saunders, Wm
Searle, John
Sweetland, Dionisius
Way, Moses

COMBE ST. NICHOLAS, SOMERSET
Beach, Zachary
Beavis, Thos
Bendick, Simon
Denham, John
Denham, Hugh
Fort, Thos
Griffen, Hen
Griffen, Nic
Jaell, Wm
Jarwish, Thos
Maundery, Humph
Maundery, John
Mills, Rob
Pine, Alex
Radd, Thos
Rawlins, Geo
Rawlins, Ric
Roper, John
Slade, Ric
Standerwick, Nat
Staple, Leonard, sen
Tibbs, Geo
Unwen, Rob
Way, Wm

COMBPYNE, DEVON
Cox, John
Crew (Crow), Ben
Fowler, Hen
Loring, David
Newell, Ric
Pinnell, Abel
Sandford, Ben
Stocks, Geo

COMBWICH, SOMERSET
Boyce, David
Jennings, Fras
Lott, David

COMPTON, NETHER, DORSET
Arnold, John
Beaton, Edw
Ellery, Thos
Foot, John
Keates, Ric
Westly, Wm

COMPTON, OVER, DORSET
Bishop, Hen
Rapson, Rob
Watts, Rob

**COMPTON DANDO, SOMERSET**
Sheppard, John

**CORFE, SOMERSET**
Bartlett, Wm
Burroughs, Wm
Hallett, Rob
Taylor, Humph
Tutt, Wm
Venner, Sam

**CORNWALL**
Oliver, Wm

**CORSCOMBE, DORSET**
Fawne (Foane), John
Fawne, Rob
Gale, John

**COTLEIGH, DEVON**
Evans, Ric

**COXLEY** *see* **WELLS**

**CREDITON, DEVON**
Bond, Sam (Sandford)
Brooke, Thos
Mey, John
Moore, Thos (Sandford)
Pearce, Thos (Sandford)
Reeve, Rob
Trumpe, Humph (Sandford)

**CREECH ST MICHAEL, SOMERSET**
Adams, Rob
Allen, Ric
Andrews, Hen
Cornawell, John
Exon, Bernard
Gill, Nic
Harris, Lewis
Hearne, John, sen
Hearne, Lewis
Howse, Nic, jun
Hoyle, Hen
Lane, Ben
Norman, Thos
Oateway, Thos
Parvuncle, John
Payle, John
Pine, Wm
Pitcher, John
Pole, Simon
Stephens, Wm

**CREWKERNE, SOMERSET**
Aller, John
Beard, Rog
Bennett, Wm,

Billen, And (Clapton)
Billen, John (Clapton)
Bugler, Wm
Burrage, Dan
Bury, John
Butcher, Jas
Butcher, John, jun (Clapton)
Chubb, Ric
Copp, Peter
Dare, John
Durnham, Thos
Ellby, Rob
Flittchett, Thos
Gillett, Wm
Gravener, Thos (Woolminstone)
Greene, Hen
Greenway, John
Hooper, Thos
Hooper, Wm
Hutchins, Ric (Woolminstone)
Jeffery, Hen
Marders, John
Marders, John, jun
Meacham, Rog
Merrefeild, Rob (Woolminstone)
Miller, John (Hewish)
Miller, Thos (Hewish)
Osborne, Wal
Palmer, Rog
Prew, John
Rapson, And (Clapton)
Rich, Geo
Sheppard, John
Slade, Rob
Speed, Phil
Tyler, Edw, jun
Warren, Ric
Willcox, Aaron
Willcox, John
Willes, Thos (Clapton)
Windsor, John

**CRICKET MALHERBIE, SOMERSET**
Sherward, Hugh
Turner, Sachrill
Waymouth, Phil

**CROSCOMBE, SOMERSET**
Aire, Edw
Bishop, John
Browne alias Bawler, John
Cooper, Wm
Davys, Thos
Downe, John
Fry, John
Fry, Thos
Garnsey, Edw
Hanham, Rob
Perry, John

Rendon, Laur
Sley, Rob
Walter, Mark

**CUDWORTH, SOMERSET**
Hutchings, Art
James, John, sen
Lombard, ——
Lumbard, John
Manning, Wm
Memberry, Wm
Phillips, Thos
Whittrow, Jas

**CULLOMPTON, DEVON**
Bartram, Peter
Chaffer, Sam
Comino, Nic
Cotterell, Emanuel
Dyer, Ric
Ellworthy, Sam
Norcott, Dan
Pottle, Nat
Richards, Rob
Row, Chris
Thomas, Merricke
Tottle, Sam

**CULMSTOCK, DEVON**
Tapscott, Wm

**CURLAND, SOMERSET**
Harwood, Thos
Wiseman, Ric

**CURLOAD** *see* STOKE ST GREGORY

**CURRY MALLET, SOMERSET**
Loding, Wm

**CURRY, NORTH, SOMERSET**
Bartlett, John, jun
Beavis, Nathan
Blunt, Wm (Wrantage)
Bragg, Elias
Broadbeare, Wm
Cheeke, Jonas
Cheeke, Phil
Curry, Rob
Dyer, Rob (Wrantage)
Furze, Jos
Giffard, John (Lillesdon)
Gillard, Chris
Guddridge, Laur, jun
Halesey, Wm (Lillesdon)
Hebbett, Nic
Hobart, B (Lillesdon)
Kewer, Rob
Lea, Peter

Lyddon, Gabriel
Marks alias Staple, Gabriel
Odsey, John
Osmans, Jas
Osmans, Wm
Osmond alias Seward, Phil
Rooke, Geo
Snow, Geo
Soper, Rob
Stephens, Ric (Wrantage)
Stephens, Ric
Stone, Thos (Wrantage)
Thatcher, Bernard
Toogood, Hen
Verrier, Ric
Verrier, Thos
Verrier, Wm
Walker, Rob
Walter, Rob
Watts, Edw (Wrantage)
Wensley, Wm
Young, John

**CURRY RIVEL, SOMERSET**
Bennett, Ric
Croft, Wm
Grange, Thos
Jennings, Mary (Burton)
Jennings, Maurice (Burton)
Jesse, Marmaduke
Lane, Dan
Meade, Edw
Old, Wal
Pocock, Geo, sen
Pocock, Geo, jun
Rea, Wm
Scott, Fras (Hambridge)
Wiseman, John

**DAWLISH, DEVON**
Skinner, Thos

**DEVON**
Bovett, Edm
Meade, John

**DIPFORD** *see* TRULL

**DITCHEAT, SOMERSET**
Boole, Ric
Chaplin, Ric
Collins, John
Redwood, Phil

**DONYATT, SOMERSET**
Aylen, Edw
Burrage, John
Demster, Rog
Dobb, Hen

Drake, Ambr
Dunster, Hen
Fry, Wm
Goodlane, John
Grinster, Wm
Hart, John
Middleton, Ralph
North, Wm
Page, Fras
Phorton, Wm
Scriven, Jas
Travers, Wm
Tucker, Edw
Tucker, Hen

DORCHESTER, DORSET
Lockett, John
Maler, John

DOWLISH, WEST, SOMERSET
Garnley, John
Marshall, John

DOWLISHWAKE, SOMERSET
Baker alias Barrett, John
Dyke, Jas
Dyke, John or Jonathan
Hawkins, Nic
Pyke, Hugh
Pyke, John
Pyke, John, jun
Shoale, Wm

DOWNSIDE *see* SHEPTON MALLET

DUDDLESTONE *see* PITMINSTER

DULVERTON, SOMERSET
Broome, John, jun
Fouler, Wm
Lucas, Ric
Perrott, ——
Pippen, Geo
Watts, John

DUNSTER, SOMERSET
Budd, Ric
Coffin, Wm
Dinham, Oziah
Glasse, John
Hoope alias Ellstone, Wm, jun
Horne alias Harbett, Thos
Jeul, Ric
Luckwill, Hen
Rand, Ric, sen
Reynolds, Rog
Spencer, Lancelot
Wright, John

DURLEIGH, SOMERSET
Culverwell, Ric
Facey, Bart
Hakins, John
Hearle, Wm
King, John
Tapper, And
Tutcher, Rob
Williams, Wm

DURSTON, SOMERSET
Aplyn, Wm
Aprepolling, Wm
Bryant, Wm
Mandworth, Luser
Pale, Simon

EDINGTON, SOMERSET
Plaice, Thos

EXETER, DEVON
Gaylard, Jos
Harte, Hen (South Quarter)
Poole, Wm
Roper, Wm (St David's)
Timothy, John
Tricks, Lewis

FIVEHEAD, SOMERSET
Long, Jos
Meade, Fras
Moore, Geo
Wall, Edw
Young, John

FORDE *see* THORNCOMBE

FROME, SOMERSET
Andrewes, John, sen
Andrewes, Jeremiah
Bedford, Jos
Biggott, Thos
Broxwell, Thos
Chapman, Thos
Collins, Wm
Court, Rob
Daniel, Thos
Davison, Jeremiah
Davys, Humph
Debnam, Thos
Dredge, John
Dutch, John
Erbury, Wm
Fallston, Thos
Fryer, Isaac
Gartett, Ric
Gibbons, Jas, jun
Hensley, John
Hincks, Theophilus

Parricke (Parris), John
Phippen, Wm
Sansome, John

HEMINGTON, SOMERSET
Viggor, John

HEWISH *see* CREWKERNE

HILLFARRANCE, SOMERSET
Dyer, Jas
Dyer, Wm
Gotterell, Geo
Jennings, Wm
Lutley, David
Osmond, Stephen
Tracey, Geo

HINTON ST GEORGE, SOMERSET
Butcher, Ben
Butcher, John
Dunne, Amos
Dunne, John, sen
Dunne, John, jun
Gough, John
Hoare, Ric

HOLFORD, SOMERSET
Ellet, Rob
Grinham, Jos

HONITON, DEVON
Abbott, Mic
Abbott, Wm
Baker alias Wood, John
Bond, Josiah (Northcote)
Brownsey, Wm
Bucknoll, Wm
Bull, Thos
Bussell, John (Northcote)
Clarke, Adam
Clarke, Geo (Northcote)
Clarke, Jas
Clarke, Jas (Northcote)
Clarke, Rob
Clarke, Tristram
Clatworthy, Reg
Cooper, Chris
Crabb, —— (Northcote)
Croote, John, jun
Dillany (Dilling), Wm
Dolbeare, Sam
Dolbeare, Thos
Every, Jas
Foweracres, Jas (Northcote)
Foweracres, John
Fowler, Jas
Foxwell, Fras
Hocombe, John

Hollett, John
Jewell, Chris
Knight, Chris
Knight, Edw
Lee, Nic
Levermore, Phil
Loder, John (Northcote)
Lowman, Phil
Marchant, Emanuel
Marchant, Ric
Marchant, Wm
Martin, Wm
Meade, Thos
Minifie, John
Moggeridge, Tim
Parker, John
Pilling, Wm
Pine, Ric (Northcote)
Pinsent, Sam
Prowse, Sam
Redwood, Hen (Northcote)
Reynolds, Jas (Northcote)
Skinner, John
Skinner, John, jun
Slade, Humph, sen
Slade, Humph, jun
Smith, Fras
Smith, John
Thomas, Abr
Thomas, Sam (Northcote)
Thomas, Thos (Northcote)
Trood, John (Northcote)
Worthell, John (Northcote)
White, John
Whorwood, Rob

HORRINGTON, WEST, *see* WELLS

HORTON *see* ILMINSTER

HUISH EPISCOPI, SOMERSET
Barnard, Ric
Barnard, Wm
Luker, Hen

HUNTSPILL, SOMERSET
Bindon, Josias (Alston Morris)
Came, Fras
Coombe, John
Foyle, Ralph (Alston Morris)
Harris, John
Harris, Ric
Hooper, Wm
Howell, Ralph
Hurford, Thos
Leaker, John, jun
Long, John (Alston Morris)
Paine, John (Alston Morris)
Palmer, Thos (Alston Morris)

Pryor, John
Turner, John (Alston Morris)

ILCHESTER, SOMERSET
Cordilion, Peter
Game, Rob
Jones, John
Lockyer, Thos
Lyde, John
Raymond, Geo
Salisbury, Thos
Trent, Sam

ILMINSTER, SOMERSET
Barrett, John, jun
Broome, John (Horton)
Broome, Thos (Horton)
Burrow, Thos
Callaway, Edw
Callaway, Rob
Callaway, Wm
Carner, Alex
Carner, Edw
Carrier, Jas
Chick, John
Chick, Stephen, jun
Clarke, Ric
Cornelius, Jos
Eames, Maurice
Fort, Thos
Foxwell, Wm
Frost, Abr
Goodlane, Thos
Gunt, Geo
Hill, John
Hockaday, Thos
Holmes, Jos
Horsey, Phil
House, Nat, jun
Kempson, Jas
Key, Alex
Key, Sam
Leete, Rob
Marshall, Wm
Mitchell, Geo
Moore, John, jun
Parsons, John
Paull, Geo
Paull, John
Paull, Thos
Paull, Wm
Pitcher, Ric
Pope, Ben
Pope, Hen, jun
Robens, Phil
Slade, John
Slade, Wm
Smith, Ric
Smith, Rob

Speke, John
Standerwick, Jos
Towell, Edw
Townsend, Sam
Tresane, John, jun
Tresham, Rob, jun
Turner, John
Turner, Sam
Walrond, John
White, Thos
Wilmott, John
Wootten, Sam

ILTON, SOMERSET
Mitchell, Rob
Paull, Rob

ISLE ABBOTS, SOMERSET
Burnester, Edw
Grange, Wm
Hendy, John, jun
Mitchell, Wm
Pinney, Nat

ISLE BREWERS, SOMERSET
Taylor, Marmaduke

KENTON DEVON
Eastabrooke, Hen

KILMINGTON, DEVON
Cooke, Thos
White, John

KINGSBURY EPISCOPI, SOMERSET
Baker, Thos
Braine, Wm
Bright, John
Butter, John
Gifford, John
Godden, Edw
Humphrey, Jos
Humphrey, Thos
Isaak, Geo
Isaak, Thos
Jeanes, Jos
King, John
Ley, John
Ley, Sam
Moore, Jas
Ostler, John
Pittard, Geo
Pittard, Rob
Pittard, Thos
Pittard, Wm
Sampson,, Wm
Sibley, Edw
Stuckey, Hen
Taylor, Blase

Tibbs, Wm
Tole, David
Toleman, Tim
Willey, Geo
Willey, John
Winn, Rob

KINGSTON ST MARY, SOMERSET
Acastle, Rob
Baynham, Jacob (Nailsbourne)
Carswell, Rob (Nailsbourne)
Cornish, Phil
Farthing, Wm
Harle, Ric
Harris, Sam
Kent, Edw (Nailsbourne)
Trottle, Sam

KITTISFORD, SOMERSET
Bray, John
Farmer, Isaac
Hollings, Geo

KNOWLE ST GILES, SOMERSET
Atkins, John
Browne, Wm
Evan, Griffen
Garnley, Sydeock
Grinham, Jonas
Hodges, Giles
Orchard, John
Pitts, John
Pitts, Jonathan
Weaver, John

LANGFORD BUDVILLE, SOMERSET
Bodley, Chris
Brock, John
Brock, Wm
Hogley, Ambr
Hogley, Humph
Hogley, John
Pasmore, Sam
Winter, John

LANGPORT, SOMERSET
Bishop, Humph
Doleman, Rob
Feddell, John
Hurd, Jas
Hurd, Jedidiah
Hurd, Thos
Pavior, Geo
Pavior, Geo
Which, Geo
Which, John

LEIGH, DORSET
Keate, Thos, jun

LEIGH *see* PITMINSTER; WINSHAM

LEIGH ON MENDIP, SOMERSET
Adams, Abr
Adams, Jacob
Fineer, Ric
Moore, Moses
Roster, Ric
Worrell, Stephen

LILLESDON *see* CURRY, NORTH

LLANGARVAN, HEREFORD
Rawlins, Thos

LOCKING, SOMERSET
Plumley, Wm

LOPEN, SOMERSET
Adams, John
Best, Rob
Gillett, Hen
Hooper, Geo
Paull, Rob
Thorne, Thos
Wills, Hen

LOVINGTON, SOMERSET
Andrewes, Jos

LUPPITT, DEVON
Bird, Bernard
Bird, John
Bird, Nat
Braddick, John
Bradley, Geo
Bradley, Jas
Broome, John
Browne, John
Burrough, Ezekiel
Burrow, John (Wick)
Coleman, Jas
Coombe, John
Dare, Gideon
Deeme, John, sen
Deeme, John, jun
Evans, Edw
Farmer, Jos
Ferrer, Jos
Francklin, Thos
Hamme, Edw
Huggins, John
Huggins, Jos
Huggins, Ric
Lambert, John, jun
Lowman, Geo
Middleton, John
Pulman, Thos, jun
Quick, Thos

Pick, Edw
Shore, John

MARK, SOMERSET
Hellier, John

MARNHULL, DORSET
Burge, Wm
Stronge, Stephen

MARSHWOOD, DORSET
Hallett, Jos
Hellier, Sam
Houndsell, And
Orchard, Jas
Roper, John
Roper, Wm, sen
Roper, Wm, jun
Snooke, Hen
Snooke, Thos
Webber, Nat

MARSTON BIGOT, SOMERSET
Dredge, John
Humphreys, John
Richards, John

MARTOCK, SOMERSET
Bisse, Geo
Bull, Thos
Chubb, Thos, jun
Dymond, John
Francklen, Jos
Galler, Wm
Galler, Wm, jun
Gardiner, John
Gee, John
Gee, Rob
Hardman, John
Jeanes, Wm, sen
Lea, Thos
Palmer, John, jun
Prew, Abr
Prist, John, jun
Strickland, Wm
Sybly, Peter
Symonds, Jos
Westcott, Sam

MEARE, SOMERSET
Patch, Edw

MELLS, SOMERSET
Cooke, Hen
Heeles, Fras
Hill, Geo
Maynard, Ric
Morris, Thos
Russell, Wm
Sparke, Ben

MELSBURY *see* WELLS

MEMBURY, DEVON
Bovett, Thos
Bowditch, John, sen
Bowditch, John, jun
Brinsdon (Brunsdon), Wm
Bucknoll (Buckerell), Thos
Dare, Geo
Fyldy, Edm
Harris, Wm
Harvey, Wm, sen
Harvey, Wm, jun
Long, Bernard
Long, Wm
Loring, Wm
Mitchell, John
Mitchell, Mic
Mitchell, Nic
Newberry, John
Newberry, John
Newberry, Sam
Parsons, Thos
Quick, Thos
Sprake, Edw
Viddy, Edw
Walter, Wm

MERRIOTT, SOMERSET
Durdant, John
French, Maurice
Goodfellow, Ric
Hutchins, Thos
Lawrence, John
Lawrence alias Turke, Thos
Mitchell, Jas
Mitchell, John
Mitchell, Peter
Moore, Rob
Osborne, Alex
Phelps, John
Pitcher, Amos
Share, Hen
Templeman, John
Templeman, Ric
Templeman, Thos
Wansey, Art
Wansey, Jos
Whittle, Giles
Woodland, Nat
Woodland, Rob

MIDSOMER NORTON, SOMERSET
Somers, Ric

MILBORNE PORT, SOMERSET
Gardiner, John
Jones, Thos

MILVERTON, SOMERSET
  Baker, Jas
  Bayly, Wm
  Bessom, Blose
  Burridge, Jas
  Burston, John
  Bussom, John
  Colborne, Rog
  Coleman, John
  Crocker, Thos
  Davy, Bart
  Farils, Geo
  Farmer, Wm
  Ferris, Thos
  Ford, Edw, jun
  Furse alias Brooke, Morris
  Gill, Wm
  Hilman, Jas
  Holeman, Art
  Holmes, John, sen
  Holmes, John, jun
  Hughes, Dan
  Hurley, John
  Jennings alias Appledore, Rob
  Lake, John
  Lockbeare, Elias
  Loquier, John
  Lundon, Ric, jun
  Milton, Amos
  Milton, Hen, jun
  Milton, John
  Moore, Thos
  Morris, Jas
  Onwin, Ric
  Onwyns, Hen, sen
  Onwyns, Hen, jun
  Parsons, John
  Pearce, Chas
  Pearce, Humph
  Pearce, Jos
  Perkins, Ric
  Poole, Sylvester
  Priddy, Ric
  Pring, Ben
  Pring, Wm
  Richards, Fras
  Richards, Jas
  Richards, John
  Rugg, Ric
  Rugg, Rob, sen
  Rugg, Rob, jun
  Saunders, Thos
  Saunders, Wm
  Small, Rob
  Stutt, John
  Upham, Thos
  Vertue, Nic
  Vertue, Wm
  Warren, Geo, sen

  Warren, John
  Waters, Gabriel
  Wear, Ric

MINEHEAD, SOMERSET
  Bishop, John
  Bryant, Wm, jun
  Chibbett (Kitnor), Thos
  Gitton, John
  Williams, Thos

MOLTON, SOUTH, DEVON
  Howard, And

MONKTON, WEST, SOMERSET
  Brock, Jas
  Brock, Thos, jun
  Francklin, Nic
  Hare, John
  Hare, Wm
  Macey, John
  Pacey, John
  Savage, John
  Sims, Hen (Bathpool)
  Woolcott, Geo

MONKTON WYLD, DORSET
  Gay, John
  Hayward, Thos
  Hoskins, Rob
  Lathie, Nic
  Rockett, Solomon
  Webber, Nic

MOSTERTON, DORSET
  Edgar, Ric

MUSBURY, DEVON
  Ashford, Ambrose
  Baker, John
  Bird, John
  Browne, Ric
  Butcher, Ric
  Cox, Ric
  Cox, Thos
  Cox, Wm, sen
  Cox, Wm, jun
  Cross, Jonas
  French, Ric
  French, Wm
  Hoare, Dan
  Hobbes, Oliver
  Hutchins, Humph
  Loveridge, Bernard
  Loveridge, Sam
  Loveridge, Thos
  Loveridge, Wm
  Rockett, Rob
  Salter, Jas

Smith, Aaron
Standerwick, Jos
Trevitt, Edw
Willcox, Peter

NAILSBOURNE *see* KINGSTON ST
MARY

NEATH, GLAMORGAN
Powell, Nic

NETHERBURY, DORSET
Camnbden, Wm
Hellier, Edw (Stoke Atrum)
Symes, John (Stoke Altrum)
Taylor, Sam (Stoke Atrum)

NORTHCOTE *see* HONITON

NORTHLEIGH, DEVON
Greene, Ric

NORTHOVER, SOMERSET
Raymond, Wm

NORTON FITZWARREN, SOMERSET
Ball, Jas
Ball, Wm
Woolcott, Jas

NORTON SUB HAMDON, SOMERSET
Browne, Thos
Dennick, Nathan
Dennick, Tim

NOTTINGHAM
Temple, Ben

OAKE, SOMERSET
Speed, And, sen
Speed, nd, jun

OATHILL *see* WAYFORD

OFFWELL, DEVON
Hawker, Emanuel
Turner, Joshua

ORCHARDLEIGH, SOMERSET
Fry, John

OTHERY, SOMERSET
Allford, Ric
Andersey, Thos
Chin, Thos, jun
Kerle, Ric
Kimber, Dan
Pillick, Phil

OTTERFORD, SOMERSET
Townsend, Alex

OTTERY ST MARY, DEVON
Deard, Ric
Bond, Thos
Burch, Edw
Burch, Wal, jun
Carter, Jas
Channon, John
Dodridge alias Spiller, John
Forward, Nic
Kent, Peter
Knight, Wm
Leacott, Ric
Stockdale, Wm
Turner, Jacob
Ware, Wm

PAWLETT, SOMERSET
Henson, John
Godins, Fras

PENNARD, WEST, SOMERSET
Burgis, Thos
Champion, Edw
Clothier, Mic
Hill, Ric
Hollway, Wm

PETHERTON, SOMERSET
Chappell, John

PETHERTON, NORTH, SOMERSET
Aplyn, Wm
Bennett, Wm
Bray, John
Bray, Thos
Henson, John
Jervis, Fras
Mandworth, Luser
Mortimore, John
Nation, John
Palmer, Matt
Puckeridge, Geo, sen
Puckeridge, Ralph
Puckeridge, Ric
Reckett, Wm
Rew, John
Robbins, Thos
Rose, Ric
Rose, Theodore
Stodgell, Nic
Tapper, And
Trott, John
Warner, Wm
Warren, Wm
Wiltsheir, John

PETHERTON, SOUTH, SOMERSET
Bagg, Edw
Baker, Rog
Bartlett, John (Stratton)
Batt, Stephen
Braine, Hugh (Stratton)
Chaffy, Ben
Edmonds, Hen
Edmonds, John, jun
Edmonds, Jonathan
England, Thos
Fort, Jas
Gawler, Sam
Geer, Chris (Southarp)
Godden, John
Holland, Hugh
Holland, Wm
Knight, Geo, jun
Knight, John
Lever, Sam
Lincock, Thos
Patten, Jas
Patten, Rob, sen (Southarp)
Smith, John
Symes, John
Tibbs, Abr, sen
Vincent, Rob (Stratton)
Wyne, John
Yelverton, Sam

PILSDON, DORSET
Gardiner, John
Gollopp, Jas
Lovelace, John, sen
Lovelace, John, jun
Smith, Rob

PILTON, SOMERSET
Duncarton, Geo

PITMINSTER, SOMERSET
Baller, Fras
Bartlett, John
Bartlett, Thos
Booby, Chas
Borman, Amos
Broadbeare, Thos, jun
Bruford, John
Bugler, Thos
Buriman, Chas
Burneham, John, sen
Burneham, John
Butcher, Rog
Coombe, Jas
Drake, Sam
Drayton, Peter (Leigh)
Every, Geo (Leigh)
Every, Symeon (Leigh)
Gill, Wm (South Trendle)

Gillard, Geo (South Trendle)
Groves, Jos
Groves, Simon
Hamlyn, Simon
Harcombe, John (South Trendle)
Herring, Jas
Herring, Sam
Herring, Thos, sen
Herring, Thos, jun
Herring, Wm
Hoskins, John
Hutchins, Isaac
Jesse, Rob
Keene, Edw
Joyce, Rob (Blagdon)
Luttley, Bernard
Mills, Wm
Mogridge, Ames
Mogridge, Chas
Mogridge, John, sen
Mogridge, John, jun
Mogridge, Wm
Mownstone, Ric (South Trendle)
Mountstephen, Sam
Newman, Stephen
Perry, Jas
Preist, Fras
Preist, Jas
Priest, Thos
Scadding, Nic (Blagdon Green)
Scaddon, John
Spring, Wm
Strong, Peter
Thompson, John (Duddlestone)
Tucker, Jas
Verncombe, Hugh
Westcott, John
Westcott, Ric

PLYMTREE, DEVON
Cockney, Thos
Stone, Thos

POWERSTOCK, DORSET
Fawne, Rob
Fawne, Wm

PURITON, SOMERSET
Barnard, Sam
Gold, Wm
Hucker, Wm
Palmer, Thos
Pitt, Fras
Preist, Hen

QUEEN CHARLTON, SOMERSET
Boulter, John
Harris, John, jun

RODDEN, SOMERSET
Leversedge, Alleyn

RODE, SOMERSET
Attwood, John
Beaman, Rob
Coward, Rob
Edghill, Ric
Froston, Wm
Greenland, Wm
Guy, Edw
Harris, Thos
Harris, Wm
Hoell, Edw
Hoell, John
Holland, Wm
Holman, Wm
Holman, Stephen
Howell, John
Hussey, John
Linn, Ric
Nash, Fras
Payne, Wm
Piccard, Geo
Pryor, Edw
Reman, John
Smith, Thos
Smith, Wm
Stone, John
Whittock, John
Wilkins, Wm
Willis, John
Willis, Rob
Wilsher, Wal

RUISHTON, SOMERSET
Baker, Wal
Chillcott, Wm
Coleman, John
Elliott, Rob
Gray, John
Greeneham, John
Lock, Rob
Martin, John
Moore, Wm
Patten, John
Pullen, Edw
Sellick, Thos
Turner, Chris

SALISBURY, WILTSHIRE
Bennett, Thos

SAMPFORD ARUNDELL, SOMERSET
Halfyard, Geo
Moatyard, Thos

SAMPFORD COURTNEY, DEVON
Davy, Jacob

SAMPFORD PEVERELL, DEVON
Cantlebury, John

SANDFORD *see* CREDITON

SANDFORD ORCAS, DORSET
Pitman, Wm

SARUM WELLS *see* WHITECHURCH
CANONICORUM

SAWLEY
Poddington, Ric

SEATON, DEVON
Daniel, Ric (Beer)
French, Rog
Lucas, Rob
Parsons, Edw (?Beer)
Parsons, Edw, jun (?Beer)
Parsons, John (?Beer)

SEAVINGTON ST MARY, SOMERSET
Drewer, Geo
Dunn, Sam
Gummer, Rog
Gummer, Sam
Rawlins, John
Swayne, John
Tappell, Wm (Seavington Abbott)

SEAVINGTON ST MICHAEL,
SOMERSET
Drewer, Jos
Willey, John

SHAFTESBURY, DORSET
Andrewes, Phil
Baker, John
Long alias Baker, Rob
Thomas alias Bisse, Wal

SHAPWICK, SOMERSET
Swaine, John

SHELDON, DEVON
Baker, Mark
Baker, Wm

SHEPTON MALLET, SOMERSET
Allen, Hen
Bakehouse, Geo
Dunscarton, Edw
Ford, Edw
Penny, Rob
Strode, Edw (Downside)
Tucker, John
Webb, John

STOGURSEY, SOMERSET
Bluecock, Ric
Gilbert, Wm
Kirkham, Ric, sen
Wickham, Ric

STOKE ABBOTT, DORSET
Hellier, Edw
Hellier, Nic

STOKE ATRUM *see* NETHERBURY

STOKE CANON, DEVON
Wells, Geo

STOKE ST GREGORY, SOMERSET
Bartlett, John, jun
Biddle, Wm (Curload)
Chedzoy, Edw
Chedzoy, Rob, jun
Coombe, ?Wm
Crosseman, John
Furze, Thos, jun
Furze, Wm
Gattley, Wm
Gent, Chris (Curload)
Godfrey, Wm
House, Chris (Curload)
Lea, Sam
Leakey, John
Leakey, Ric, jun (Curload)
Leakey, Rob
Leakey, Thos, jun
Lockyer, John
Lockyer, Thos
Powell, Isaac, sen
Powell, Isaac, jun
Powell, Wm
Robbins, John
Rosewell, Rob
Sams, Ric
Soper, Rob
Staple, John
Thatcher, Bernard
Webber, Rob
Wilmott, Odes

STOKE ST MARY, SOMERSET
Coleman, John, jun
Cornish, Phil
Dyer, Thos
Earle, Rob
Griffen, ——
Manning, Dan
Satchell, John

STOKE SUB HAMDON, SOMERSET
Axe, And
Dymick, Caleb

Haynes, John
Pryor, John
Rayson, Thos

STOKE TRISTER, SOMERSET
Bollster, Edw
Bollster, Israel,
Bollster, Jas

STOWELL, SOMERSET
Lacke, John

STRATTON *see* PETHERTON, SOUTH

STREET, SOMERSET
Crane, Giles
Crane, John
Crane, Wm
Pick, Stephen
Reeves, John
Reeves, Thos
Seley, Nic

STREET *see* WINSHAM

SUTTON, SOMERSET
Davison, Sam

SUTTON, LONG, SOMERSET
Barnett, Wm
Fanam, Wm
Field, Jas, sen
Field, Jas, jun
Smart, John
Tucker, Reg
Wallis, Jasper

SUTTON MALLET, SOMERSET
Jones, Geo
Jones, Thos

SWELL, SOMERSET
Pocock, John

SYMONDSBURY, DORSET
Barnes, Rob
Battiscomb, Chris
Moore, John

TAUNTON, SOMERSET
Atkins, Jeremiah
Burges, John
Burrage, Chas
Burroughs, Geo
Dare, Thos
Dare, Thos
Dawe, Wm
Dewdney, Sam
Easton, Rob
Farmer, John
Guppy, Justinian

Lock, John (Extraportam)
Masters, Ric
Mays, John (Extraportam)
Mays, Wm (Extraportam)
Melliner, Wm
Middleton, Thos
Mullens, Geo, sen
Newton, Thos
Nowell, Geo
Parker, Wm,
Pomeroy, Dan
Pope, Humph
Quant, Hen
Read, Osmund
Reeves, Wm
Savage, John (Extraportam)
Savage, John (Extraportam)
Seaman, Rob
Stacey, Simon, sen
Taylor, Hen
Trickey, Thos
Walter, John
Whetham, Jos
Whettcombe, Josias
Williams, Art (Extraportam)
Williams, John, sen (Extraportam)
Williams, John, jun (Extraportam)

TAUNTON, SOMERSET, PARISH OF
ST JAMES
Adams, John
Adams, Sam
Alford, Ben
Arnold, Fras
Ashford, Thos
Ashford, Wm
Bagg, Rob
Bond, Geo
Bristowe, Chris
Channell, Humph
Chedzoy, Rob
Clarke, Wm
Cooksley, John
Court, Jas
Cross, Chris
Davey, Edw
Dinham, Thos
Dinning, Wm
Dolphin, Thos
Dyer, Geo
Dyer, Wm
Ellory, Rob
Evered, Wm, sen
Evered, Wm, jun
Ford, Ben
Ford, John, sen
Ford, John, jun
Ford, Jos
Ford, Sam

Fowler, John, jun
Gill, John, sen
Gill, John, jun
Gill, Rob
Gooding, Isaac
Greene, Wm
Gulley, Wm
Henson, Rog
Herring, John
Hilliard, Jos
Hutchins, Simon
Jay, Chris
Keates, Thos
Knight, John
Lissant, Geo
Lissant, Wm
Lloyd, John
Maber, Jos
Minifie, John
Minifie, Jos (or Jas)
Nicholls, Ric
Norton, Hen
Noss, Peter
Odams, Nic
Parr, Thos
Parsons, Thos
Perry, Peter
Phelps, John
Poole, Hen
Poole, Wm
Pound, Fras
Purdy, Bart
Purdy, Wm
Resdon, John
Rossiter, Chas
Short, Sam
Simons, Rog
Slape, Peter
Slape, Ric
Stacey, John
Stacey, Simon, jun
Stone, Geo
Sweete, Ric
Symons, Benedict
Thompson, John
Trott, Chas, sen
Trott, Chas, jun
Tutt, And
Tuttwell, John
Waddams, Nic
Warmouth, John
Webber, Rob
Westlake, John
Wilkins, Taverner, jun
Woodvine, John

TAUNTON, SOMERSET, PARISH OF
ST MARY
Adams, Thos

Adder, John
Amerey, Simon
Andrewes, Sam
Ash, Wm
Ashley, John
Atkins, John
Atkins, Phil
Baker, Caleb
Bartlett, Fras
Beavis, Fras
Beavis, Fras
Bellringer, John
Bennett, John, sen
Bennett, John, jun
Bennett, Wm
Bird, John
Bird, Thos
Blackmore, Ric
Blake, Wm
Blanchflower, Geo
Bond, John
Bond, Phil
Bond, Thos, sen
Bond, Thos, jun
Boone, Rob
Bovett, Edm
Bovett, John, sen
Bovett, John, jun
Bovett, Ric
Branscombe, Osmund
Bray, Thos
Broadbeare, John
Brocas, Sam
Brooke, Simon
Browne, Jas
Browne, John
Bryant, Gerrard
Bryant, Hugh
Burgen, John, sen
Burges, Peter
Burges, Thos, sen
Burges, Thos
Burnett, John
Buttley, Edw
Buttley, Thos
Camm, John
Cardy, Abr
Case, Wm
Chare, Sam
Christopher, Thos
Clarke, John
Clatworthy, Marmaduke
Clatworthy, Rob
Clogg, Thos
Cloud, John
Cockram, Jeremiah
Cockram, Ric
Cole, Edw
Cole, Wm

Collick, John
Collins, Thos
Coombe, Ric
Cornish, Nic
Cornish, Phil
Cornish, Phil
Cox, John, sen
Cox, John, jun
Cox, Thos
Cox, Wm, sen
Cox, Wm, jun
Crooke, Wm
Cross, Nic
Dauphin, Rob
Dell, Sam
Dicker, Geo
Dinning, Elias
Doman, John
Dryer, John
Dyer, Bart
Eastabrooke, Ric
England, John
England, Rob
England, Wm, sen
England, Wm, jun
Fane, Jos
Farmer, Jos
Faulkner, John
Fleming, Thos
Flower, Wm
Floyd, Thos
Follett, John
Follett, Nat
Fox, Rob
French, Geo, sen
French, Geo, jun
Fry, Wm
Gale, Edw
Gale, Jas
Gamagè, Thos, sen
Gamage, Thos, jun
Gibbs, Chris
Gibbs, Rob
Gibbons, Hen
Gillard, Humph
Gillett, Sam
Glanville, David
Gold, John
Goldsworthy, Ric
Gollopp, Rob
Graunt, Ric
Grigg, Jas
Groode, John
Grove, John
Gullhampton, Jos
Gunstone, Art
Hamlyn, Simon, jun
Hammond, Thos
Hannon, Jas

Stibbs, Geo
Stibbs, Jas
Stocker, Wm
Strickland, John
Stuckey, Wm
Talbott, Max
Tapley, John
Taylor, Chris
Taylor, Rob, jun
Terry, And
Thompson, Geo
Tucker, Ric
Tucker, Thos
Verrier, John
Vickery, John
Vincent, Jos
Vincent, Nic
Warren, Edw
Wash, Edw
Wash, Thos
Waterman, John
Way, John
Weaver, Jasper
Webb, John
Webb, Rog
Webber, John
Westover, Sam
Whittley, Ric
Williams, Hen
Willis, John
Wilkins, Jas
Woodall, John
Woolavington, Edw
Woolcott, Rob
Worrell, Rog
Yende, Jas, jun

TAVISTOCK, DEVON
Rowe, Peter

THORNCOMBE, DORSET
Bowditch, Dan
Bowditch, John
Bragg, John
Bragg, Matt
Bragg, Matt, jun
Bryant, Bernard
Croft, Matt
Dolling, Silvanus
Ellis alias Cossins, And
Forsey, Thos
Hacker, Tim
Hallett, Geo
Hardman, John
Hardman, Nat
Hardman, Wm
Hawker, Tim
Haynes, Wm
Hitchcock, Humph

Hitchcock, John
James, Rob
James, Sam
Liggens, Wm (Forde)
Machell, Rob
Mitchell, John
Morris, John
Phelps, Dan
Philly, Rob
Pinney, Rob
Polling, Sylvanus
Prideaux, Edm (Forde)
Slade, Thos
Smith, Ric
Sprake, John
Staple, Jas
Staple, John
Staple, Matt

Staple, Nat
Staple, Sam
Stoodley, John
Swaffield, Nat
Tiggins, Wm
Trencher, John
Wakely, John
Wakely, Nic
Wakely, Rob
Webb, John
Whetham, Wm
Wythell, Thos

THORNFALCON, SOMERSET
Andrews, John
Bowell, Wm
Cheeke, Jonas
Cheeke, Phil
Clarke, Thos, sen
Clarke, 'Thos, jun
Cornish, Jas
Deane, John
Gattley, Wm
Hallswell, Rob
House, Chris
Lea, Oates
Leakey, Ric, jun
Lockyer, Thos
Powell, Isaac, sen
Powell, Thos
Robbins, John
Snow, Thos
Thatcher, Bernard

THORVERTON, DEVON
Greenway, Geo

THURLBEAR, SOMERSET
Hawker, Chris
Hawker, Ric

Robjount, Edw
Salter, Nic
Salter, Rob
Smith, Edw
Smith, Jas
Smith, John
Smith, Wm, jun
Sparke, Rog
Stamp, Malachi
Troubridge, Moses
Ward, Zach
Warren, Jas
Warren, John, sen
Warren, John jun
Yorke, John

WALTON, SOMERSET
Collins, Wm
Everdall, John
Harman, Wm

WANSTROW, SOMERSET
Coward, John

WAREHAM, DORSET
Clarke, Wm
Reekeman, John

WAYFORD, SOMERSET
Bowditch, Mic (Oathill)
Chapple, Jas (Oathill)
Davy, Godfrey (Oathill)
Fry, Wm
Hewes, Rob
Norris, Giles
Turner, John (Oathill)
Williams, Giles

WEARE, SOMERSET
Hellier, John

WEDMORE, SOMERSET
Barrell, Rob
Bussell, Fras
Buxton, Edw
Carter, Wm
Charell, John
Counsell, John
Cox, Rob
Feare, Nic
Fisher, Chas
Fudge, Fras
Honan, Ric
Jenkins, Wm
Lader, Wm
Latcham, Ric
Lye, Geo
Lye, Wm
Smith, John

Smith, Thos
Taylor, Wm
Thatcher, Rob
Walch, Wm

WELLINGTON, SOMERSET
Andrews, Rob
Baker, John
Bennett, Chas
Bennett, John
Bennett, John
Bickham, Ric
Bishop, Wm
Bisse, John
Bovett, Phil
Bowring, Wm
Boyte, And
Burrow, Chris
Carswell, Rog
Chambers, Hen
Clarke, John
Clatworthy, Hugh
Clatworthy, Thos
Colborne, John
Colborne, Wm
Cole, Dan
Cross, John
Cross, Simon
Dawe, Rob
Dinning, Phil
Giles, Ric, sen
Giles, Ric, jun
Gill, John, sen
Gill, John, jun
Govett, John, sen
Govett, John jun
Hart, John
Hill, Hannibal
Hill, Thos
Hurford, Cornelius
Hurley (Hussey), Lawrence
Hussey, Simon
Jordan, Chris
Liscombe, Wm
Lock, Art
Lock, Ric
Lugg, Edw or Edm
Mercy, Geo
Mercy, Jas
Mercy, John
Norman, John
Norman, Wm
Northam, John
Nurton, Wm
Parsons, John
Patil, Art
Peeters, Jas
Pine, Cornelius, jun
Pinney, John

Ralph, Edw
Ralph, Geo
Read, Rob, jun
Rugg, John
Rutter, Dan
Rutter, Thos
Southey, Rob
Syle, Edw
Taylor, Rob
Timewell, Wm
Toleman, Nic
Tottle, Sam
Trock, Thos
Walters, Hen
Warren, Jos
Weaver, Wm
Winter, Chris
Winter, John
Winter, Ric
Woodford, Thos
Yeo, John

**WELLOW, SOMERSET**
Bigg, Jas, jun
Buckler, Hen
White, Ric, jun

**WELLS, SOMERSET**
Carter, John (Coxley)
Chinn, Ric
Cross, Wm, sen (West Horrington)
Cross, Wm, jun (West Horrington)
Hillier, John (Coxley)
Hippisley, Geo (Melsbury)
Oram, John (Worminster)
Oram, Thos (Worminster)
Willcox, Ric (West Horrington)

**WESTBURY, WILTSHIRE**
Aldridge, Ralph
Clift, Jas
Dagg, Fras
Goyce, Thos
Short, Ben
Wheler, Jeremiah

**WESTONZOYLAND, SOMERSET**
Baker, Geo
Baker, Wal, sen
Baker, Wal, jun
Galhampton, Thos
Godfrey, Thos
Goodland, John
Miller, Wm
Wilkins, Thos

**WHATLEY, SOMERSET**
Hodges, Rog
Maynard, Jas

Thatcher, Wm

**WHITECHURCH      CANONICORUM, DORSET**
Bartlett, John (Abbotts Wootton)
Beavis, John (Abbotts Wootton)
Hodder, Wm
Orchard, Jas
Orchard, Wm (Abbotts Wootton)
Pearce, Wm
Phelps, Jos
Salter, Geo (Sarum Wells)
Snooke, Thos
Taylor, Sam (Sarum Wells)
Trattle, John
Trattle, Sam
Watts, Hen

**WHITELACKINGTON, SOMERSET**
Bereman, John
Blatchford, Alex
Lake, Mic
Mailard, Wm
Miller, Geo
Rogers, John
Speke, Chas
Stuckey, Geo

**WHITESTAUNTON, SOMERSET**
Griffin, Nic
Parys, Aaron

**WHITFORD, DEVON**
Bushells, John
Hooper, Edw
Hooper, wm
Searle, Wm

**WICK** *see* **LUPPITT**

**WILLAND, DEVON**
Ellis, Thos

**WILLITON, SOMERSET**
Fowler, John, sen

**WILTON, SOMERSET**
Barton, Ric
Blinman, Ames (Galmington)
Browne, John
Clement, Geo
Cooke, Chris
Cooke, Stephen
Daniel, Thos
Dunstar, John
Edwards, John, sen (Galmington)
Edwards, John, jun
Evans, John
Gale, Thos

Gardiner, Rob
Gold (Gould), Enoch
Greeneham, Jeremiah
Hallett, Dan
Hallett, John
Hammett (Hammond), Hen
Hutchins, Thos
Lockston, John
Miles, Matt
Stephens, John
Street, Wm
Symes, Hugh
Thorne, Simon
Thorne, Wm
Wyatt, Thos
Wyatt, Zachary

## WINCANTON, SOMERSET

Cooke, Jonathan
Creed, Laurence
Cuttler, John
Davidge, Nic
Frith, Maurice
Gilbert, Edw
Glisson, John
Gulley, John
Hillard, Ben
Hurman, Thos
Norvell, Wm
Poynter, Ric
Thick, John
Vyning, Ambr
Vyning, John
Vyning, Simon
White, Nic
White, Thos

## WINSHAM, SOMERSET

Bennett, Hen
Bennett, John (Street and Leigh)
Bennett, Wm
Briddell, Thos
Coggan, Bernard (Street and Leigh)
Edwards, Wm
Paull, Maurice
Phelps, Humph
Rushell, Abr (Street)
Scriven, Geo (Street)
Scriven, Thos
Sprake, John
Stuckey, Wm (Street)
Whiterow, Geo

## WITHAM FRIARY, SOMERSET

Richards, Chris
Smart, Gabriel

## WITTINGTON

Osborne, Wm

## WOODLANDS, EAST, FROME, SOMERSET

Balston, John
Biggott, Thos, sen
Biggott, Thos, jun
Bryant, Ric
Case, Matt
Dowell, John
Eyres, Matt
Gay, Isaac
Gay, John
Hole, Ric
Horton, Peter
Merriweather, Thos
Nipperett, And
Parker, Wal
Pope, Jas
Rossiter, Ric, jun
Smart, Thos, sen
Wittington, Wm

## WOODLANDS, WEST, FROME, SOMERSET

Adlam, Tim
Attwood, Ric
Clay, John
Garland, Edw
George, Ric
George, Wm
Godwin, Edw
Hacker (Hackett), Wal
Iles, Jos
Millard, Rob
Redway, Stephen
Reeve, Rob
Rogers, John
Saunders, Ric
Smith, Jas
West, Ric, jun

## WOOKEY, SOMERSET

Bolting, John (Yarley)
Cooke, John
Hippisley, Thos (Burcott)
Little, John (Burcott)

## WOOLAVINGTON, SOMERSET

Graham, Ric
Mew alias Seller, Thos

## WOOLMINSTONE *see* CREWKERNE

## WOOTTON FITZPAINE, DORSET

Avant, Fras
Bagg, Geo
Bowditch, Edw
Bowditch, John
Bowditch, Matt
Bowditch, Wm